empowered™

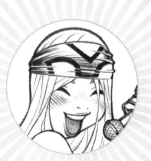

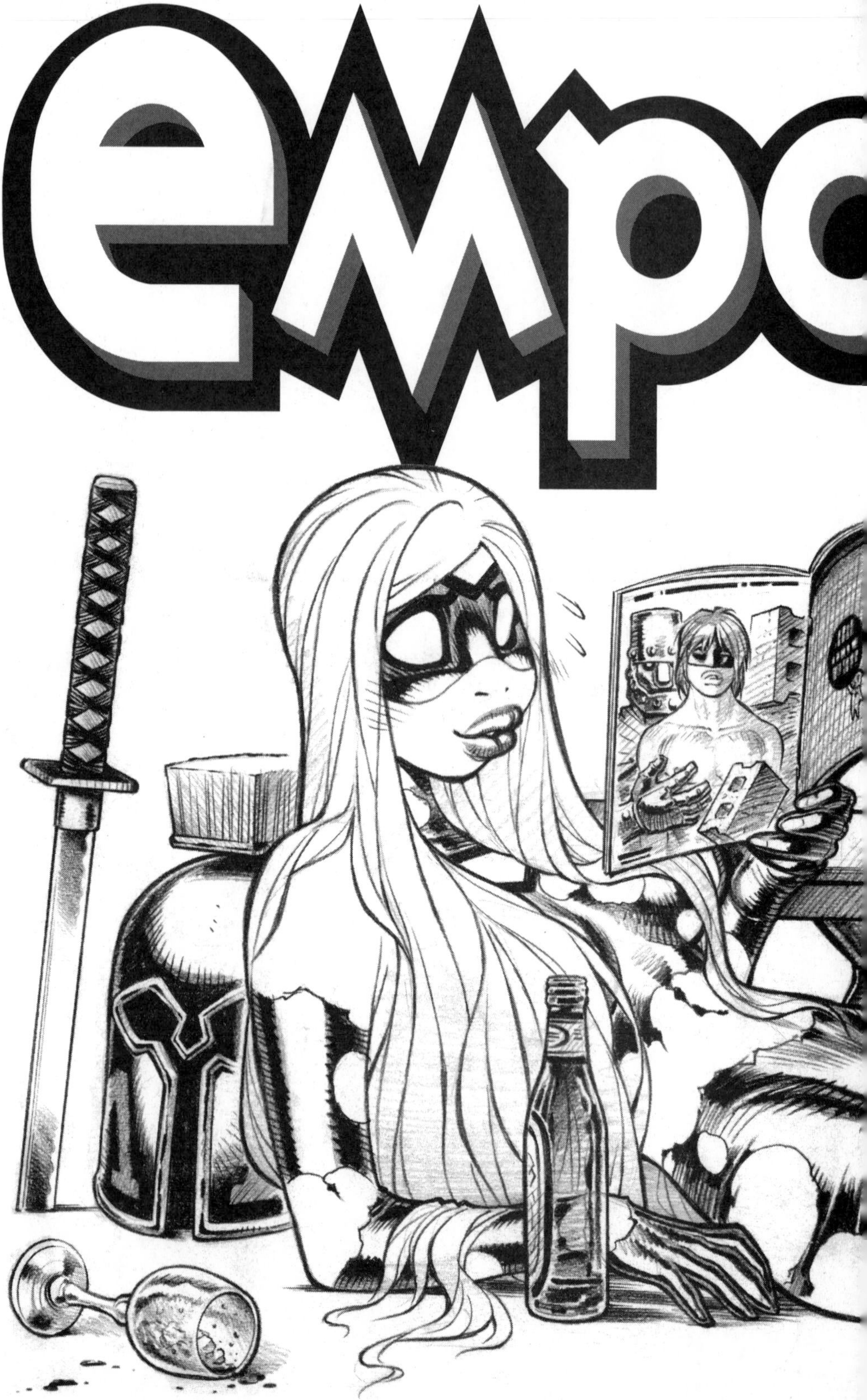

™

volume **3**

Empowered

by ADAM WARREN

ninjutsu linguistic assistance and dōjinshi artwork by **JO CHEN** and **TOMOKO SAITO**

cover colors by **LEE DUHIG** for **GURUeFX**   empowered logo by **EUGENE WANG**

DARK HORSE BOOKS®

publisher
Mike Richardson

editor
Chris Warner

designer
Joshua Elliott

art director
Lia Ribacchi

EMPOWERED VOLUME 3

© 2008 by Adam Warren. Empowered, Ninjette, Thugboy, and all prominent characters and their distinctive likenesses are trademarks of Adam Warren. All rights reserved. Dark Horse Books® and the Dark Horse logo are registered trademarks of Dark Horse Comics, Inc. All rights reserved. No portion of this publication may be reproduced, in any form or by any means, without the express written permission of the copyright holders. Names, characters, places, and incidents featured in this publication are either the product of the author's imagination or are used fictitiously. Any resemblance to actual persons (living or dead), events, institutions, or locales, without satiric intent, is coincidental.

Dark Horse Books
A division of Dark Horse Comics, Inc.
10956 SE Main Street
Milwaukie, OR 97222

darkhorse.com

To find a comics shop in your area, call the Comic Shop
Locator Service toll-free at 1-888-266-4226

First edition: March 2008
ISBN 978-1-59307-870-6

1 3 5 7 9 10 8 6 4 2

Printed in Canada

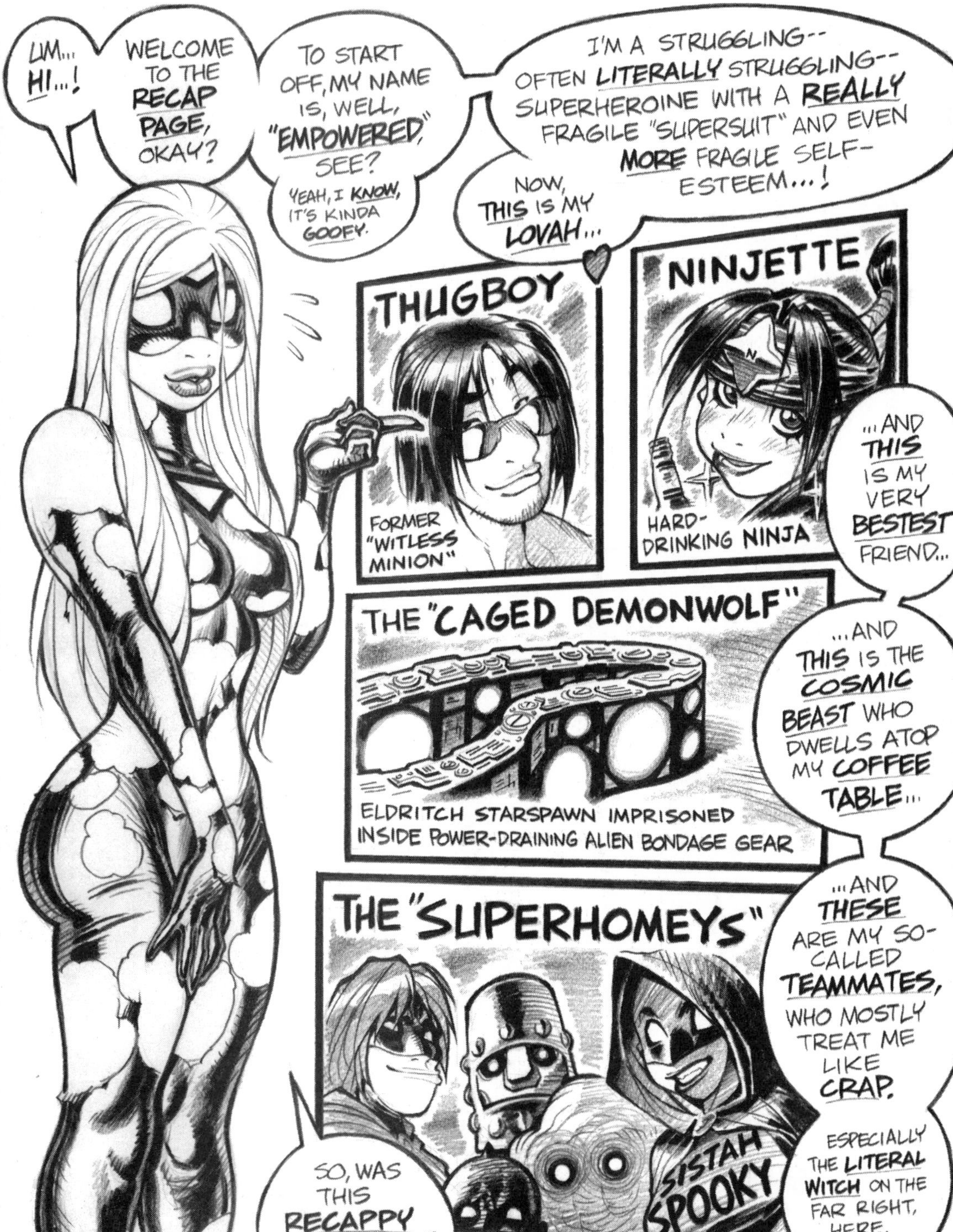
UM... HI...!
WELCOME TO THE RECAP PAGE, OKAY?
TO START OFF, MY NAME IS, WELL, "EMPOWERED," SEE?
YEAH, I KNOW, IT'S KINDA GOOFY.
I'M A STRUGGLING-- OFTEN LITERALLY STRUGGLING-- SUPERHEROINE WITH A REALLY FRAGILE "SUPERSUIT" AND EVEN MORE FRAGILE SELF-ESTEEM...!
NOW, THIS IS MY LOVAH...
THUGBOY
FORMER "WITLESS MINION"
NINJETTE
HARD-DRINKING NINJA
...AND THIS IS MY VERY BESTEST FRIEND...
THE "CAGED DEMONWOLF"
ELDRITCH STARSPAWN IMPRISONED INSIDE POWER-DRAINING ALIEN BONDAGE GEAR
...AND THIS IS THE COSMIC BEAST WHO DWELLS ATOP MY COFFEE TABLE...
THE "SUPERHOMEYS"
...AND THESE ARE MY SO-CALLED TEAMMATES, WHO MOSTLY TREAT ME LIKE CRAP.
SISTAH SPOOKY
ESPECIALLY THE LITERAL WITCH ON THE FAR RIGHT, HERE.
BOO, HISS.
SO, WAS THIS RECAPPY ENOUGH...? HOPE SO...!

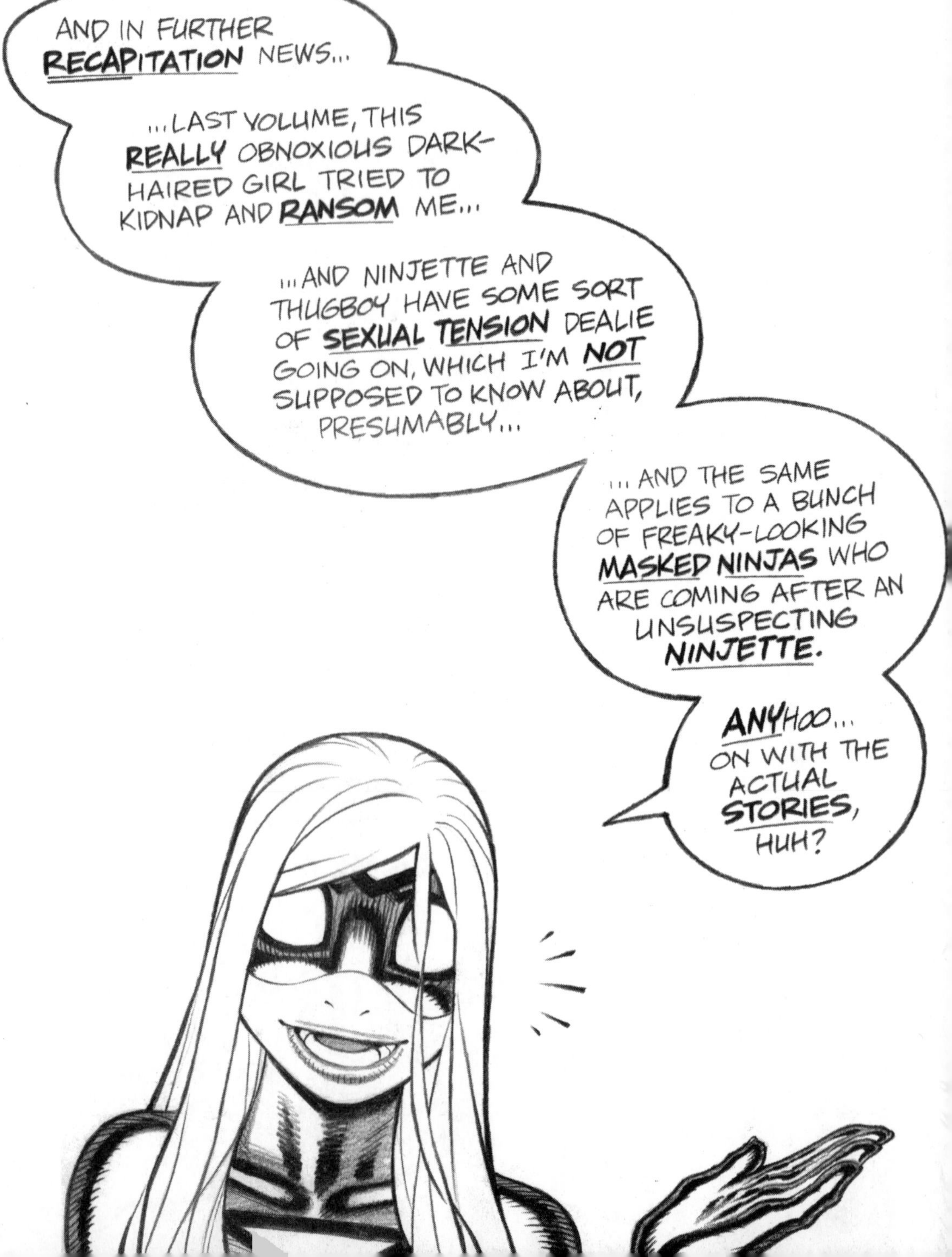
AND IN FURTHER RECAPITATION NEWS...
...LAST VOLUME, THIS REALLY OBNOXIOUS DARK-HAIRED GIRL TRIED TO KIDNAP AND RANSOM ME...
...AND NINJETTE AND THUGBOY HAVE SOME SORT OF SEXUAL TENSION DEALIE GOING ON, WHICH I'M NOT SUPPOSED TO KNOW ABOUT, PRESUMABLY...
...AND THE SAME APPLIES TO A BUNCH OF FREAKY-LOOKING MASKED NINJAS WHO ARE COMING AFTER AN UNSUSPECTING NINJETTE.
ANYHOO... ON WITH THE ACTUAL STORIES, HUH?

Empowered™

Feel the Überburn

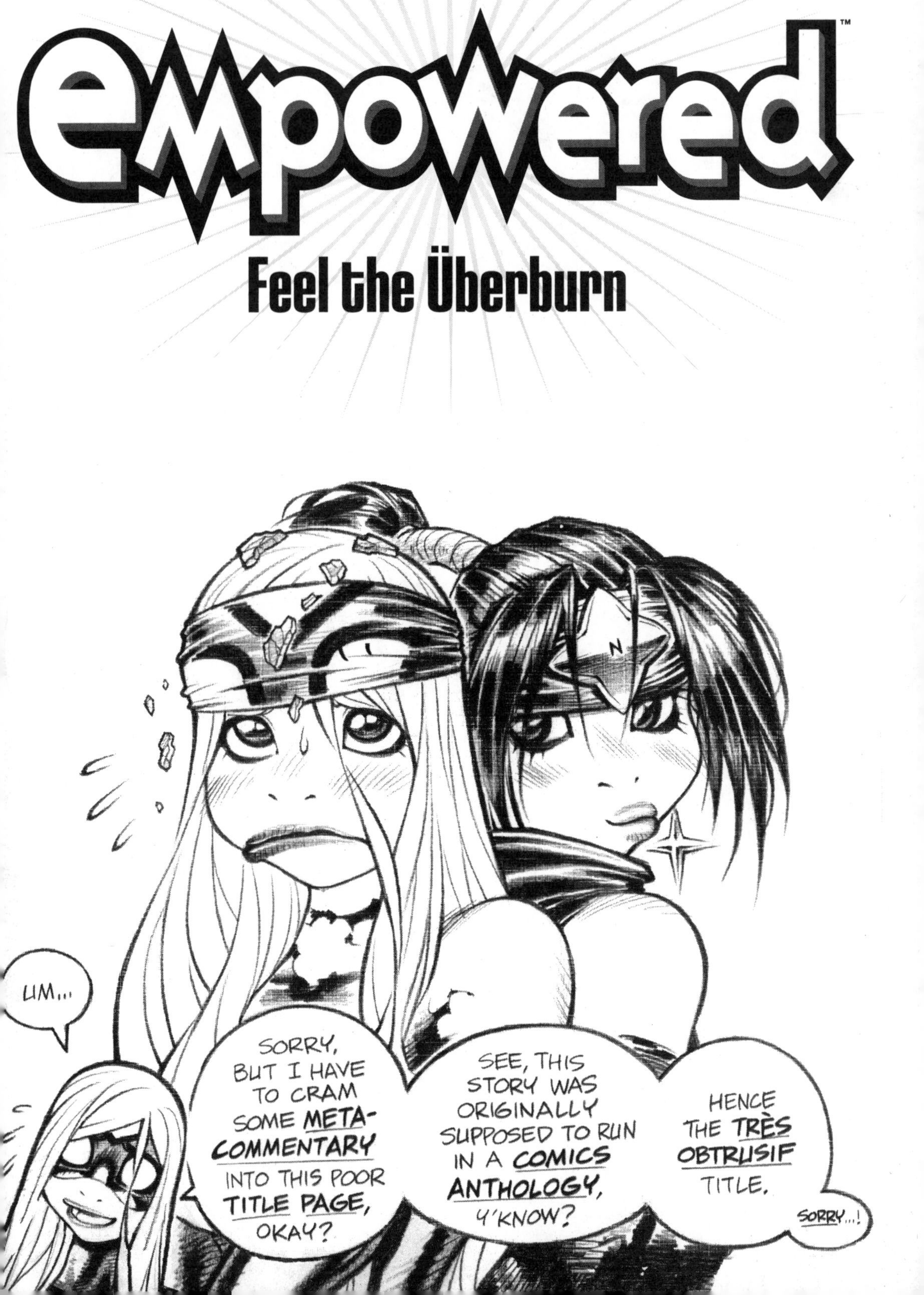
UM...
SORRY, BUT I HAVE TO CRAM SOME META-COMMENTARY INTO THIS POOR TITLE PAGE, OKAY?
SEE, THIS STORY WAS ORIGINALLY SUPPOSED TO RUN IN A COMICS ANTHOLOGY, Y'KNOW?
HENCE THE TRÈS OBTRUSIF TITLE.
SORRY...!

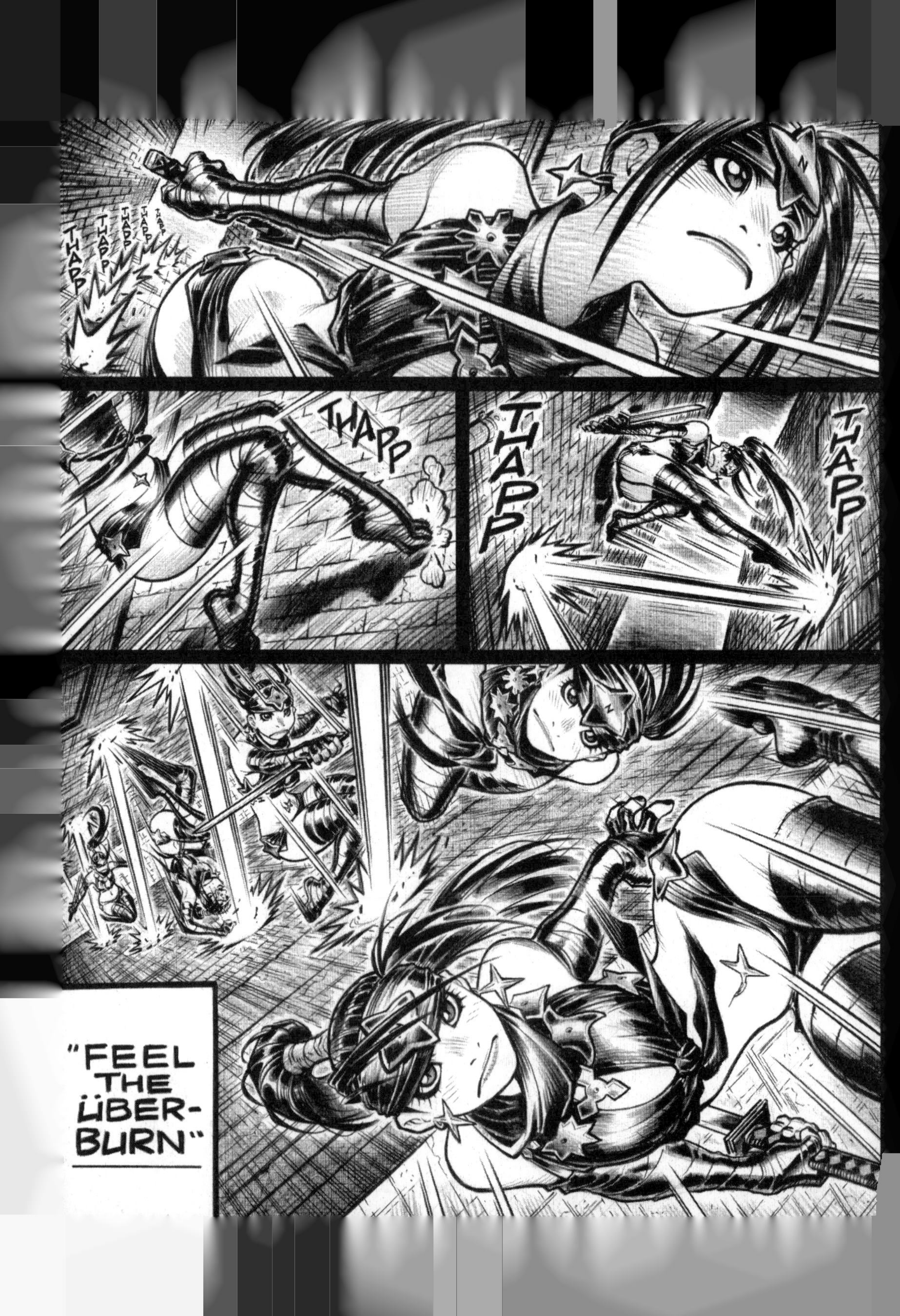
THAPP
THAPP
THAPP
THAPP
THAPP
THAPP
THAPP
THAPP
"FEEL THE ÜBER-BURN"

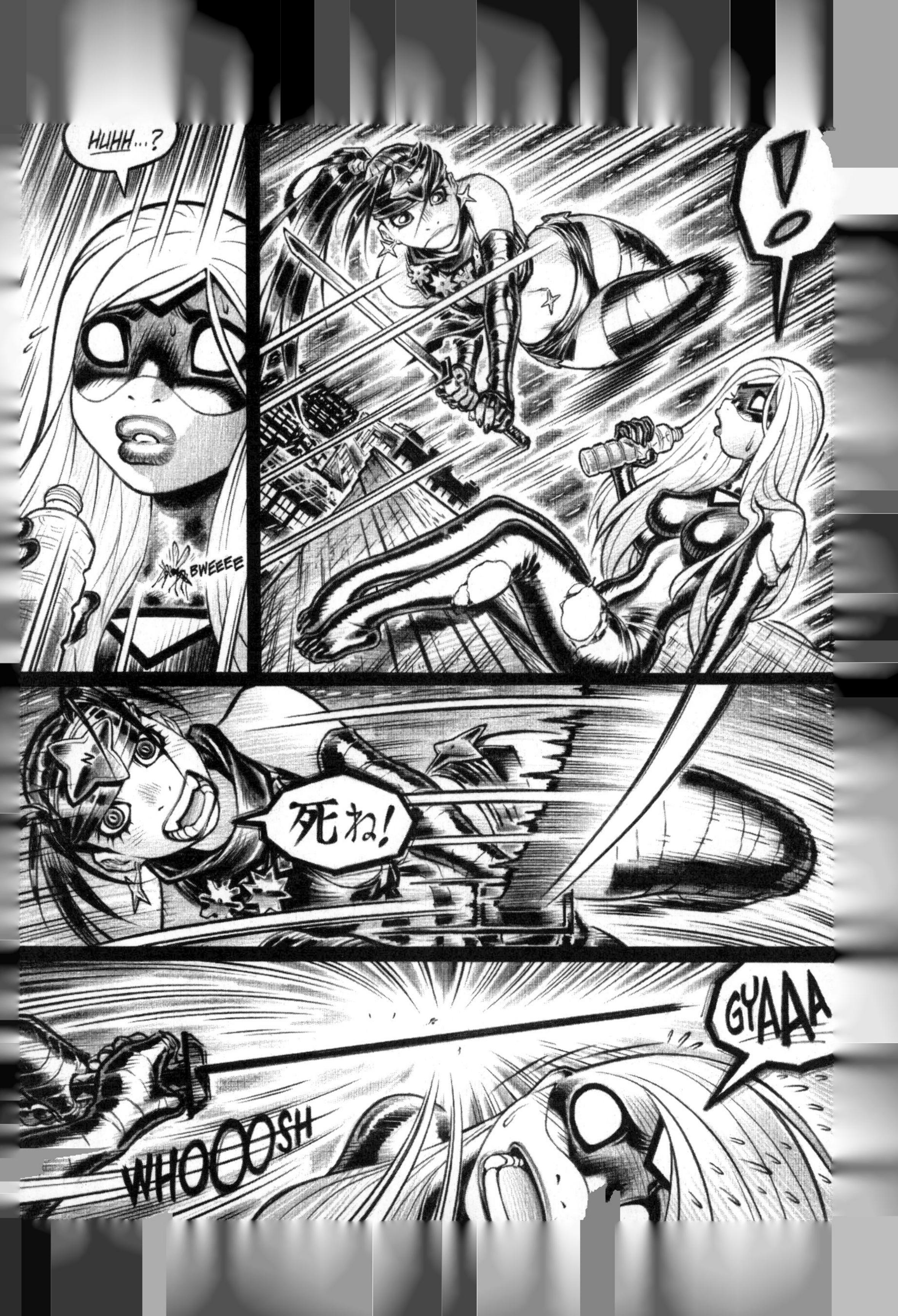
HUHH...?
BWEEEE
!?
死ね!
GYAAA
WHOOOSH

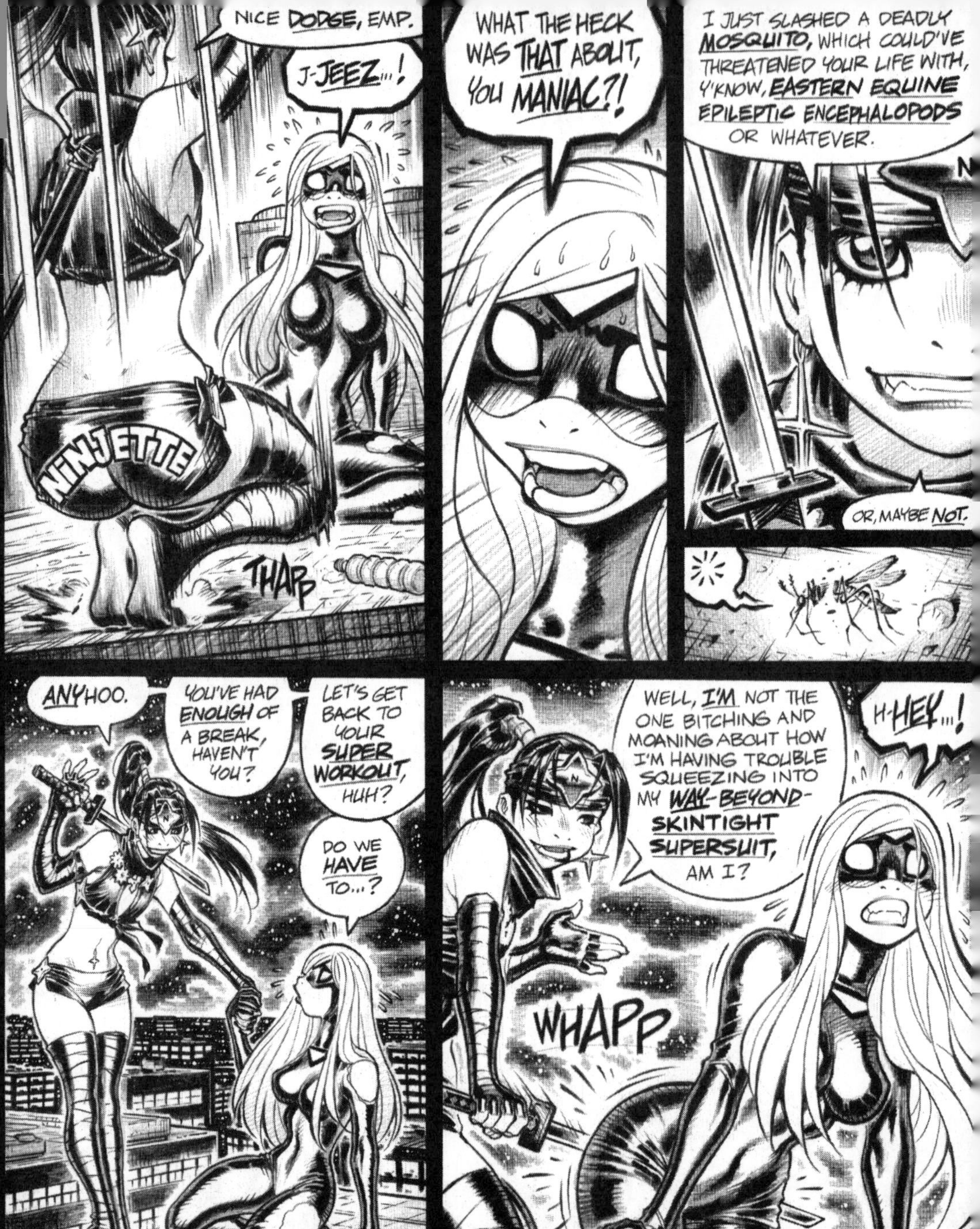
NICE DODGE, EMP.
J-JEEZ...!
THAPP
WHAT THE HECK WAS THAT ABOUT, YOU MANIAC?!
I JUST SLASHED A DEADLY MOSQUITO, WHICH COULD'VE THREATENED YOUR LIFE WITH, Y'KNOW, EASTERN EQUINE EPILEPTIC ENCEPHALOPODS OR WHATEVER.
OR, MAYBE NOT.
ANYHOO.
YOU'VE HAD ENOUGH OF A BREAK, HAVEN'T YOU?
LET'S GET BACK TO YOUR SUPER WORKOUT, HUH?
DO WE HAVE TO...?
WELL, I'M NOT THE ONE BITCHING AND MOANING ABOUT HOW I'M HAVING TROUBLE SQUEEZING INTO MY WAY-BEYOND-SKINTIGHT SUPERSUIT, AM I?
H-HEY...!
WHAPP

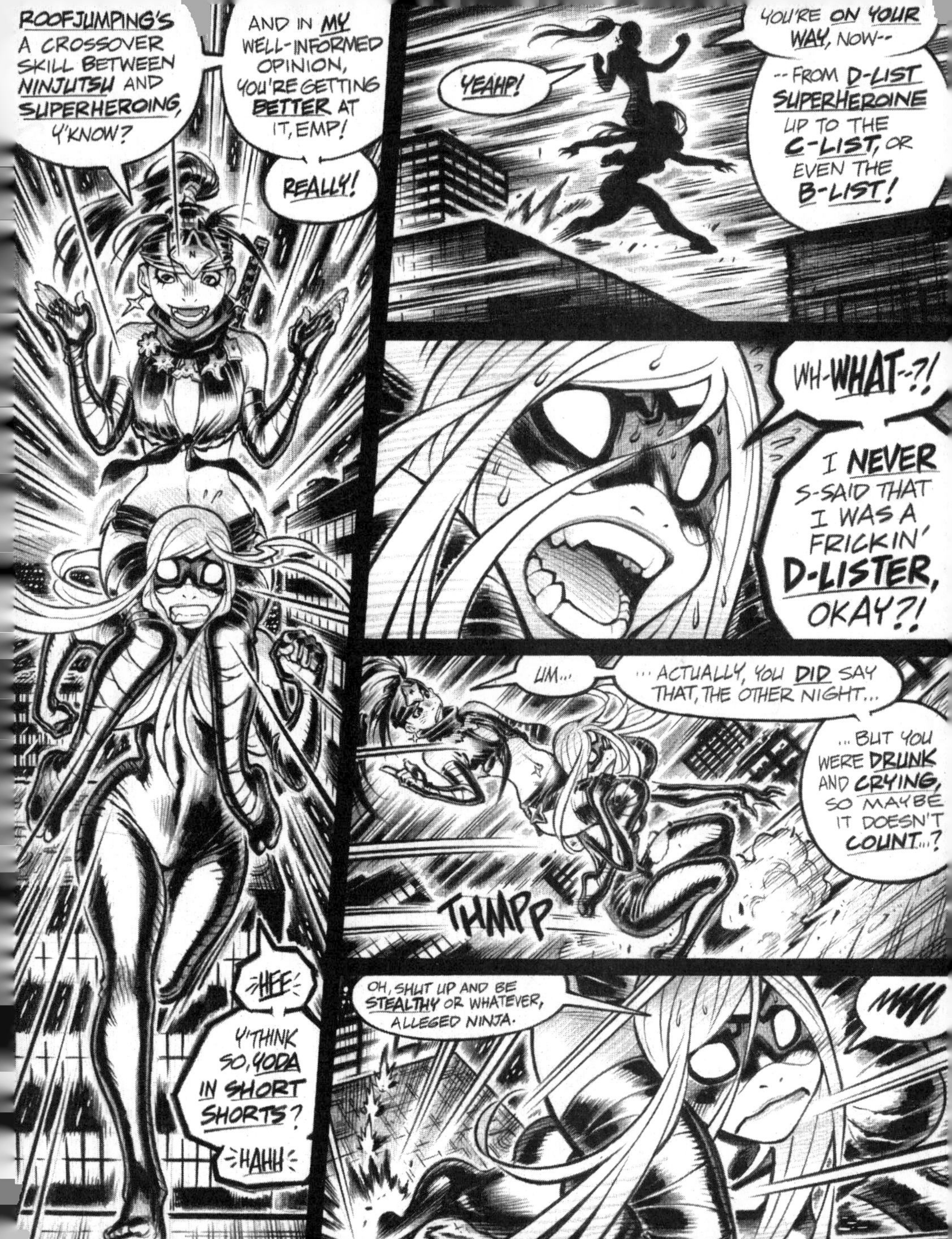
ROOFJUMPING'S A CROSSOVER SKILL BETWEEN NINJUTSU AND SUPERHEROING, Y'KNOW?
AND IN MY WELL-INFORMED OPINION, YOU'RE GETTING BETTER AT IT, EMP!
REALLY!
YEAHP!
YOU'RE ON YOUR WAY, NOW--
--FROM D-LIST SUPERHEROINE UP TO THE C-LIST, OR EVEN THE B-LIST!
HEE
Y'THINK SO, YODA IN SHORT SHORTS?
HAHH
WH-WHAT--?!
I NEVER S-SAID THAT I WAS A FRICKIN' D-LISTER, OKAY?!
UM...
...ACTUALLY, YOU DID SAY THAT, THE OTHER NIGHT...
...BUT YOU WERE DRUNK AND CRYING, SO MAYBE IT DOESN'T COUNT...?
THMPP
OH, SHUT UP AND BE STEALTHY OR WHATEVER, ALLEGED NINJA.
NNN

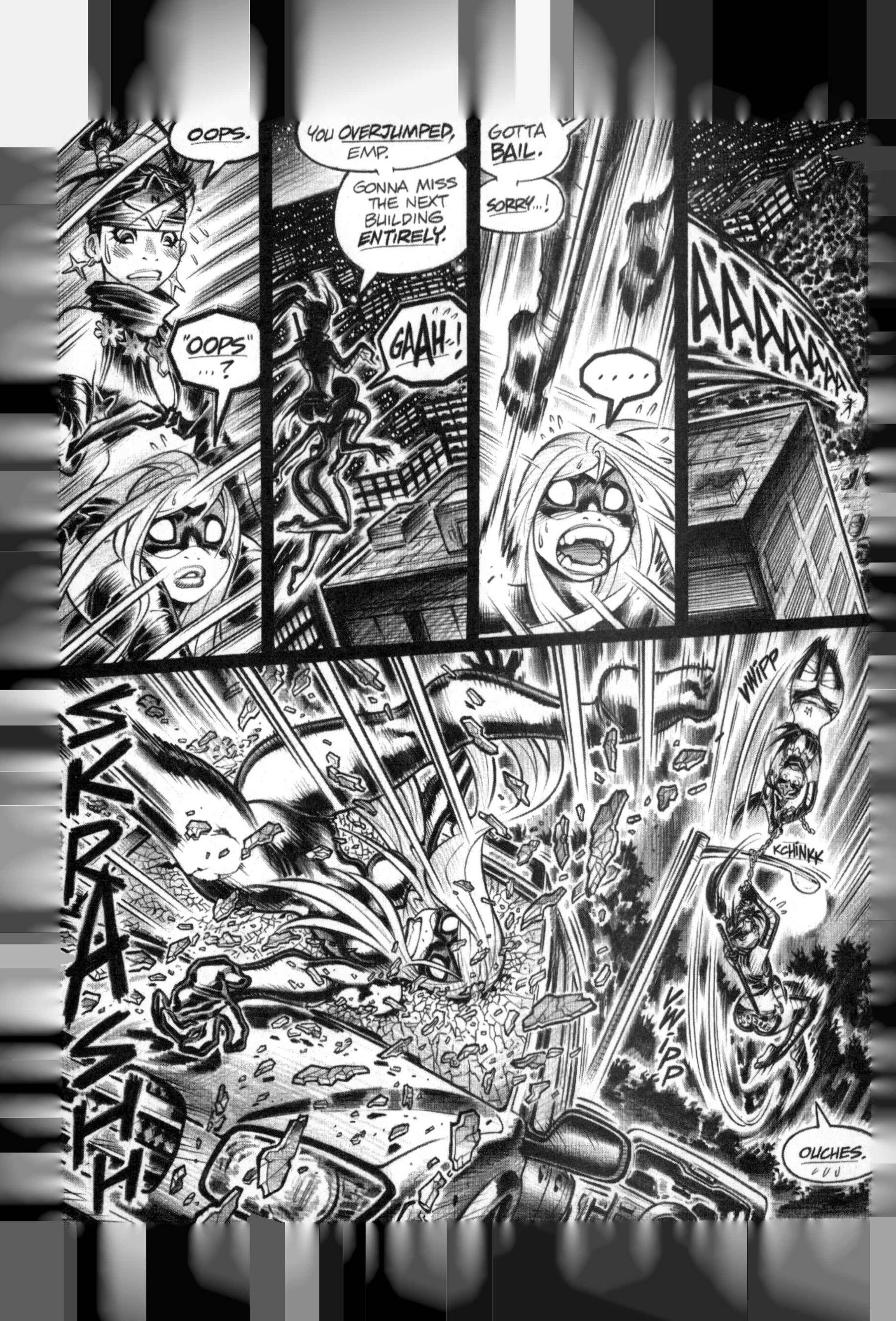

OOPS.
"OOPS" ...?
YOU OVERJUMPED, EMP.
GONNA MISS THE NEXT BUILDING ENTIRELY.
GAAH-!
GOTTA BAIL.
SORRY...!
. . . .
AAAAAAAAAA
SKRASHH
VWIPP
KCHINKK
VWIPP
OUCHES.

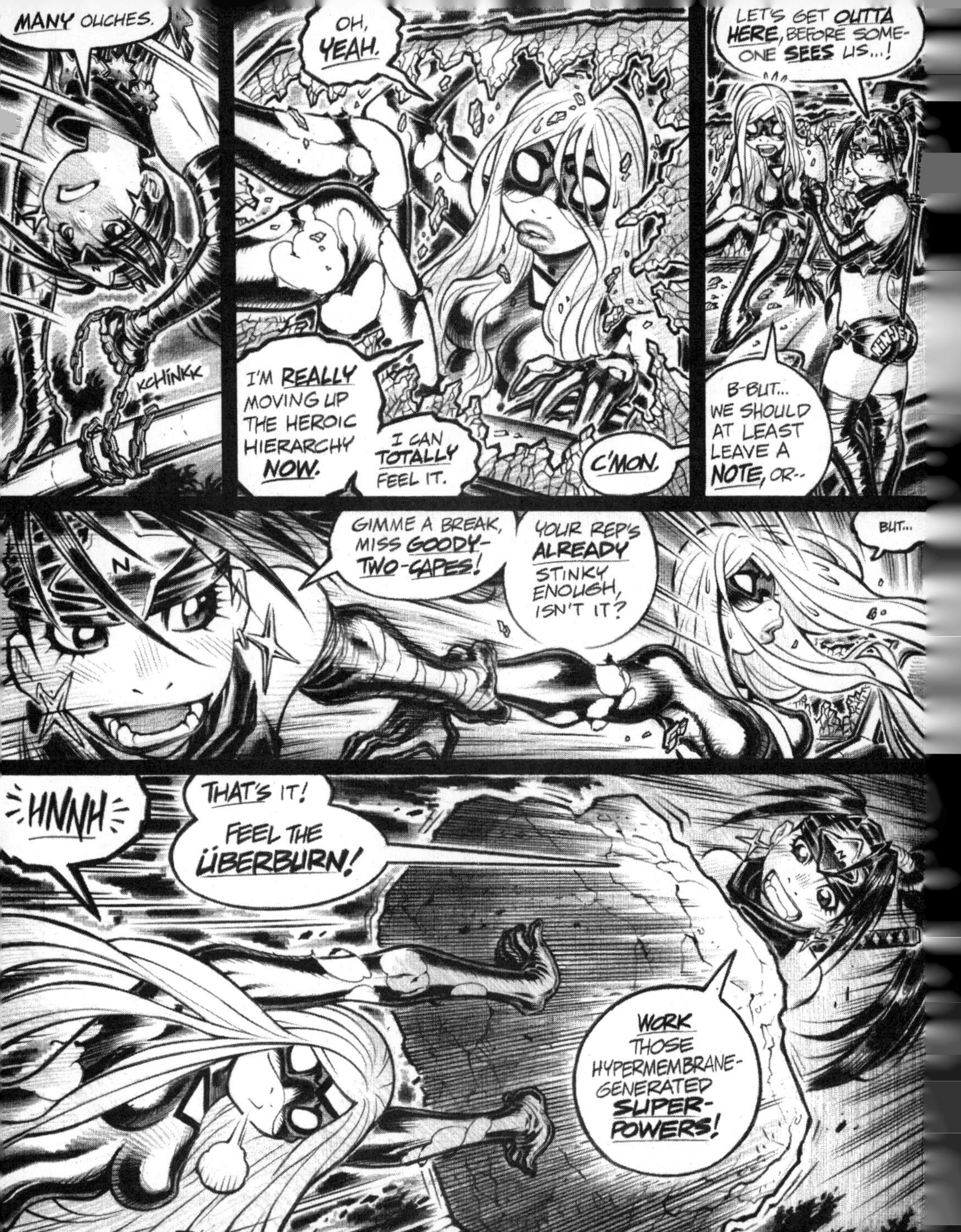
MANY OUCHES.
KCHINKK
OH, YEAH.
I'M REALLY MOVING UP THE HEROIC HIERARCHY NOW.
I CAN TOTALLY FEEL IT.
C'MON.
LET'S GET OUTTA HERE, BEFORE SOME-ONE SEES US...!
B-BUT... WE SHOULD AT LEAST LEAVE A NOTE, OR--
GIMME A BREAK, MISS GOODY-TWO-CAPES!
YOUR REP'S ALREADY STINKY ENOUGH, ISN'T IT?
BUT...
HNNH
THAT'S IT!
FEEL THE ÜBERBURN!
WORK THOSE HYPERMEMBRANE-GENERATED SUPER-POWERS!

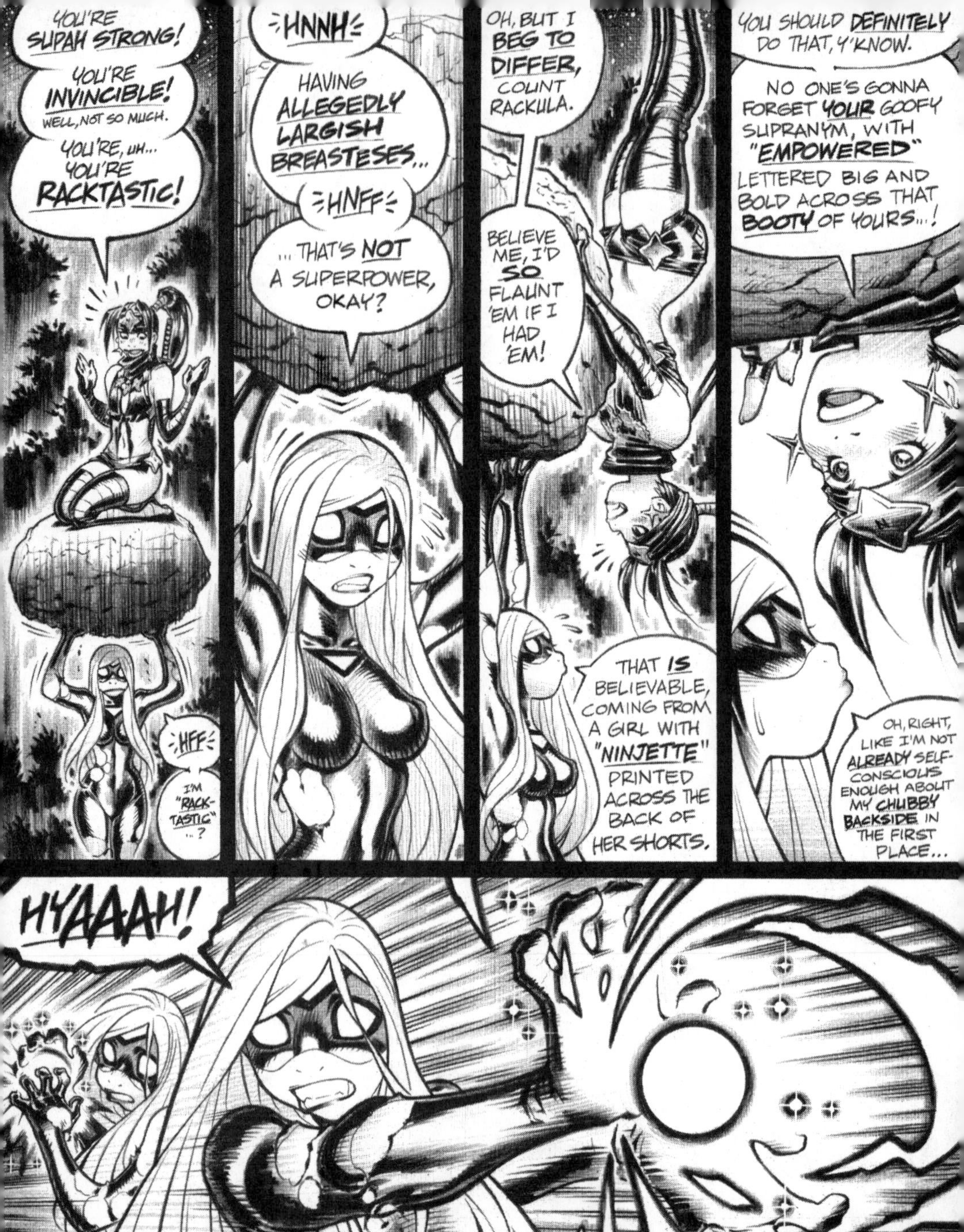
YOU'RE SUPAH STRONG!
YOU'RE INVINCIBLE! WELL, NOT SO MUCH.
YOU'RE, UH... YOU'RE RACKTASTIC!
HFF
I'M "RACK-TASTIC"...?
HNNH
HAVING ALLEGEDLY LARGISH BREASTESES...
HNFF
...THAT'S NOT A SUPERPOWER, OKAY?
OH, BUT I BEG TO DIFFER, COUNT RACKULA.
BELIEVE ME, I'D SO FLAUNT 'EM IF I HAD 'EM!
THAT IS BELIEVABLE, COMING FROM A GIRL WITH "NINJETTE" PRINTED ACROSS THE BACK OF HER SHORTS.
YOU SHOULD DEFINITELY DO THAT, Y'KNOW.
NO ONE'S GONNA FORGET YOUR GOOFY SUPRANYM, WITH "EMPOWERED" LETTERED BIG AND BOLD ACROSS THAT BOOTY OF YOURS...!
OH, RIGHT, LIKE I'M NOT ALREADY SELF-CONSCIOUS ENOUGH ABOUT MY CHUBBY BACKSIDE IN THE FIRST PLACE...
HYAAAH!

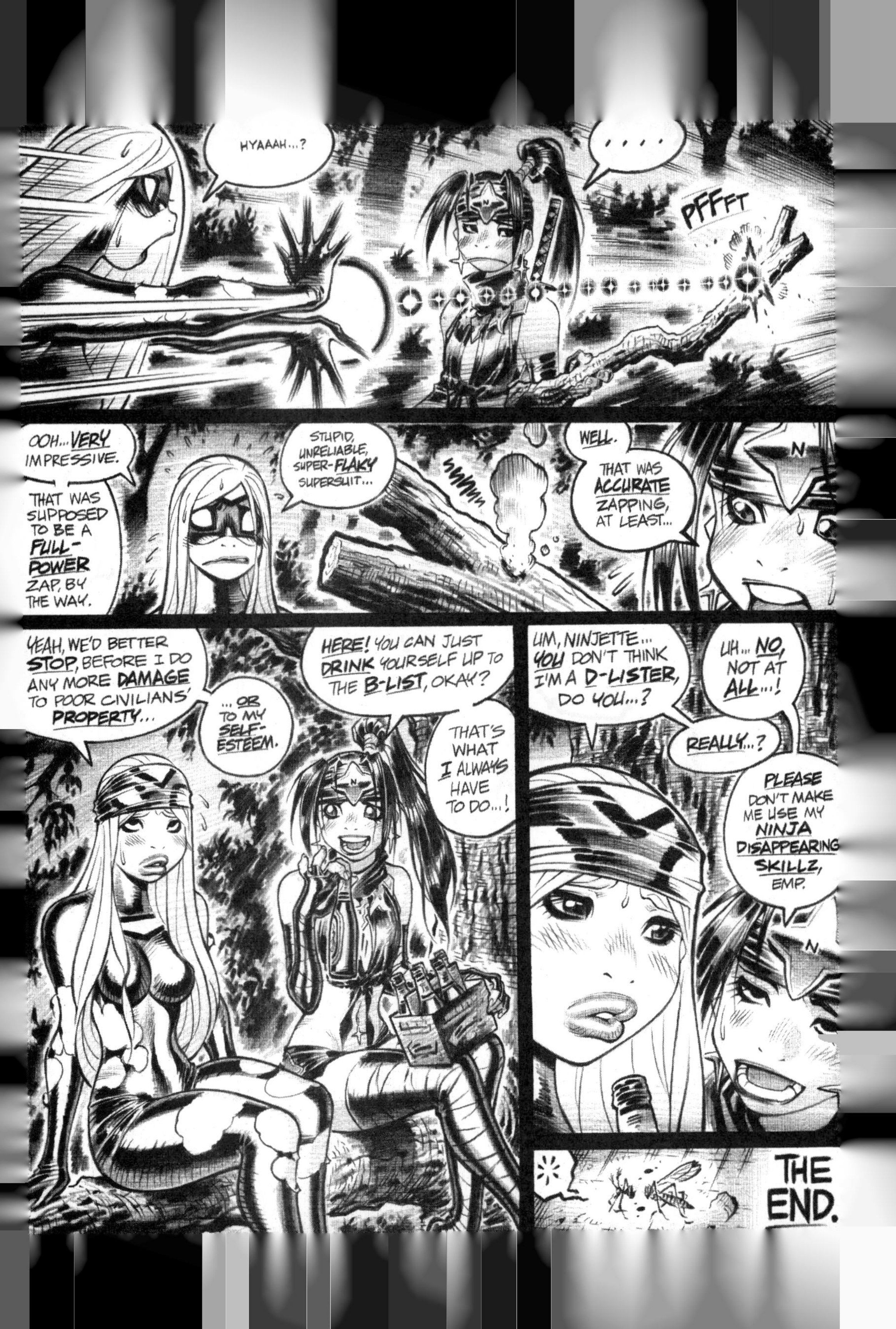
HYAAAH...?
....
PFFFFT
OOH... VERY IMPRESSIVE.
THAT WAS SUPPOSED TO BE A FULL-POWER ZAP, BY THE WAY.
STUPID, UNRELIABLE, SUPER-FLAKY SUPERSUIT...
WELL.
THAT WAS ACCURATE ZAPPING, AT LEAST...
YEAH, WE'D BETTER STOP, BEFORE I DO ANY MORE DAMAGE TO POOR CIVILIANS' PROPERTY...
...OR TO MY SELF-ESTEEM.
HERE! YOU CAN JUST DRINK YOURSELF UP TO THE B-LIST, OKAY?
THAT'S WHAT I ALWAYS HAVE TO DO...!
UM, NINJETTE... YOU DON'T THINK I'M A D-LISTER, DO YOU...?
UH... NO, NOT AT ALL...!
REALLY...?
PLEASE DON'T MAKE ME USE MY NINJA DISAPPEARING SKILLZ, EMP.
THE END.

Empowered™

Heroine Hold 'Em

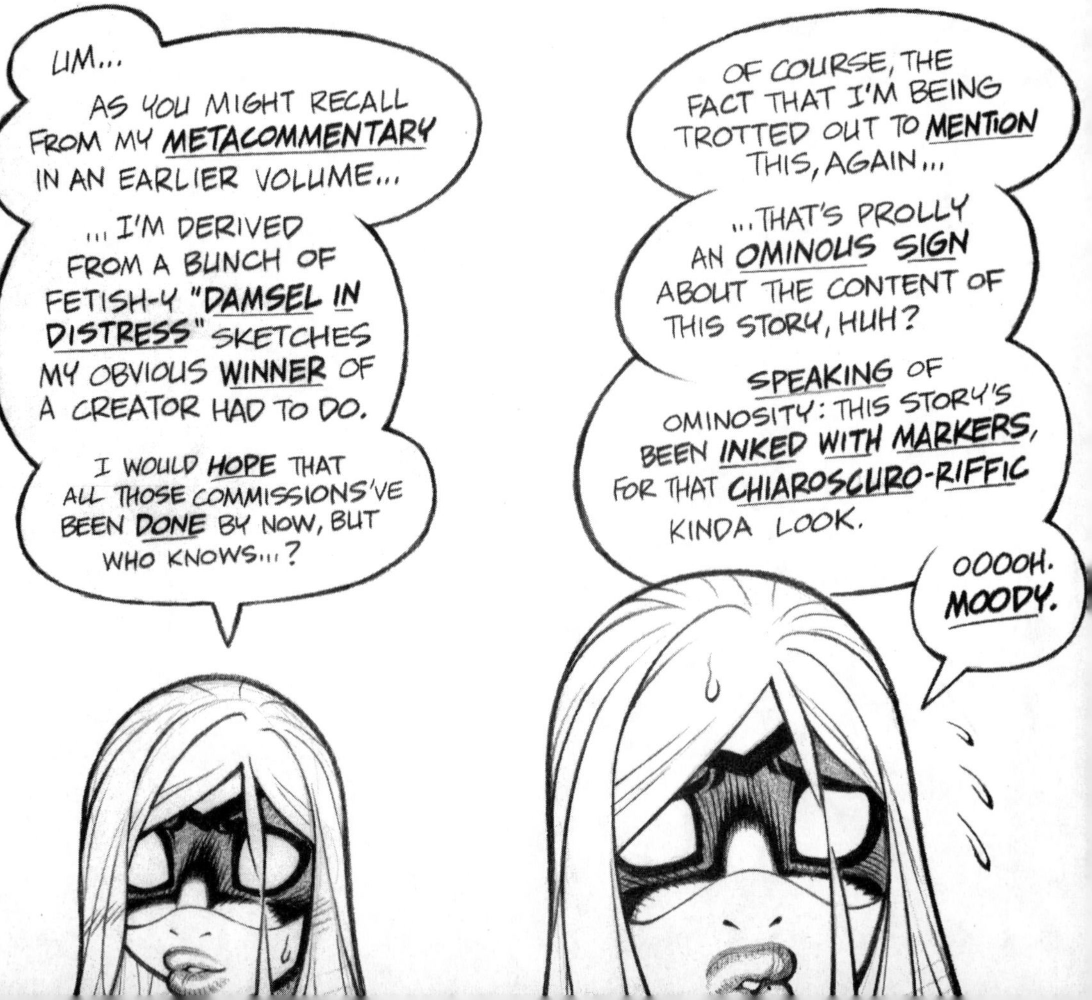
UM...
AS YOU MIGHT RECALL FROM MY METACOMMENTARY IN AN EARLIER VOLUME...
...I'M DERIVED FROM A BUNCH OF FETISH-Y "DAMSEL IN DISTRESS" SKETCHES MY OBVIOUS WINNER OF A CREATOR HAD TO DO.
I WOULD HOPE THAT ALL THOSE COMMISSIONS'VE BEEN DONE BY NOW, BUT WHO KNOWS...?
OF COURSE, THE FACT THAT I'M BEING TROTTED OUT TO MENTION THIS, AGAIN...
...THAT'S PROLLY AN OMINOUS SIGN ABOUT THE CONTENT OF THIS STORY, HUH?
SPEAKING OF OMINOSITY: THIS STORY'S BEEN INKED WITH MARKERS, FOR THAT CHIAROSCURO-RIFFIC KINDA LOOK.
OOOOH. MOODY.

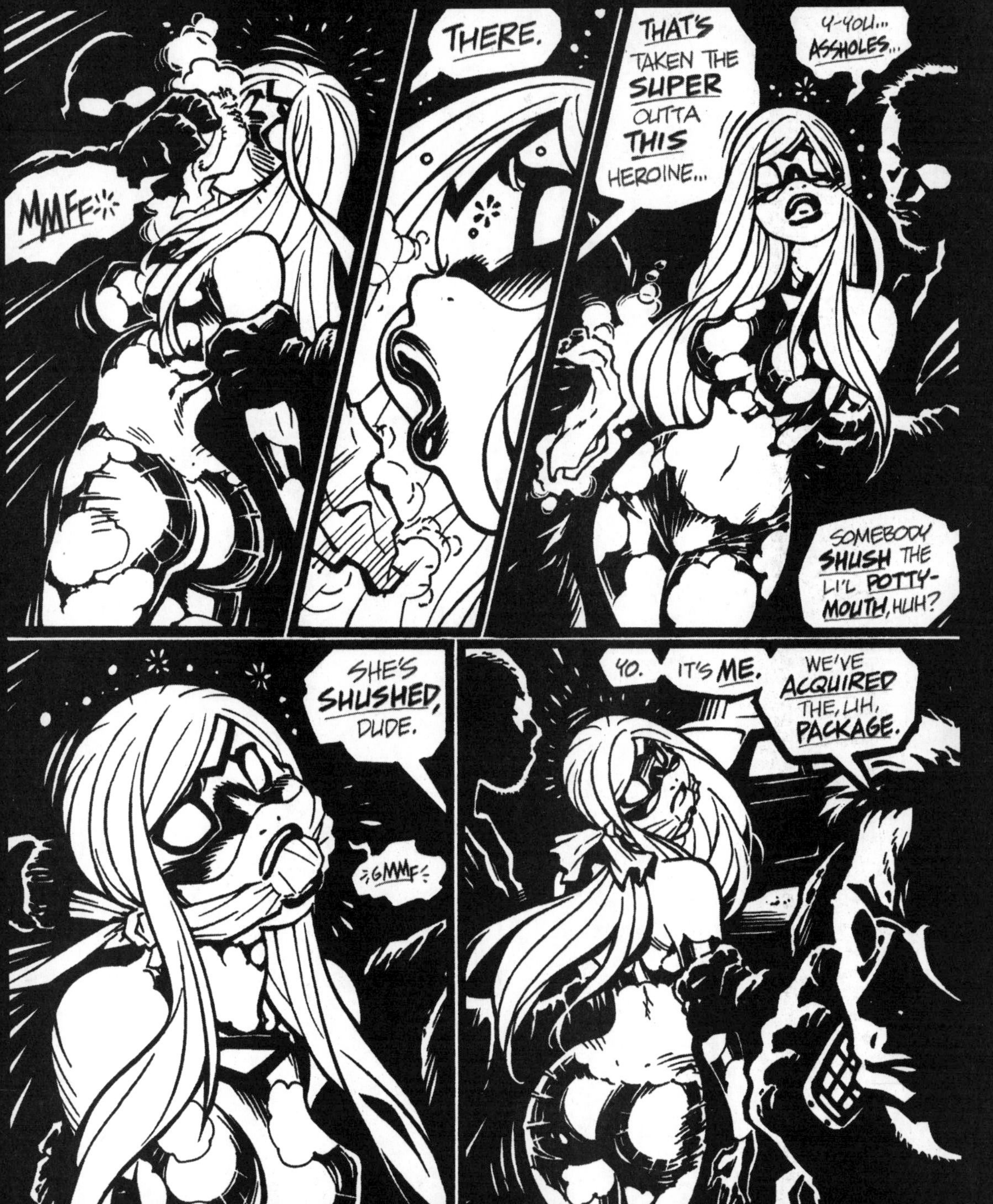
MMFF
THERE.
THAT'S TAKEN THE SUPER OUTTA THIS HEROINE...
Y-YOU... ASSHOLES...
SOMEBODY SHUSH THE LI'L POTTY-MOUTH, HUH?
SHE'S SHUSHED, DUDE.
GMMF
YO.
IT'S ME.
WE'VE ACQUIRED THE, UH, PACKAGE.

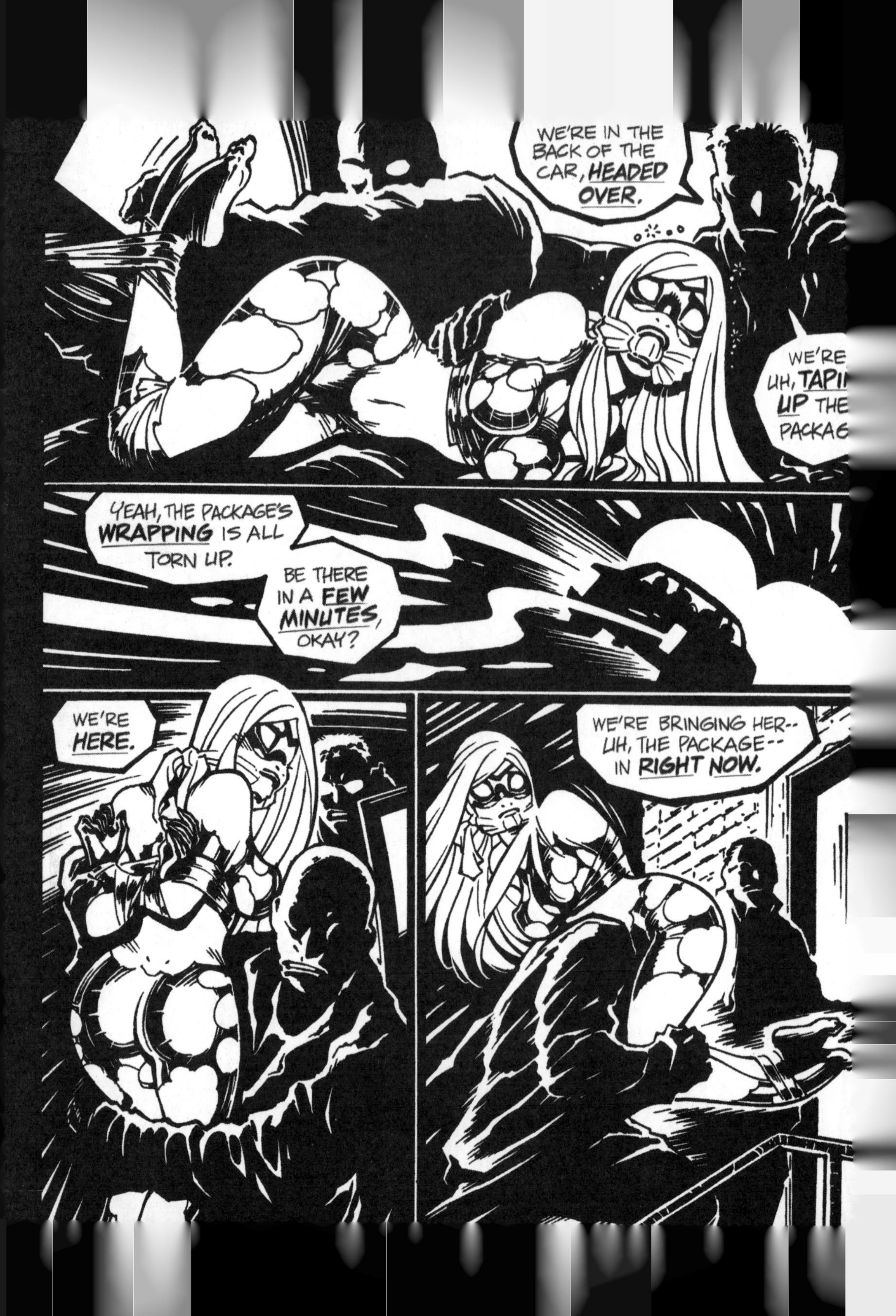
WE'RE IN THE BACK OF THE CAR, HEADED OVER.
WE'RE UH, TAPI UP THE PACKAG
YEAH, THE PACKAGE'S WRAPPING IS ALL TORN UP.
BE THERE IN A FEW MINUTES, OKAY?
WE'RE HERE.
WE'RE BRINGING HER-- UH, THE PACKAGE-- IN RIGHT NOW.

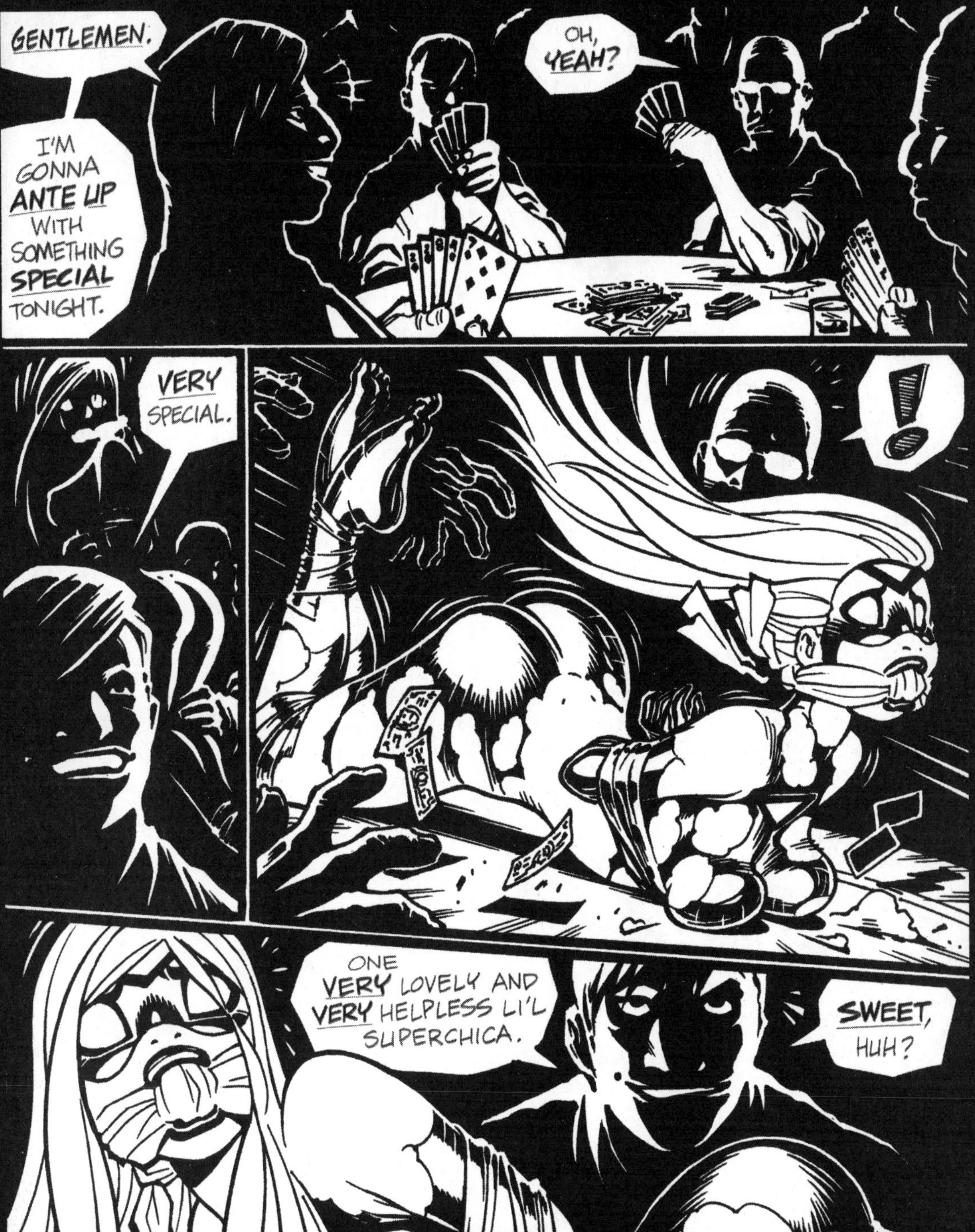

GENTLEMEN.
I'M GONNA ANTE UP WITH SOMETHING SPECIAL TONIGHT.
OH, YEAH?
VERY SPECIAL.
!
ONE VERY LOVELY AND VERY HELPLESS LI'L SUPERCHICA.
SWEET, HUH?

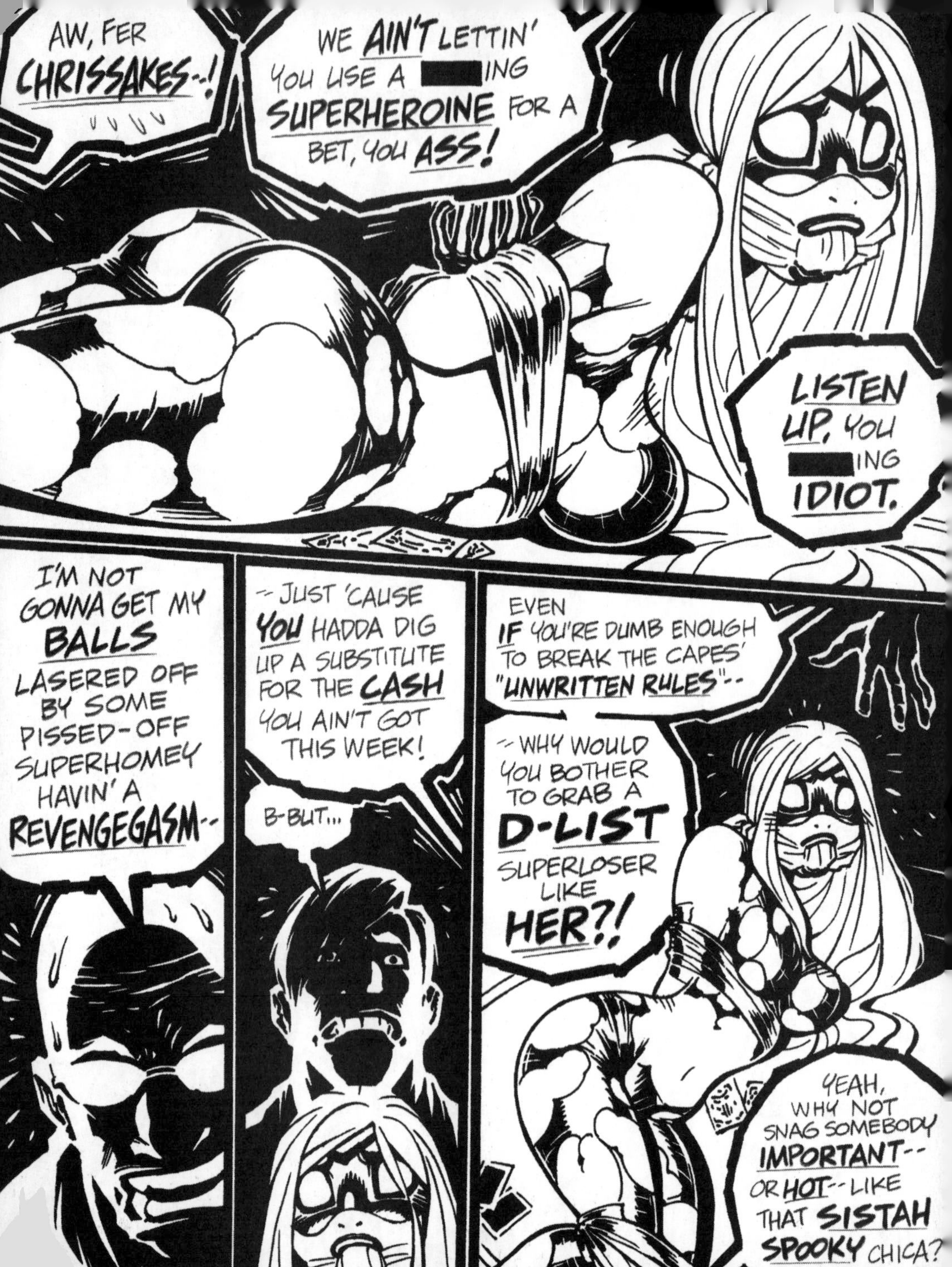
AW, FER CHRISSAKES--!
WE AIN'T LETTIN' YOU USE A [redacted]ING SUPERHEROINE FOR A BET, YOU ASS!
LISTEN UP, YOU [redacted]ING IDIOT.
I'M NOT GONNA GET MY BALLS LASERED OFF BY SOME PISSED-OFF SUPERHOMEY HAVIN' A REVENGEGASM--
--JUST 'CAUSE YOU HADDA DIG UP A SUBSTITUTE FOR THE CASH YOU AIN'T GOT THIS WEEK!
B-BUT...
EVEN IF YOU'RE DUMB ENOUGH TO BREAK THE CAPES' "UNWRITTEN RULES"--
--WHY WOULD YOU BOTHER TO GRAB A D-LIST SUPERLOSER LIKE HER?!
YEAH, WHY NOT SNAG SOMEBODY IMPORTANT-- OR HOT--LIKE THAT SISTAH SPOOKY CHICA?

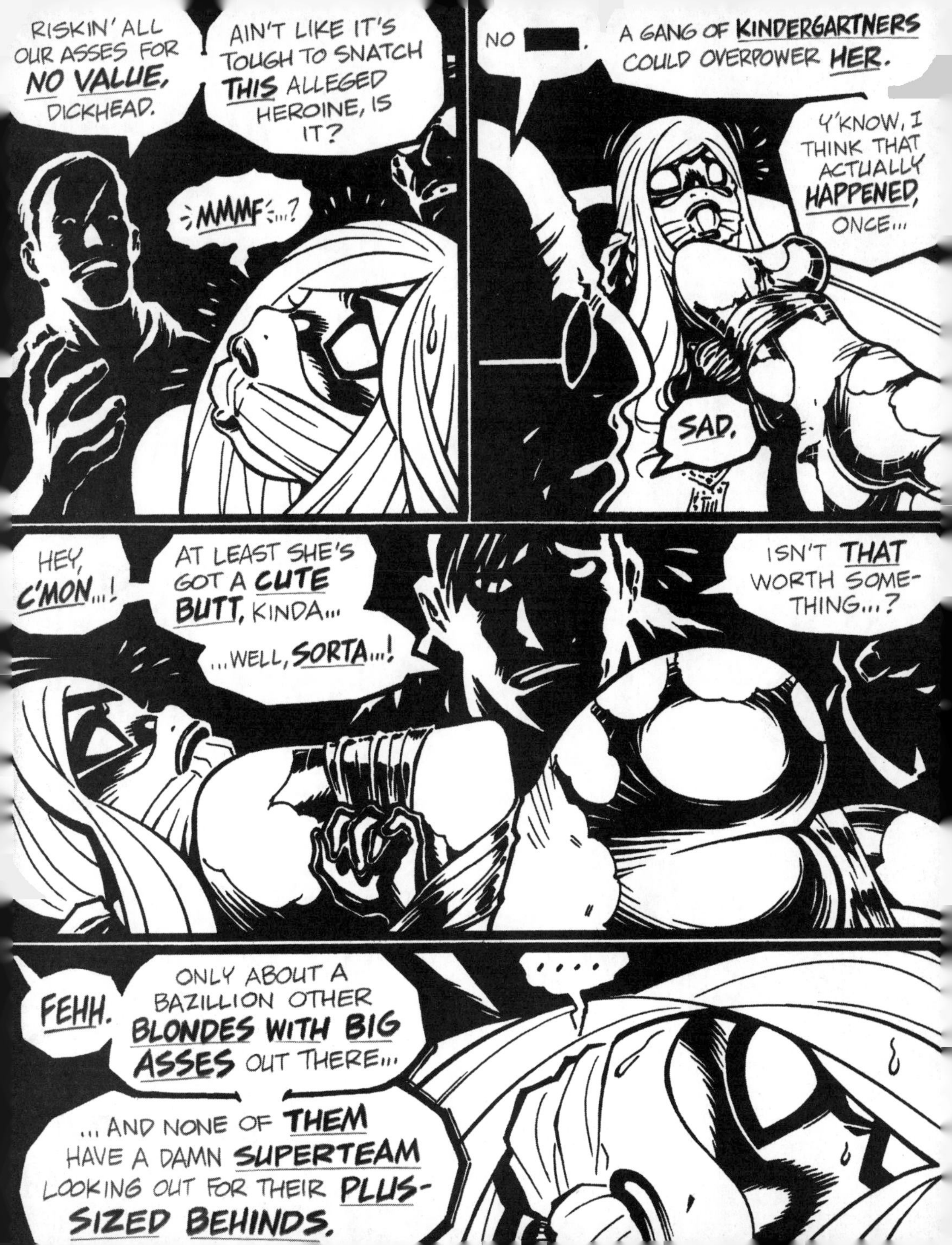
RISKIN' ALL OUR ASSES FOR NO VALUE, DICKHEAD.
AIN'T LIKE IT'S TOUGH TO SNATCH THIS ALLEGED HEROINE, IS IT?
MMMF...?
NO [redacted].
A GANG OF KINDERGARTNERS COULD OVERPOWER HER.
Y'KNOW, I THINK THAT ACTUALLY HAPPENED, ONCE...
SAD.
HEY, C'MON...!
AT LEAST SHE'S GOT A CUTE BUTT, KINDA...
...WELL, SORTA...!
ISN'T THAT WORTH SOME-THING...?
FEHH.
ONLY ABOUT A BAZILLION OTHER BLONDES WITH BIG ASSES OUT THERE...
...AND NONE OF THEM HAVE A DAMN SUPERTEAM LOOKING OUT FOR THEIR PLUS-SIZED BEHINDS.
....

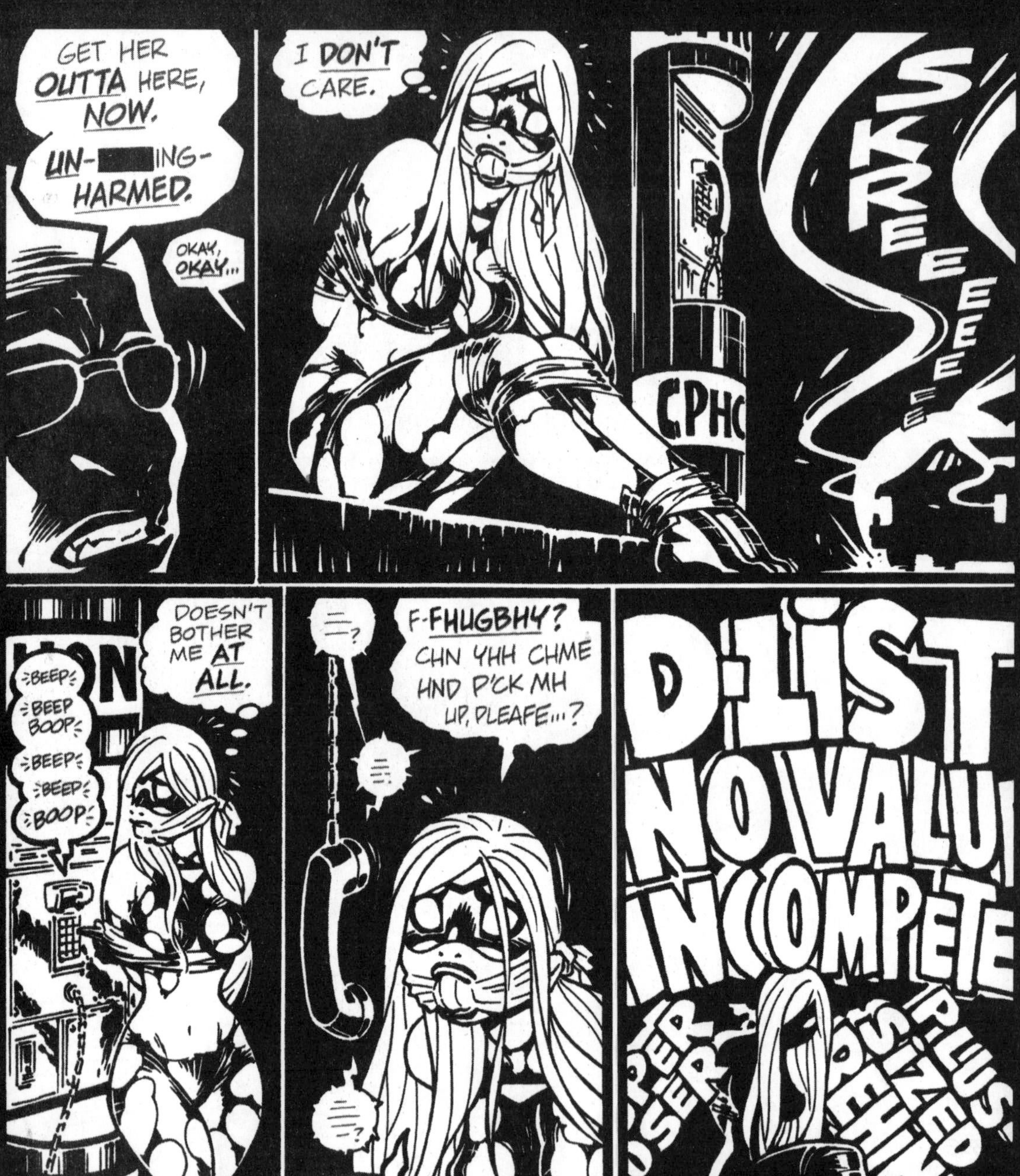
GET HER OUTTA HERE, NOW.
UN-[redacted]ING-HARMED.
OKAY, OKAY...
I DON'T CARE.
CPHC
SKREEEEEE
DOESN'T BOTHER ME AT ALL.
BEEP
BEEP BOOP
BEEP
BEEP
BOOP
F-FHUGBHY? CHN YHH CHME HND P'CK MH UP, PLEAFE...?
CHRNHR UF MHRKHT UN' FOUFH WHLLOW.
FHANKF, FWEETIE.
D-LIST
NO VALU
INCOMPETE
PER
OSER
PLUS-SIZED
BEHIND
I DON'T CARE.

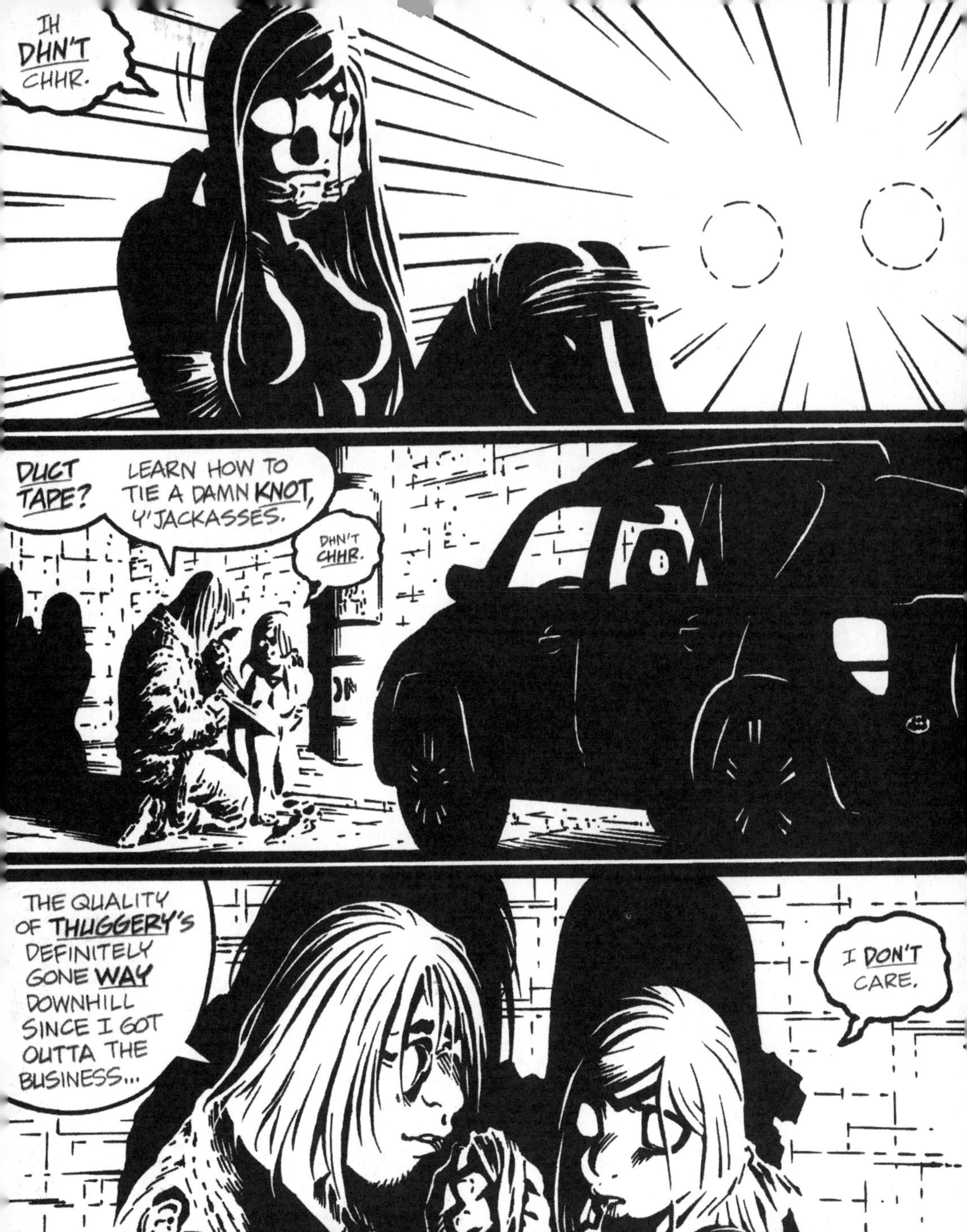
IH DHN'T CHHR.
DUCT TAPE?
LEARN HOW TO TIE A DAMN KNOT, Y'JACKASSES.
DHN'T CHHR.
THE QUALITY OF THUGGERY'S DEFINITELY GONE WAY DOWNHILL SINCE I GOT OUTTA THE BUSINESS...
I DON'T CARE.

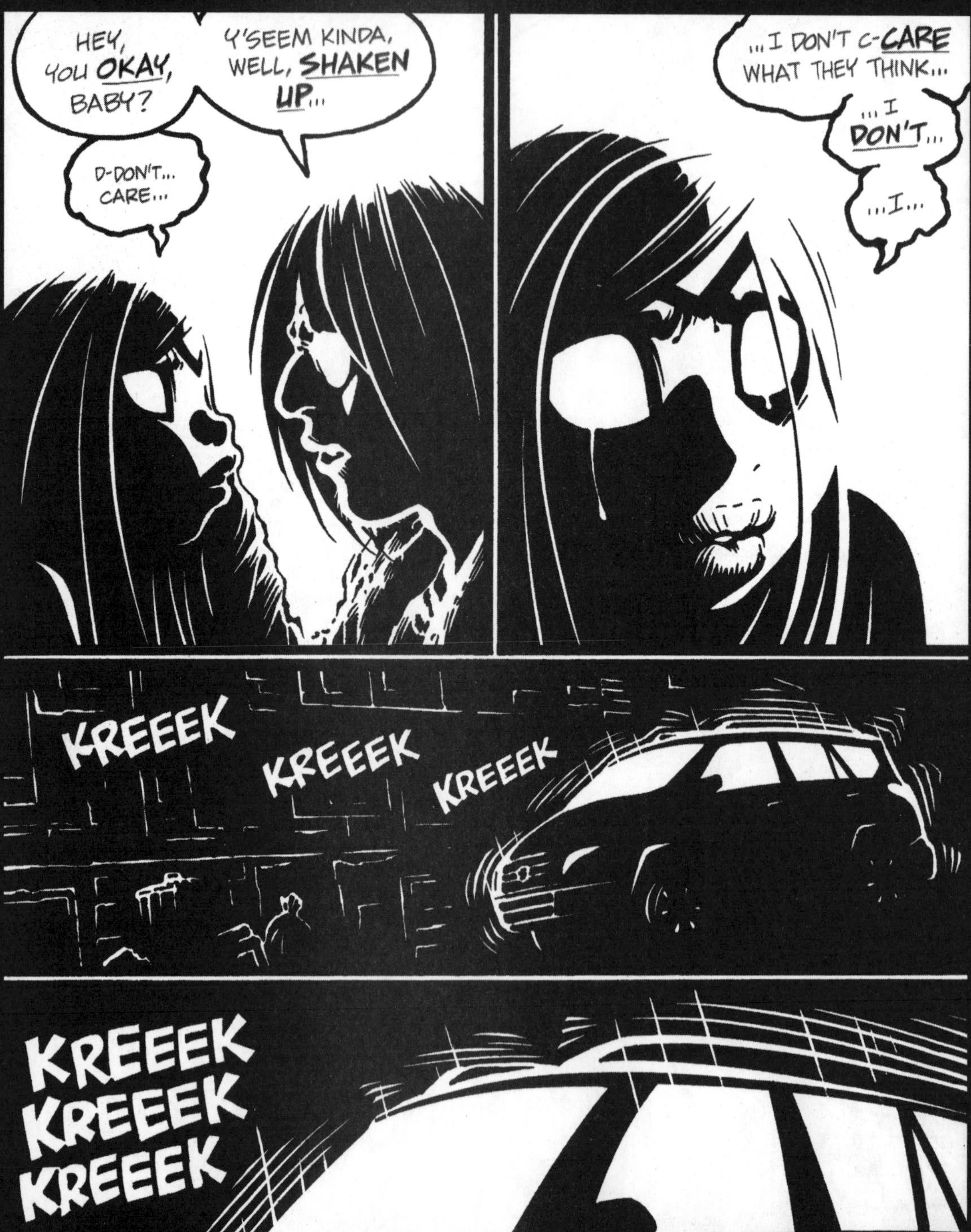

HEY, YOU OKAY, BABY?
Y'SEEM KINDA, WELL, SHAKEN UP...
D-DON'T... CARE...
...I DON'T C-CARE WHAT THEY THINK...
...I DON'T...
...I...
KREEEK
KREEEK
KREEEK
KREEEK
KREEEK
KREEEK

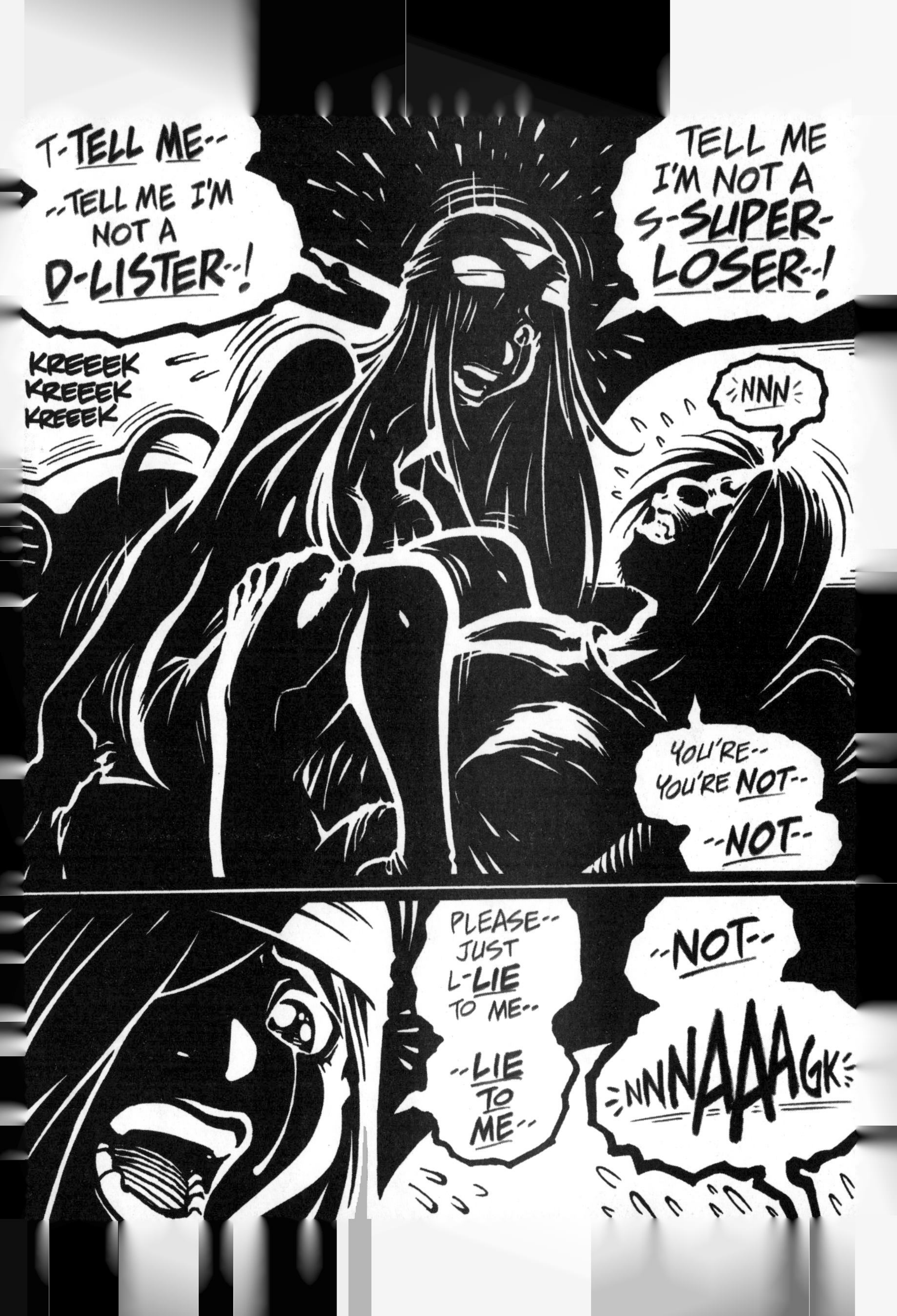
T-TELL ME--
--TELL ME I'M NOT A D-LISTER--!
TELL ME I'M NOT A S-SUPER-LOSER--!
KREEEK KREEEK KREEEK
NNN
YOU'RE-- YOU'RE NOT--
--NOT--
PLEASE-- JUST L-LIE TO ME--
--LIE TO ME--
--NOT--
NNNNAAAGK

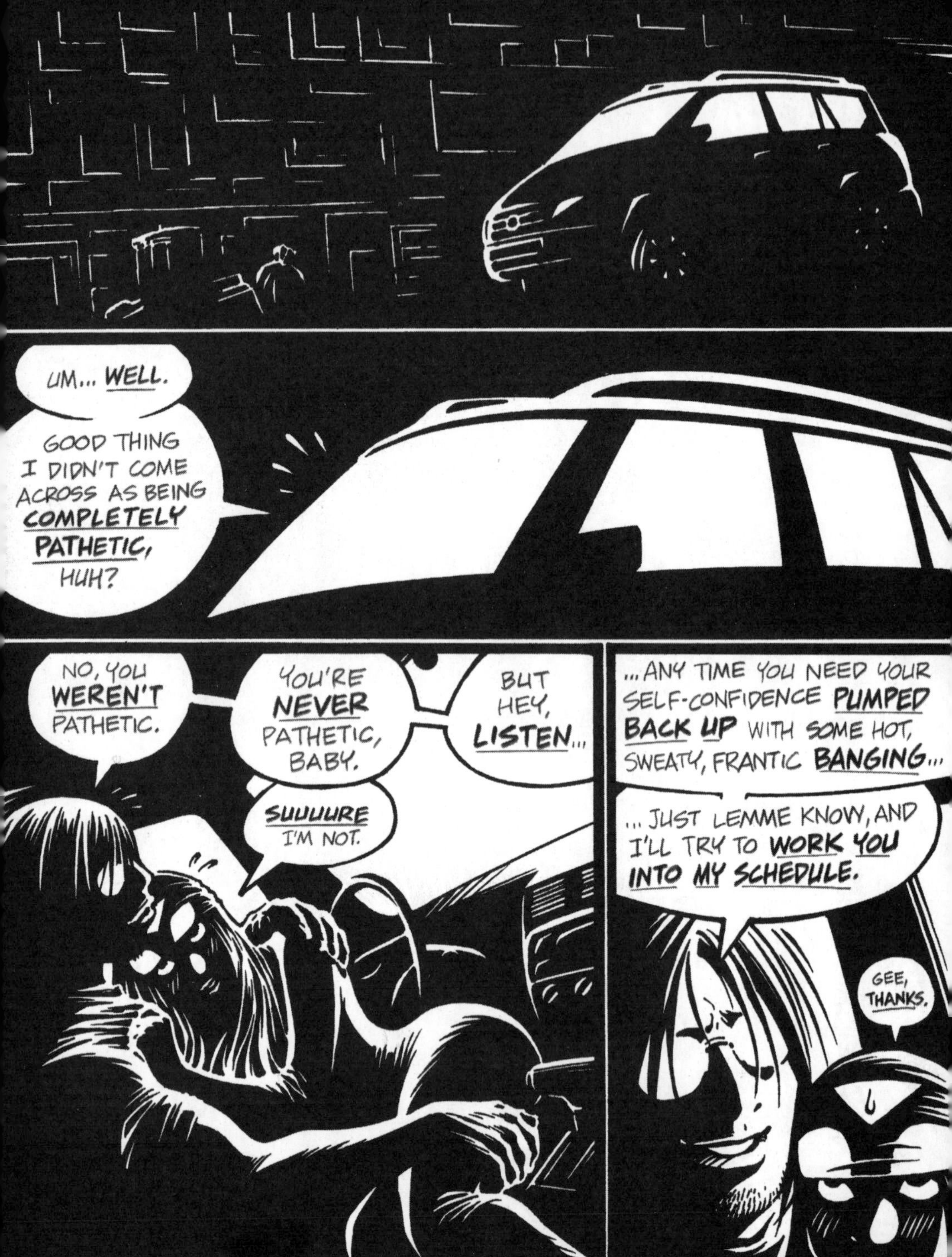
UM... WELL.
GOOD THING I DIDN'T COME ACROSS AS BEING COMPLETELY PATHETIC, HUH?
NO, YOU WEREN'T PATHETIC.
YOU'RE NEVER PATHETIC, BABY.
SUUUURE I'M NOT.
BUT HEY, LISTEN...
...ANY TIME YOU NEED YOUR SELF-CONFIDENCE PUMPED BACK UP WITH SOME HOT, SWEATY, FRANTIC BANGING...
...JUST LEMME KNOW, AND I'LL TRY TO WORK YOU INTO MY SCHEDULE.
GEE, THANKS.

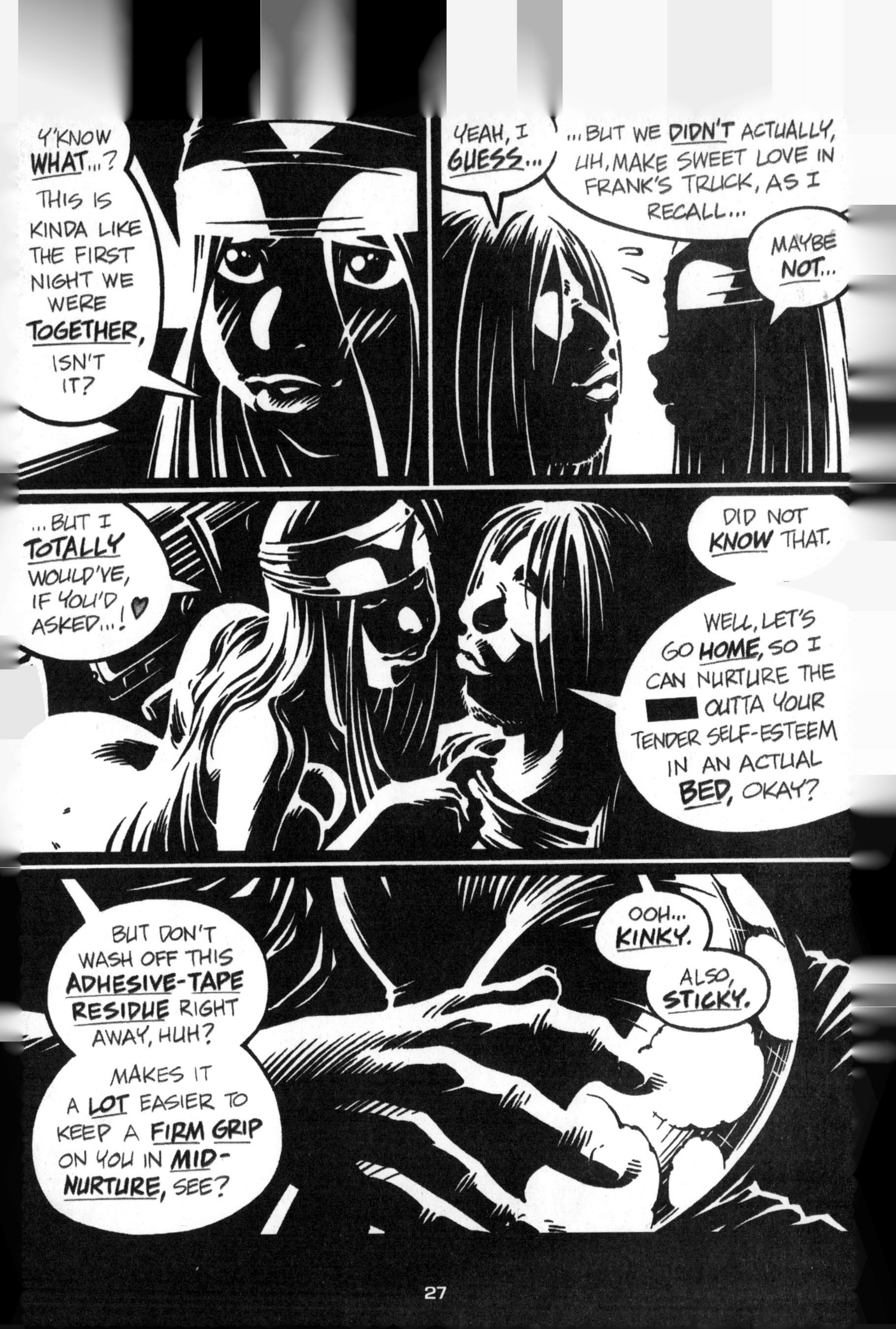
Y'KNOW WHAT...?
THIS IS KINDA LIKE THE FIRST NIGHT WE WERE TOGETHER, ISN'T IT?
YEAH, I GUESS...
...BUT WE DIDN'T ACTUALLY, UH, MAKE SWEET LOVE IN FRANK'S TRUCK, AS I RECALL...
MAYBE NOT...
...BUT I TOTALLY WOULD'VE, IF YOU'D ASKED...! ♥
DID NOT KNOW THAT.
WELL, LET'S GO HOME, SO I CAN NURTURE THE [redacted] OUTTA YOUR TENDER SELF-ESTEEM IN AN ACTUAL BED, OKAY?
BUT DON'T WASH OFF THIS ADHESIVE-TAPE RESIDUE RIGHT AWAY, HUH?
MAKES IT A LOT EASIER TO KEEP A FIRM GRIP ON YOU IN MID-NURTURE, SEE?
OOH... KINKY.
ALSO, STICKY.

Karaoke Rocket Sled and the Eye of the Tippling Tiger

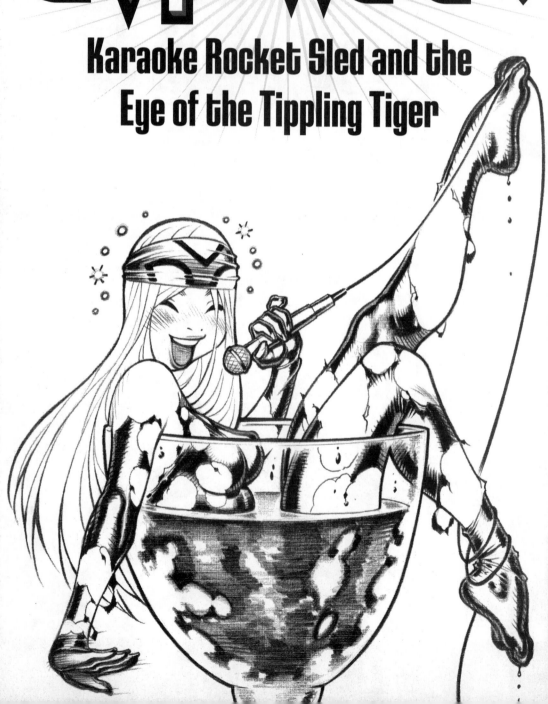

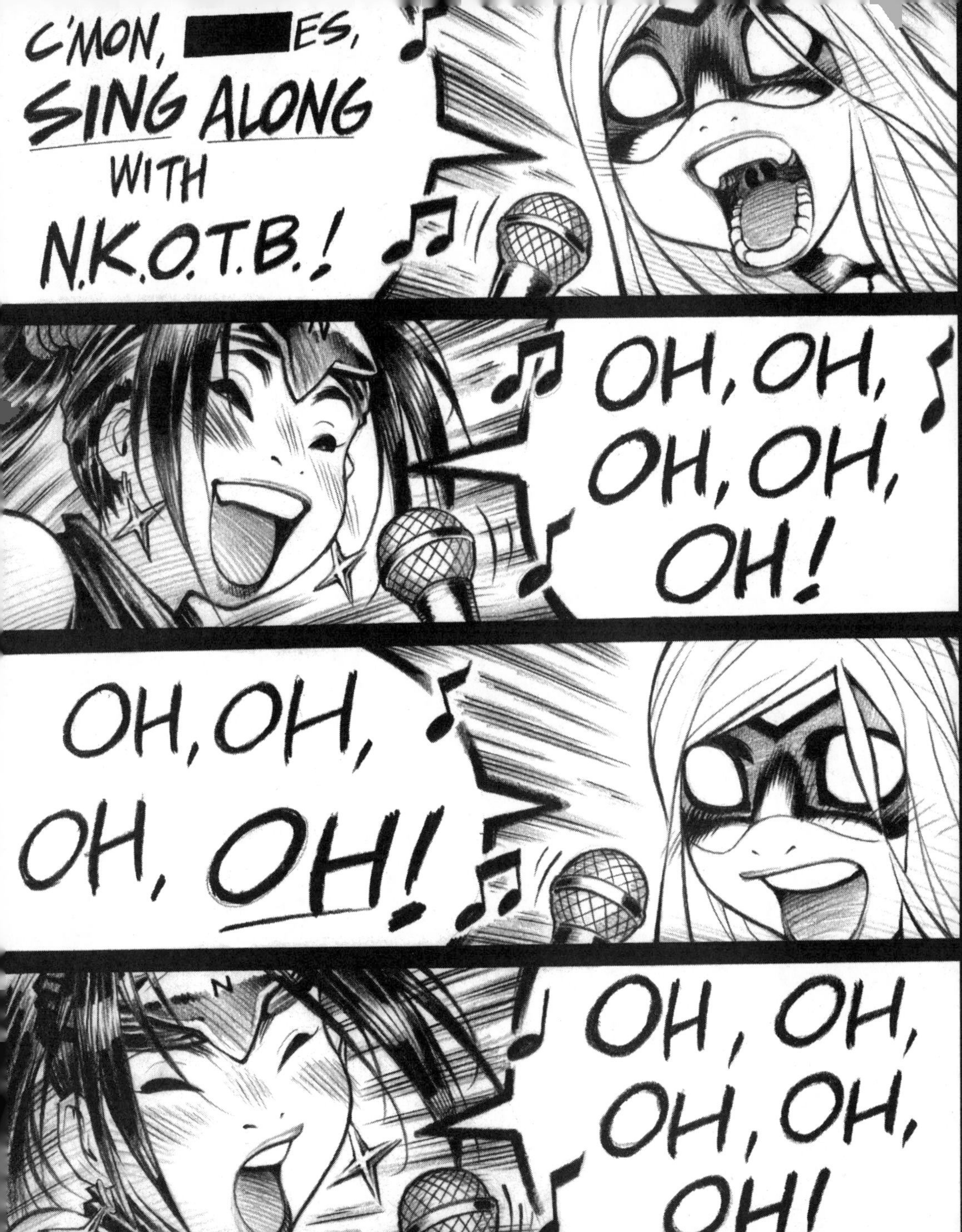
C'MON, [redacted]ES, SING ALONG WITH N.K.O.T.B.!
OH, OH, OH, OH, OH!
OH, OH, OH, OH!
OH, OH, OH, OH, OH!

THE RIGHT STUFF!
THE RIGHT STUFF
THE RIGHT STUFF
XTREME KARAOKE

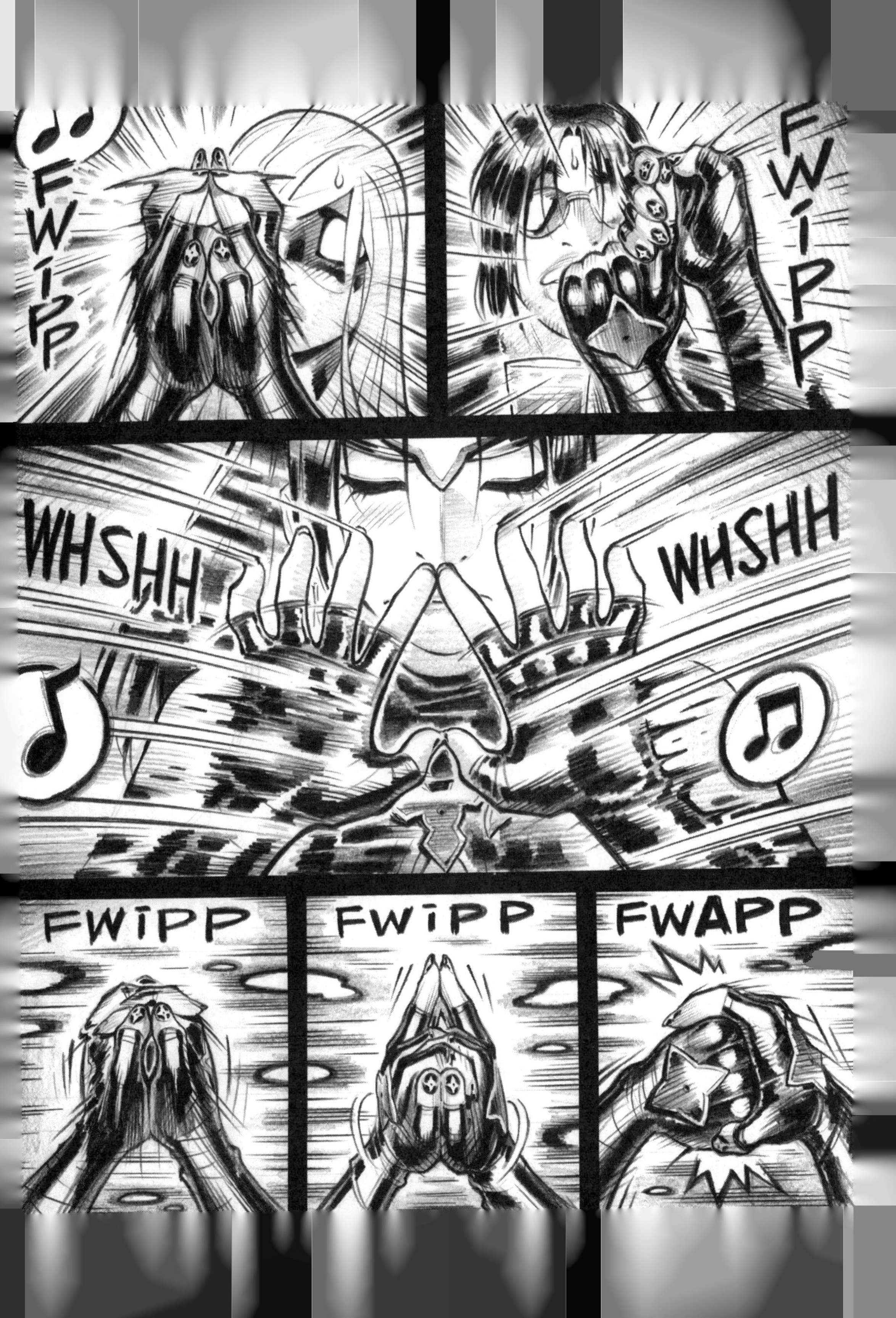
FWIPP
FWIPP
WHSHH
WHSHH
FWIPP
FWIPP
FWAPP

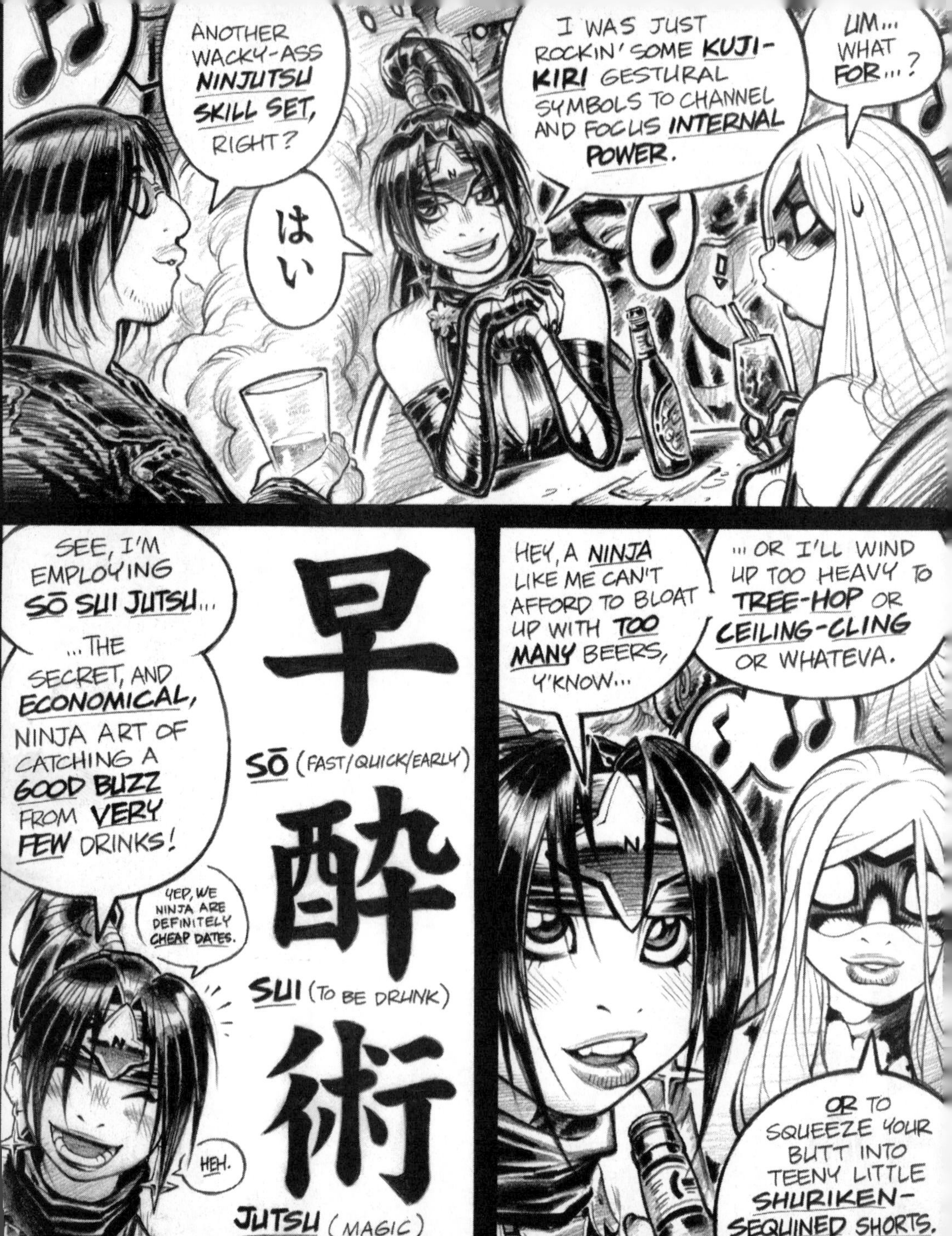
ANOTHER WACKY-ASS NINJUTSU SKILL SET, RIGHT?
はい
I WAS JUST ROCKIN' SOME KUJI-KIRI GESTURAL SYMBOLS TO CHANNEL AND FOCUS INTERNAL POWER.
UM... WHAT FOR...?
SEE, I'M EMPLOYING SŌ SUI JUTSU...
...THE SECRET, AND ECONOMICAL, NINJA ART OF CATCHING A GOOD BUZZ FROM VERY FEW DRINKS!
早
SŌ (FAST/QUICK/EARLY)
酔
SUI (TO BE DRUNK)
術
JUTSU (MAGIC)
YEP, WE NINJA ARE DEFINITELY CHEAP DATES.
HEH.
HEY, A NINJA LIKE ME CAN'T AFFORD TO BLOAT UP WITH TOO MANY BEERS, Y'KNOW...
...OR I'LL WIND UP TOO HEAVY TO TREE-HOP OR CEILING-CLING OR WHATEVA.
OR TO SQUEEZE YOUR BUTT INTO TEENY LITTLE SHURIKEN-SEQUINED SHORTS.

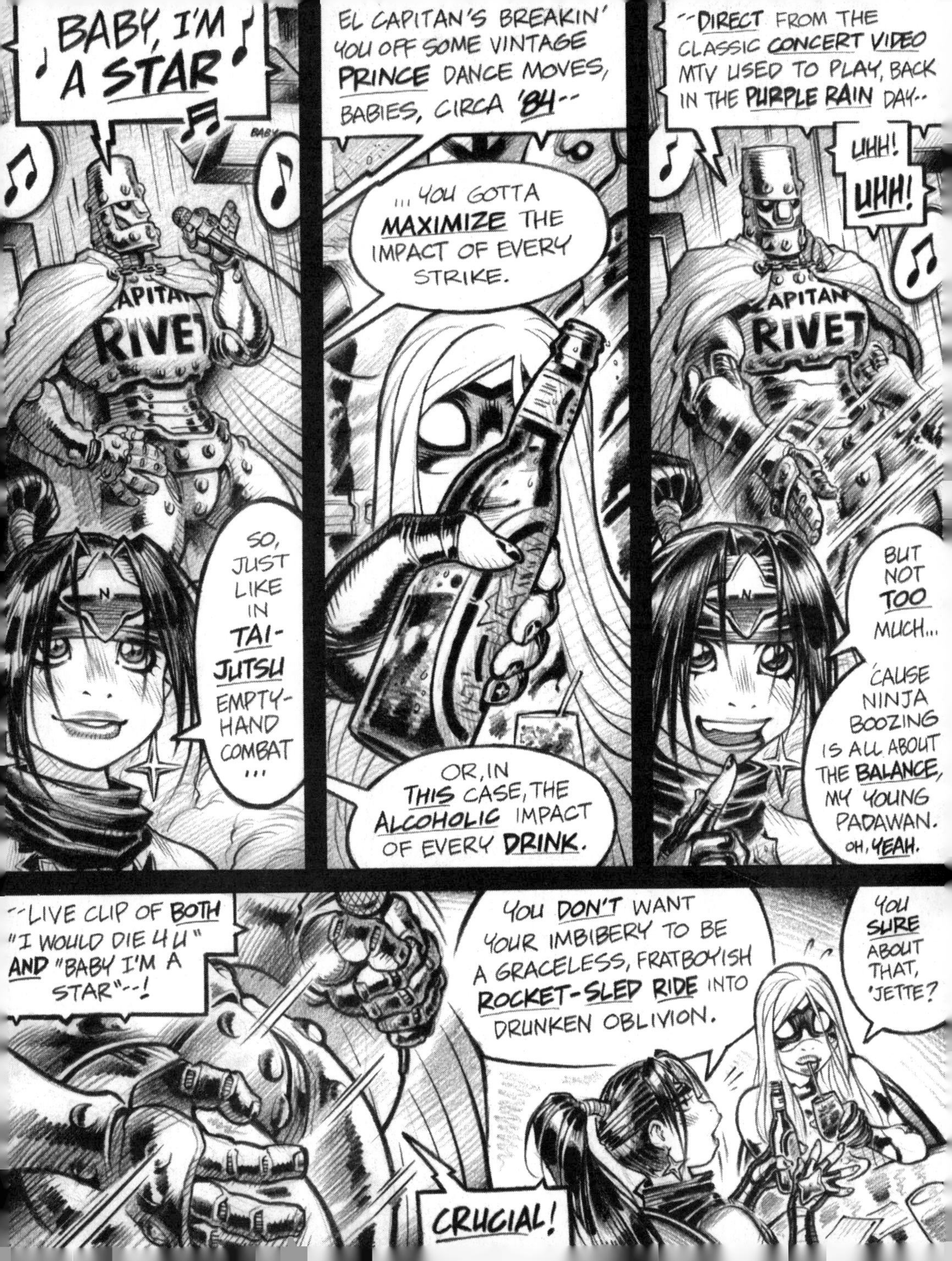
BABY, I'M A STAR
BABY
SO, JUST LIKE IN TAI-JUTSU EMPTY-HAND COMBAT ...
EL CAPITAN'S BREAKIN' YOU OFF SOME VINTAGE PRINCE DANCE MOVES, BABIES, CIRCA '84--
... YOU GOTTA MAXIMIZE THE IMPACT OF EVERY STRIKE.
OR, IN THIS CASE, THE ALCOHOLIC IMPACT OF EVERY DRINK.
--DIRECT FROM THE CLASSIC CONCERT VIDEO MTV USED TO PLAY, BACK IN THE PURPLE RAIN DAY--
UHH! UHH!
BUT NOT TOO MUCH...
'CAUSE NINJA BOOZING IS ALL ABOUT THE BALANCE, MY YOUNG PADAWAN. OH, YEAH.
--LIVE CLIP OF BOTH "I WOULD DIE 4 U" AND "BABY I'M A STAR"--!
YOU DON'T WANT YOUR IMBIBERY TO BE A GRACELESS, FRATBOYISH ROCKET-SLED RIDE INTO DRUNKEN OBLIVION.
YOU SURE ABOUT THAT, 'JETTE?
CRUCIAL!

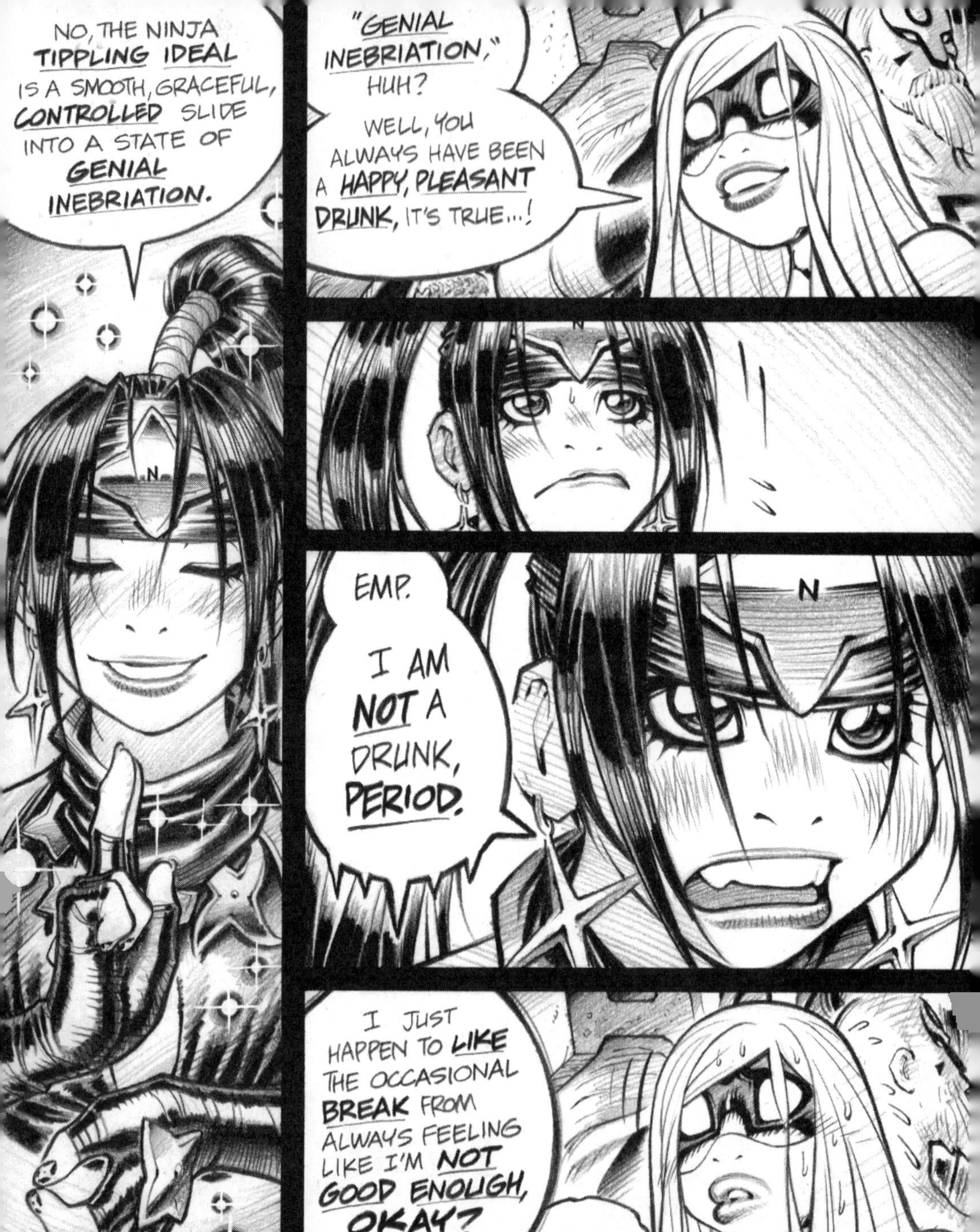
NO, THE NINJA TIPPLING IDEAL IS A SMOOTH, GRACEFUL, CONTROLLED SLIDE INTO A STATE OF GENIAL INEBRIATION.
"GENIAL INEBRIATION," HUH?
WELL, YOU ALWAYS HAVE BEEN A HAPPY, PLEASANT DRUNK, IT'S TRUE...!
EMP.
I AM NOT A DRUNK, PERIOD.
I JUST HAPPEN TO LIKE THE OCCASIONAL BREAK FROM ALWAYS FEELING LIKE I'M NOT GOOD ENOUGH, OKAY?
OOPS.

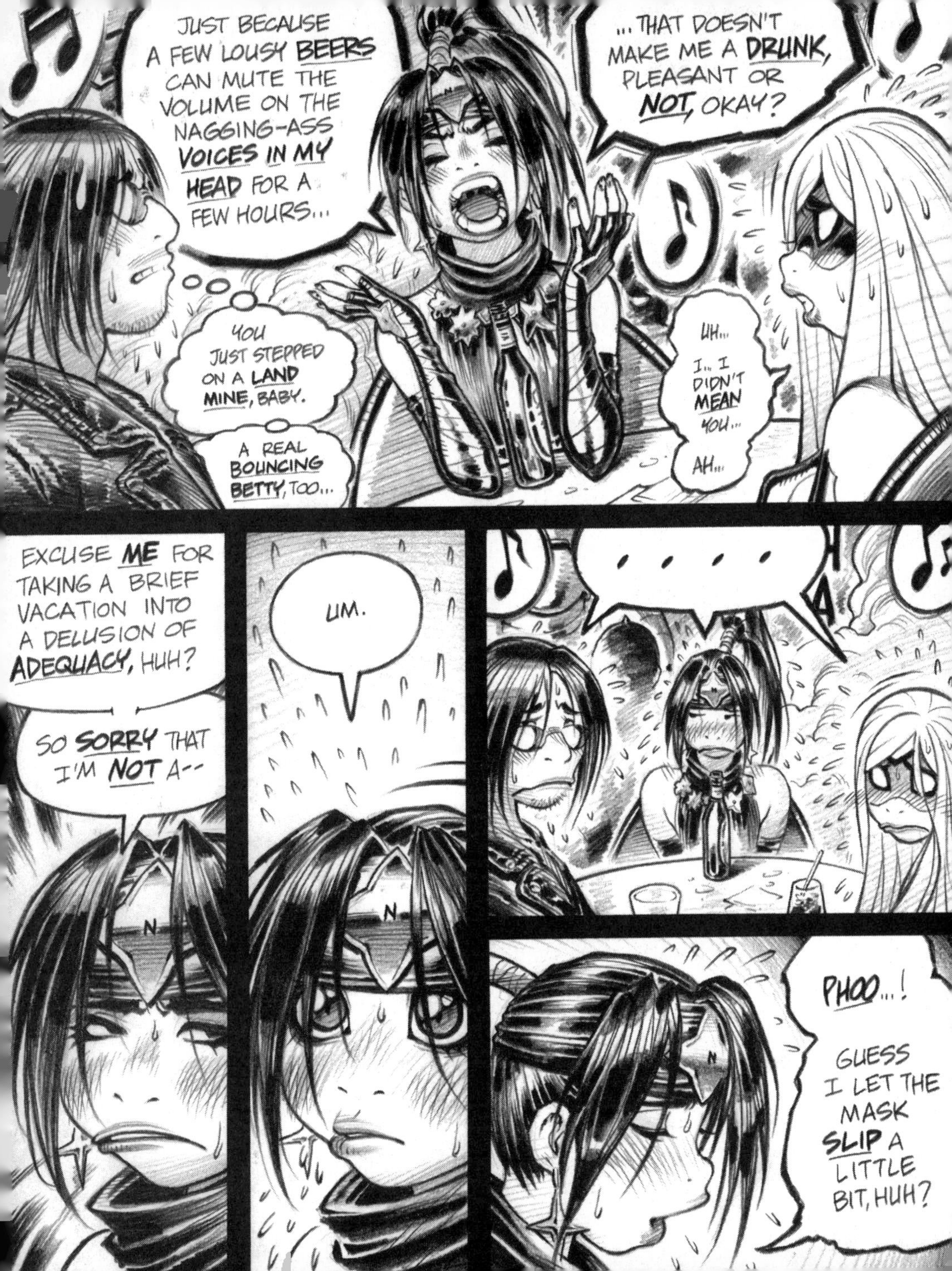
JUST BECAUSE A FEW LOUSY BEERS CAN MUTE THE VOLUME ON THE NAGGING-ASS VOICES IN MY HEAD FOR A FEW HOURS...
...THAT DOESN'T MAKE ME A DRUNK, PLEASANT OR NOT, OKAY?
YOU JUST STEPPED ON A LAND MINE, BABY.
A REAL BOUNCING BETTY, TOO...
UH... I... I DIDN'T MEAN YOU... AH...
EXCUSE ME FOR TAKING A BRIEF VACATION INTO A DELUSION OF ADEQUACY, HUH?
SO SORRY THAT I'M NOT A--
UM.
. . . .
PHOO...!
GUESS I LET THE MASK SLIP A LITTLE BIT, HUH?

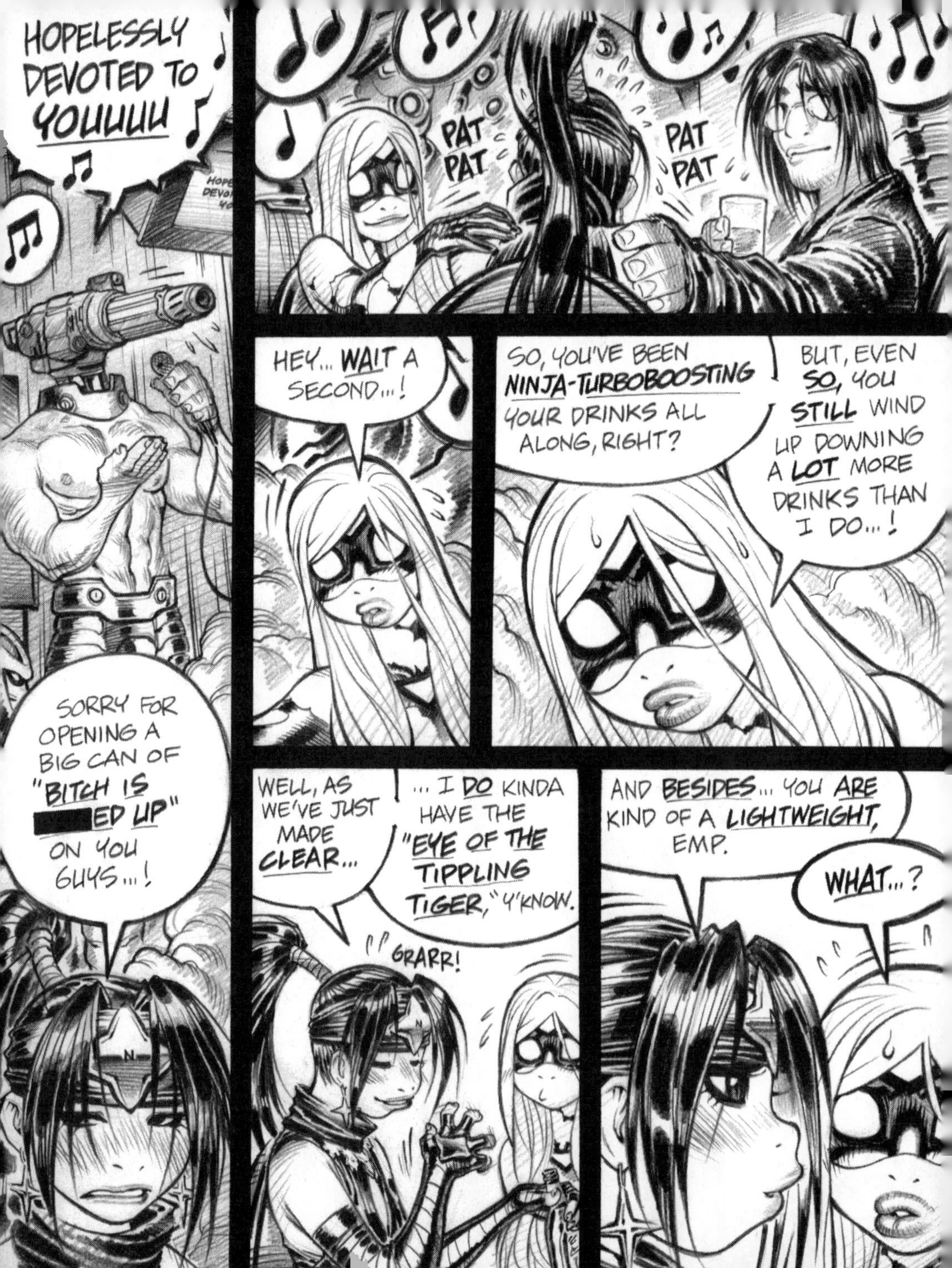
HOPELESSLY DEVOTED TO YOUUUU
PAT PAT
PAT PAT
HEY... WAIT A SECOND...!
SO, YOU'VE BEEN NINJA-TURBOBOOSTING YOUR DRINKS ALL ALONG, RIGHT?
BUT, EVEN SO, YOU STILL WIND UP DOWNING A LOT MORE DRINKS THAN I DO...!
SORRY FOR OPENING A BIG CAN OF "BITCH IS [redacted]ED UP" ON YOU GUYS...!
WELL, AS WE'VE JUST MADE CLEAR...
... I DO KINDA HAVE THE "EYE OF THE TIPPLING TIGER," Y'KNOW.
GRARR!
AND BESIDES... YOU ARE KIND OF A LIGHTWEIGHT, EMP.
WHAT...?

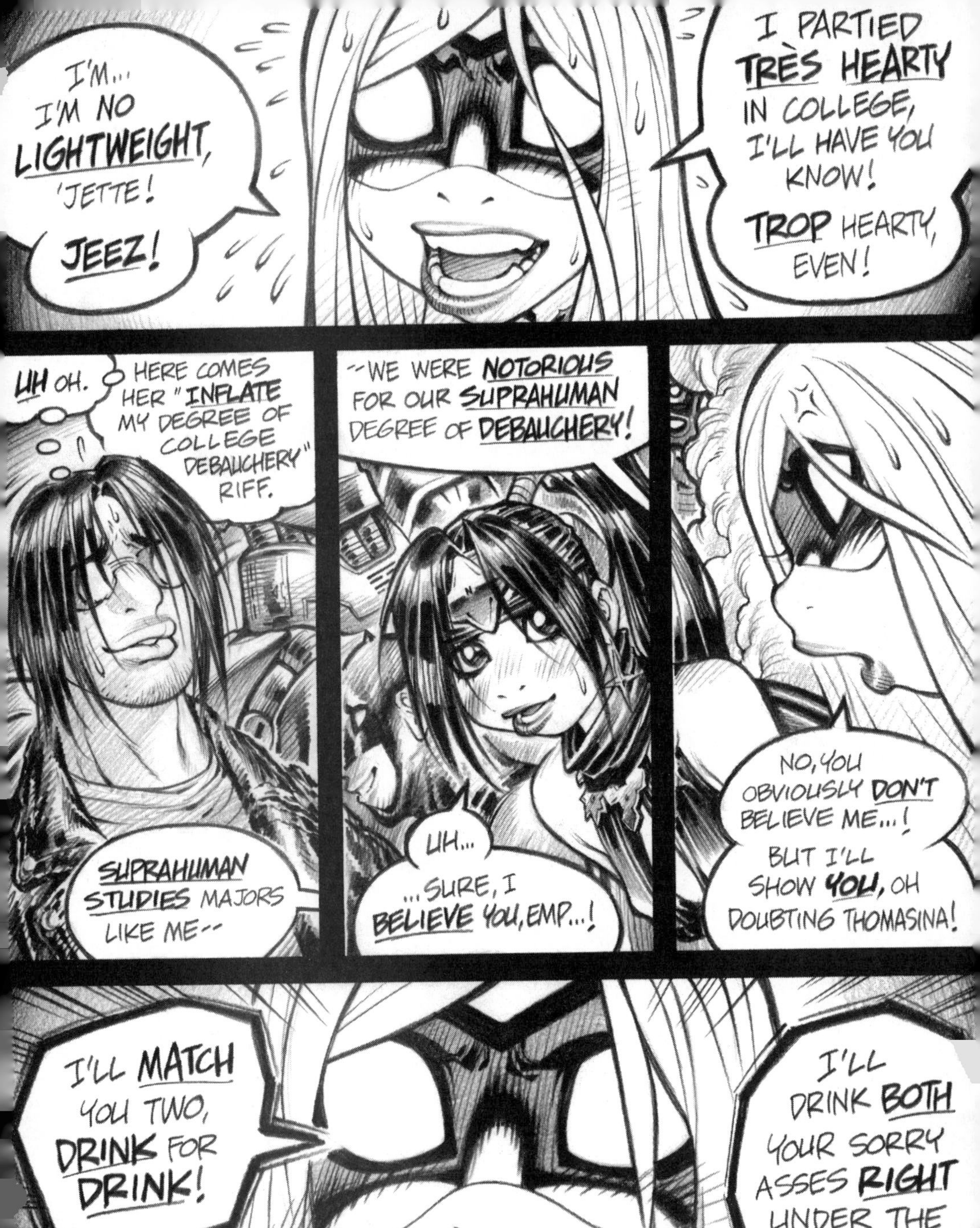
I'M... I'M NO LIGHTWEIGHT, 'JETTE! JEEZ!
I PARTIED TRÈS HEARTY IN COLLEGE, I'LL HAVE YOU KNOW! TROP HEARTY, EVEN!
UH OH.
HERE COMES HER "INFLATE MY DEGREE OF COLLEGE DEBAUCHERY" RIFF.
SUPRAHUMAN STUDIES MAJORS LIKE ME--
--WE WERE NOTORIOUS FOR OUR SUPRAHUMAN DEGREE OF DEBAUCHERY!
UH... ...SURE, I BELIEVE YOU, EMP...!
NO, YOU OBVIOUSLY DON'T BELIEVE ME...! BUT I'LL SHOW YOU, OH DOUBTING THOMASINA!
I'LL MATCH YOU TWO, DRINK FOR DRINK!
I'LL DRINK BOTH YOUR SORRY ASSES RIGHT UNDER THE TABLE!

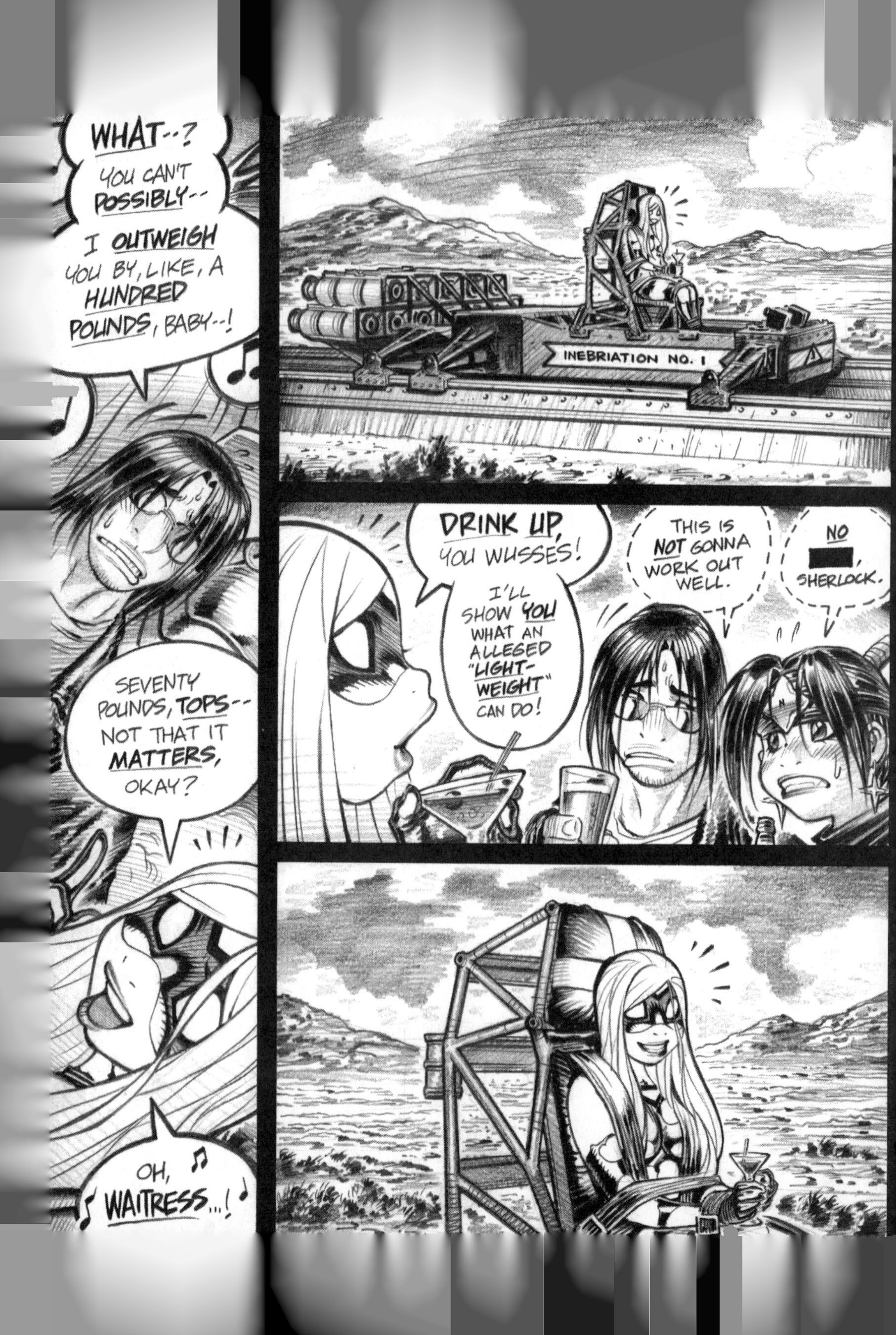
WHAT--? YOU CAN'T POSSIBLY-- I OUTWEIGH YOU BY, LIKE, A HUNDRED POUNDS, BABY--!
SEVENTY POUNDS, TOPS-- NOT THAT IT MATTERS, OKAY?
OH, WAITRESS...!
INEBRIATION NO. 1
DRINK UP, YOU WUSSES!
I'LL SHOW YOU WHAT AN ALLEGED "LIGHT-WEIGHT" CAN DO!
THIS IS NOT GONNA WORK OUT WELL.
NO [redacted], SHERLOCK.

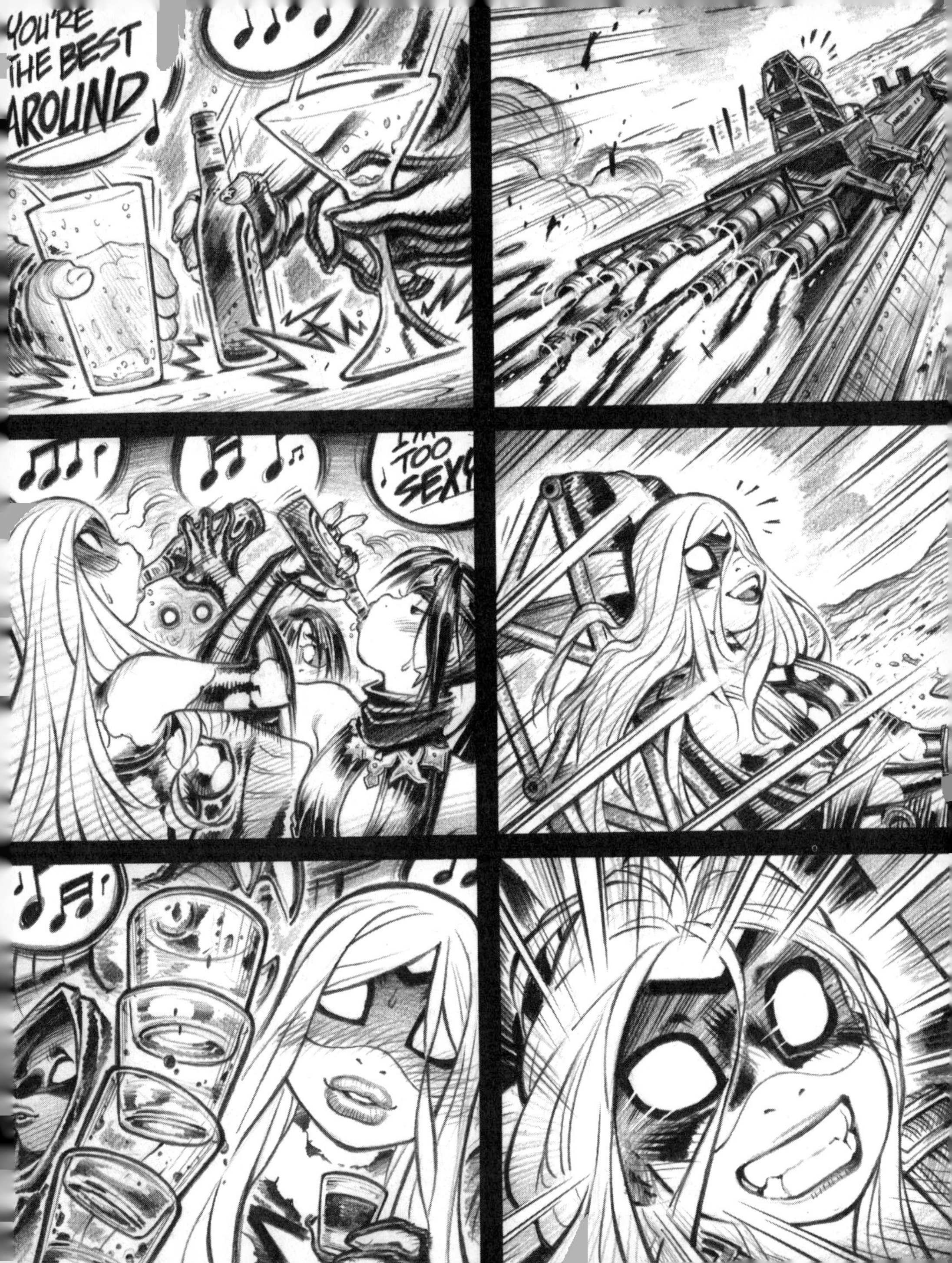
YOU'RE THE BEST AROUND
TOO SEX

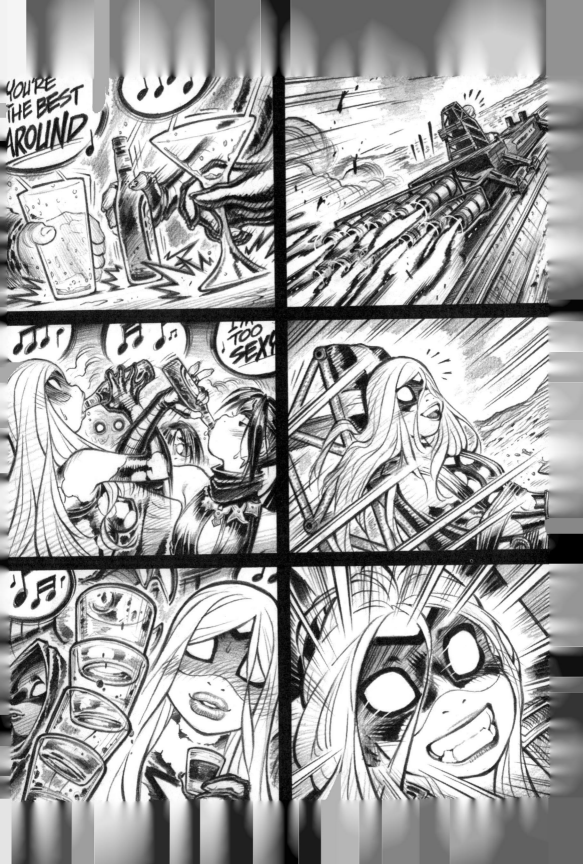

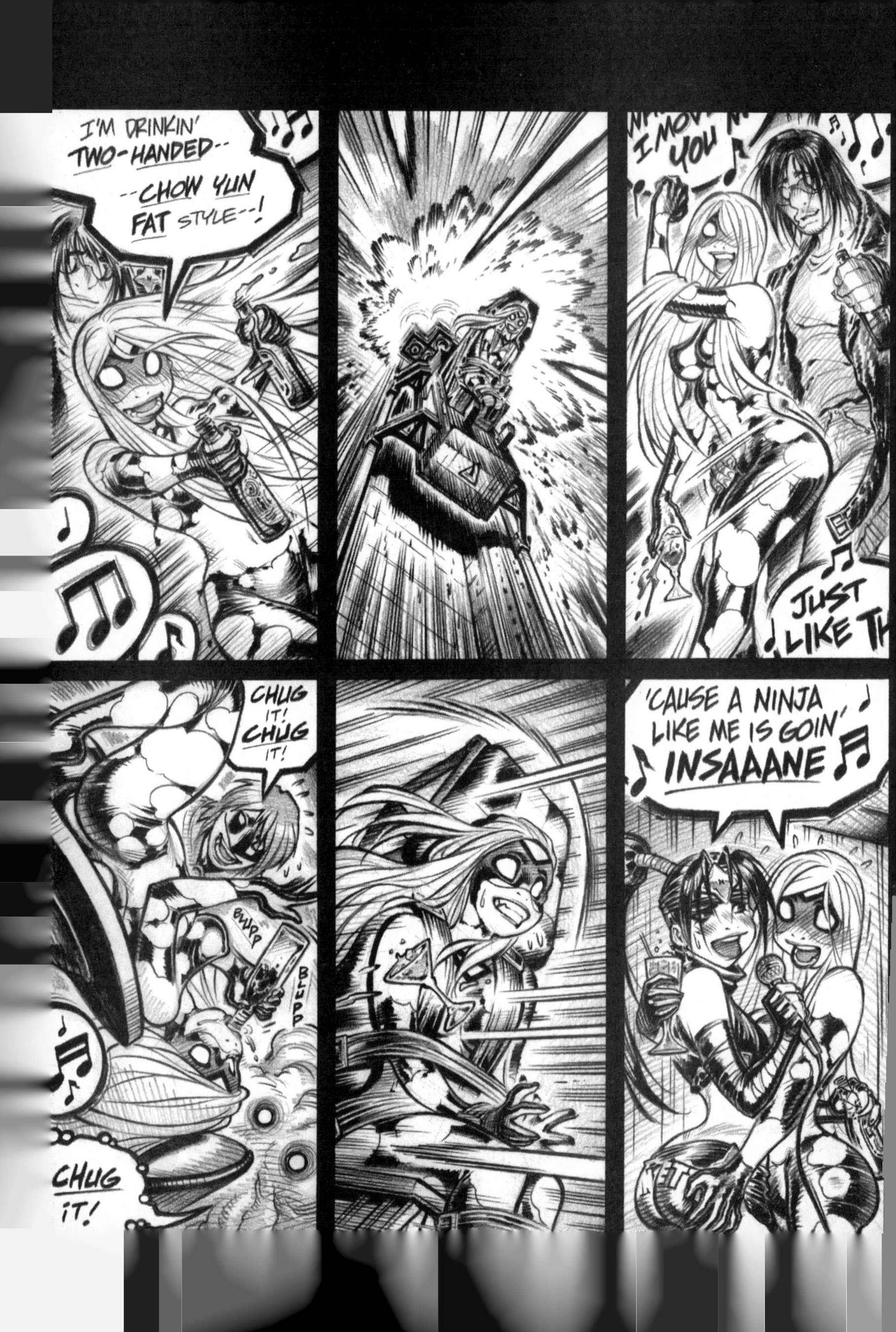
I'M DRINKIN' TWO-HANDED--
--CHOW YUN FAT STYLE--!
CHUG IT! CHUG IT!
BLUPP
BLUPP
CHUG IT!
'CAUSE A NINJA LIKE ME IS GOIN' INSAAANE

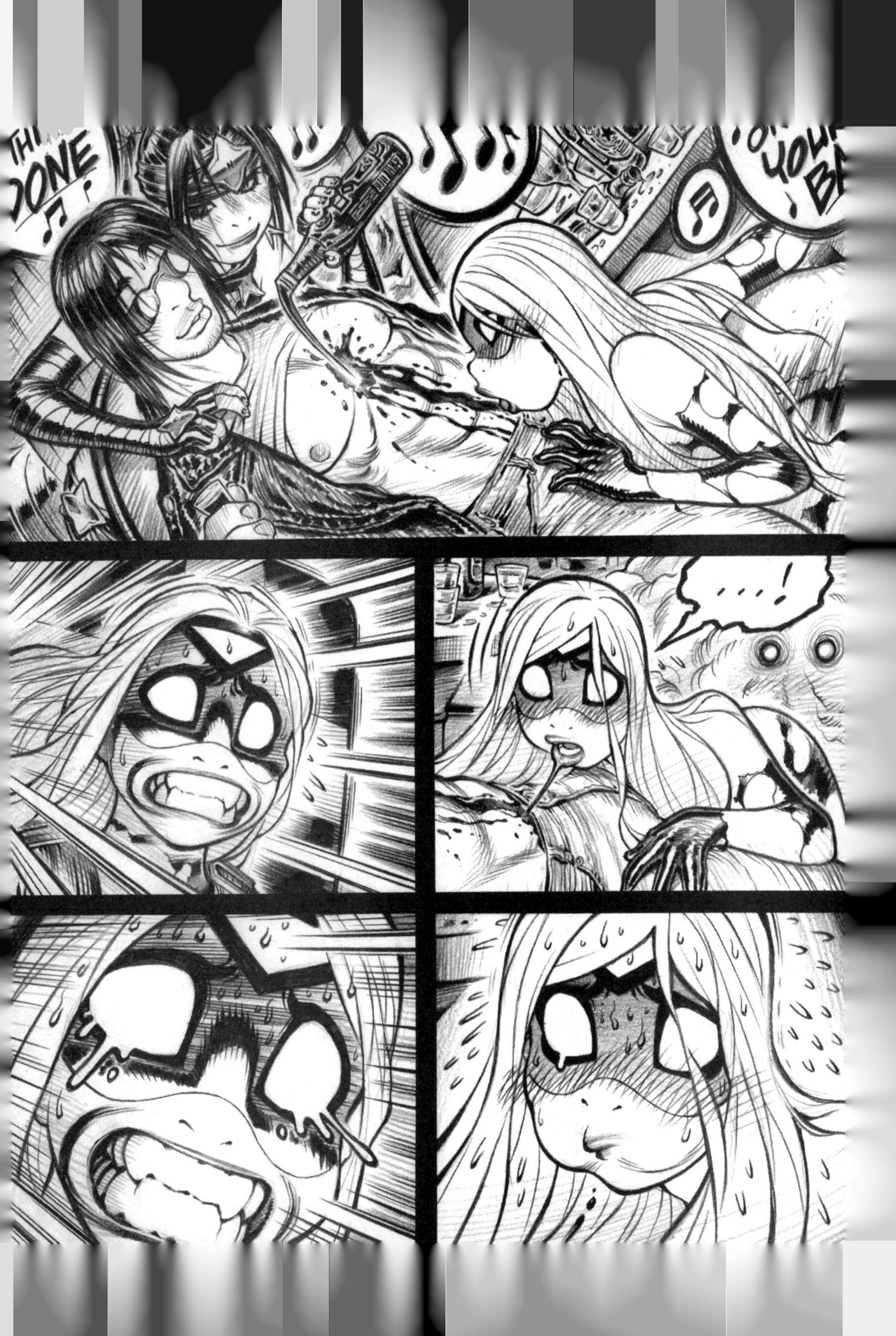
DONE
...!

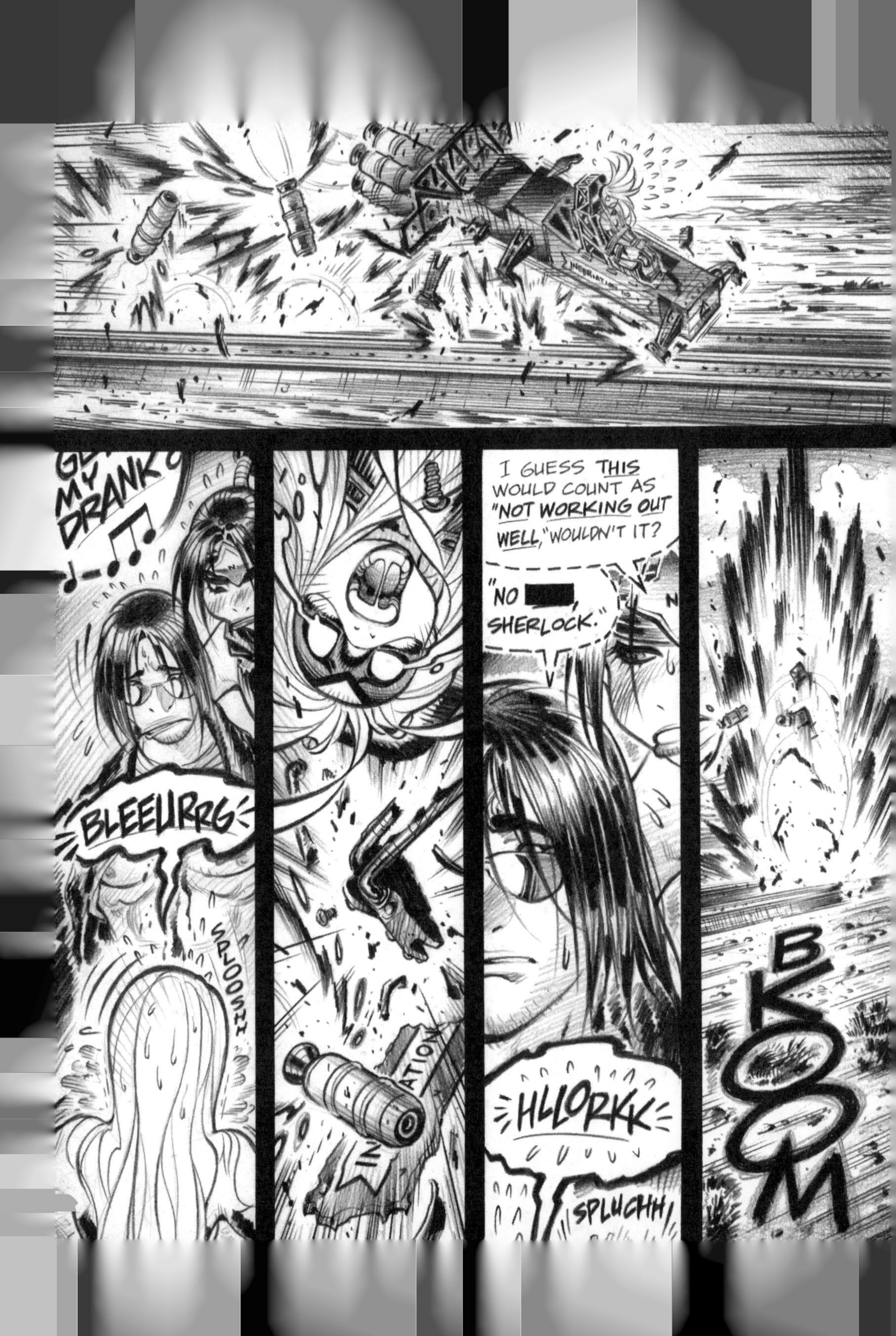

MY DRANK
BLEEURRG
SPLOOSHH
I GUESS THIS WOULD COUNT AS "NOT WORKING OUT WELL," WOULDN'T IT?
"NO [redacted], SHERLOCK."
HLLORKK
SPLUCHH
BKOOM

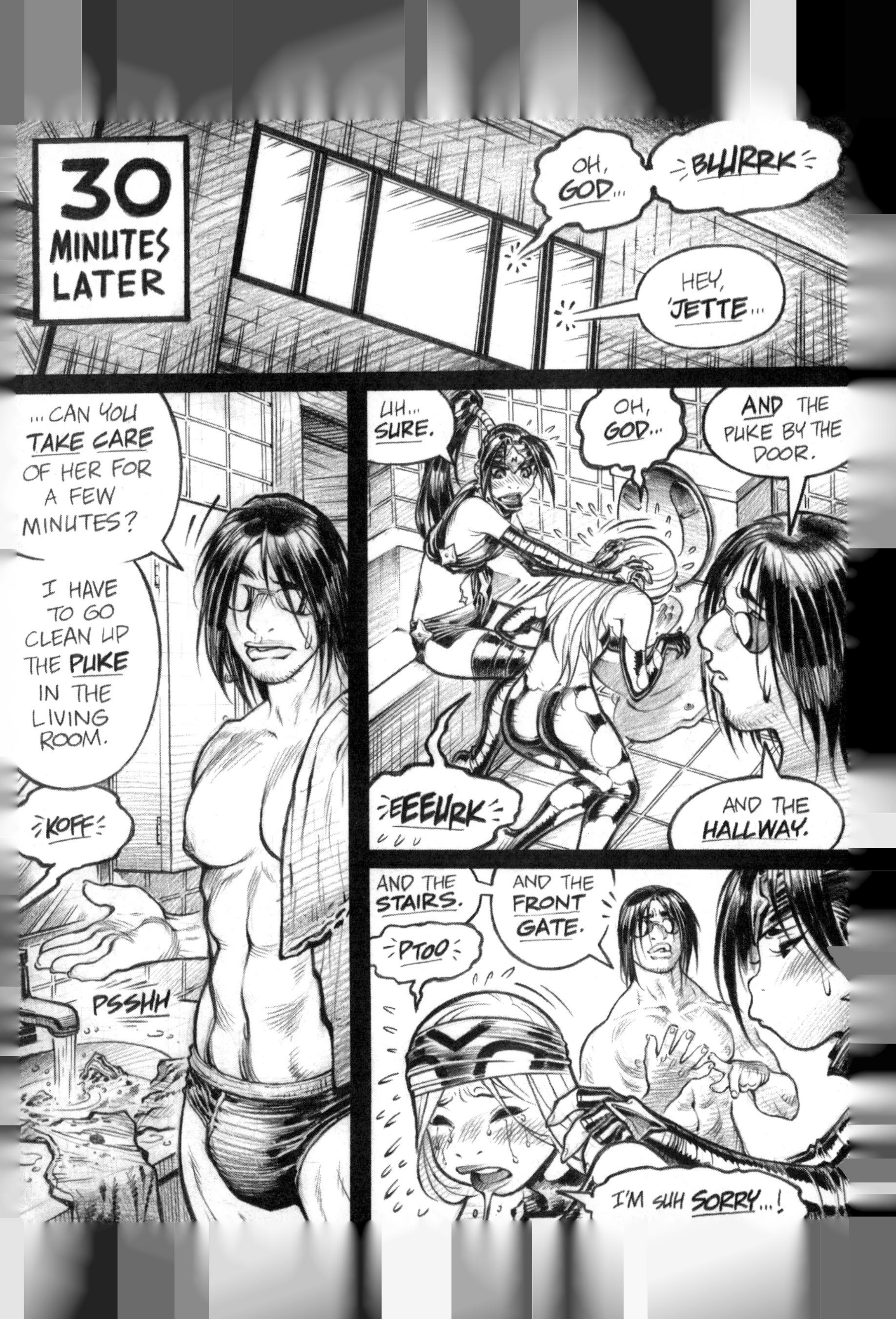
30 MINUTES LATER
OH, GOD...
BLURRK
HEY, 'JETTE...
...CAN YOU TAKE CARE OF HER FOR A FEW MINUTES?
I HAVE TO GO CLEAN UP THE PUKE IN THE LIVING ROOM.
KOFF
PSSHH
UH... SURE.
OH, GOD...
AND THE PUKE BY THE DOOR.
EEEURK
AND THE HALLWAY.
AND THE STAIRS.
AND THE FRONT GATE.
PTOO
I'M SUH SORRY...!

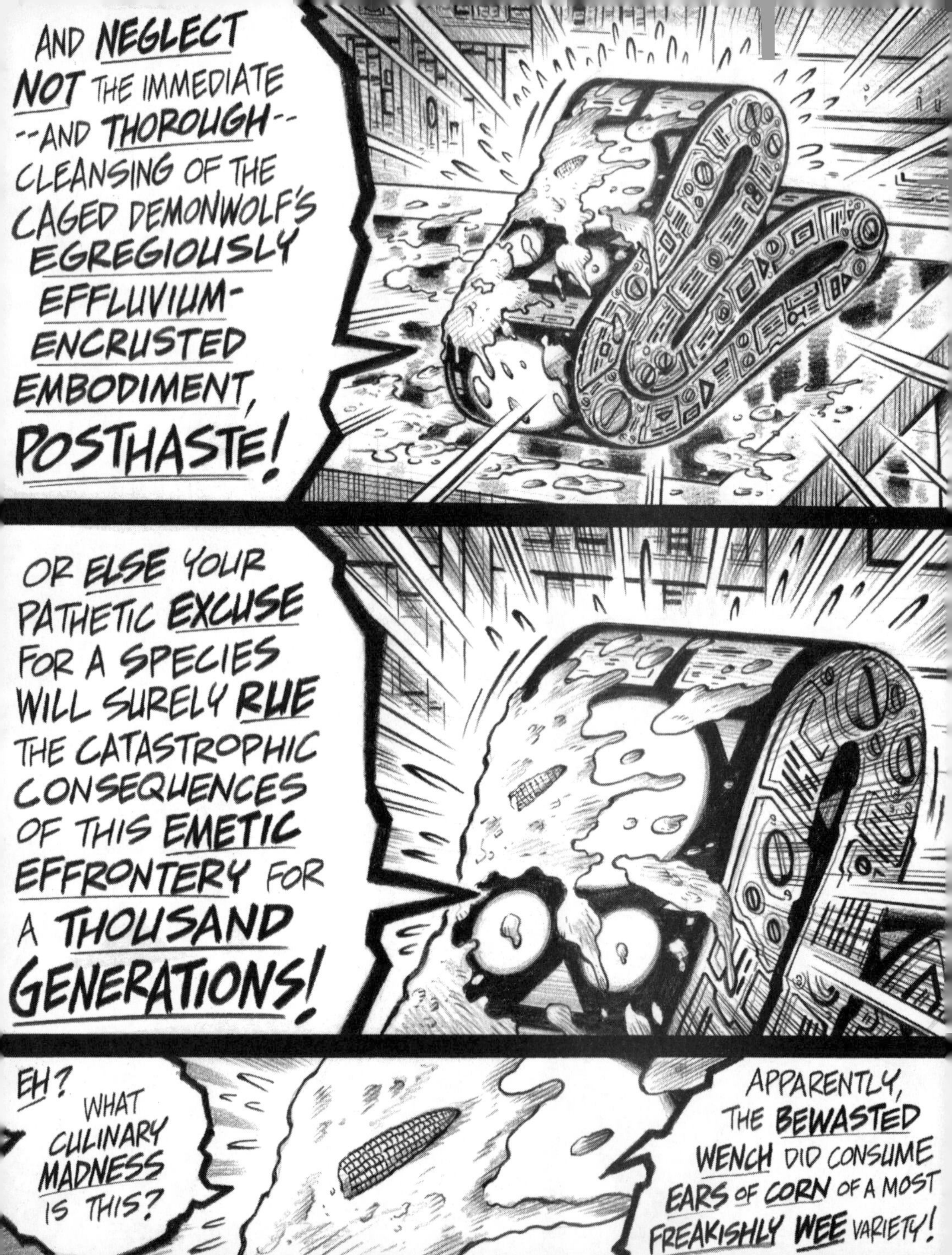
AND NEGLECT NOT THE IMMEDIATE --AND THOROUGH-- CLEANSING OF THE CAGED DEMONWOLF'S EGREGIOUSLY EFFLUVIUM-ENCRUSTED EMBODIMENT, POSTHASTE!
OR ELSE YOUR PATHETIC EXCUSE FOR A SPECIES WILL SURELY RUE THE CATASTROPHIC CONSEQUENCES OF THIS EMETIC EFFRONTERY FOR A THOUSAND GENERATIONS!
EH? WHAT CULINARY MADNESS IS THIS?
APPARENTLY, THE BEWASTED WENCH DID CONSUME EARS OF CORN OF A MOST FREAKISHLY WEE VARIETY!

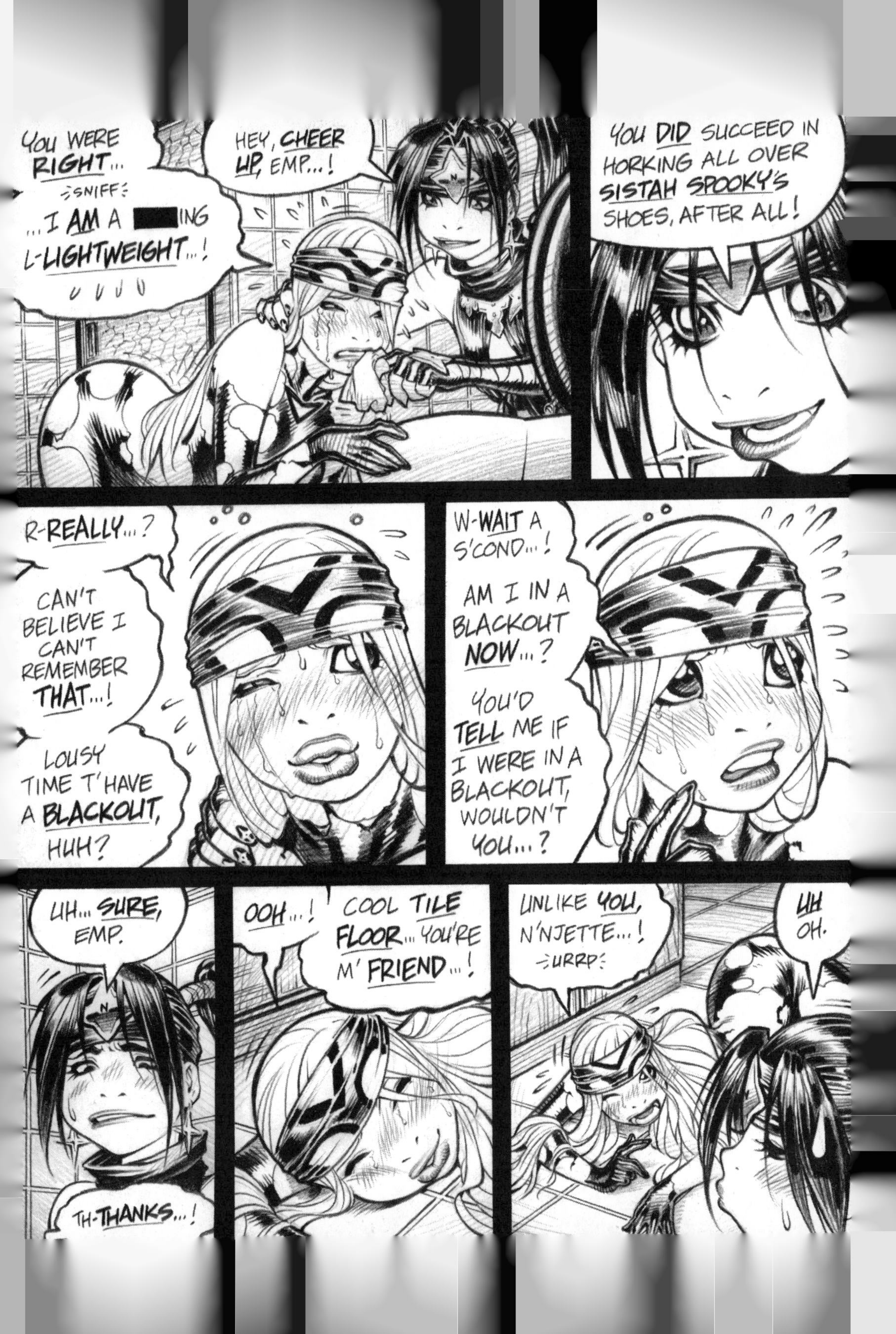

YOU WERE RIGHT...
SNIFF
...I AM A [redacted]ING L-LIGHTWEIGHT...!
HEY, CHEER UP, EMP...!
YOU DID SUCCEED IN HORKING ALL OVER SISTAH SPOOKY'S SHOES, AFTER ALL!
R-REALLY...?
CAN'T BELIEVE I CAN'T REMEMBER THAT...!
LOUSY TIME T'HAVE A BLACKOUT, HUH?
W-WAIT A S'COND...!
AM I IN A BLACKOUT NOW...?
YOU'D TELL ME IF I WERE IN A BLACKOUT, WOULDN'T YOU...?
UH... SURE, EMP.
TH-THANKS...!
OOH...!
COOL TILE FLOOR... YOU'RE M' FRIEND...!
UNLIKE YOU, N'NJETTE...!
URRP
UH OH.

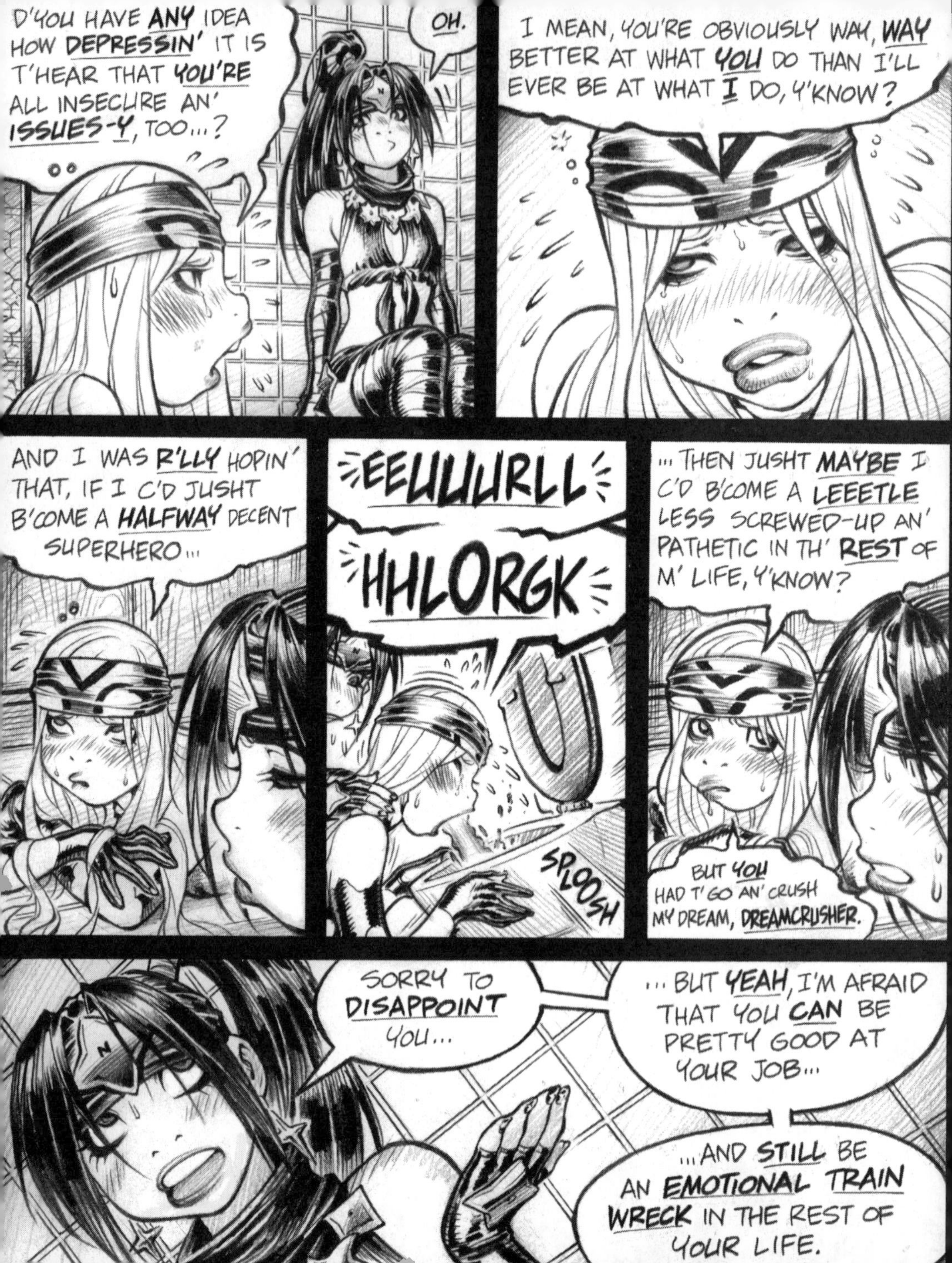
D'YOU HAVE ANY IDEA HOW DEPRESSIN' IT IS T'HEAR THAT YOU'RE ALL INSECURE AN' ISSUES-Y, TOO...?
OH.
I MEAN, YOU'RE OBVIOUSLY WAY, WAY BETTER AT WHAT YOU DO THAN I'LL EVER BE AT WHAT I DO, Y'KNOW?
AND I WAS R'LLY HOPIN' THAT, IF I C'D JUSHT B'COME A HALFWAY DECENT SUPERHERO...
EEUUUURLL
HHLORGK
SPLOOSH
...THEN JUSHT MAYBE I C'D B'COME A LEEETLE LESS SCREWED-UP AN' PATHETIC IN TH' REST OF M' LIFE, Y'KNOW?
BUT YOU HAD T'GO AN' CRUSH MY DREAM, DREAMCRUSHER.
SORRY TO DISAPPOINT YOU...
...BUT YEAH, I'M AFRAID THAT YOU CAN BE PRETTY GOOD AT YOUR JOB...
...AND STILL BE AN EMOTIONAL TRAIN WRECK IN THE REST OF YOUR LIFE.

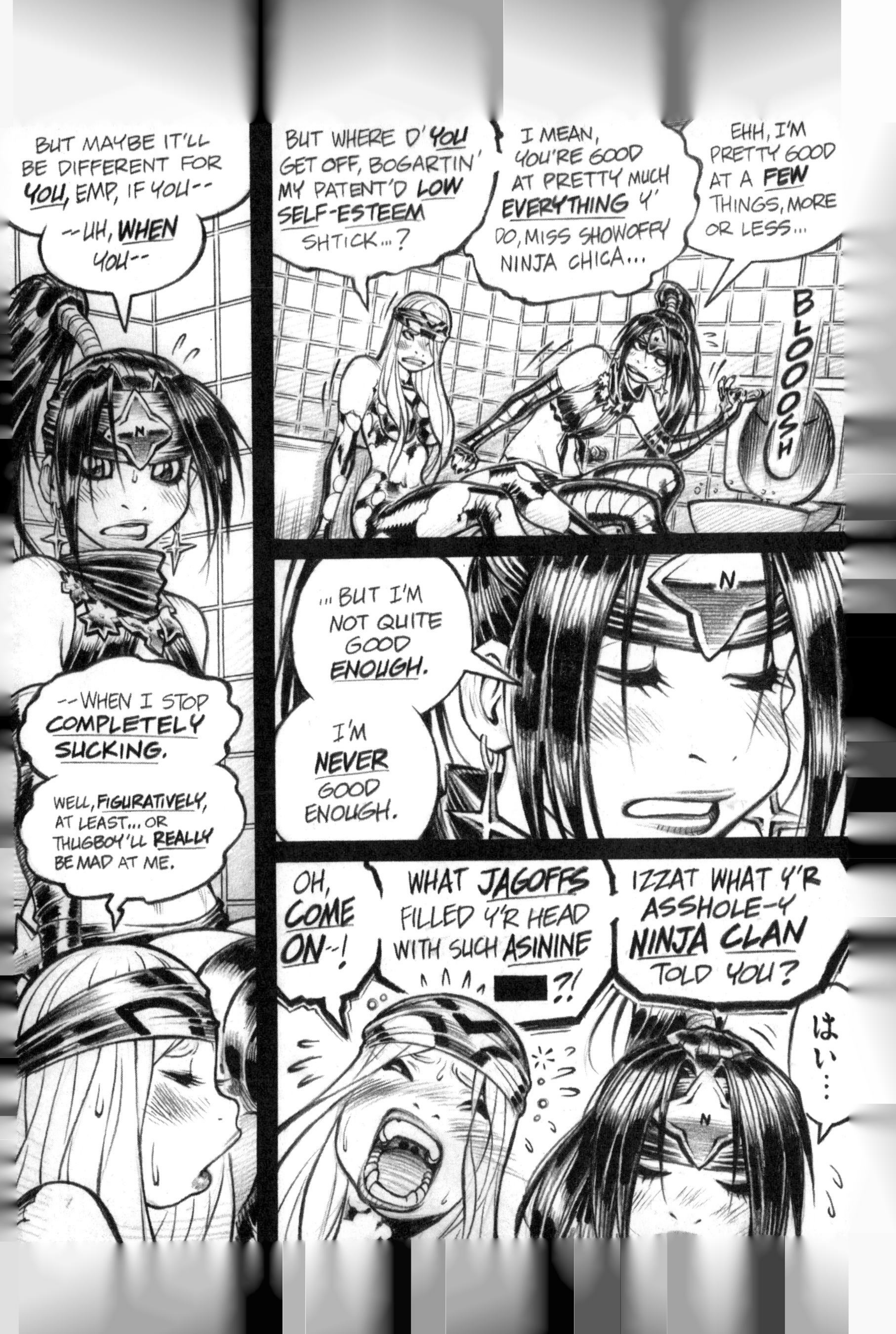
BUT MAYBE IT'LL BE DIFFERENT FOR YOU, EMP, IF YOU--
--UH, WHEN YOU--
--WHEN I STOP COMPLETELY SUCKING.
WELL, FIGURATIVELY, AT LEAST... OR THUGBOY'LL REALLY BE MAD AT ME.
BUT WHERE D'YOU GET OFF, BOGARTIN' MY PATENT'D LOW SELF-ESTEEM SHTICK...?
I MEAN, YOU'RE GOOD AT PRETTY MUCH EVERYTHING Y' DO, MISS SHOWOFFY NINJA CHICA...
EHH, I'M PRETTY GOOD AT A FEW THINGS, MORE OR LESS...
BLOOOOSH
...BUT I'M NOT QUITE GOOD ENOUGH.
I'M NEVER GOOD ENOUGH.
OH, COME ON--!
WHAT JAGOFFS FILLED Y'R HEAD WITH SUCH ASININE [redacted]?!
IZZAT WHAT Y'R ASSHOLE-Y NINJA CLAN TOLD YOU?
はい…

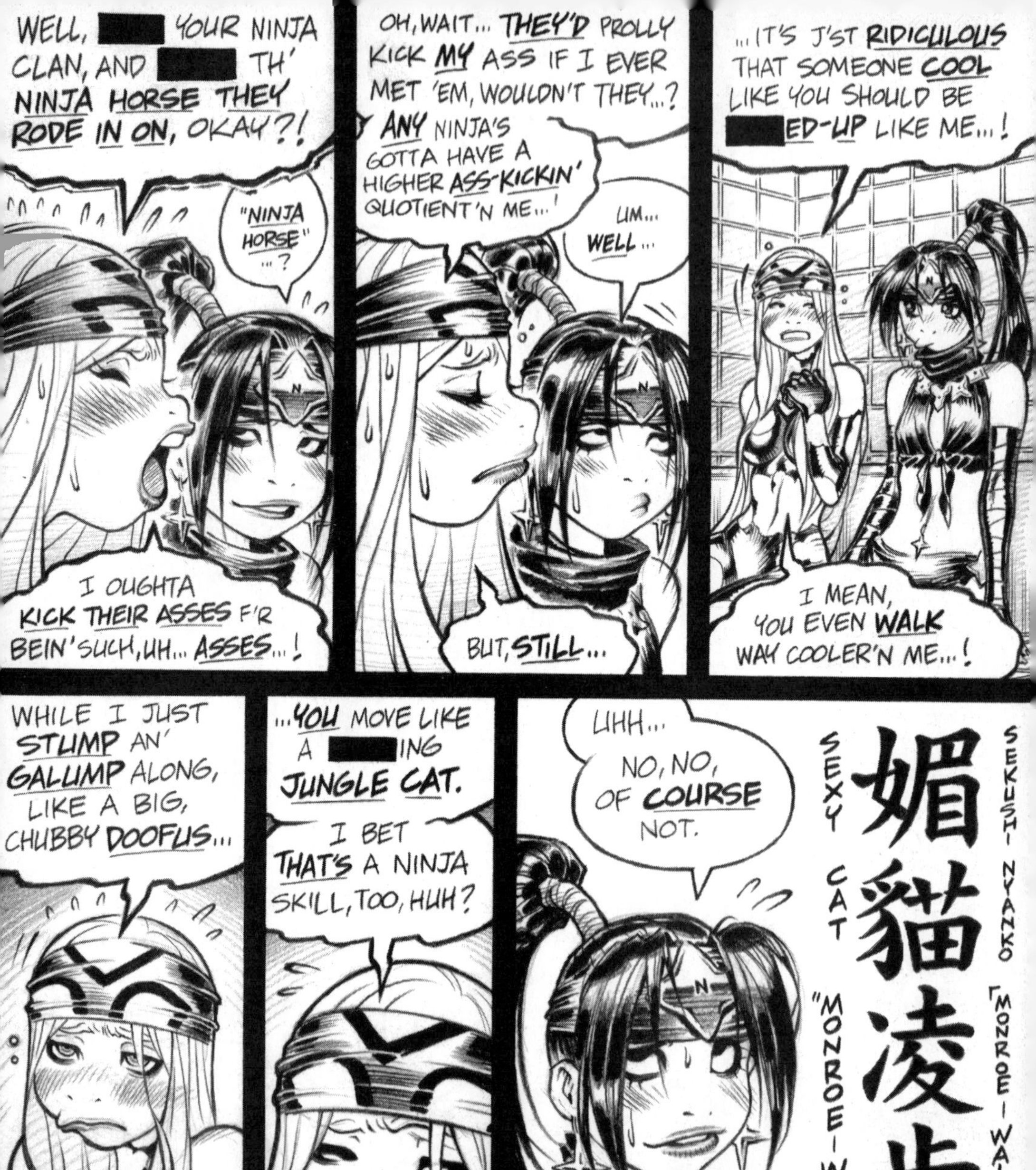
WELL, [redacted] YOUR NINJA CLAN, AND [redacted] TH' NINJA HORSE THEY RODE IN ON, OKAY?!
"NINJA HORSE"...?
I OUGHTA KICK THEIR ASSES F'R BEIN' SUCH, UH... ASSES...!
OH, WAIT... THEY'D PROLLY KICK MY ASS IF I EVER MET 'EM, WOULDN'T THEY...?
ANY NINJA'S GOTTA HAVE A HIGHER ASS-KICKIN' QUOTIENT'N ME...!
UM... WELL...
BUT, STILL...
...IT'S J'ST RIDICULOUS THAT SOMEONE COOL LIKE YOU SHOULD BE [redacted]ED-UP LIKE ME...!
I MEAN, YOU EVEN WALK WAY COOLER'N ME...!
WHILE I JUST STUMP AN' GALUMP ALONG, LIKE A BIG, CHUBBY DOOFUS...
...YOU MOVE LIKE A [redacted]ING JUNGLE CAT.
I BET THAT'S A NINJA SKILL, TOO, HUH?
UHH...
NO, NO, OF COURSE NOT.
SEKUSHI NYANKO 「MONROE-WALK」 NO JUTSU
媚貓凌歩術
SEXY CAT "MONROE-WALK" MAGIC

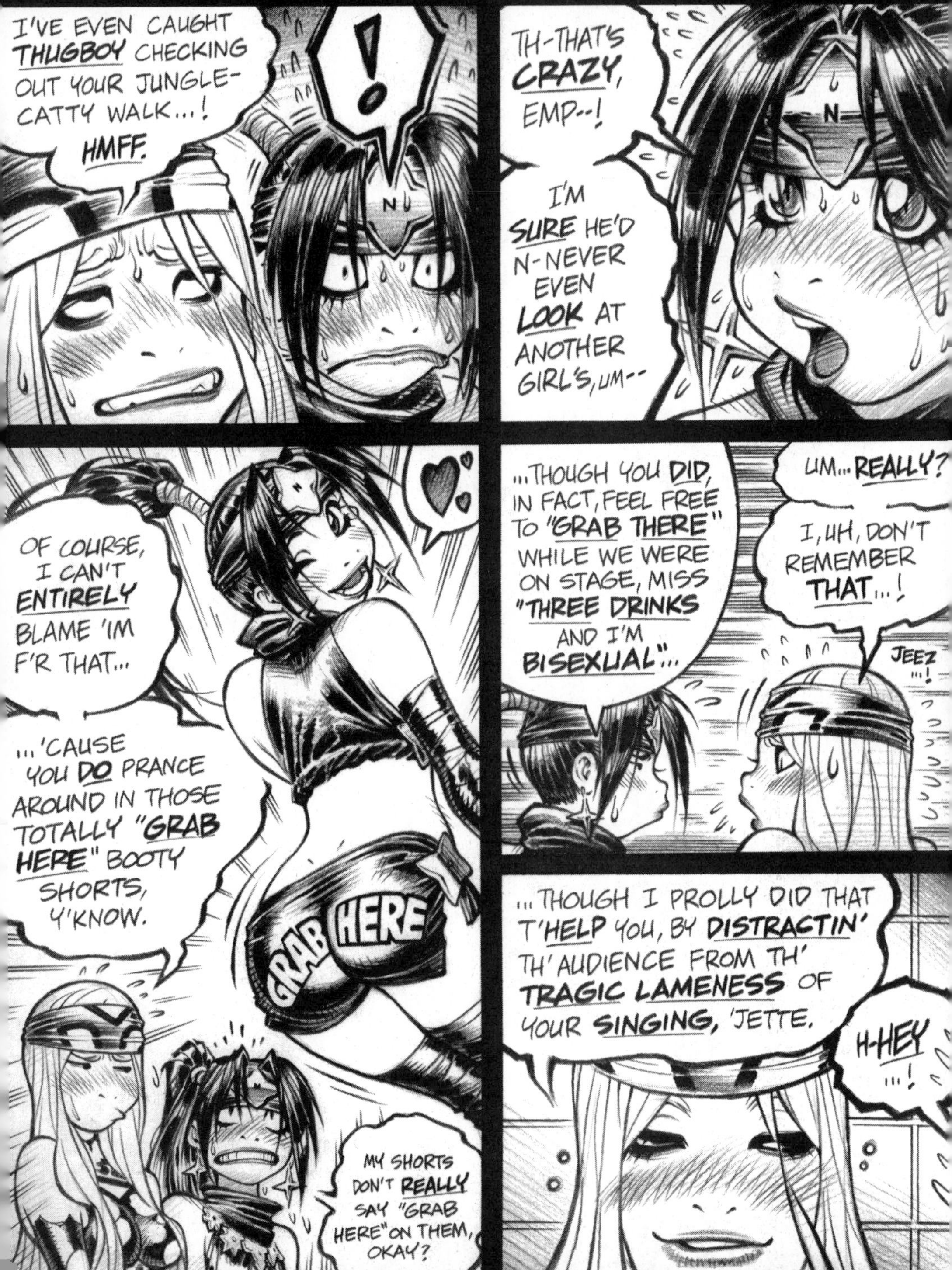
I'VE EVEN CAUGHT THUGBOY CHECKING OUT YOUR JUNGLE-CATTY WALK...! HMFF.
!
TH-THAT'S CRAZY, EMP--!
I'M SURE HE'D N-NEVER EVEN LOOK AT ANOTHER GIRL'S, UM--
N
OF COURSE, I CAN'T ENTIRELY BLAME 'IM F'R THAT...
...'CAUSE YOU DO PRANCE AROUND IN THOSE TOTALLY "GRAB HERE" BOOTY SHORTS, Y'KNOW.
GRAB HERE
MY SHORTS DON'T REALLY SAY "GRAB HERE" ON THEM, OKAY?
...THOUGH YOU DID, IN FACT, FEEL FREE TO "GRAB THERE" WHILE WE WERE ON STAGE, MISS "THREE DRINKS AND I'M BISEXUAL"...
UM...REALLY?
I, UH, DON'T REMEMBER THAT...!
JEEZ ...!
...THOUGH I PROLLY DID THAT T'HELP YOU, BY DISTRACTIN' TH' AUDIENCE FROM TH' TRAGIC LAMENESS OF YOUR SINGING, 'JETTE.
H-HEY ...!

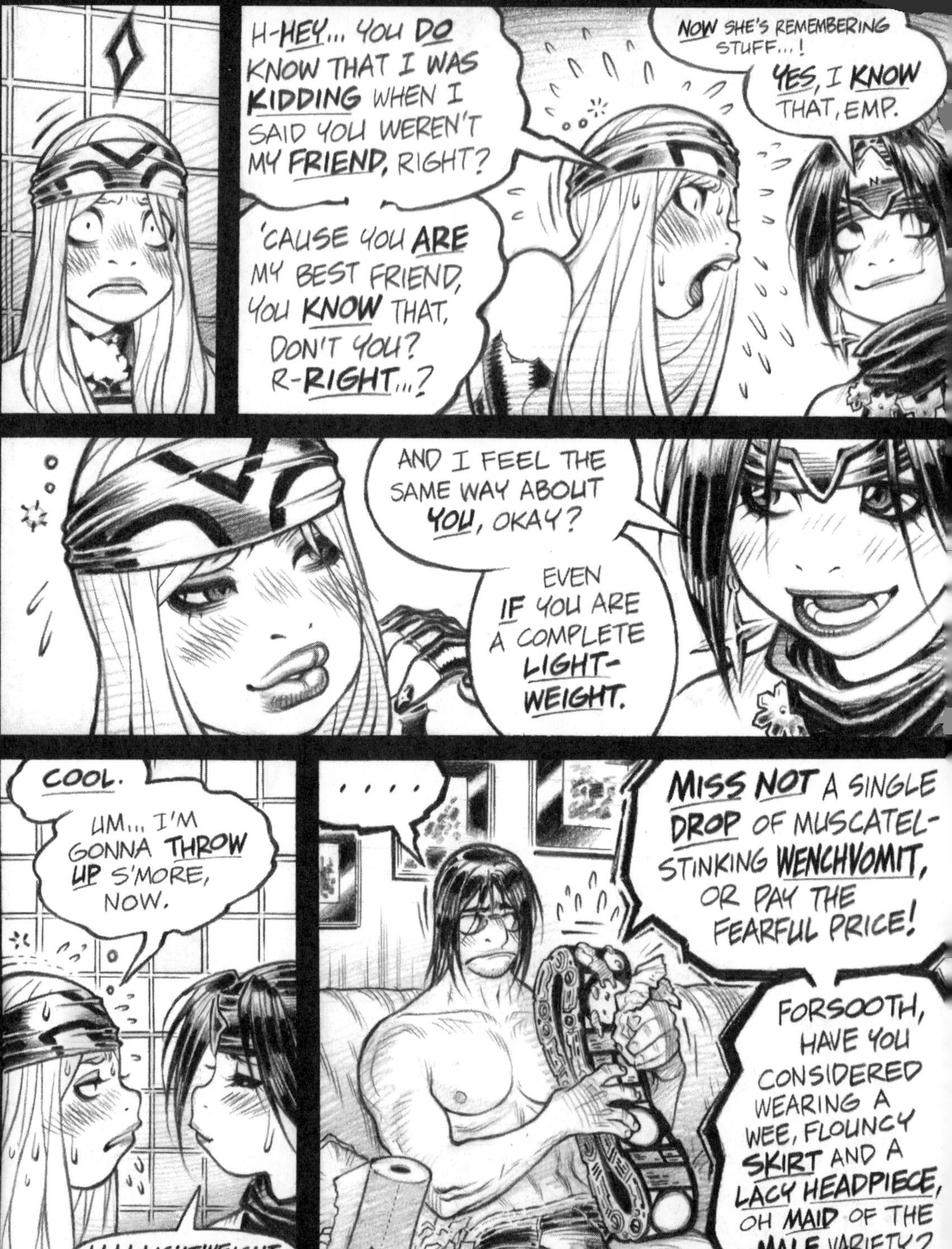

H-HEY... YOU DO KNOW THAT I WAS KIDDING WHEN I SAID YOU WEREN'T MY FRIEND, RIGHT?
'CAUSE YOU ARE MY BEST FRIEND, YOU KNOW THAT, DON'T YOU? R-RIGHT...?
NOW SHE'S REMEMBERING STUFF...!
YES, I KNOW THAT, EMP.
AND I FEEL THE SAME WAY ABOUT YOU, OKAY?
EVEN IF YOU ARE A COMPLETE LIGHT-WEIGHT.
COOL.
UM... I'M GONNA THROW UP S'MORE, NOW.
LLLLLIGHTWEIGHT.
....
MISS NOT A SINGLE DROP OF MUSCATEL-STINKING WENCHVOMIT, OR PAY THE FEARFUL PRICE!
FORSOOTH, HAVE YOU CONSIDERED WEARING A WEE, FLOUNCY SKIRT AND A LACY HEADPIECE, OH MAID OF THE MALE VARIETY?

eMpoWered™

A Day at the Dentist's

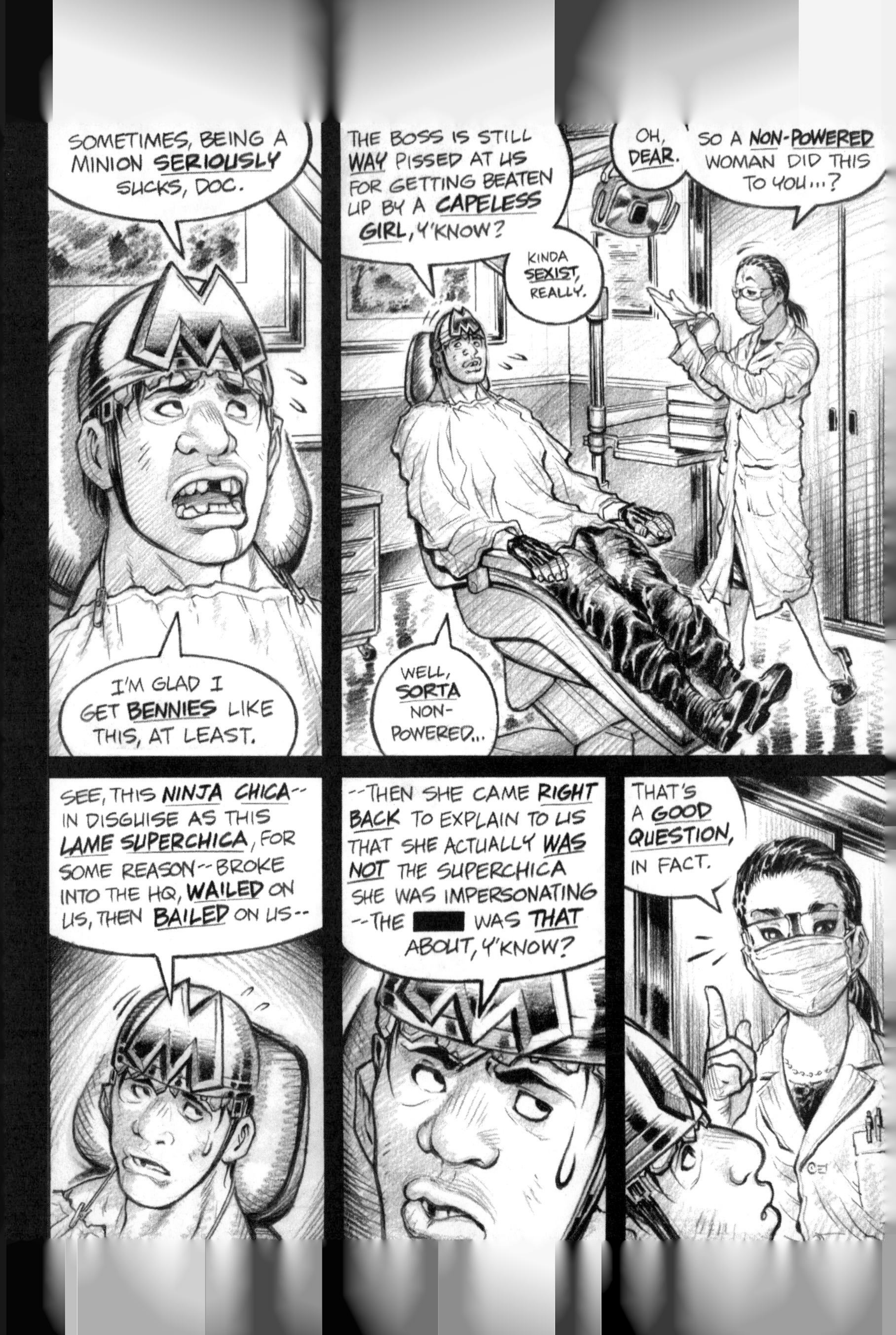
SOMETIMES, BEING A MINION SERIOUSLY SUCKS, DOC.
I'M GLAD I GET BENNIES LIKE THIS, AT LEAST.
THE BOSS IS STILL WAY PISSED AT US FOR GETTING BEATEN UP BY A CAPELESS GIRL, Y'KNOW?
KINDA SEXIST, REALLY.
OH, DEAR.
SO A NON-POWERED WOMAN DID THIS TO YOU...?
WELL, SORTA NON-POWERED...
SEE, THIS NINJA CHICA-- IN DISGUISE AS THIS LAME SUPERCHICA, FOR SOME REASON--BROKE INTO THE HQ, WAILED ON US, THEN BAILED ON US--
--THEN SHE CAME RIGHT BACK TO EXPLAIN TO US THAT SHE ACTUALLY WAS NOT THE SUPERCHICA SHE WAS IMPERSONATING --THE [redacted] WAS THAT ABOUT, Y'KNOW?
THAT'S A GOOD QUESTION, IN FACT.

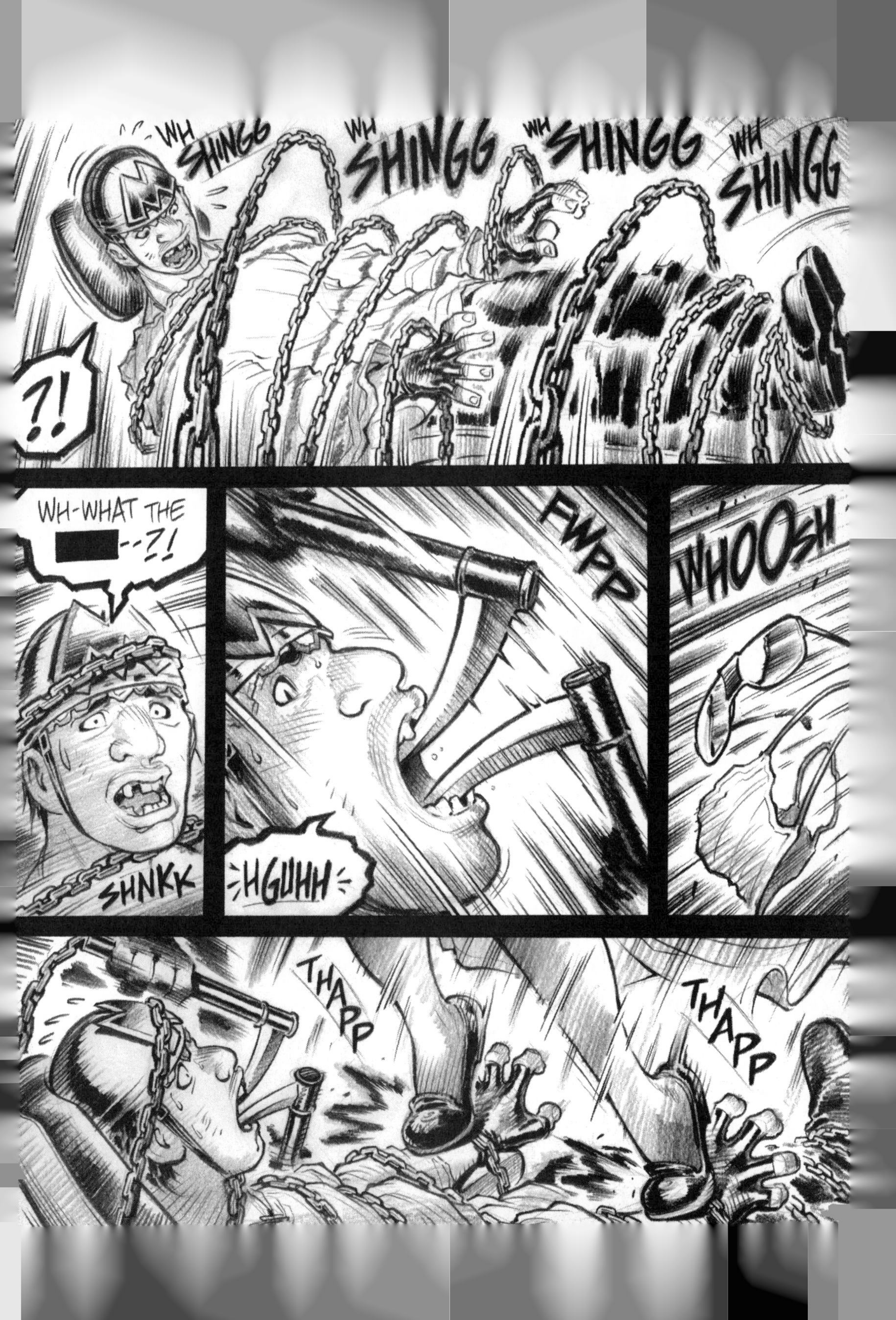
WH SHINGG
WH SHINGG
WH SHINGG
WH SHINGG
?!
WH-WHAT THE [redacted]--?!
SHNKK
FWPP
HGUHH
WHOOSH
THAPP
THAPP

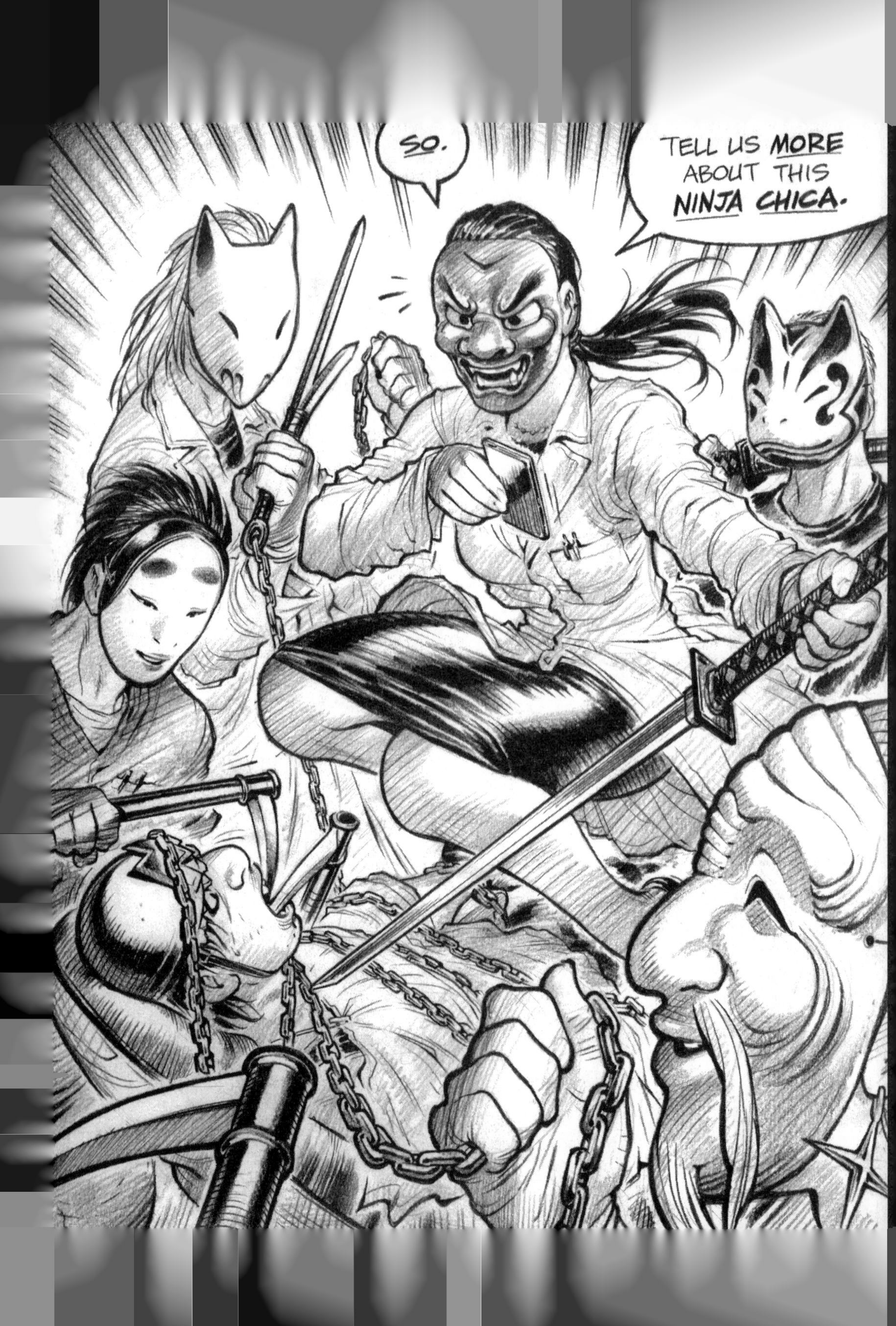
SO.
TELL US MORE ABOUT THIS NINJA CHICA.

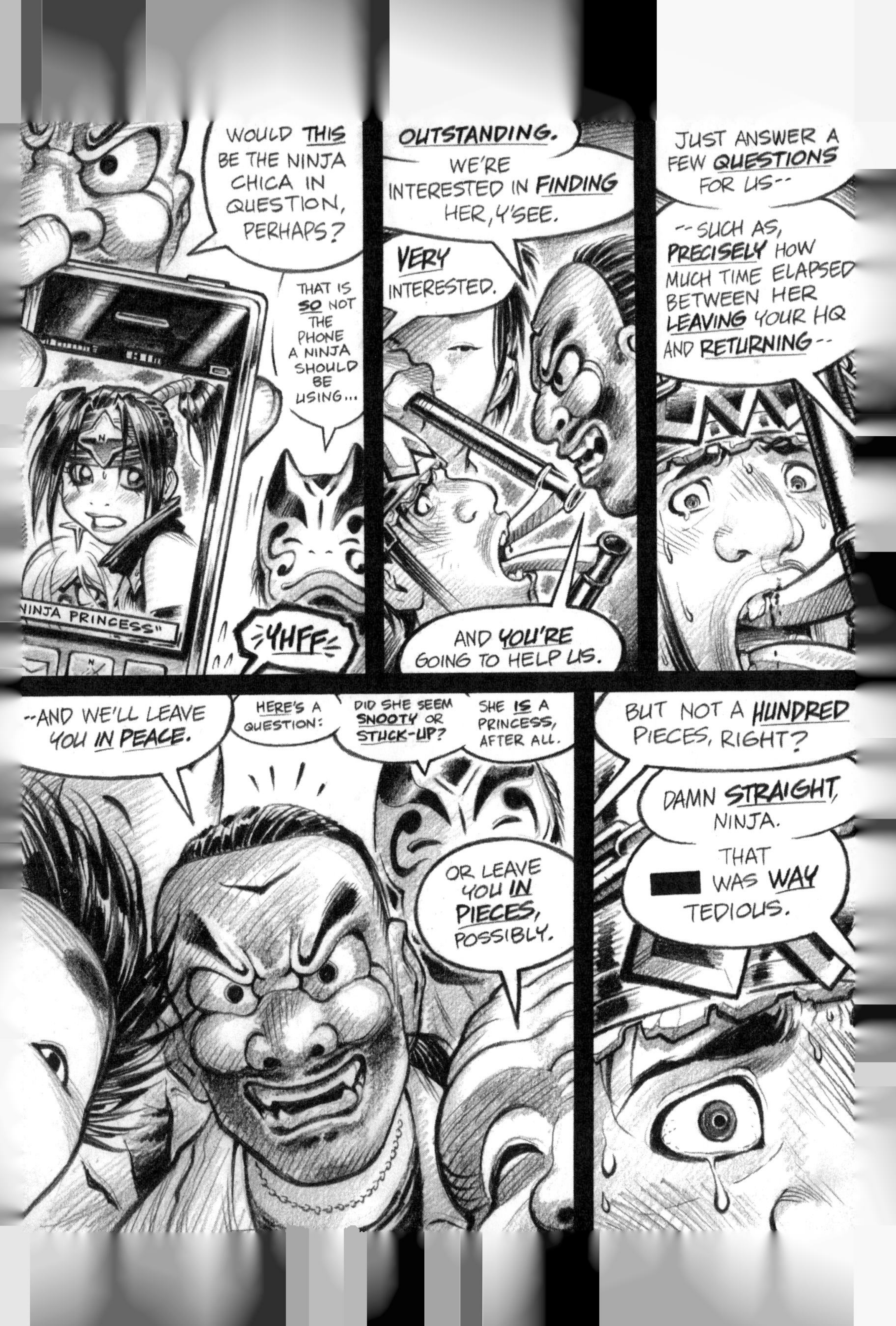
WOULD THIS BE THE NINJA CHICA IN QUESTION, PERHAPS?
"NINJA PRINCESS"
THAT IS SO NOT THE PHONE A NINJA SHOULD BE USING...
YHFF
OUTSTANDING.
WE'RE INTERESTED IN FINDING HER, Y'SEE.
VERY INTERESTED.
AND YOU'RE GOING TO HELP US.
JUST ANSWER A FEW QUESTIONS FOR US--
--SUCH AS, PRECISELY HOW MUCH TIME ELAPSED BETWEEN HER LEAVING YOUR HQ AND RETURNING--
--AND WE'LL LEAVE YOU IN PEACE.
HERE'S A QUESTION:
DID SHE SEEM SNOOTY OR STUCK-UP?
SHE IS A PRINCESS, AFTER ALL.
OR LEAVE YOU IN PIECES, POSSIBLY.
BUT NOT A HUNDRED PIECES, RIGHT?
DAMN STRAIGHT, NINJA.
THAT [redacted] WAS WAY TEDIOUS.

Empowered™

Not Quite Perfect

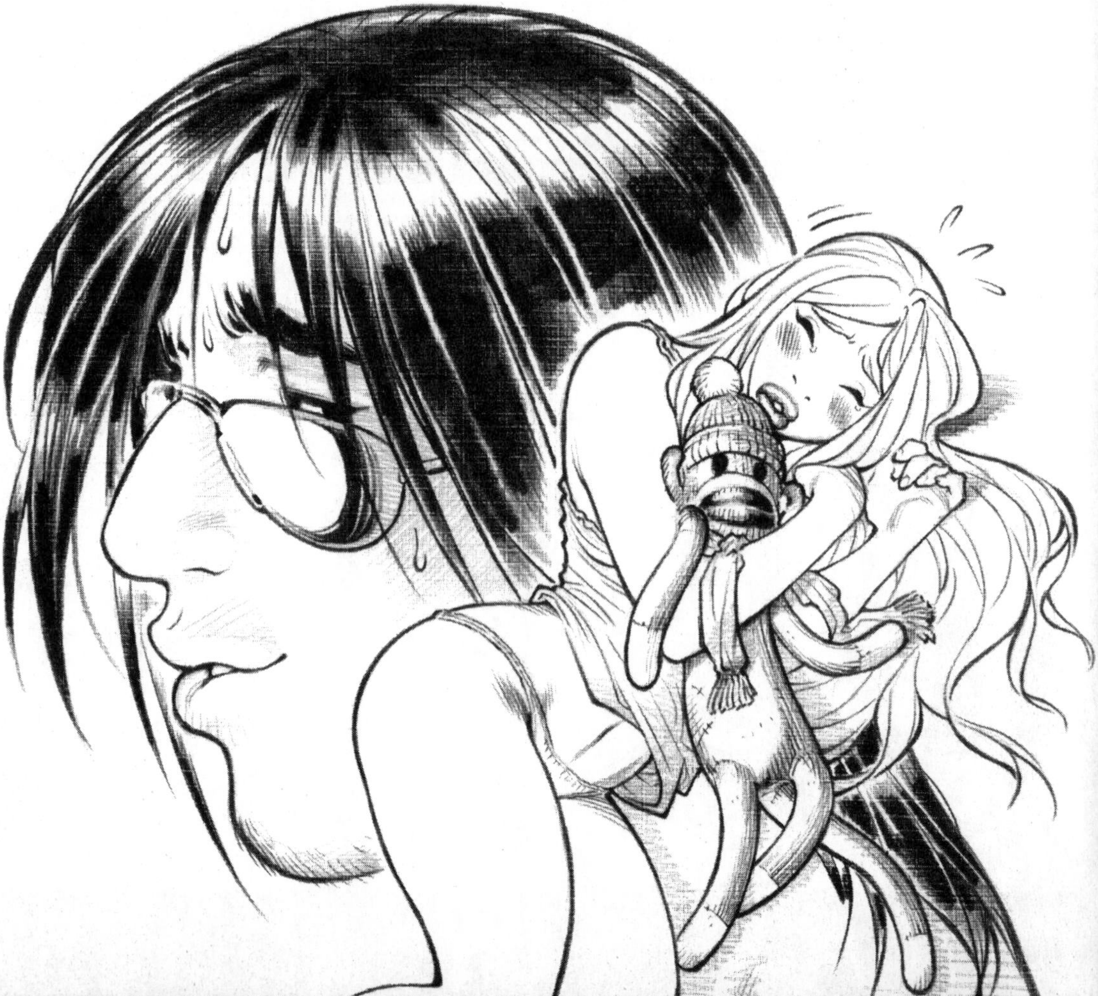

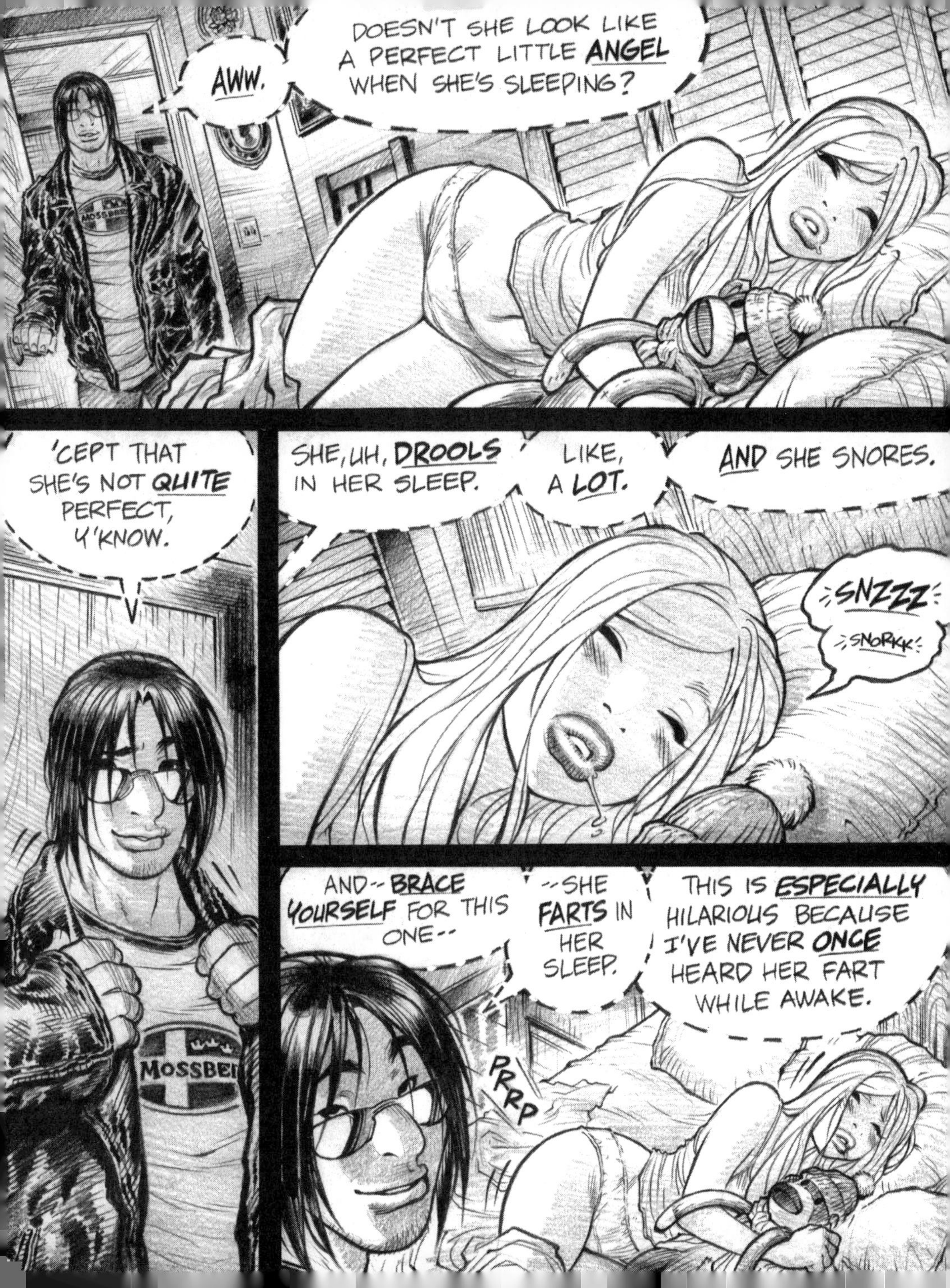
AWW.
DOESN'T SHE LOOK LIKE A PERFECT LITTLE ANGEL WHEN SHE'S SLEEPING?
'CEPT THAT SHE'S NOT QUITE PERFECT, Y'KNOW.
SHE, UH, DROOLS IN HER SLEEP.
LIKE, A LOT.
AND SHE SNORES.
SNZZZ
SNORKK
AND-- BRACE YOURSELF FOR THIS ONE--
--SHE FARTS IN HER SLEEP.
THIS IS ESPECIALLY HILARIOUS BECAUSE I'VE NEVER ONCE HEARD HER FART WHILE AWAKE.
PRRP

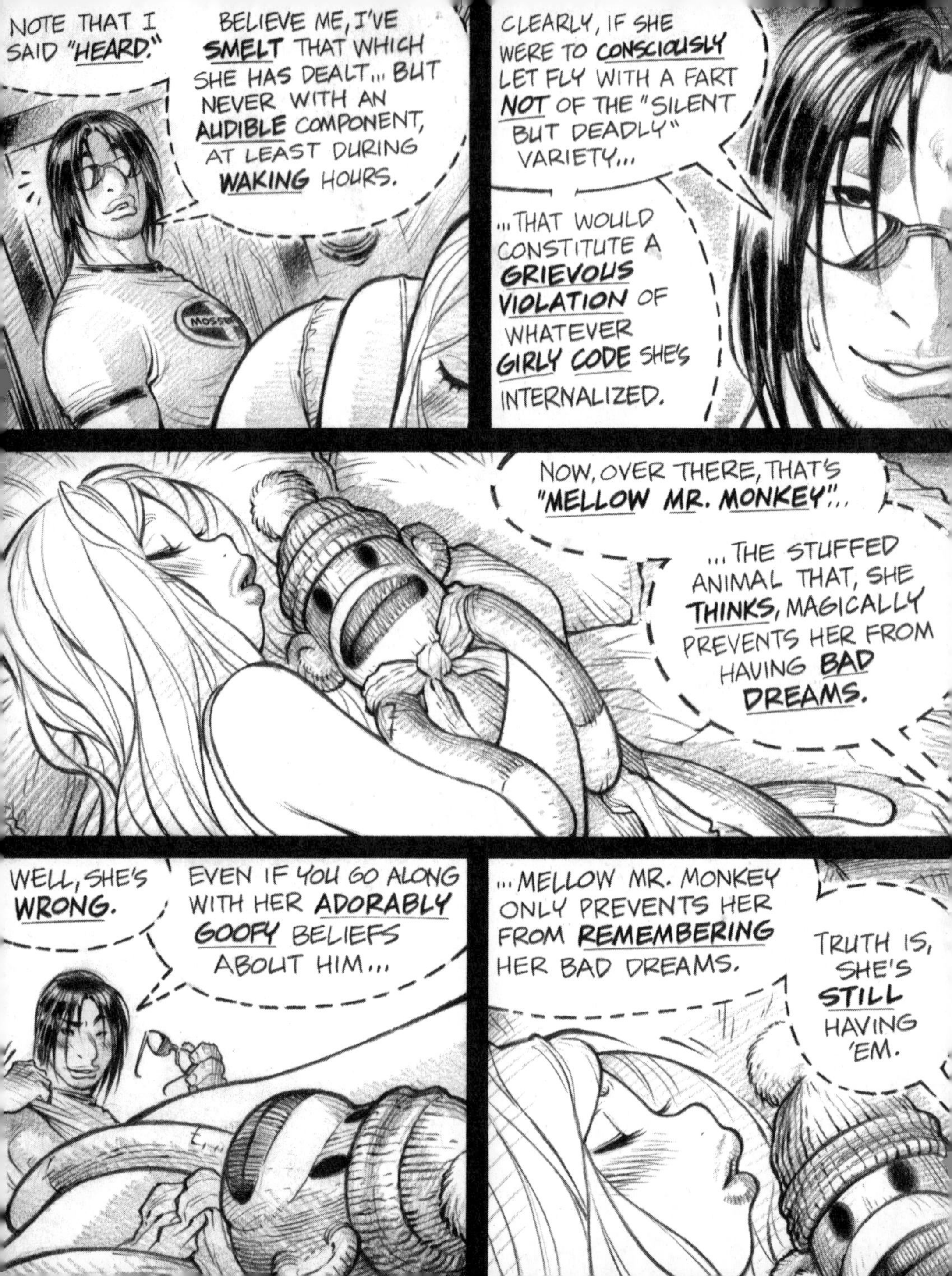
NOTE THAT I SAID "HEARD."
BELIEVE ME, I'VE SMELT THAT WHICH SHE HAS DEALT... BUT NEVER WITH AN AUDIBLE COMPONENT, AT LEAST DURING WAKING HOURS.
CLEARLY, IF SHE WERE TO CONSCIOUSLY LET FLY WITH A FART NOT OF THE "SILENT BUT DEADLY" VARIETY...
...THAT WOULD CONSTITUTE A GRIEVOUS VIOLATION OF WHATEVER GIRLY CODE SHE'S INTERNALIZED.
NOW, OVER THERE, THAT'S "MELLOW MR. MONKEY"...
...THE STUFFED ANIMAL THAT, SHE THINKS, MAGICALLY PREVENTS HER FROM HAVING BAD DREAMS.
WELL, SHE'S WRONG.
EVEN IF YOU GO ALONG WITH HER ADORABLY GOOFY BELIEFS ABOUT HIM...
...MELLOW MR. MONKEY ONLY PREVENTS HER FROM REMEMBERING HER BAD DREAMS.
TRUTH IS, SHE'S STILL HAVING 'EM.

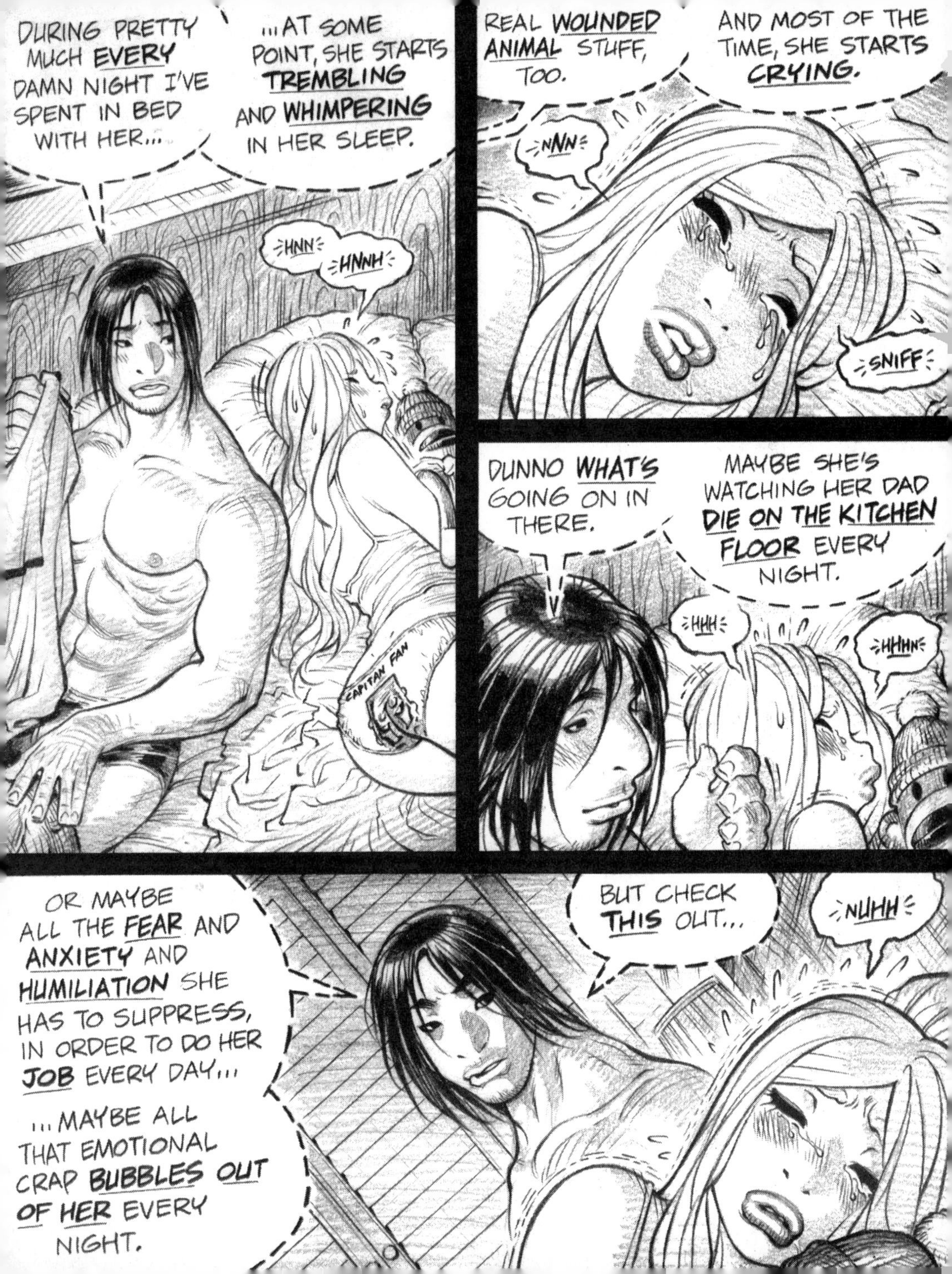
DURING PRETTY MUCH EVERY DAMN NIGHT I'VE SPENT IN BED WITH HER...
...AT SOME POINT, SHE STARTS TREMBLING AND WHIMPERING IN HER SLEEP.
HNN
HNNH
CAPITAN FAN
REAL WOUNDED ANIMAL STUFF, TOO.
AND MOST OF THE TIME, SHE STARTS CRYING.
NNN
SNIFF
DUNNO WHAT'S GOING ON IN THERE.
MAYBE SHE'S WATCHING HER DAD DIE ON THE KITCHEN FLOOR EVERY NIGHT.
HHH
HHHN
OR MAYBE ALL THE FEAR AND ANXIETY AND HUMILIATION SHE HAS TO SUPPRESS, IN ORDER TO DO HER JOB EVERY DAY...
...MAYBE ALL THAT EMOTIONAL CRAP BUBBLES OUT OF HER EVERY NIGHT.
BUT CHECK THIS OUT...
NUHH

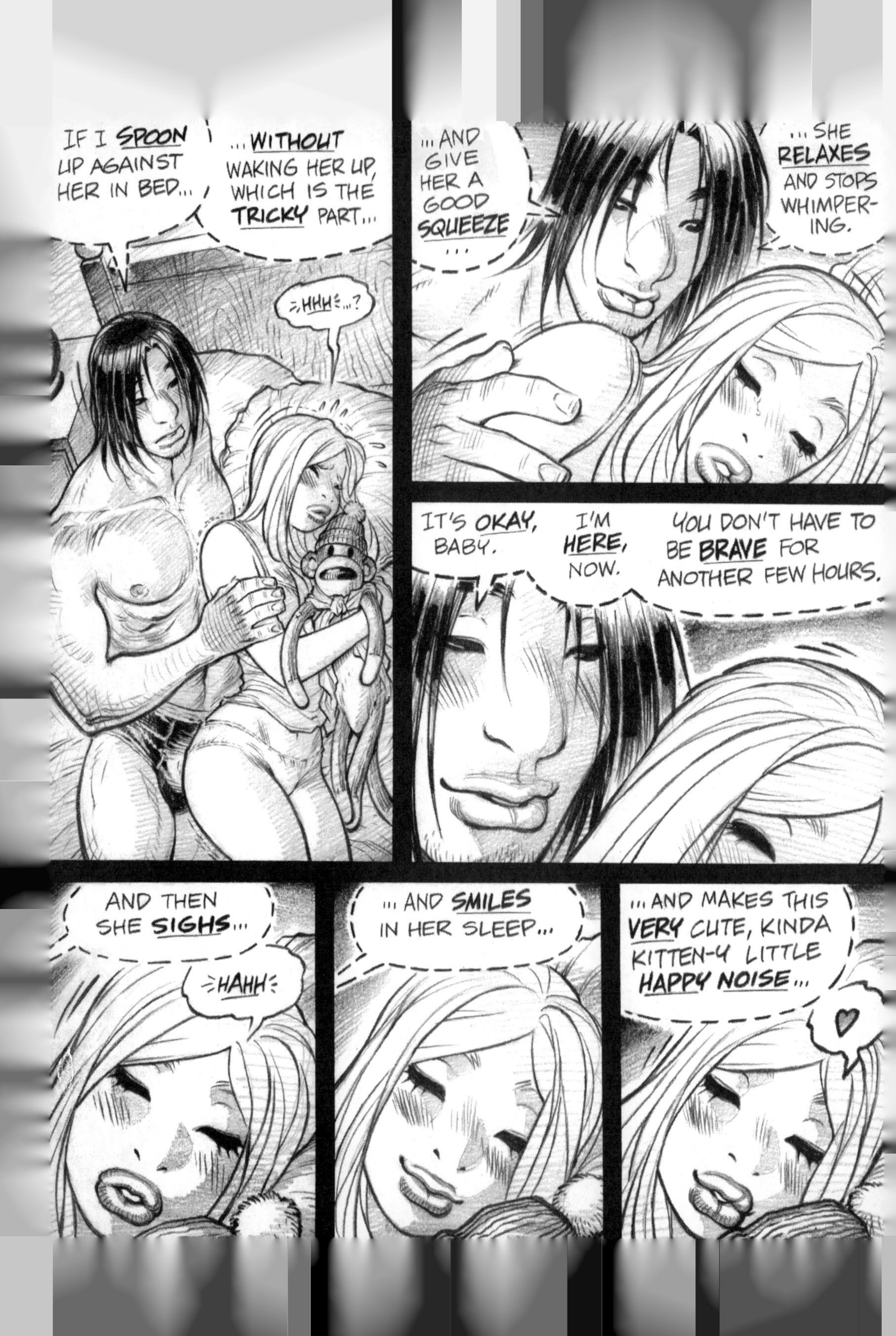
IF I SPOON UP AGAINST HER IN BED...
...WITHOUT WAKING HER UP, WHICH IS THE TRICKY PART...
HHH...?
...AND GIVE HER A GOOD SQUEEZE...
...SHE RELAXES AND STOPS WHIMPER-ING.
IT'S OKAY, BABY.
I'M HERE, NOW.
YOU DON'T HAVE TO BE BRAVE FOR ANOTHER FEW HOURS.
AND THEN SHE SIGHS...
HAHH
...AND SMILES IN HER SLEEP...
...AND MAKES THIS VERY CUTE, KINDA KITTEN-Y LITTLE HAPPY NOISE...

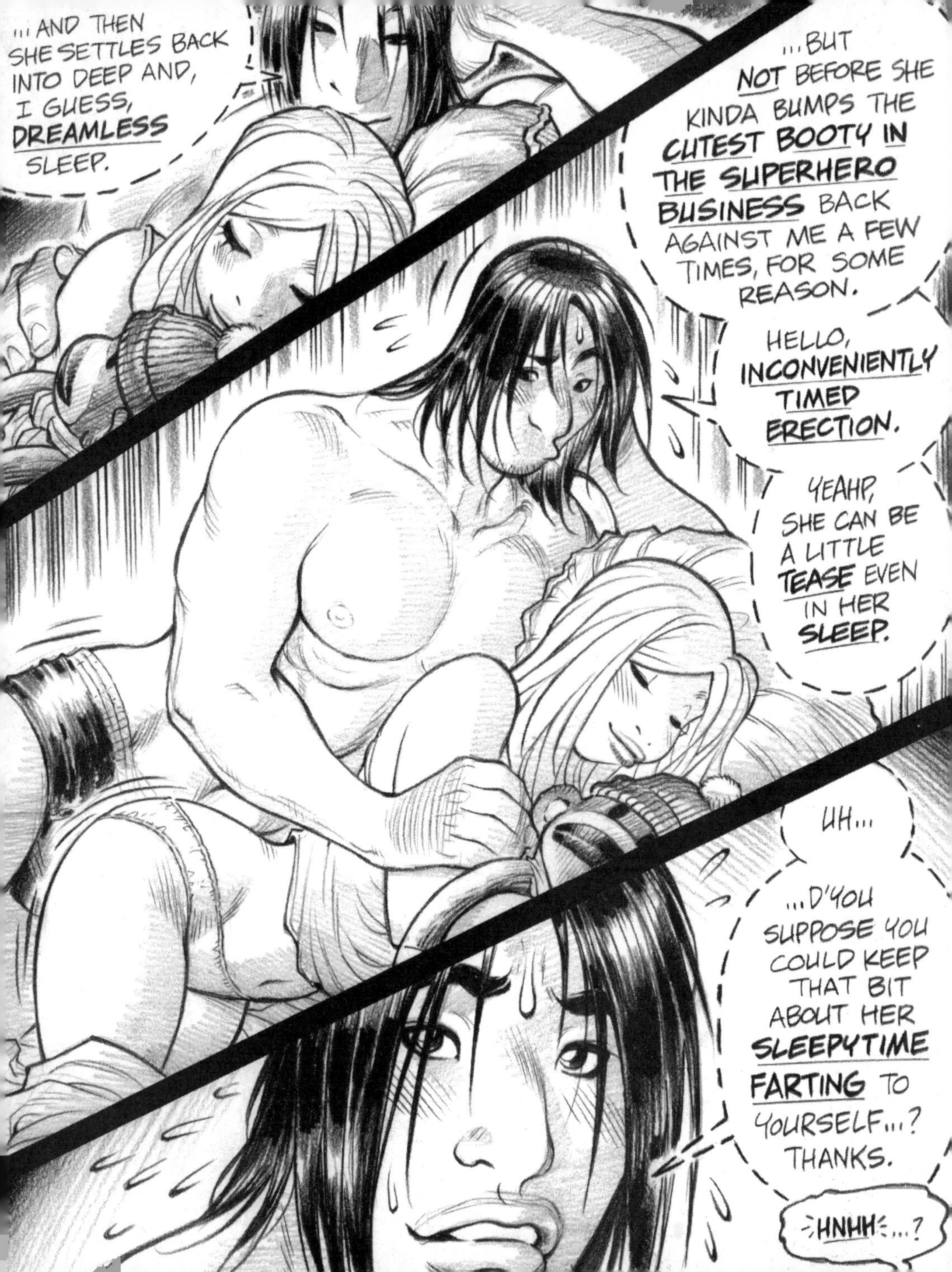
...AND THEN SHE SETTLES BACK INTO DEEP AND, I GUESS, **DREAMLESS** SLEEP.
...BUT **NOT** BEFORE SHE KINDA BUMPS THE **CUTEST BOOTY IN THE SUPERHERO BUSINESS** BACK AGAINST ME A FEW TIMES, FOR SOME REASON.
HELLO, **INCONVENIENTLY TIMED ERECTION**.
YEAHP, SHE CAN BE A LITTLE **TEASE** EVEN IN HER **SLEEP**.
UH...
...D'YOU SUPPOSE YOU COULD KEEP THAT BIT ABOUT HER **SLEEPYTIME FARTING** TO YOURSELF...? THANKS.
HNHH...?

EMPOWERED™

Chlorosexuality

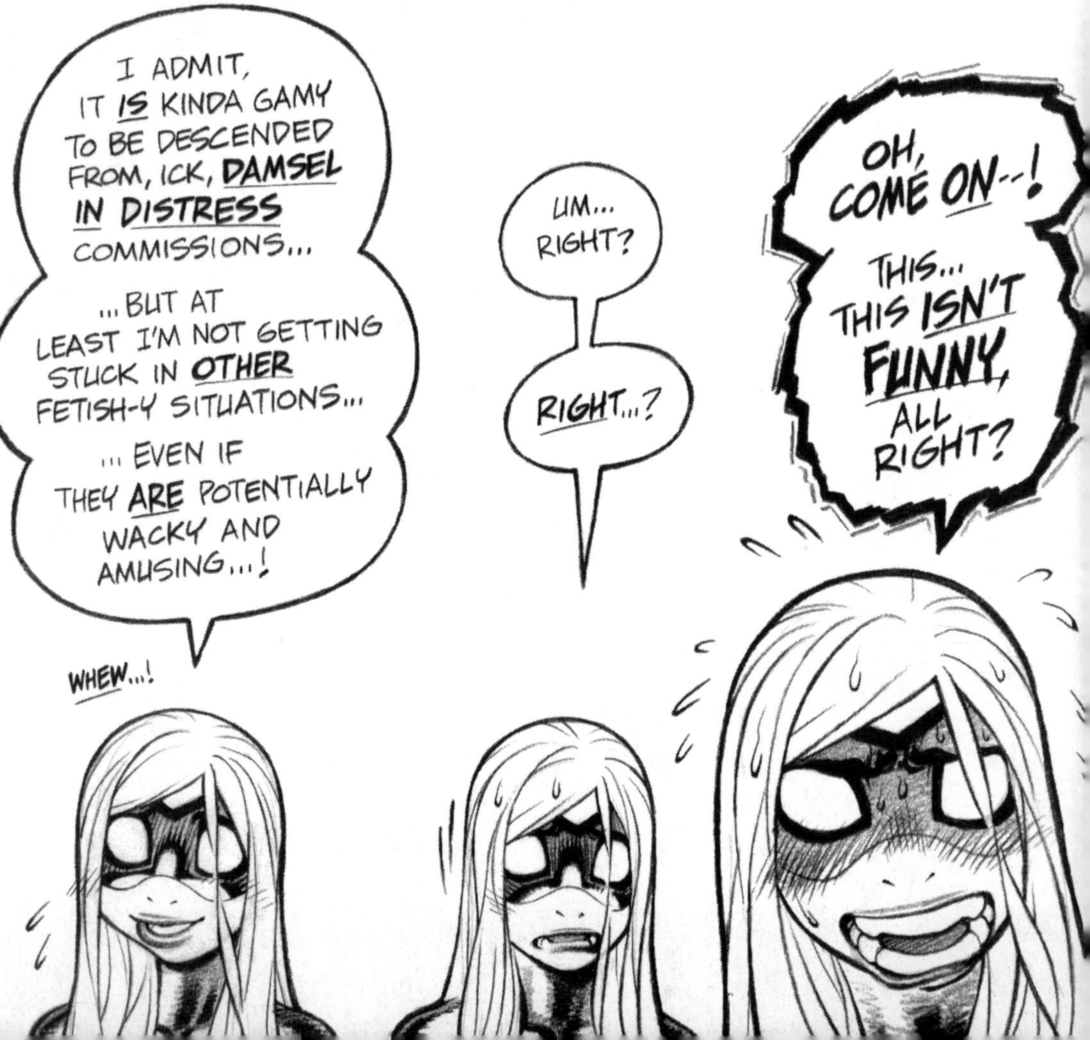
I ADMIT, IT IS KINDA GAMY TO BE DESCENDED FROM, ICK, DAMSEL IN DISTRESS COMMISSIONS...
...BUT AT LEAST I'M NOT GETTING STUCK IN OTHER FETISH-Y SITUATIONS...
...EVEN IF THEY ARE POTENTIALLY WACKY AND AMUSING...!
WHEW...!
UM... RIGHT?
RIGHT...?
OH, COME ON--!
THIS... THIS ISN'T FUNNY, ALL RIGHT?

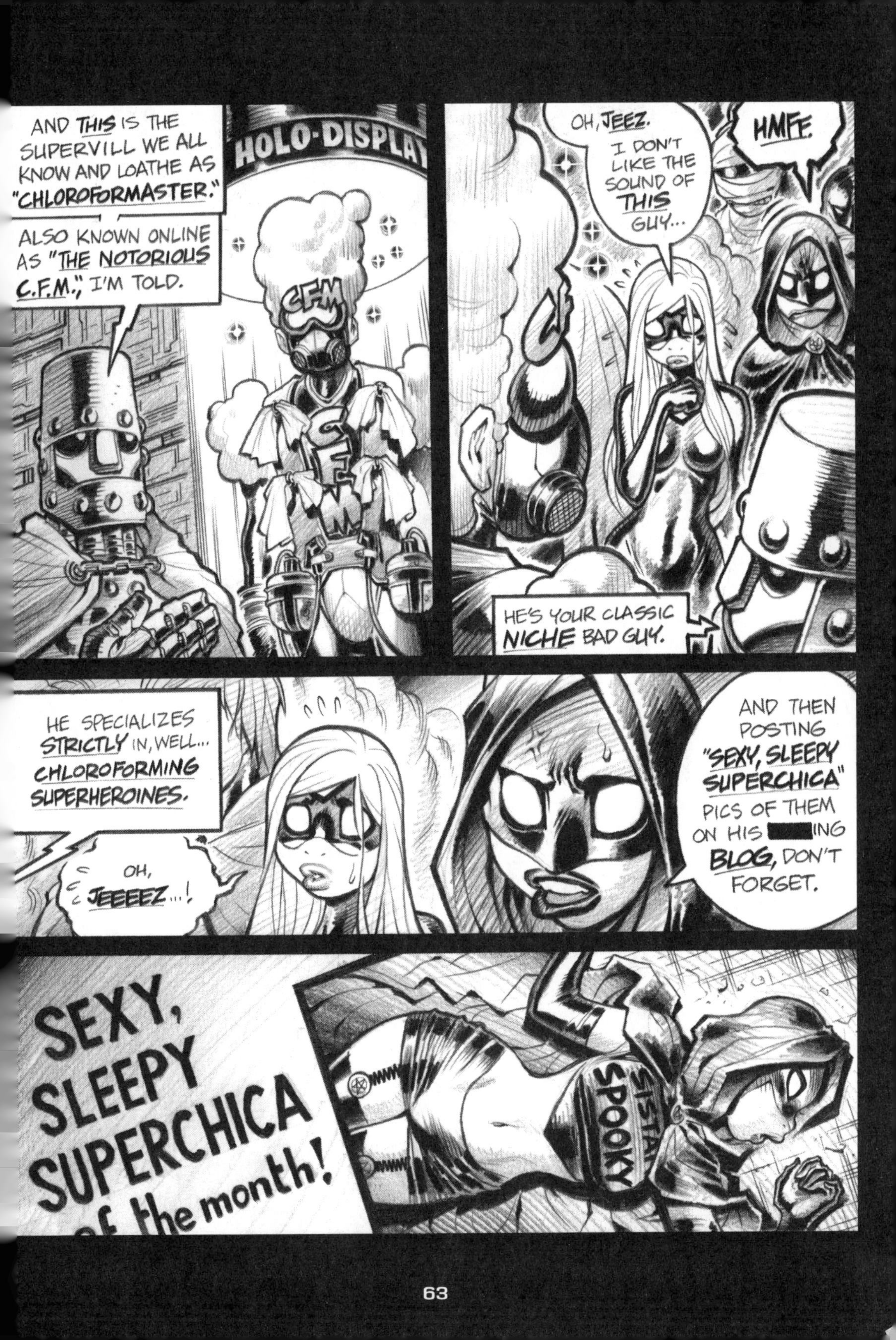
HOLO-DISPLAY
AND THIS IS THE SUPERVILL WE ALL KNOW AND LOATHE AS "CHLOROFORMASTER."
ALSO KNOWN ONLINE AS "THE NOTORIOUS C.F.M.," I'M TOLD.
CFM
OH, JEEZ.
I DON'T LIKE THE SOUND OF THIS GUY...
HMFF.
HE'S YOUR CLASSIC NICHE BAD GUY.
HE SPECIALIZES STRICTLY IN, WELL... CHLOROFORMING SUPERHEROINES.
OH, JEEEEZ...!
AND THEN POSTING "SEXY, SLEEPY SUPERCHICA" PICS OF THEM ON HIS [redacted]ING BLOG, DON'T FORGET.
SEXY, SLEEPY SUPERCHICA of the month!
SPOOKY SISTA

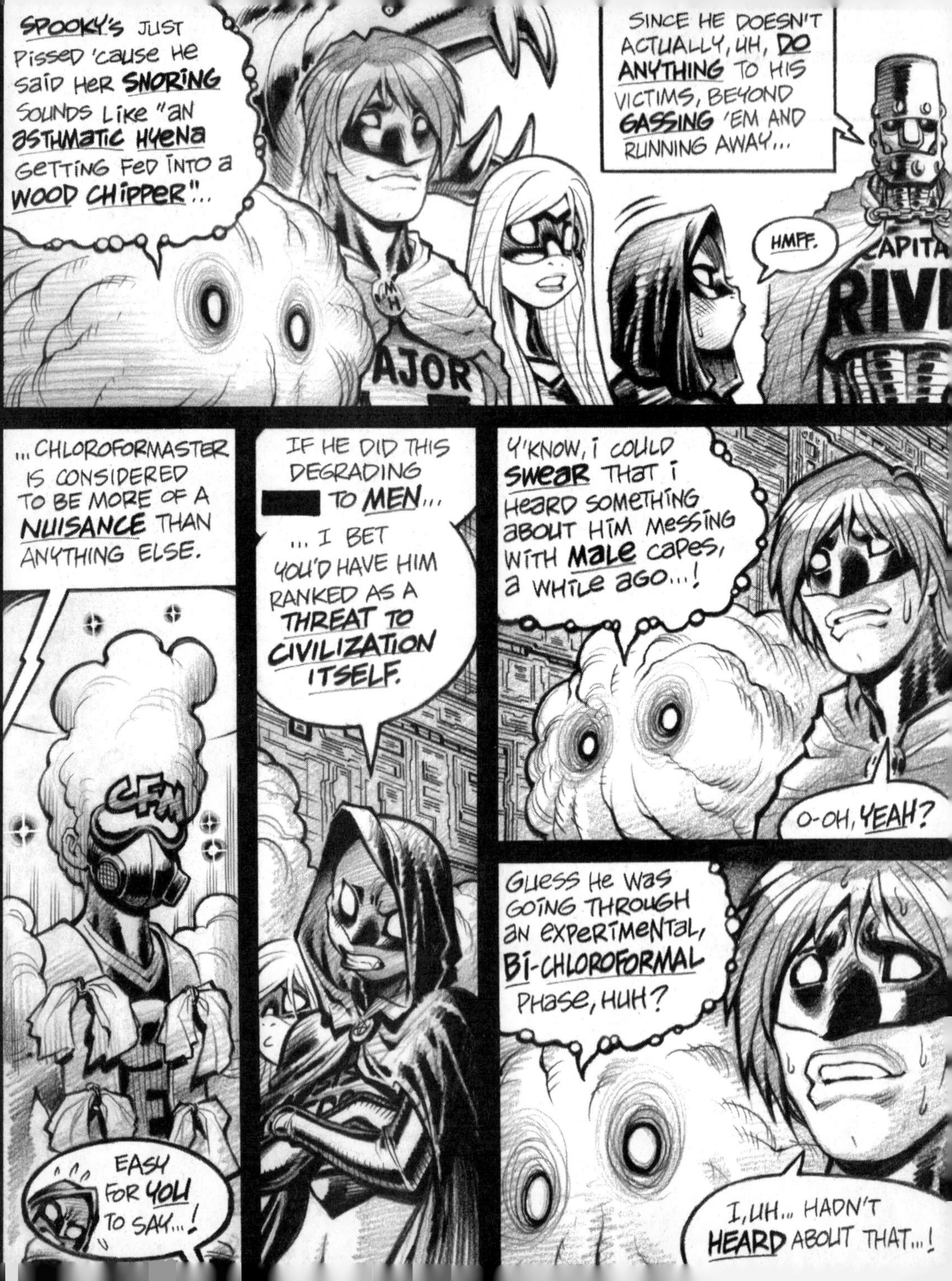
SPOOKY'S JUST PISSED 'CAUSE HE SAID HER SNORING SOUNDS LIKE "AN ASTHMATIC HYENA GETTING FED INTO A WOOD CHIPPER"...
AJOR
SINCE HE DOESN'T ACTUALLY, UH, DO ANYTHING TO HIS VICTIMS, BEYOND GASSING 'EM AND RUNNING AWAY...
HMFF.
CAPITA
RIVE
...CHLOROFORMASTER IS CONSIDERED TO BE MORE OF A NUISANCE THAN ANYTHING ELSE.
CFM
EASY FOR YOU TO SAY...!
IF HE DID THIS DEGRADING [redacted] TO MEN...
...I BET YOU'D HAVE HIM RANKED AS A THREAT TO CIVILIZATION ITSELF.
Y'KNOW, I COULD SWEAR THAT I HEARD SOMETHING ABOUT HIM MESSING WITH MALE CAPES, A WHILE AGO...!
O-OH, YEAH?
GUESS HE WAS GOING THROUGH AN EXPERIMENTAL, BI-CHLOROFORMAL PHASE, HUH?
I, UH... HADN'T HEARD ABOUT THAT...!

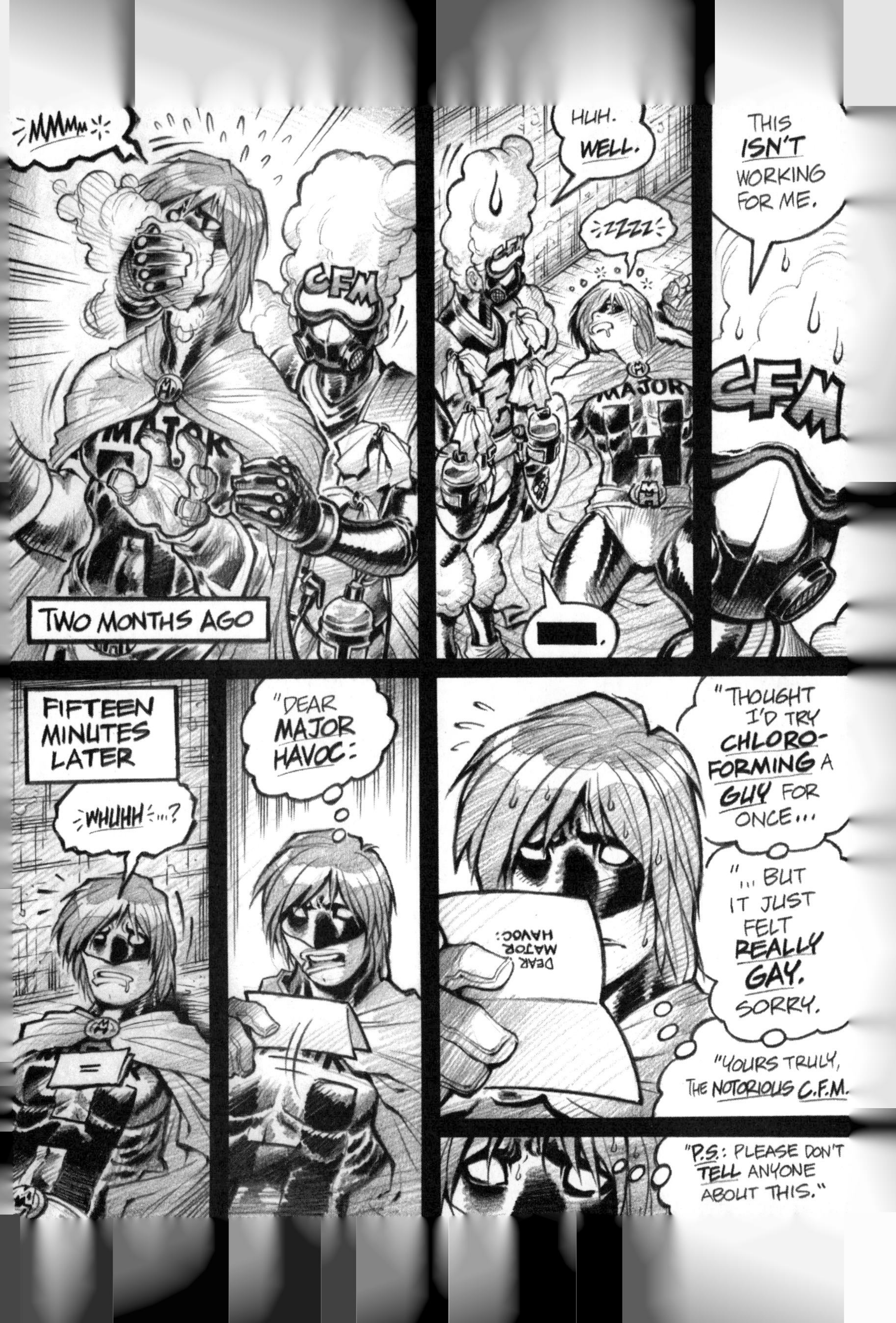
MMMmm
TWO MONTHS AGO
HUH. WELL.
ZZZZ
THIS ISN'T WORKING FOR ME.
FIFTEEN MINUTES LATER
WHUHH ...?
"DEAR MAJOR HAVOC:
"THOUGHT I'D TRY CHLORO-FORMING A GUY FOR ONCE...
"... BUT IT JUST FELT REALLY GAY. SORRY.
"YOURS TRULY, THE NOTORIOUS C.F.M.
"P.S.: PLEASE DON'T TELL ANYONE ABOUT THIS."

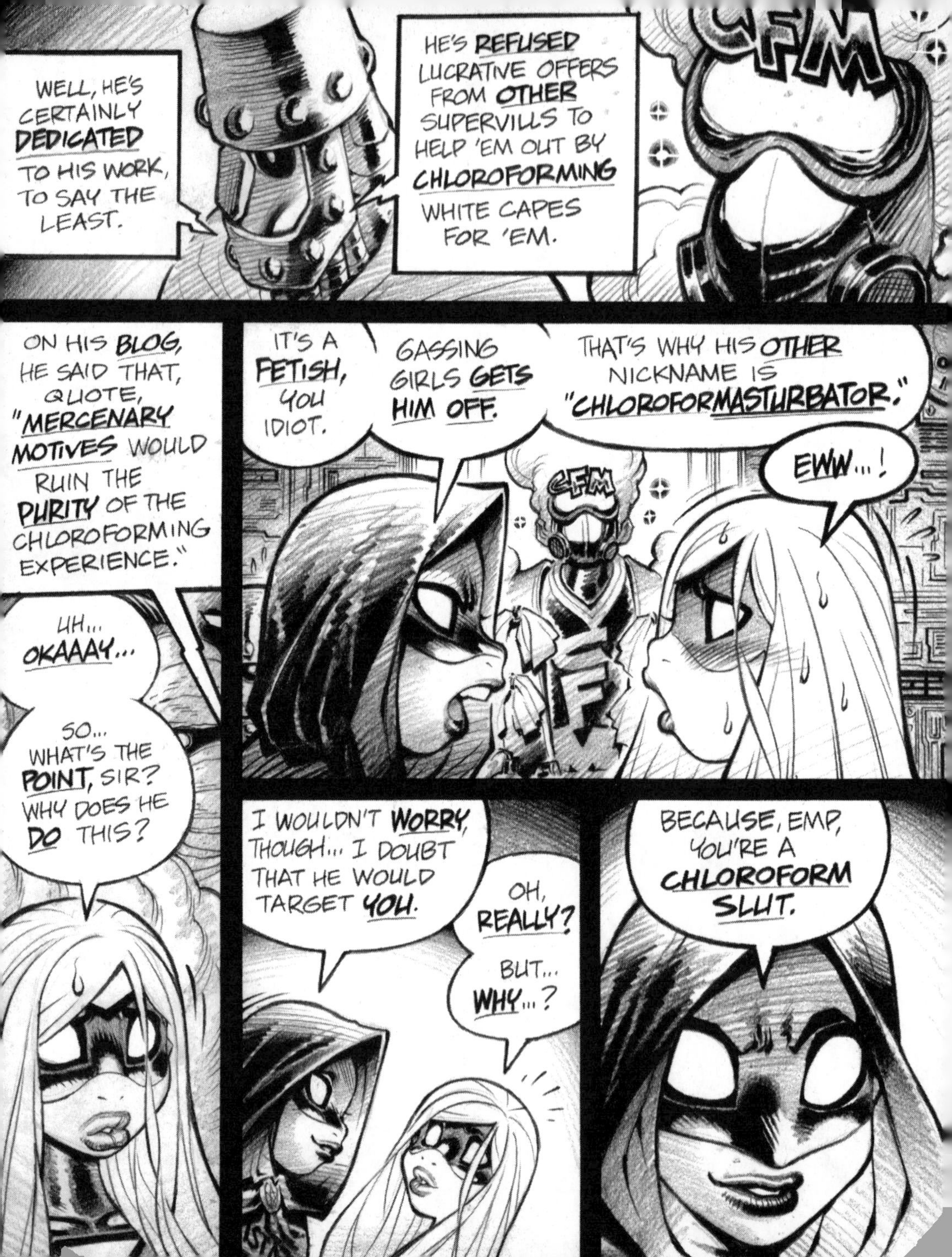
WELL, HE'S CERTAINLY DEDICATED TO HIS WORK, TO SAY THE LEAST.
HE'S REFUSED LUCRATIVE OFFERS FROM OTHER SUPERVILLS TO HELP 'EM OUT BY CHLOROFORMING WHITE CAPES FOR 'EM.
CFM
ON HIS BLOG, HE SAID THAT, QUOTE, "MERCENARY MOTIVES WOULD RUIN THE PURITY OF THE CHLOROFORMING EXPERIENCE."
UH... OKAAAY...
SO... WHAT'S THE POINT, SIR? WHY DOES HE DO THIS?
IT'S A FETISH, YOU IDIOT.
GASSING GIRLS GETS HIM OFF.
THAT'S WHY HIS OTHER NICKNAME IS "CHLOROFORMASTURBATOR."
EWW...!
CFM
I WOULDN'T WORRY, THOUGH... I DOUBT THAT HE WOULD TARGET YOU.
OH, REALLY?
BUT... WHY...?
BECAUSE, EMP, YOU'RE A CHLOROFORM SLUT.

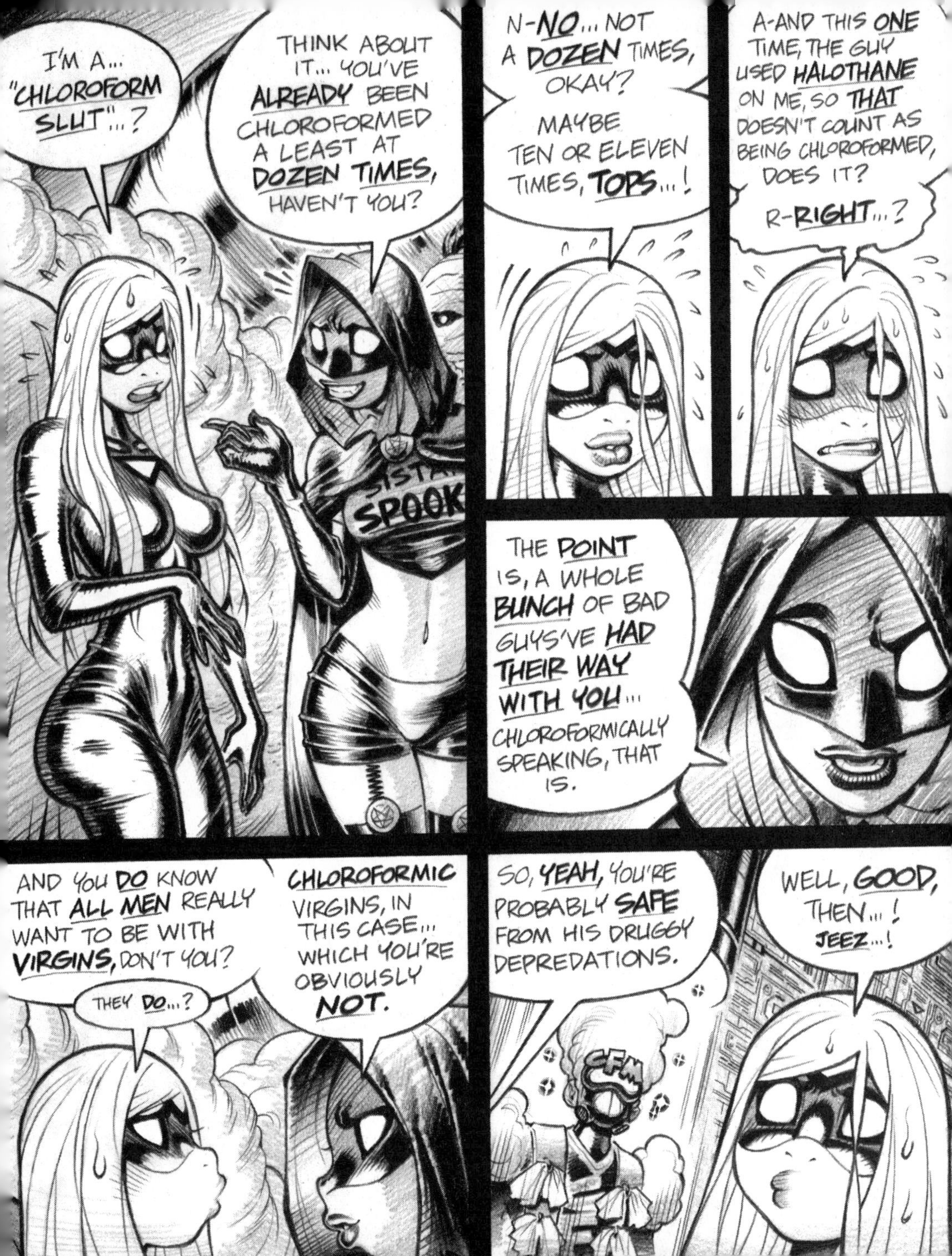
I'M A... "CHLOROFORM SLUT"...?
THINK ABOUT IT... YOU'VE ALREADY BEEN CHLOROFORMED A LEAST AT DOZEN TIMES, HAVEN'T YOU?
SPOOK
N-NO... NOT A DOZEN TIMES, OKAY?
MAYBE TEN OR ELEVEN TIMES, TOPS...!
A-AND THIS ONE TIME, THE GUY USED HALOTHANE ON ME, SO THAT DOESN'T COUNT AS BEING CHLOROFORMED, DOES IT?
R-RIGHT...?
THE POINT IS, A WHOLE BUNCH OF BAD GUYS'VE HAD THEIR WAY WITH YOU... CHLOROFORMICALLY SPEAKING, THAT IS.
AND YOU DO KNOW THAT ALL MEN REALLY WANT TO BE WITH VIRGINS, DON'T YOU?
THEY DO...?
CHLOROFORMIC VIRGINS, IN THIS CASE... WHICH YOU'RE OBVIOUSLY NOT.
SO, YEAH, YOU'RE PROBABLY SAFE FROM HIS DRUGGY DEPREDATIONS.
CFM
WELL, GOOD, THEN...! JEEZ...!

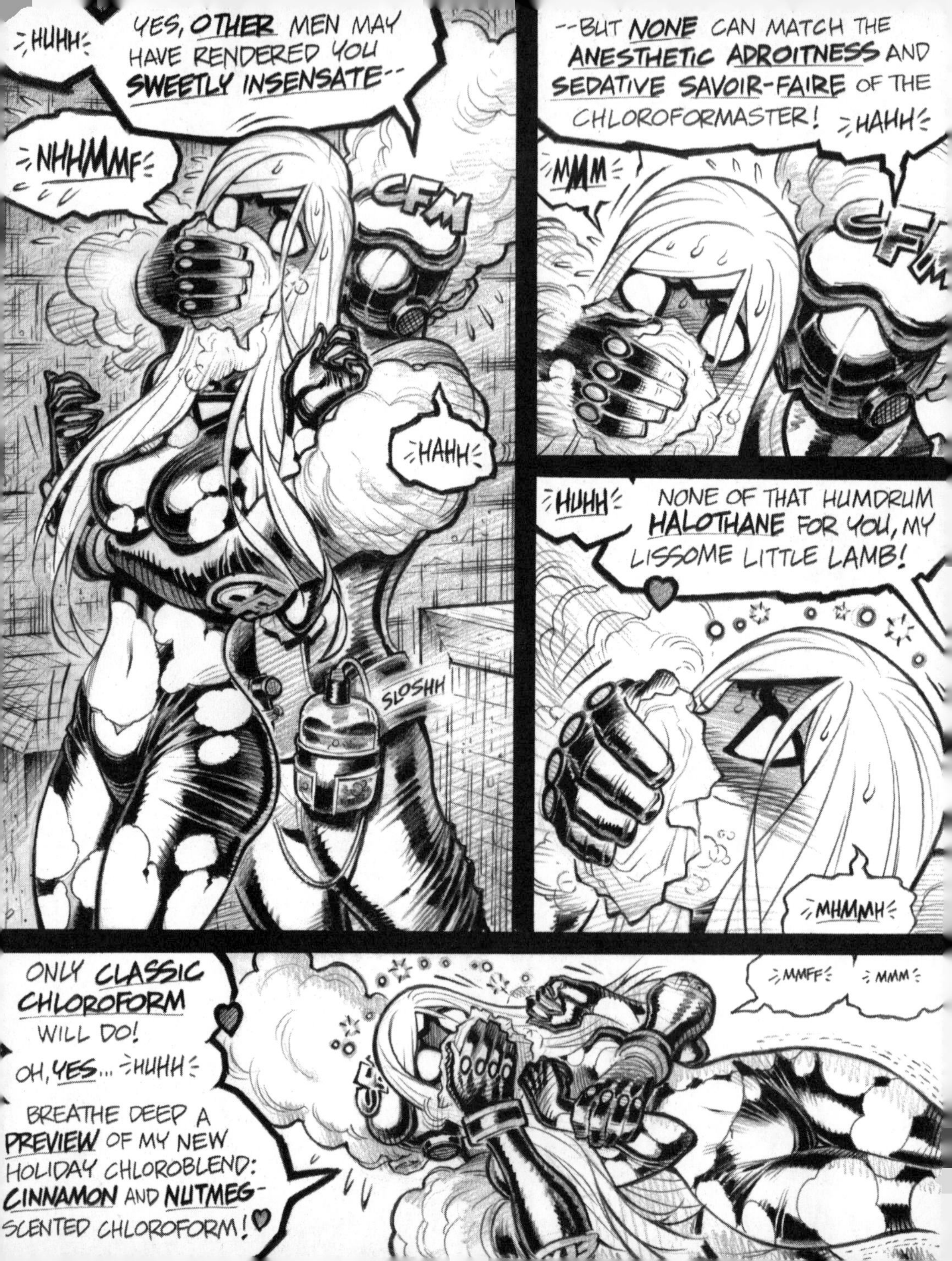

HUHH
YES, OTHER MEN MAY HAVE RENDERED YOU SWEETLY INSENSATE--
NHHMMF
CFM
HAHH
SLOSHH
--BUT NONE CAN MATCH THE ANESTHETIC ADROITNESS AND SEDATIVE SAVOIR-FAIRE OF THE CHLOROFORMASTER!
HAHH
MMM
CFM
HUHH
NONE OF THAT HUMDRUM HALOTHANE FOR YOU, MY LISSOME LITTLE LAMB!
MHMMH
ONLY CLASSIC CHLOROFORM WILL DO!
OH, YES... HUHH
BREATHE DEEP A PREVIEW OF MY NEW HOLIDAY CHLOROBLEND: CINNAMON AND NUTMEG-SCENTED CHLOROFORM!
MMFF
MMM

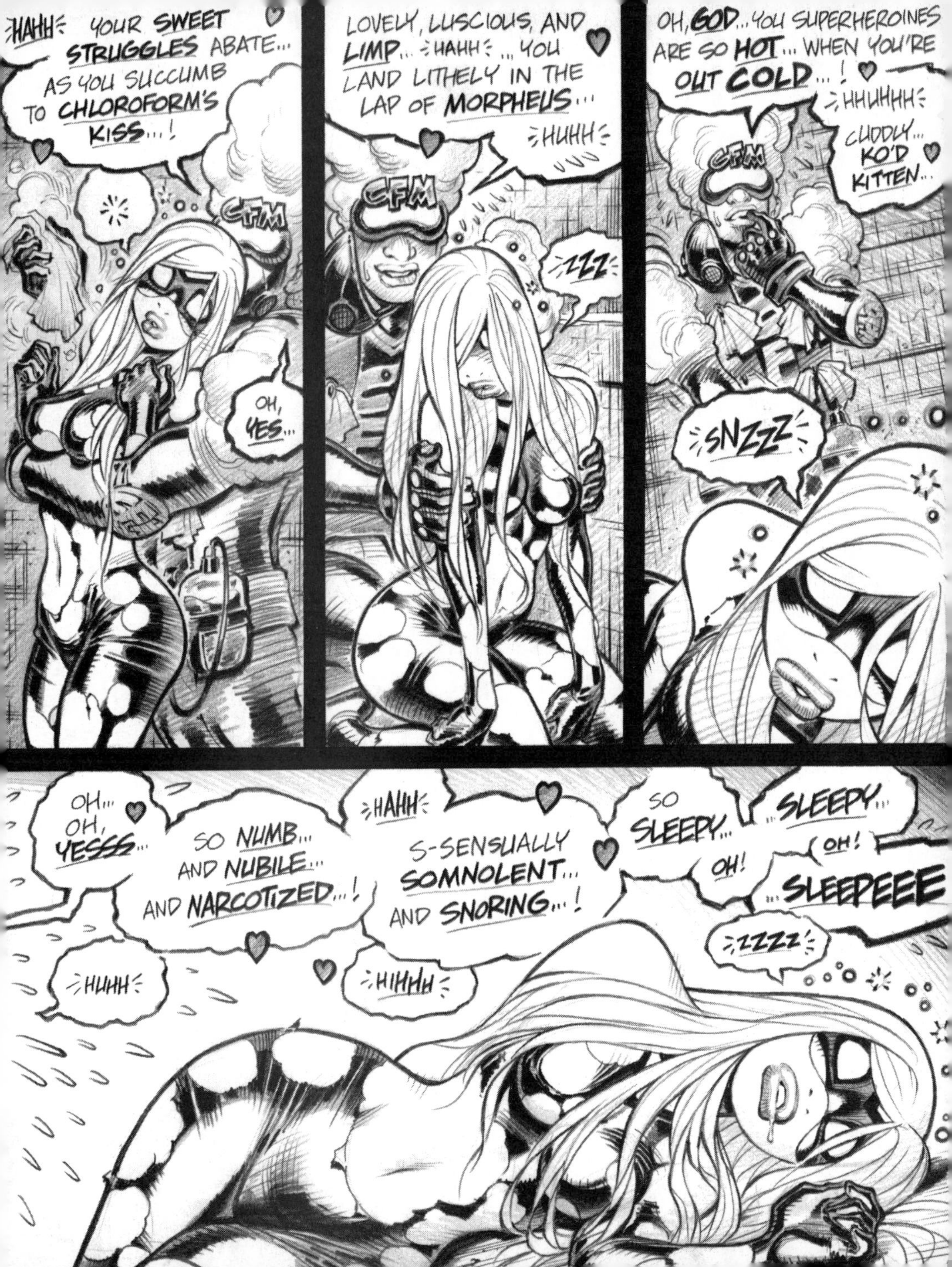
HAHH
YOUR SWEET STRUGGLES ABATE... AS YOU SUCCUMB TO CHLOROFORM'S KISS...!
CFM
OH, YES...
LOVELY, LUSCIOUS, AND LIMP... HAHH ... YOU LAND LITHELY IN THE LAP OF MORPHEUS...
HUHH
CFM
ZZZ
OH, GOD... YOU SUPERHEROINES ARE SO HOT... WHEN YOU'RE OUT COLD...!
HHUHHH
CUDDLY... KO'D KITTEN...
CFM
SNZZZ
OH... OH, YESSS...
SO NUMB... AND NUBILE... AND NARCOTIZED...!
HUHH
HAHH
S-SENSUALLY SOMNOLENT... AND SNORING...!
HIHHH
SO SLEEPY... ...SLEEPY...
OH!
OH!
...SLEEPEEE
ZZZZ

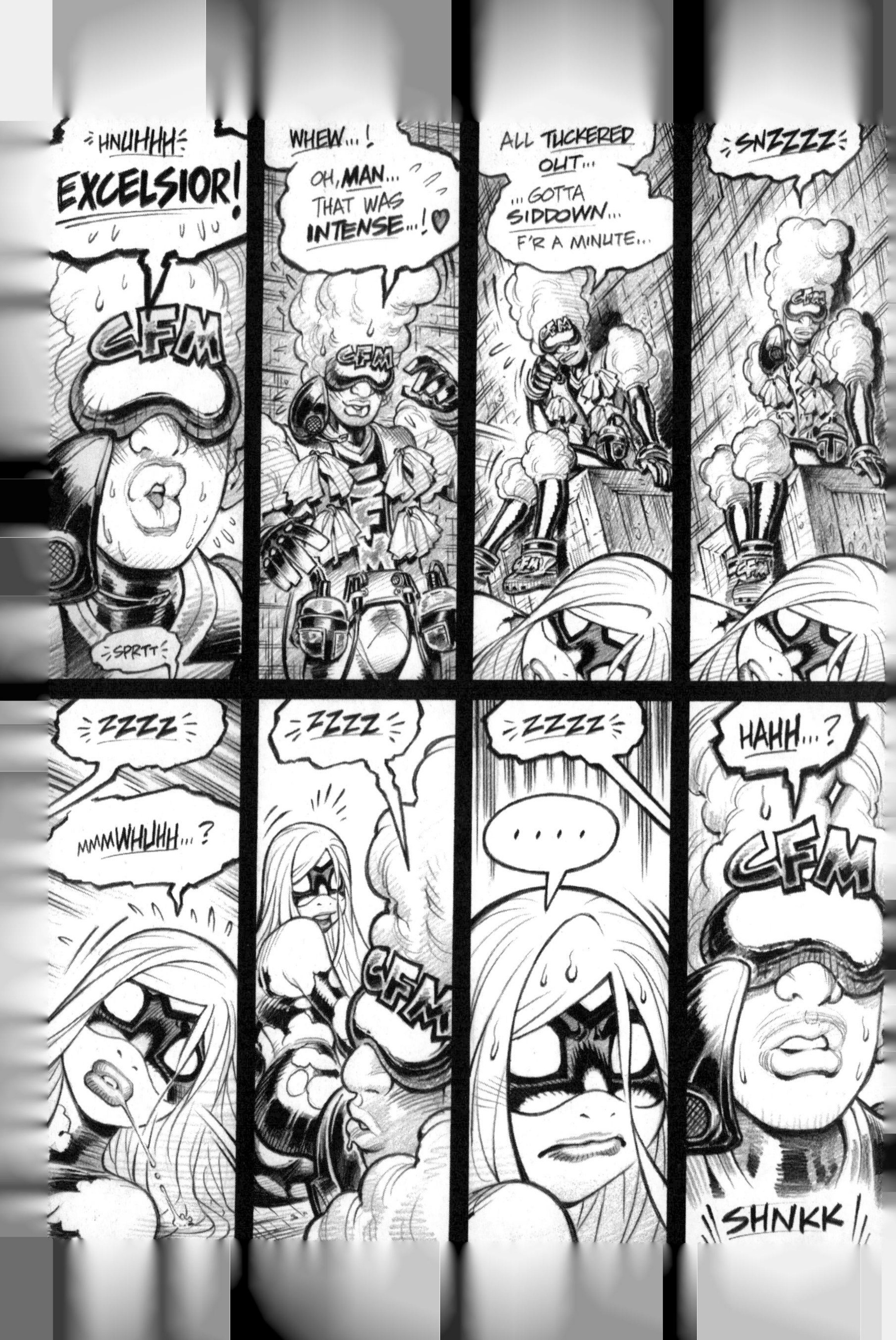
HNUHHH
EXCELSIOR!
SPRTT
WHEW...!
OH, MAN... THAT WAS INTENSE...! ♥
ALL TUCKERED OUT...
... GOTTA SIDDOWN... F'R A MINUTE...
SNZZZZ
ZZZZ
MMMWHUHH...?
ZZZZ
ZZZZ
....
HAHH...?
SHNKK

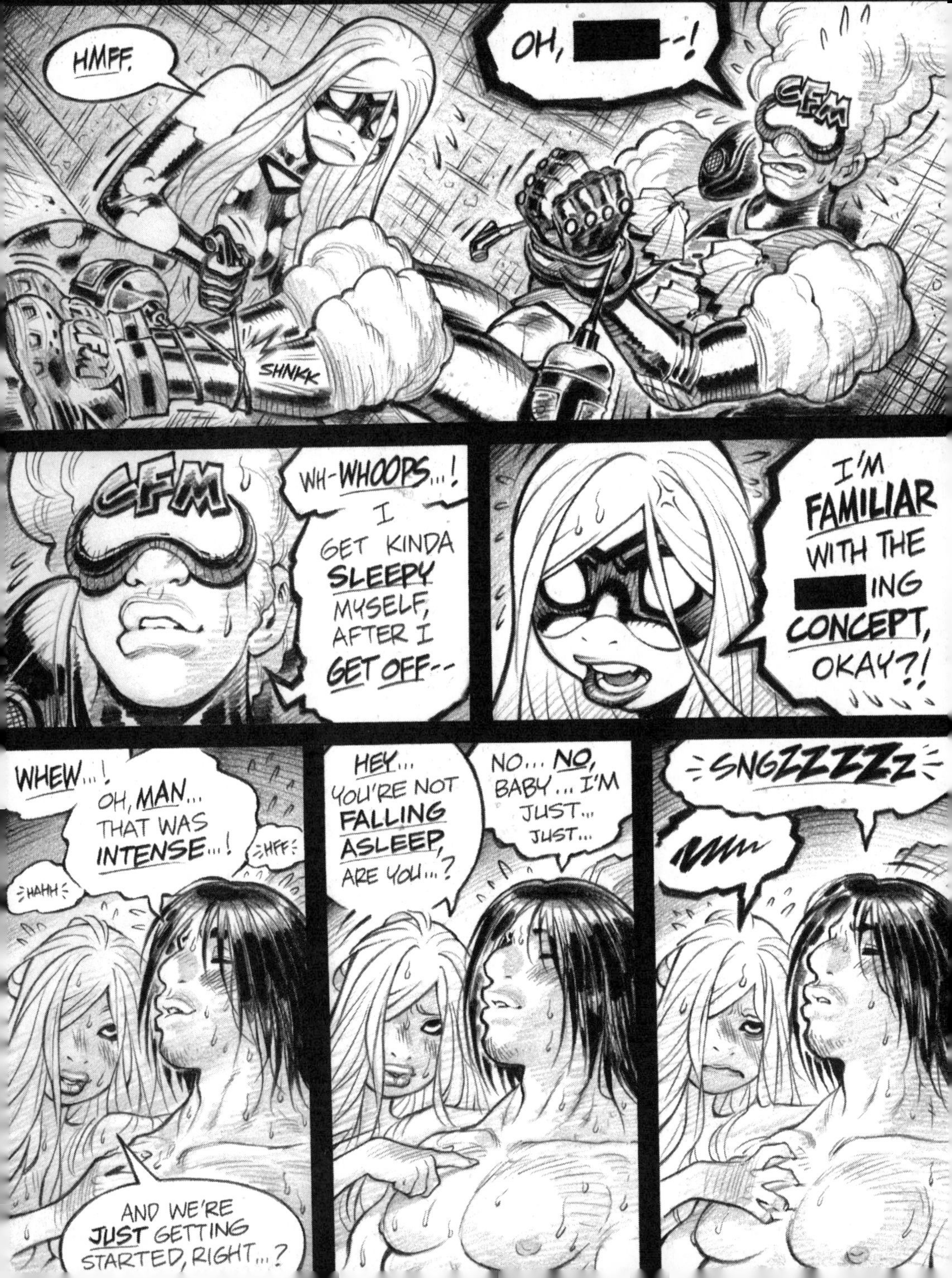
HMFF.
OH, [redacted]--!
CFM
SHNKK
CFM
WH-WHOOPS...!
I GET KINDA SLEEPY MYSELF, AFTER I GET OFF--
I'M FAMILIAR WITH THE [redacted]ING CONCEPT, OKAY?!
WHEW...!
OH, MAN... THAT WAS INTENSE...!
HFF
HAHH
AND WE'RE JUST GETTING STARTED, RIGHT...?
HEY... YOU'RE NOT FALLING ASLEEP, ARE YOU...?
NO... NO, BABY... I'M JUST... JUST...
SNGZZZZZz

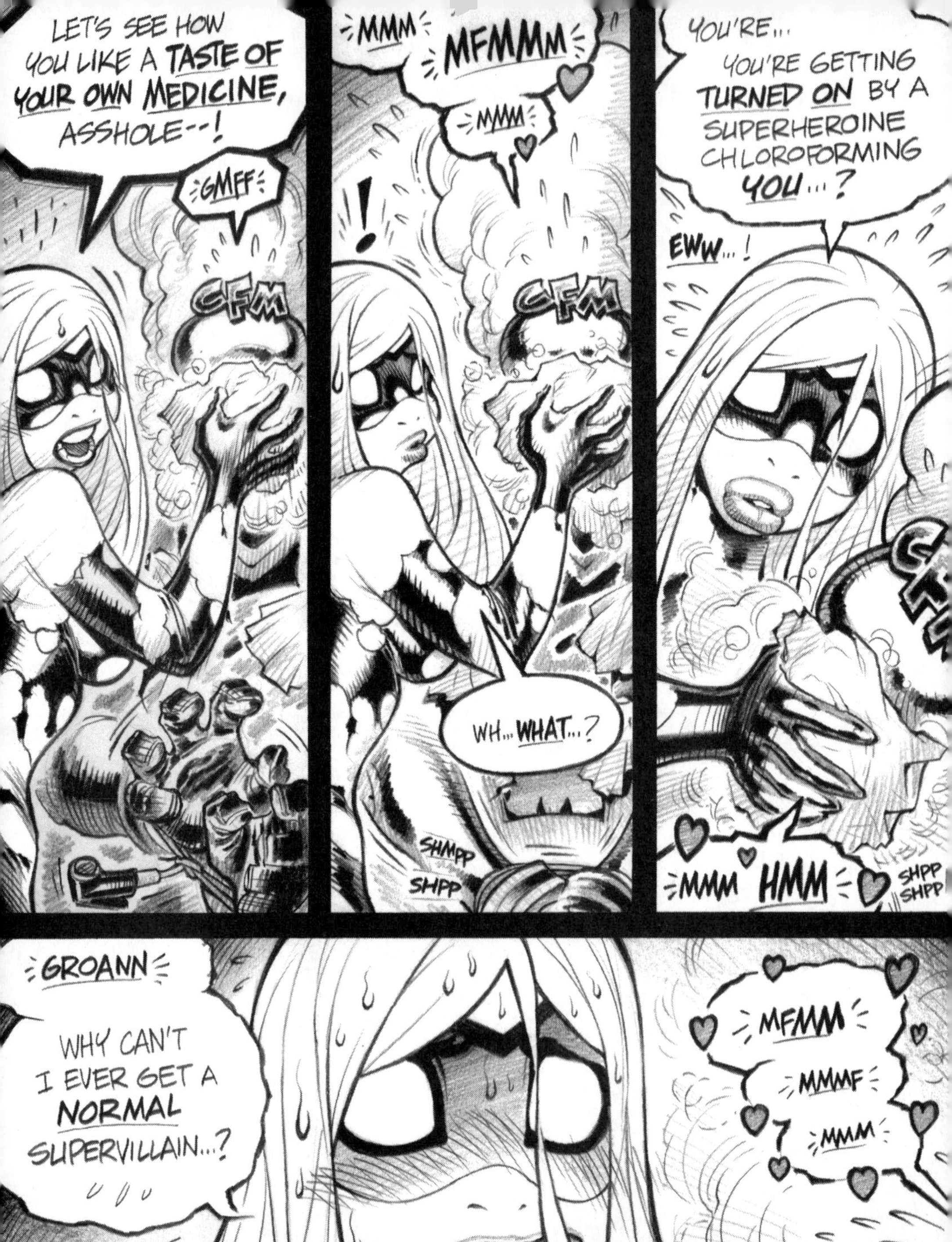
LET'S SEE HOW YOU LIKE A TASTE OF YOUR OWN MEDICINE, ASSHOLE--!
GMFF
CFM
MMM
MFMMM
MMM
!
CFM
WH... WHAT...?
SHMPP
SHPP
YOU'RE...
YOU'RE GETTING TURNED ON BY A SUPERHEROINE CHLOROFORMING YOU...?
EWW...!
MMM HMM
SHPP
SHPP
GROANN
WHY CAN'T I EVER GET A NORMAL SUPERVILLAIN...?
MFMM
MMMF
MMM

empowered™

A.R.R.!

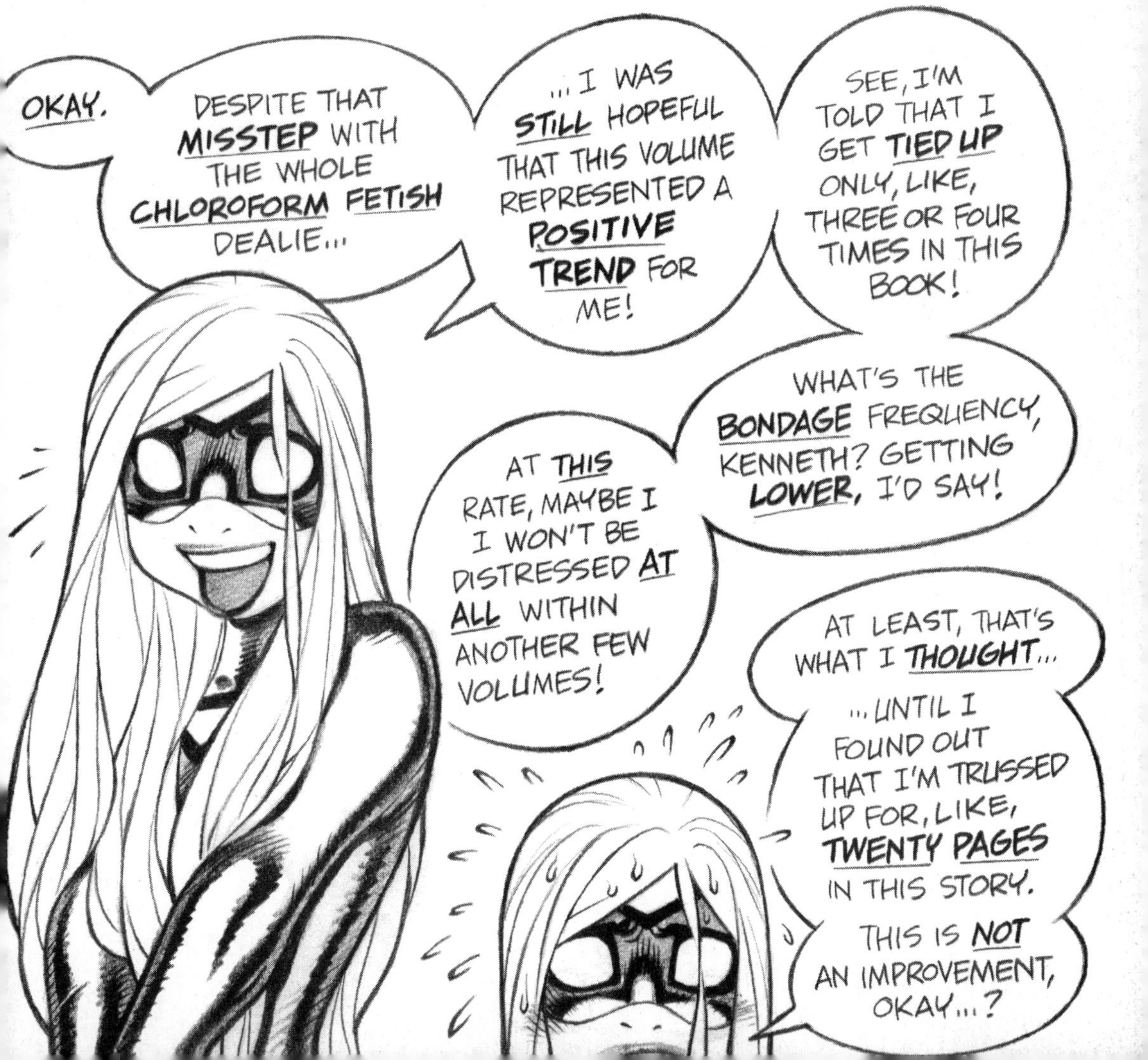

OKAY.
DESPITE THAT MISSTEP WITH THE WHOLE CHLOROFORM FETISH DEALIE...
...I WAS STILL HOPEFUL THAT THIS VOLUME REPRESENTED A POSITIVE TREND FOR ME!
SEE, I'M TOLD THAT I GET TIED UP ONLY, LIKE, THREE OR FOUR TIMES IN THIS BOOK!
WHAT'S THE BONDAGE FREQUENCY, KENNETH? GETTING LOWER, I'D SAY!
AT THIS RATE, MAYBE I I WON'T BE DISTRESSED AT ALL WITHIN ANOTHER FEW VOLUMES!
AT LEAST, THAT'S WHAT I THOUGHT...
...UNTIL I FOUND OUT THAT I'M TRUSSED UP FOR, LIKE, TWENTY PAGES IN THIS STORY.
THIS IS NOT AN IMPROVEMENT, OKAY...?

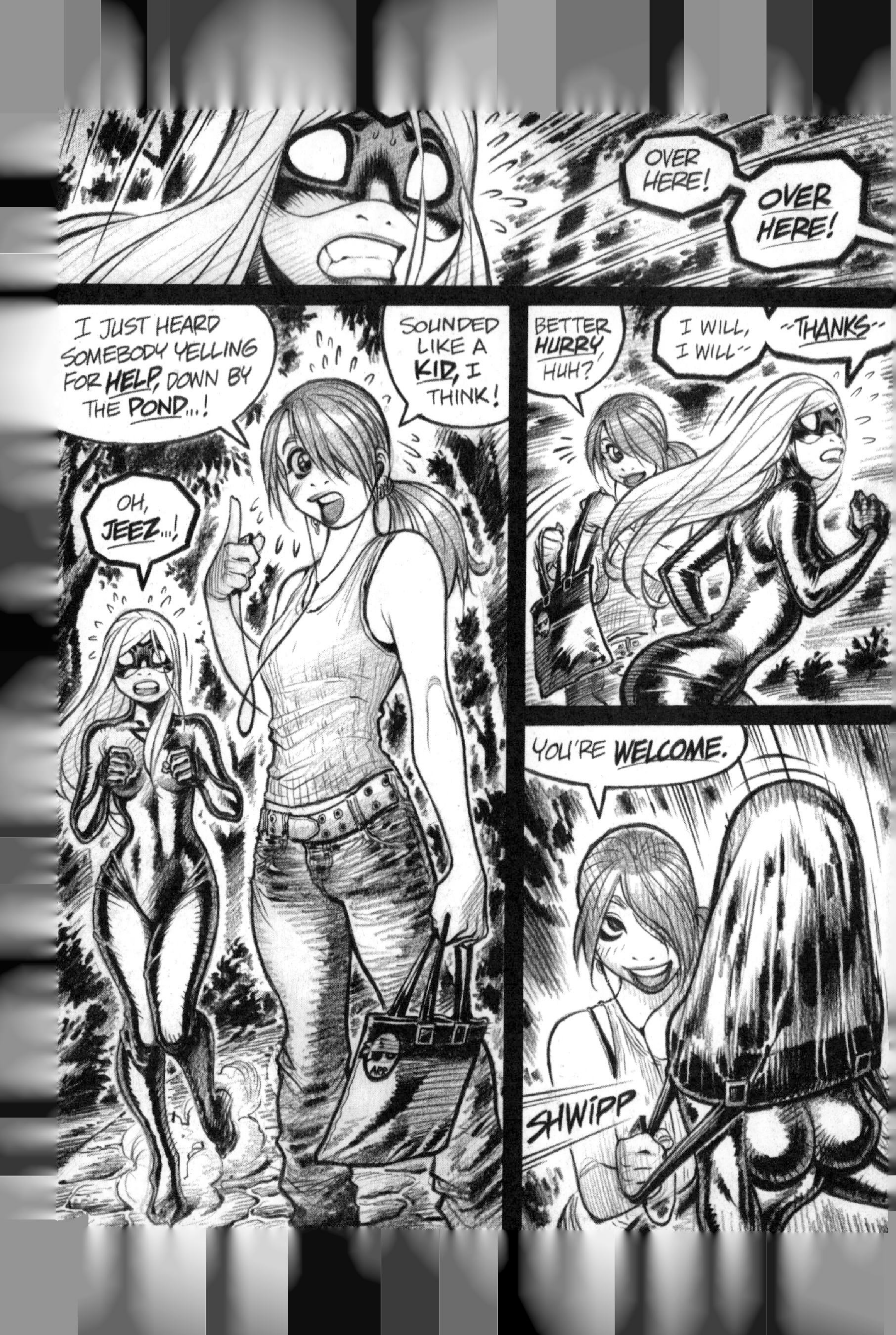
OVER HERE!
OVER HERE!
I JUST HEARD SOMEBODY YELLING FOR HELP, DOWN BY THE POND...!
SOUNDED LIKE A KID, I THINK!
OH, JEEZ...!
BETTER HURRY, HUH?
I WILL, I WILL--
--THANKS--
YOU'RE WELCOME.
SHWIPP

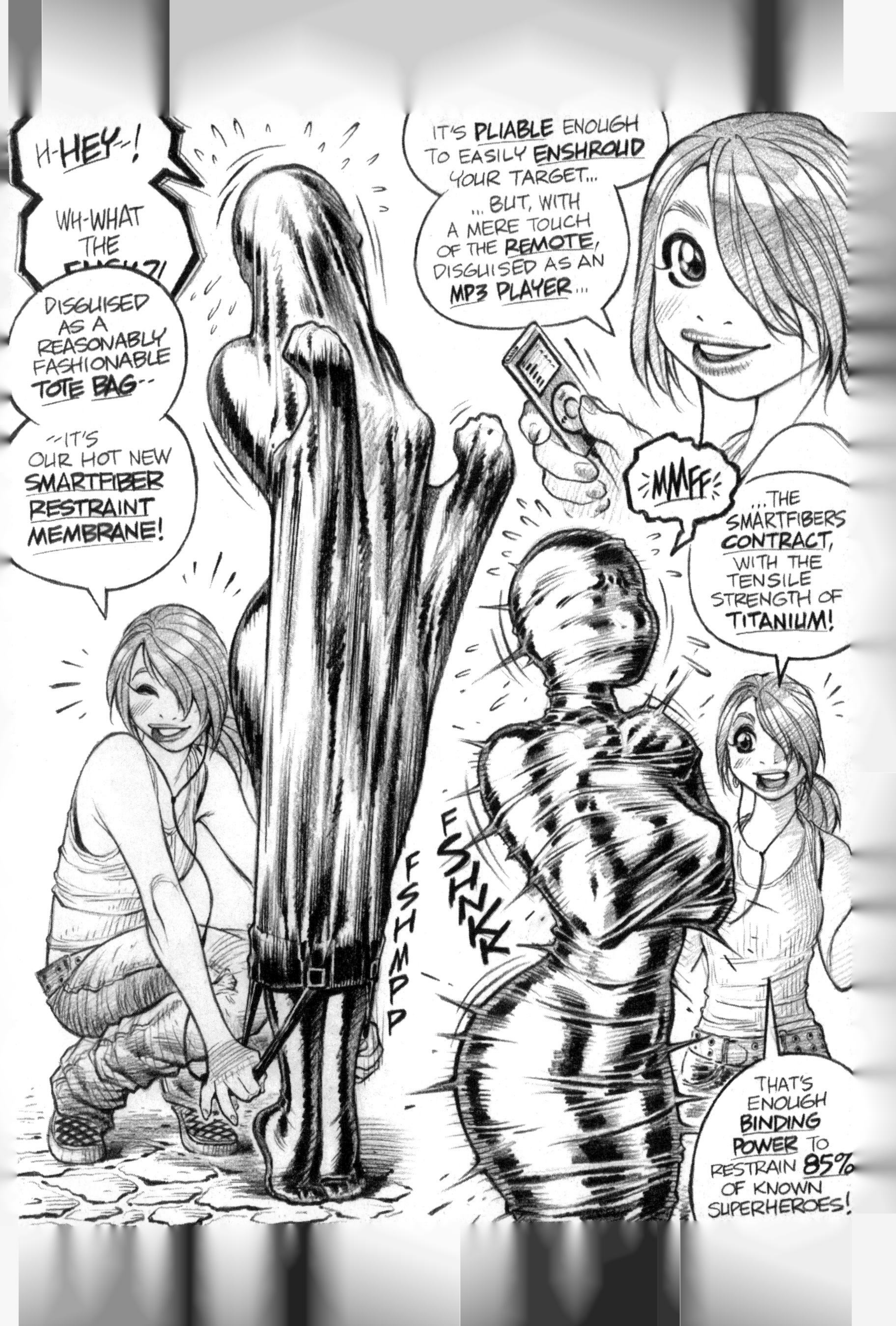
H-HEY--!
WH-WHAT THE
DISGUISED AS A REASONABLY FASHIONABLE TOTE BAG--
--IT'S OUR HOT NEW SMARTFIBER RESTRAINT MEMBRANE!
IT'S PLIABLE ENOUGH TO EASILY ENSHROUD YOUR TARGET...
...BUT, WITH A MERE TOUCH OF THE REMOTE, DISGUISED AS AN MP3 PLAYER...
MMFF
...THE SMARTFIBERS CONTRACT, WITH THE TENSILE STRENGTH OF TITANIUM!
FSHMPP
FSHNKK
THAT'S ENOUGH BINDING POWER TO RESTRAIN 85% OF KNOWN SUPERHEROES!

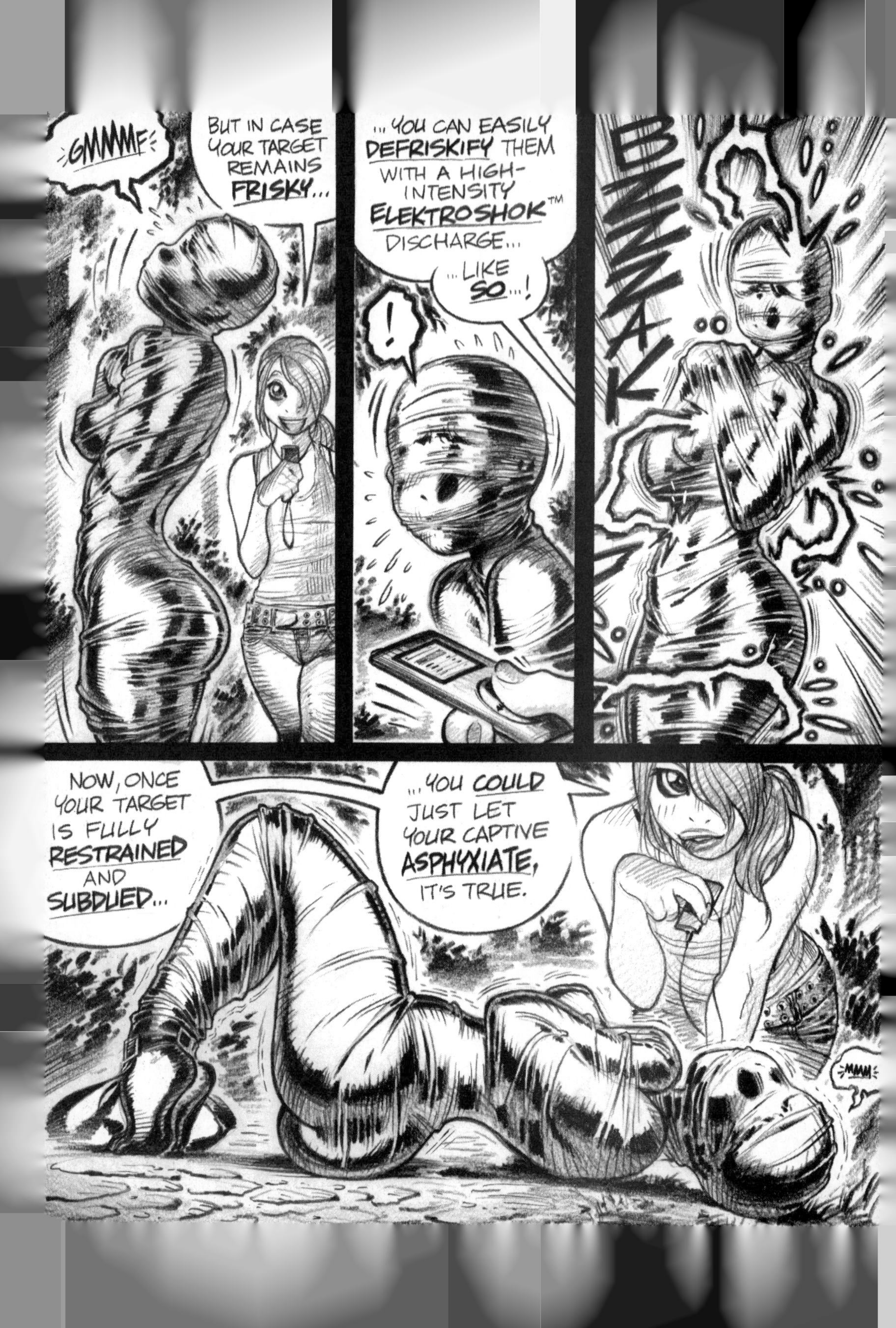
GMMMF!
BUT IN CASE YOUR TARGET REMAINS FRISKY...
...YOU CAN EASILY DEFRISKIFY THEM WITH A HIGH-INTENSITY ELEKTROSHOK™ DISCHARGE...
...LIKE SO...!
!
BZZZAK
NOW, ONCE YOUR TARGET IS FULLY RESTRAINED AND SUBDUED...
...YOU COULD JUST LET YOUR CAPTIVE ASPHYXIATE, IT'S TRUE.

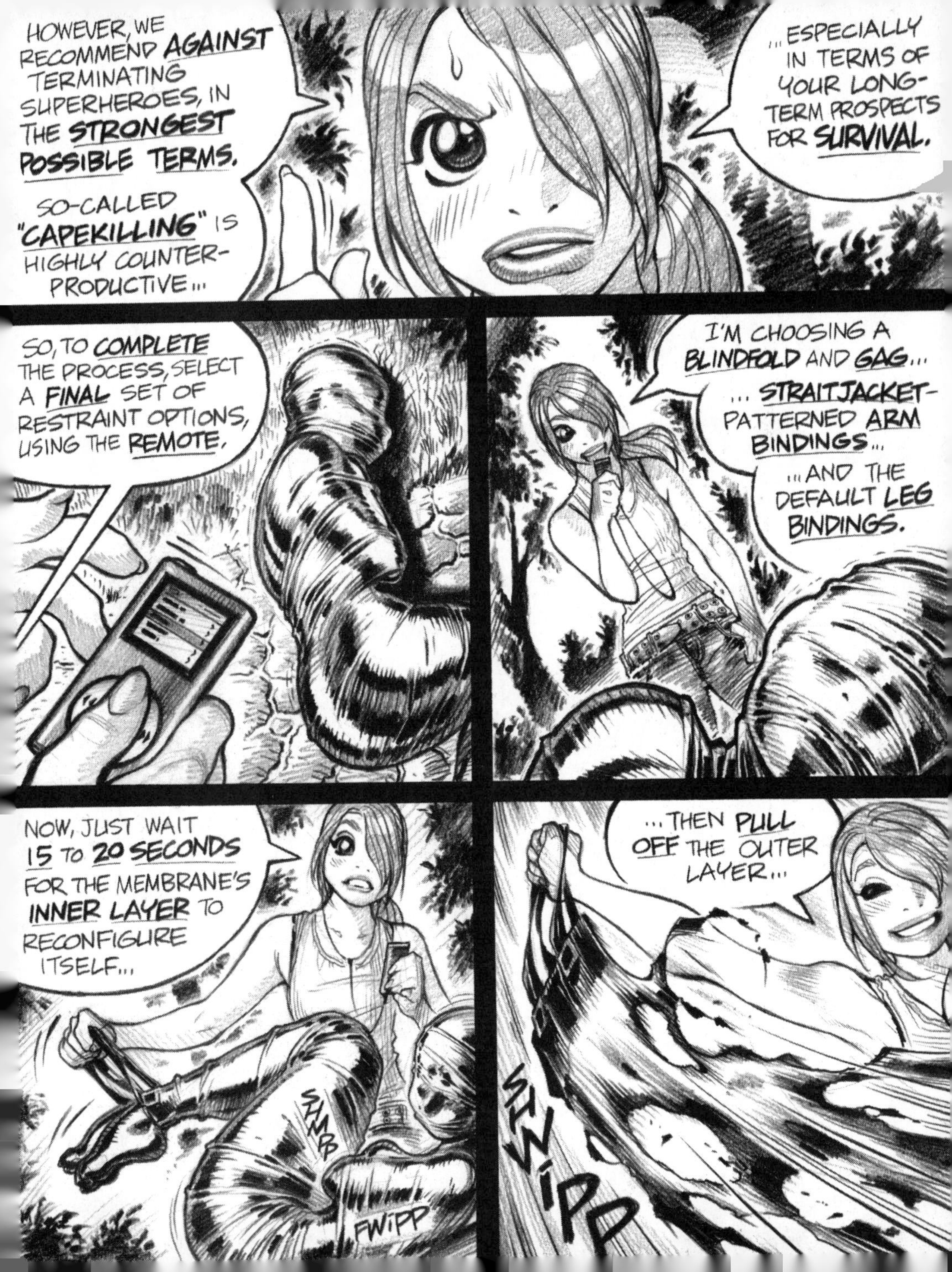
HOWEVER, WE RECOMMEND AGAINST TERMINATING SUPERHEROES, IN THE STRONGEST POSSIBLE TERMS.
SO-CALLED "CAPEKILLING" IS HIGHLY COUNTER-PRODUCTIVE...
...ESPECIALLY IN TERMS OF YOUR LONG-TERM PROSPECTS FOR SURVIVAL.
SO, TO COMPLETE THE PROCESS, SELECT A FINAL SET OF RESTRAINT OPTIONS, USING THE REMOTE.
I'M CHOOSING A BLINDFOLD AND GAG...
... STRAITJACKET-PATTERNED ARM BINDINGS...
...AND THE DEFAULT LEG BINDINGS.
NOW, JUST WAIT 15 TO 20 SECONDS FOR THE MEMBRANE'S INNER LAYER TO RECONFIGURE ITSELF...
SHNPP
FWIPP
...THEN PULL OFF THE OUTER LAYER...
SHWIPP

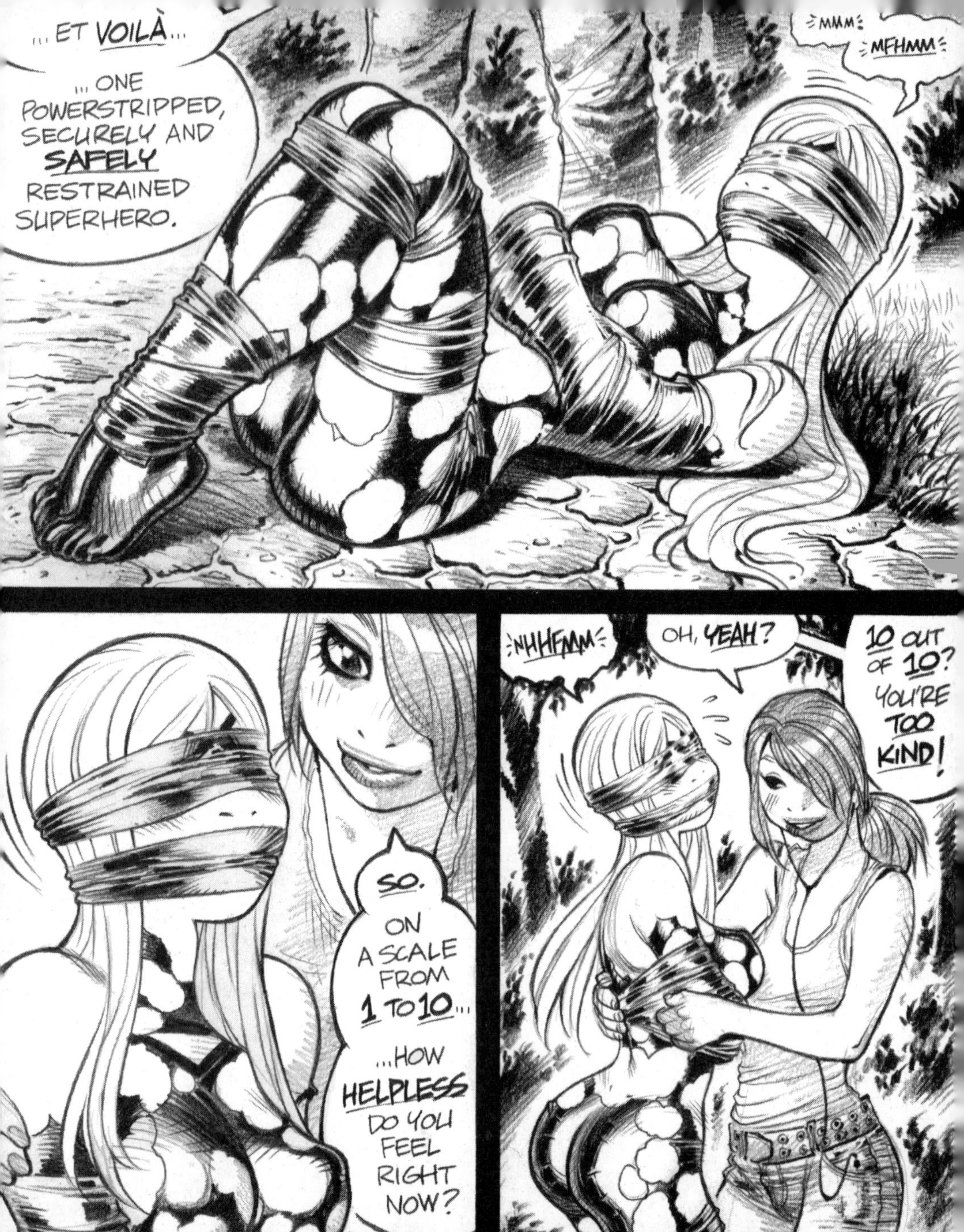
... ET VOILÀ ...
... ONE POWERSTRIPPED, SECURELY AND SAFELY RESTRAINED SUPERHERO.
MMM
MFHMM
SO.
ON A SCALE FROM 1 TO 10 ...
... HOW HELPLESS DO YOU FEEL RIGHT NOW?
NHHFMM
OH, YEAH?
10 OUT OF 10? YOU'RE TOO KIND!

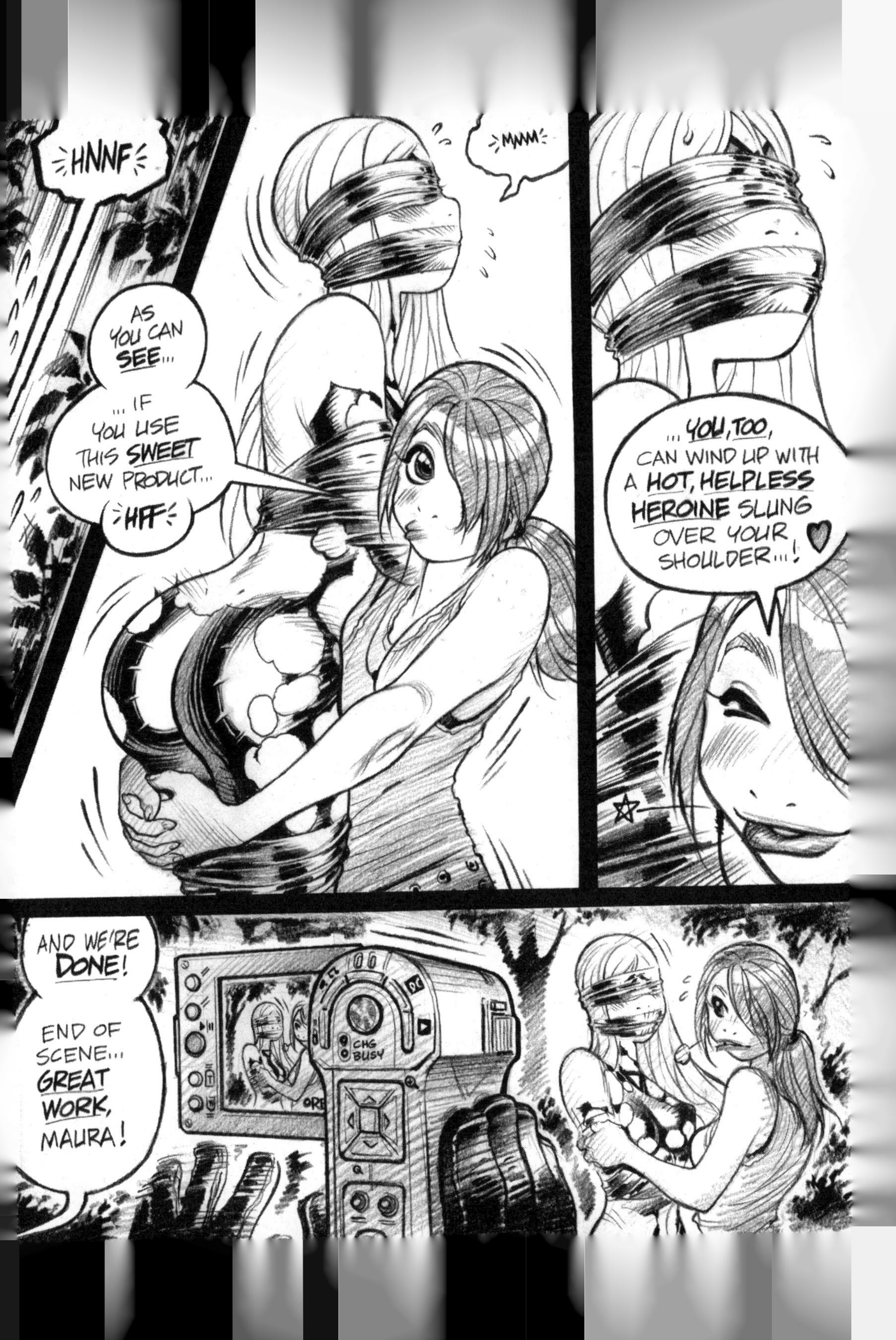
HNNF
MMM
AS YOU CAN SEE...
... IF YOU USE THIS SWEET NEW PRODUCT...
HFF
... YOU, TOO, CAN WIND UP WITH A HOT, HELPLESS HEROINE SLUNG OVER YOUR SHOULDER...!
AND WE'RE DONE!
END OF SCENE... GREAT WORK, MAURA!

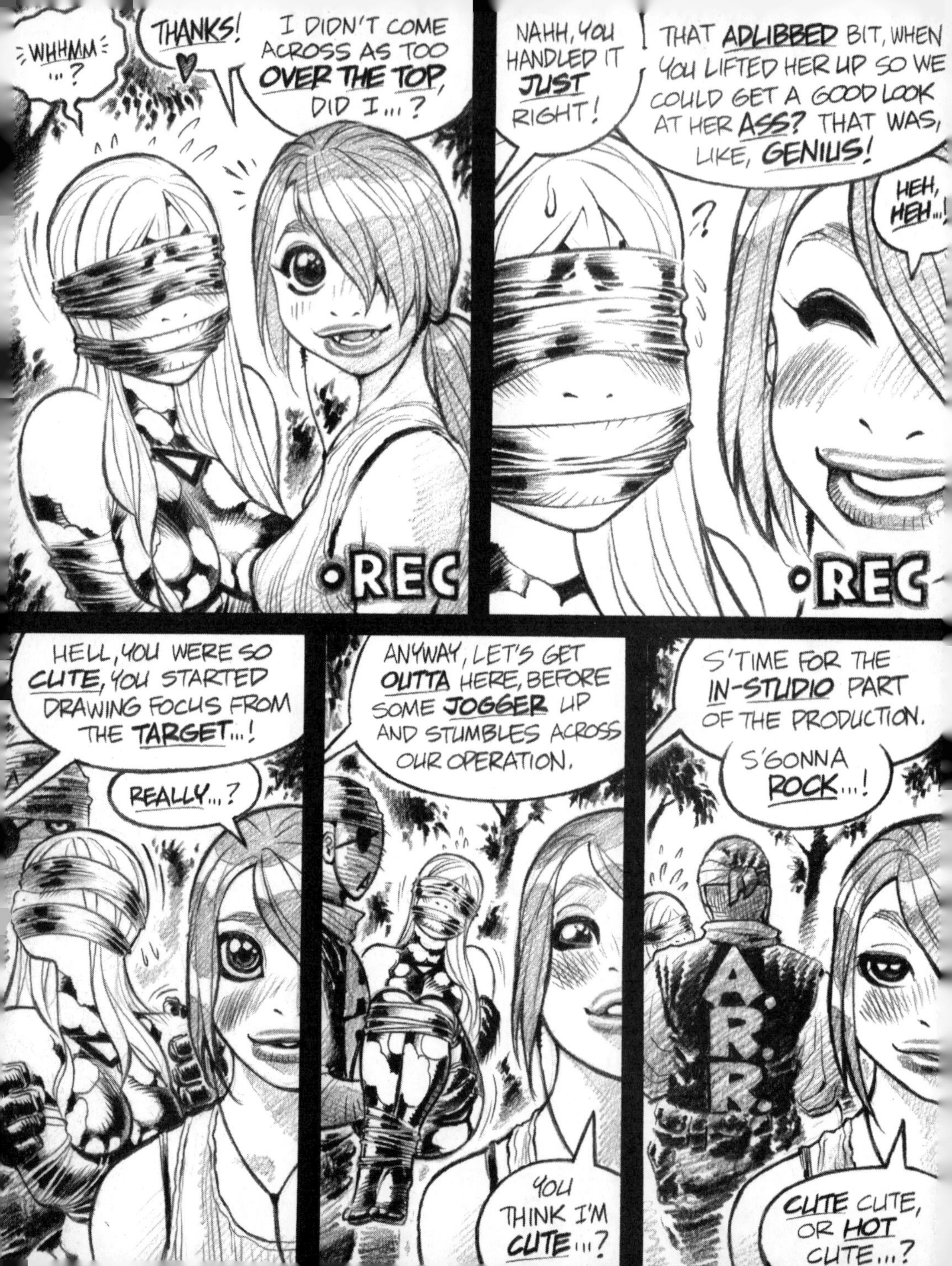
WHHMM ...?
THANKS! ♥
I DIDN'T COME ACROSS AS TOO OVER THE TOP, DID I...?
•REC
NAHH, YOU HANDLED IT JUST RIGHT!
THAT ADLIBBED BIT, WHEN YOU LIFTED HER UP SO WE COULD GET A GOOD LOOK AT HER ASS? THAT WAS, LIKE, GENIUS!
HEH, HEH...!
•REC
HELL, YOU WERE SO CUTE, YOU STARTED DRAWING FOCUS FROM THE TARGET...!
REALLY...?
ANYWAY, LET'S GET OUTTA HERE, BEFORE SOME JOGGER UP AND STUMBLES ACROSS OUR OPERATION.
YOU THINK I'M CUTE...?
S'TIME FOR THE IN-STUDIO PART OF THE PRODUCTION.
S'GONNA ROCK...!
CUTE CUTE, OR HOT CUTE...?

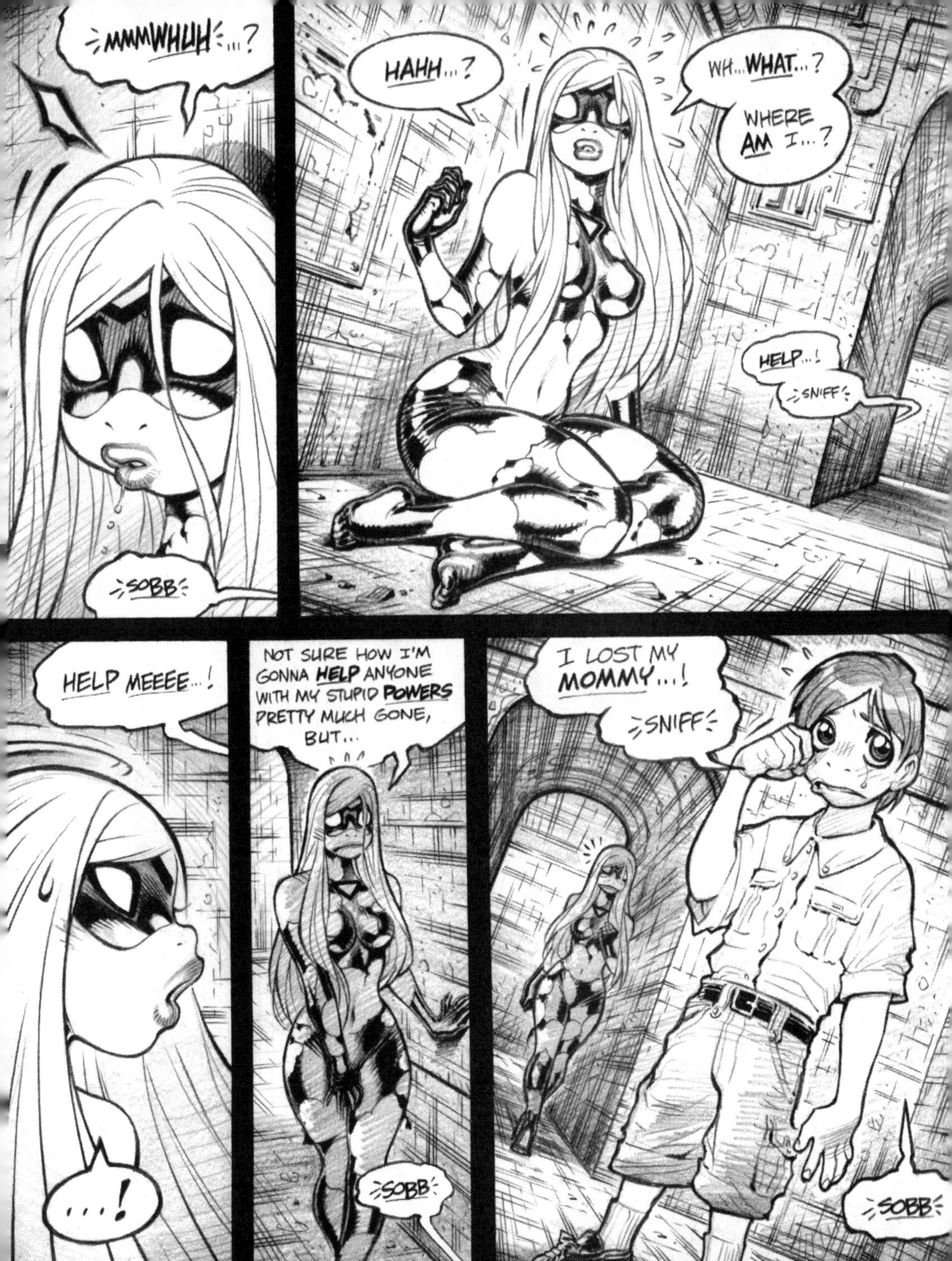
MMMWHUH...?
SOBB
HAHH...?
WH...WHAT...?
WHERE AM I...?
HELP...!
SNIFF
HELP MEEEE...!
...!
NOT SURE HOW I'M GONNA HELP ANYONE WITH MY STUPID POWERS PRETTY MUCH GONE, BUT...
SOBB
I LOST MY MOMMY...!
SNIFF
SOBB

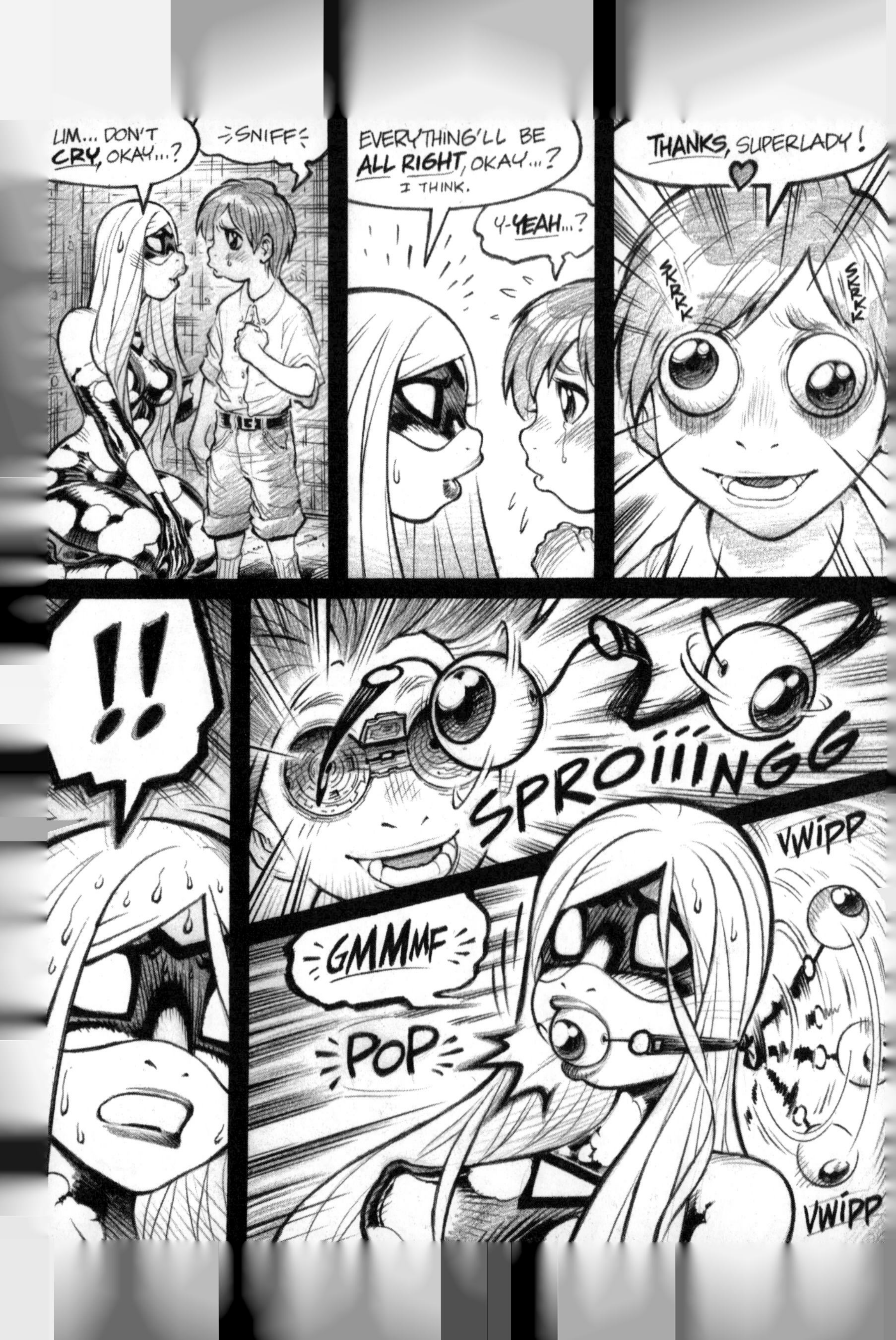
UM... DON'T CRY, OKAY...?
SNIFF
EVERYTHING'LL BE ALL RIGHT, OKAY...?
I THINK.
Y-YEAH...?
THANKS, SUPERLADY!
SKRKK
SKRKK
!!
SPROIIINGG
VWIPP
GMMMF
POP
VWIPP

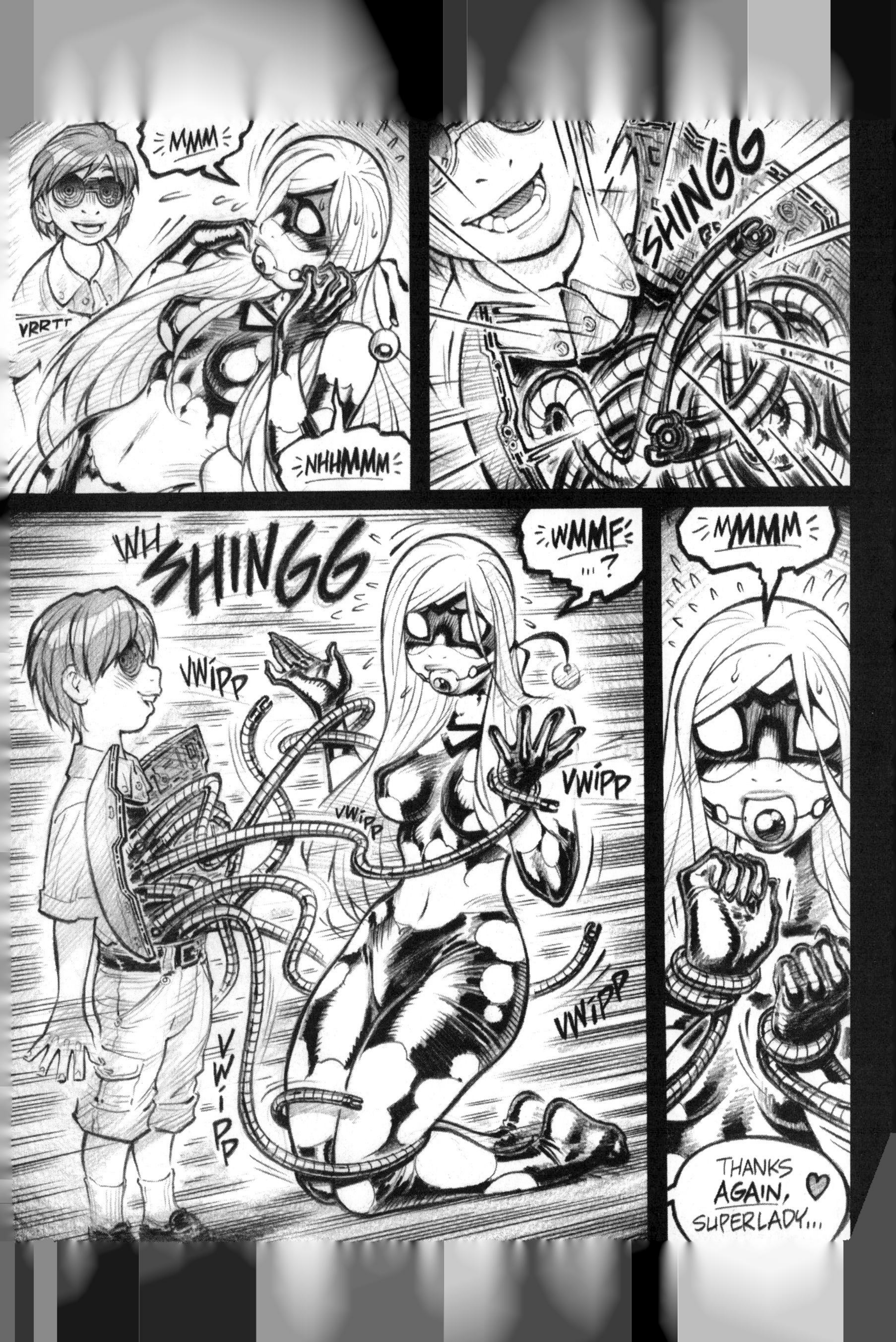
MMM
VRRTT
NHHMMM
SHINGG
WH SHINGG
WMMF ...?
VWIPP
VWIPP
VWIPP
VWIPP
VWIPP
MMMM
THANKS AGAIN, SUPERLADY...

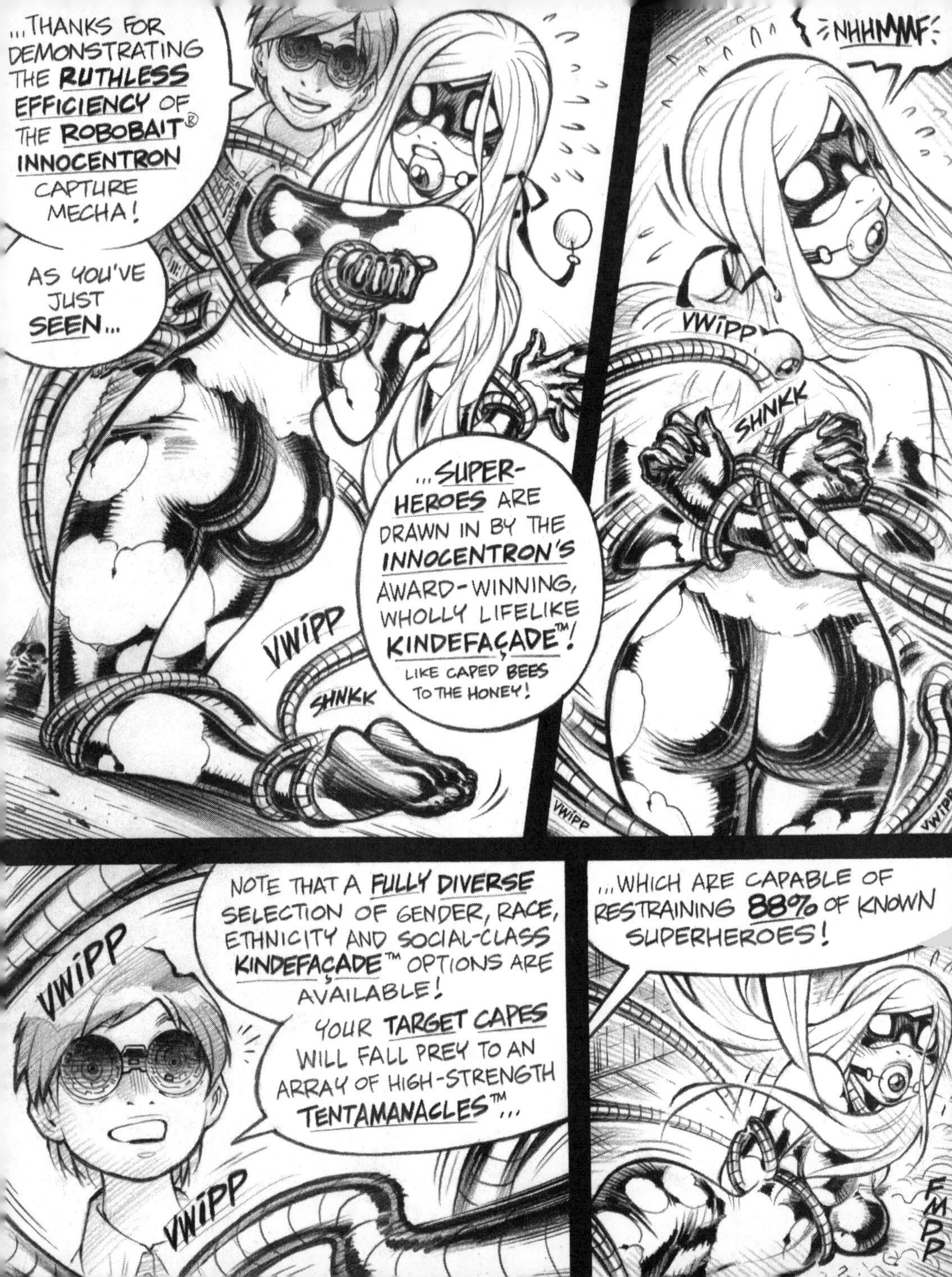
...THANKS FOR DEMONSTRATING THE RUTHLESS EFFICIENCY OF THE ROBOBAIT® INNOCENTRON CAPTURE MECHA!
AS YOU'VE JUST SEEN...
...SUPER-HEROES ARE DRAWN IN BY THE INNOCENTRON'S AWARD-WINNING, WHOLLY LIFELIKE KINDEFAÇADE™!
LIKE CAPED BEES TO THE HONEY!
VWIPP
SHNKK
NHHMMF
VWIPP
SHNKK
VWIPP
VWIPP
VWIPP
NOTE THAT A FULLY DIVERSE SELECTION OF GENDER, RACE, ETHNICITY AND SOCIAL-CLASS KINDEFAÇADE™ OPTIONS ARE AVAILABLE!
YOUR TARGET CAPES WILL FALL PREY TO AN ARRAY OF HIGH-STRENGTH TENTAMANACLES™...
VWIPP
...WHICH ARE CAPABLE OF RESTRAINING 88% OF KNOWN SUPERHEROES!
FMPP

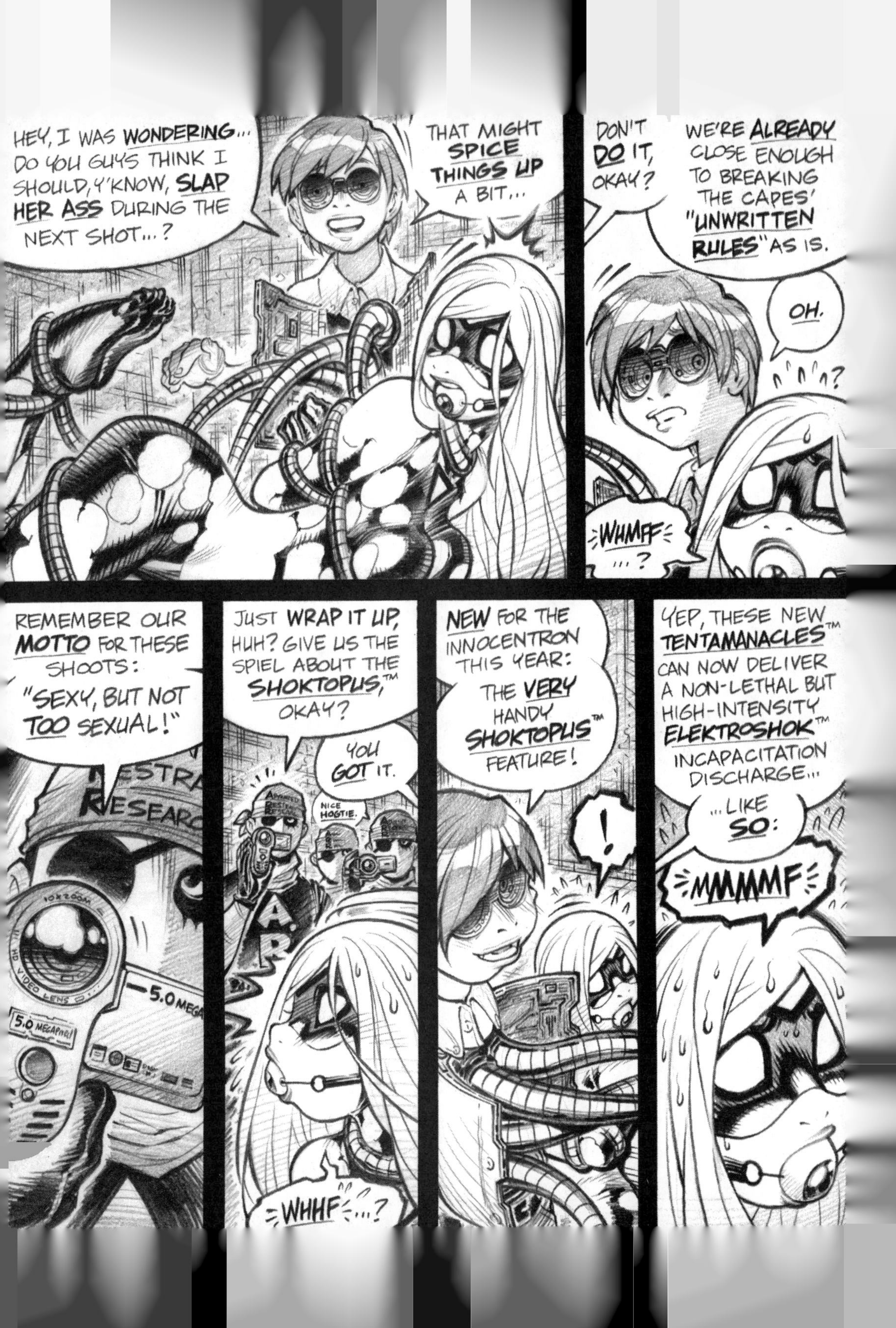
HEY, I WAS WONDERING... DO YOU GUYS THINK I SHOULD, Y'KNOW, SLAP HER ASS DURING THE NEXT SHOT...?
THAT MIGHT SPICE THINGS UP A BIT...
DON'T DO IT, OKAY?
WE'RE ALREADY CLOSE ENOUGH TO BREAKING THE CAPES' "UNWRITTEN RULES" AS IS.
OH.
WHMFF ...?
REMEMBER OUR MOTTO FOR THESE SHOOTS: "SEXY, BUT NOT TOO SEXUAL!"
JUST WRAP IT UP, HUH? GIVE US THE SPIEL ABOUT THE SHOKTOPUS,™ OKAY?
YOU GOT IT.
NICE HOGTIE.
WHHF ...?
NEW FOR THE INNOCENTRON THIS YEAR: THE VERY HANDY SHOKTOPUS™ FEATURE!
!
YEP, THESE NEW TENTAMANACLES™ CAN NOW DELIVER A NON-LETHAL BUT HIGH-INTENSITY ELEKTROSHOK™ INCAPACITATION DISCHARGE...
...LIKE SO:
MMMMMF

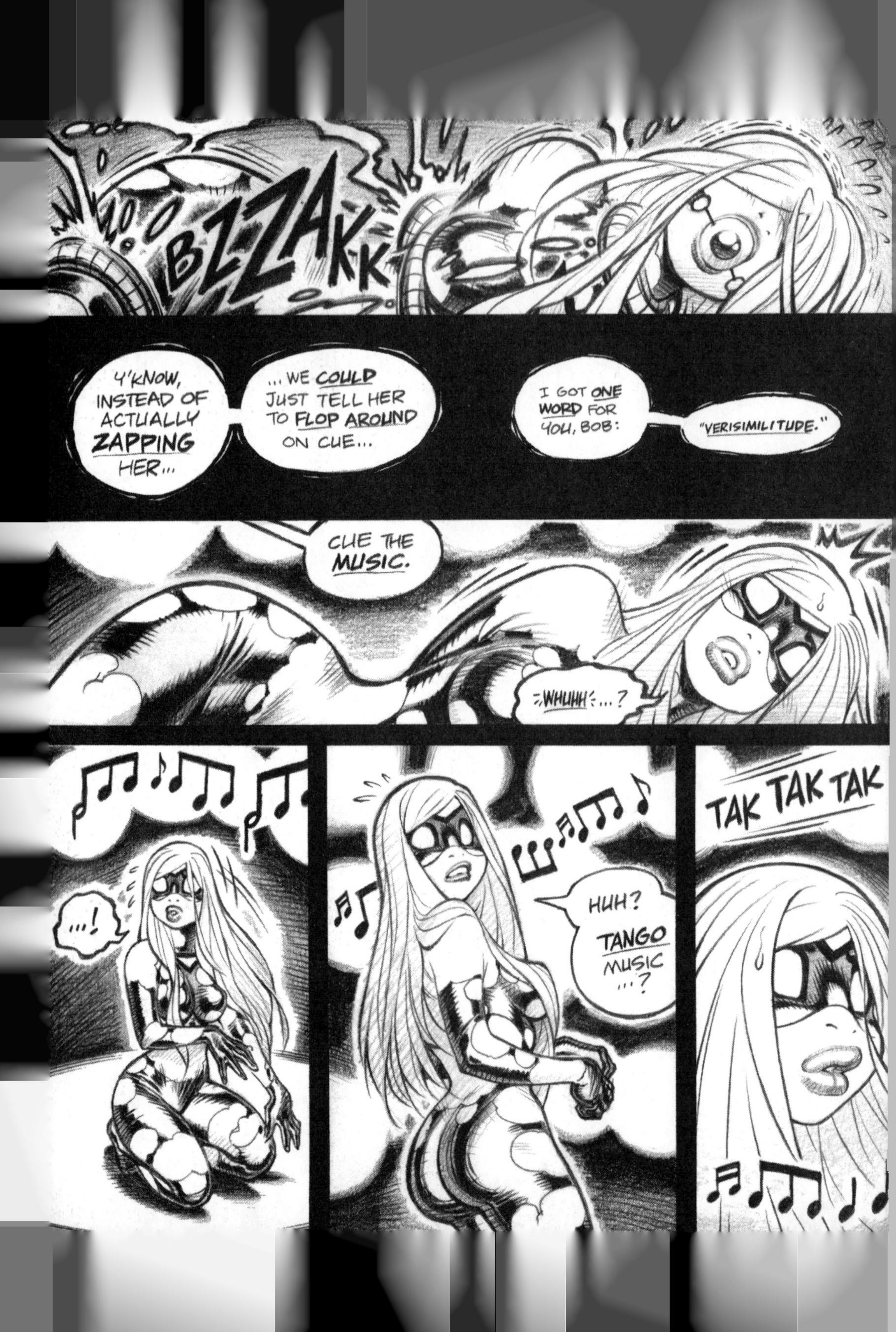
BZZAKKK
Y'KNOW, INSTEAD OF ACTUALLY ZAPPING HER...
...WE COULD JUST TELL HER TO FLOP AROUND ON CUE...
I GOT ONE WORD FOR YOU, BOB:
"VERISIMILITUDE."
CUE THE MUSIC.
WHUHH...?
...!
HUH? TANGO MUSIC ...?
TAK TAK TAK

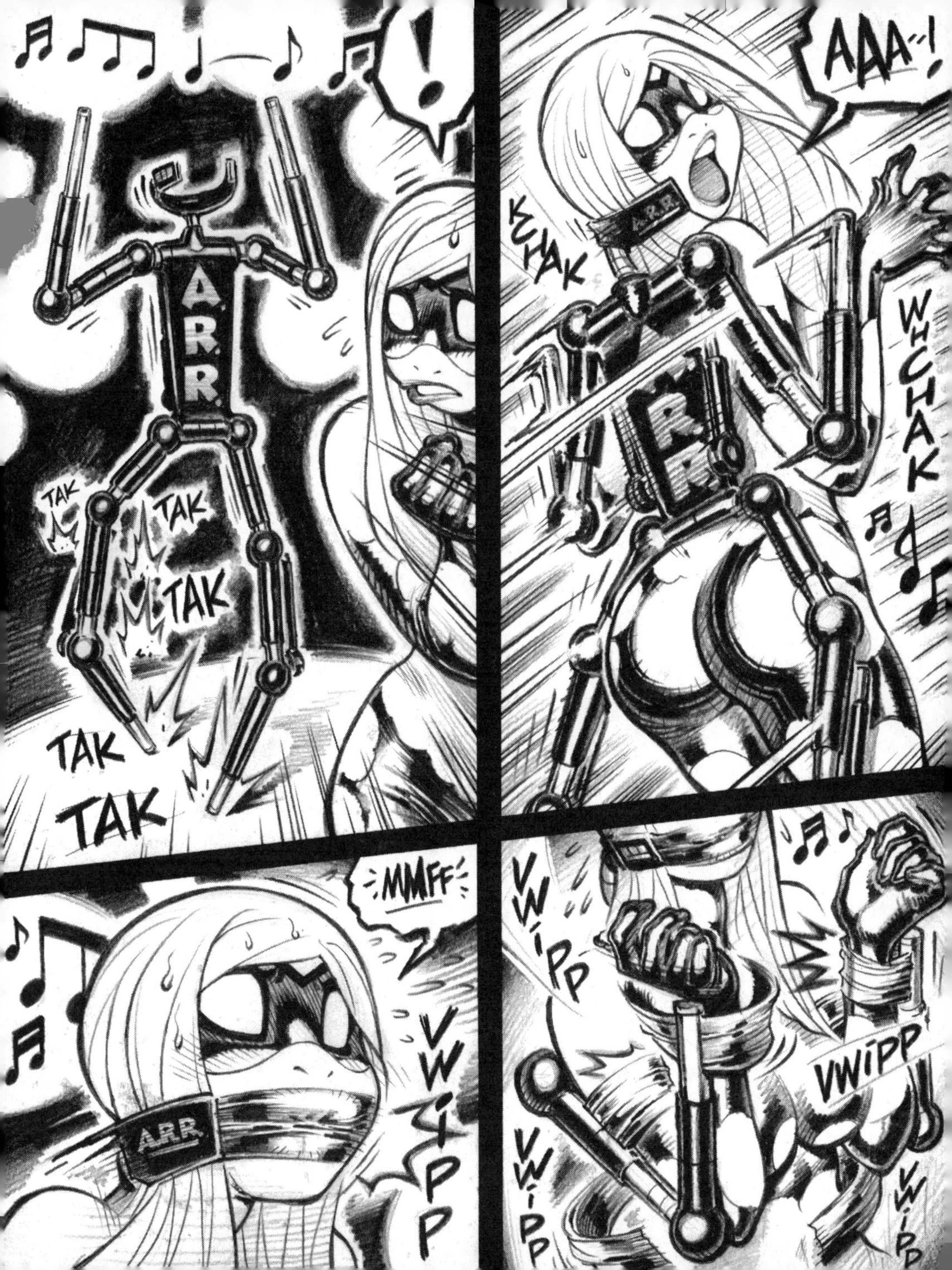
!
A.R.R.
TAK
TAK
TAK
TAK
TAK
AAA-!
KCHAK
WHCHAK
MMFF
VWIPP
A.R.R.
VWIPP
VWIPP
VWIPP
VWIPP

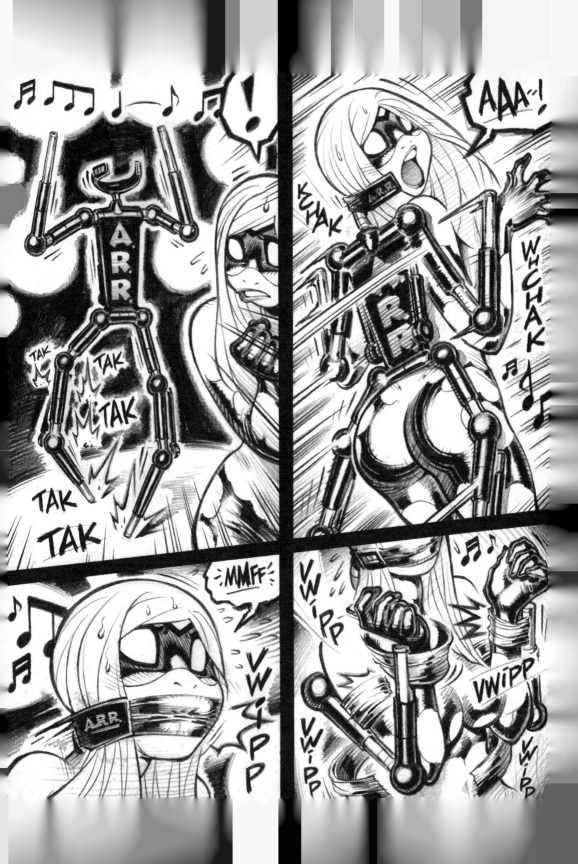

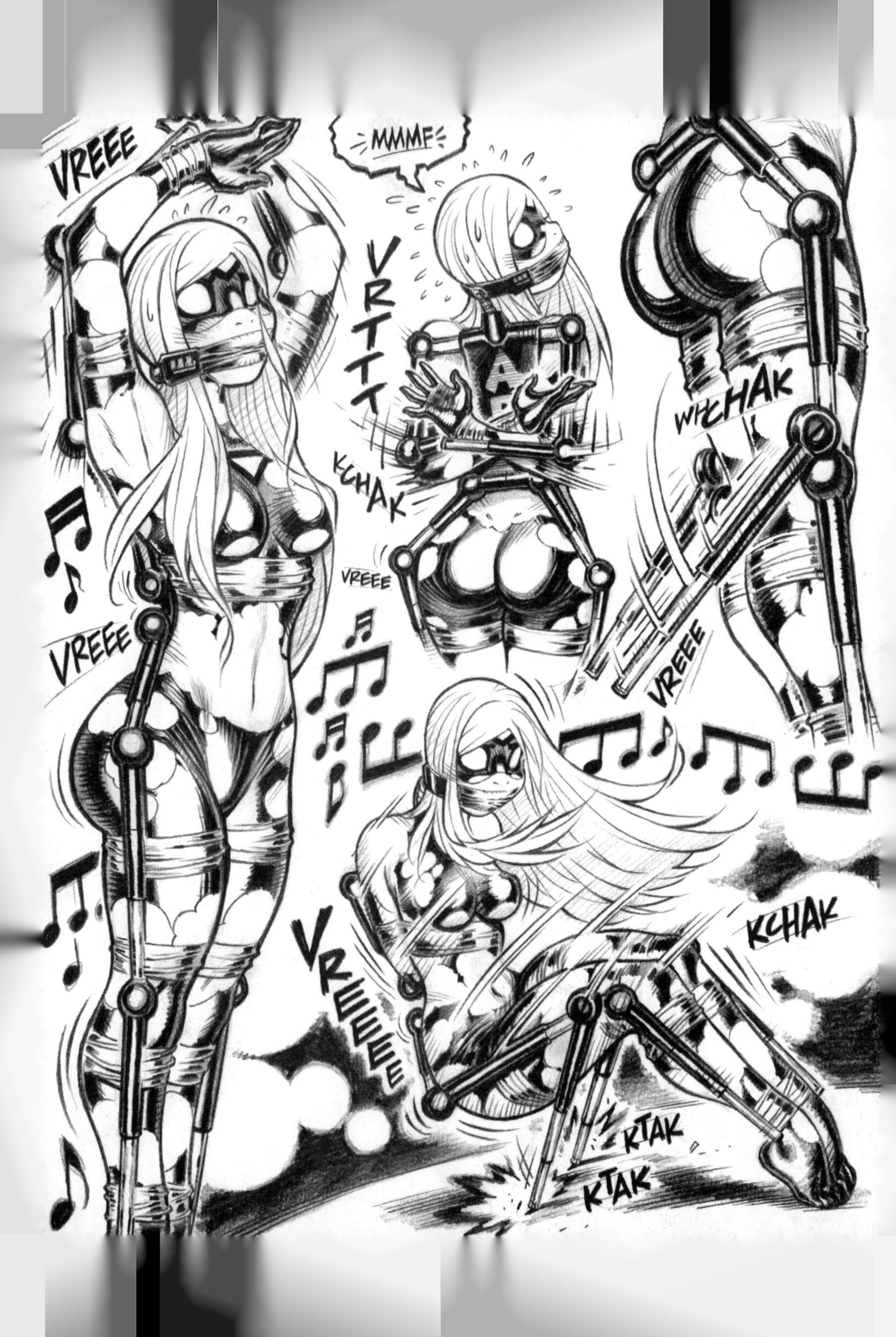
VREEE
VREEE
MMMF
VRTTTT
KCHAK
VREEE
WHCHAK
VREEE
VREEEEE
KCHAK
KTAK
KTAK

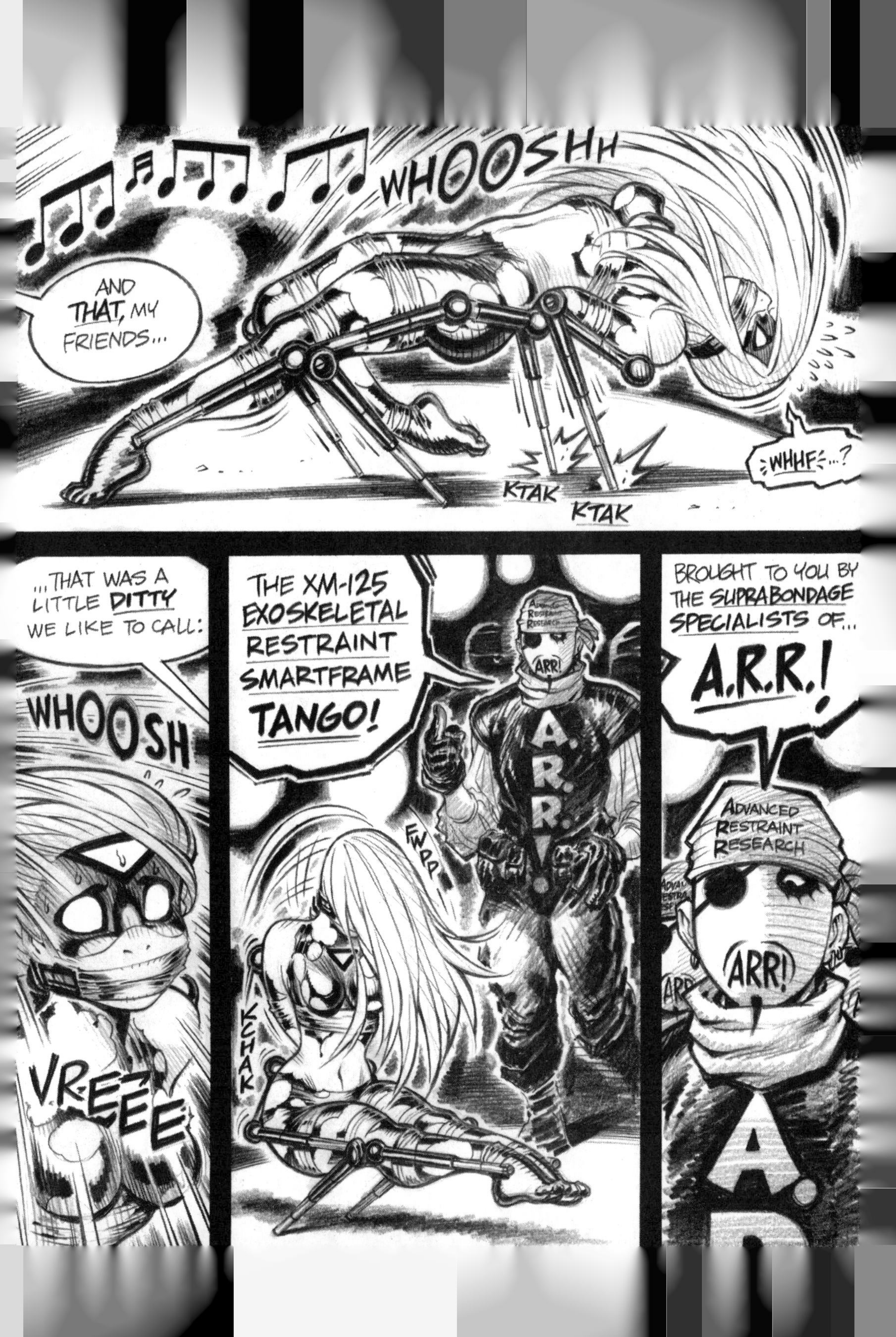
WHOOSHH
AND THAT, MY FRIENDS...
WHHF...?
KTAK
KTAK
...THAT WAS A LITTLE DITTY WE LIKE TO CALL:
WHOOSH
VREEEE
THE XM-125 EXOSKELETAL RESTRAINT SMARTFRAME TANGO!
ARR!
A.R.R.!
FWPP
KCHAK
BROUGHT TO YOU BY THE SUPRABONDAGE SPECIALISTS OF... A.R.R.!
ADVANCED RESTRAINT RESEARCH
ARR!

A!
VREEE
A.R.R.
A.R.R.
VRTTT
VREEE
VRTTT
R!
VREEE
VRTTT
VREEEE
R!
VRTTT
VREEE
KCHAK
ADVANCED RESTRAINT RESEARCH!
ADVANCED RESTRAINT RESEARCH
ADVANCED RESTRAINT RESEARCH
ADVANCED RESTRAINT RESEARCH
ARR!
ARR!
ARR!
ARR!

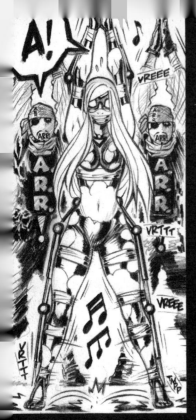

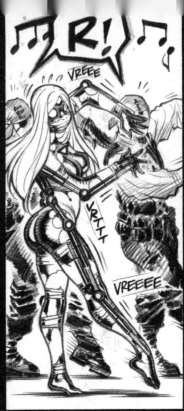

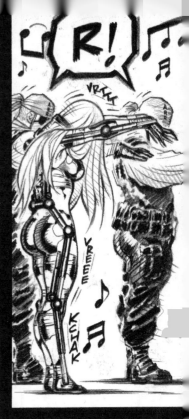

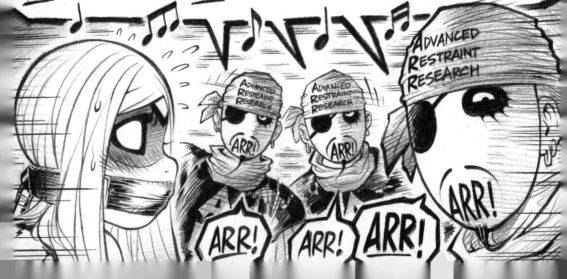

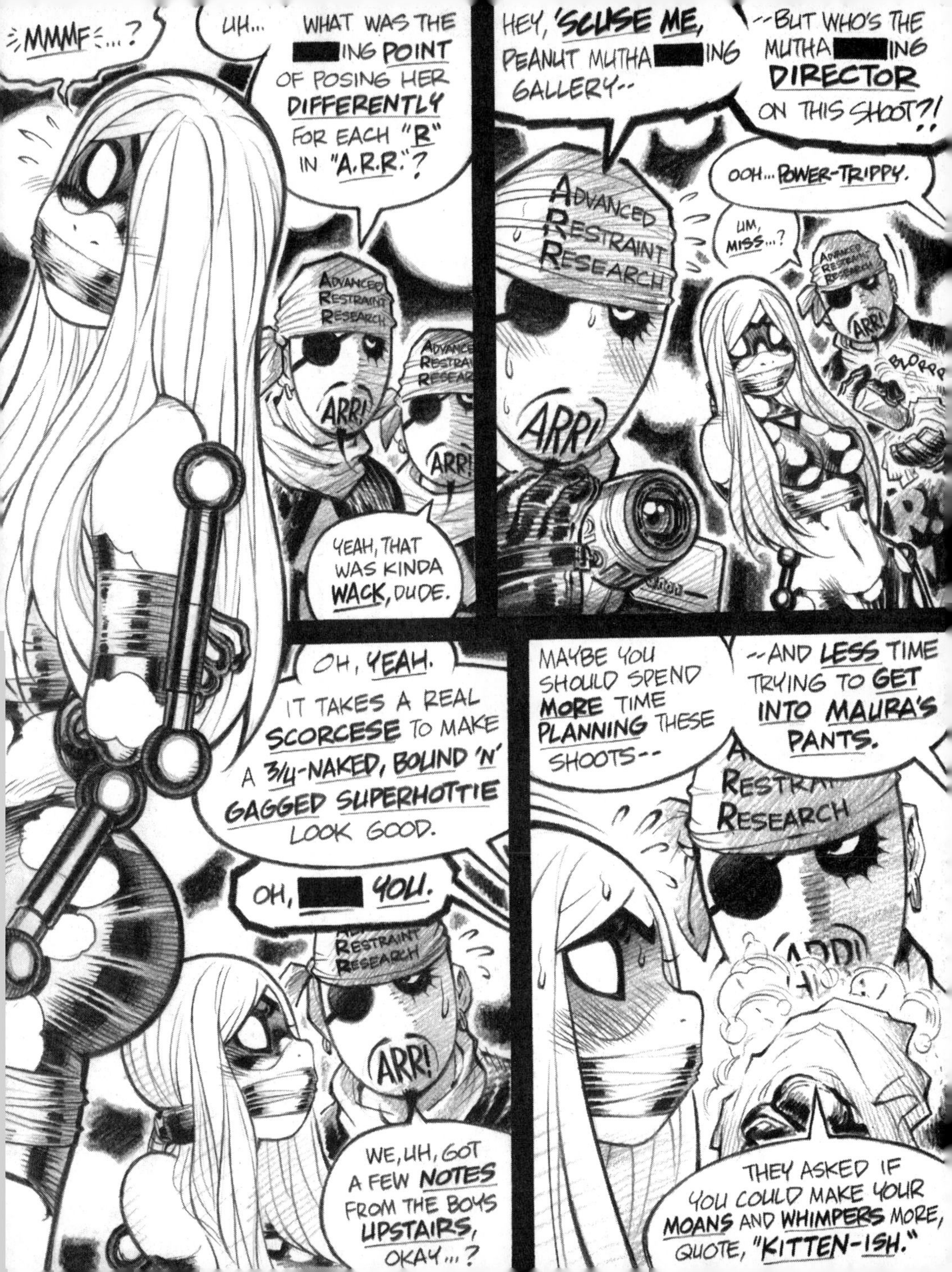
MMMF...?
UH...
WHAT WAS THE [redacted]ING POINT OF POSING HER DIFFERENTLY FOR EACH "R" IN "A.R.R."?
ADVANCED RESTRAINT RESEARCH
ARR!
ADVANCED RESTRAINT RESEARCH
ARR!
YEAH, THAT WAS KINDA WACK, DUDE.
HEY, 'SCUSE ME, PEANUT MUTHA[redacted]ING GALLERY--
--BUT WHO'S THE MUTHA[redacted]ING DIRECTOR ON THIS SHOOT?!
ADVANCED RESTRAINT RESEARCH
ARR!
OOH... POWER-TRIPPY.
UM, MISS...?
ADVANCED RESTRAINT RESEARCH
ARR!
OH, YEAH.
IT TAKES A REAL SCORCESE TO MAKE A 3/4-NAKED, BOUND 'N' GAGGED SUPERHOTTIE LOOK GOOD.
OH, [redacted] YOU.
RESTRAINT RESEARCH
ARR!
WE, UH, GOT A FEW NOTES FROM THE BOYS UPSTAIRS, OKAY...?
MAYBE YOU SHOULD SPEND MORE TIME PLANNING THESE SHOOTS--
--AND LESS TIME TRYING TO GET INTO MAURA'S PANTS.
RESEARCH
THEY ASKED IF YOU COULD MAKE YOUR MOANS AND WHIMPERS MORE, QUOTE, "KITTEN-ISH."

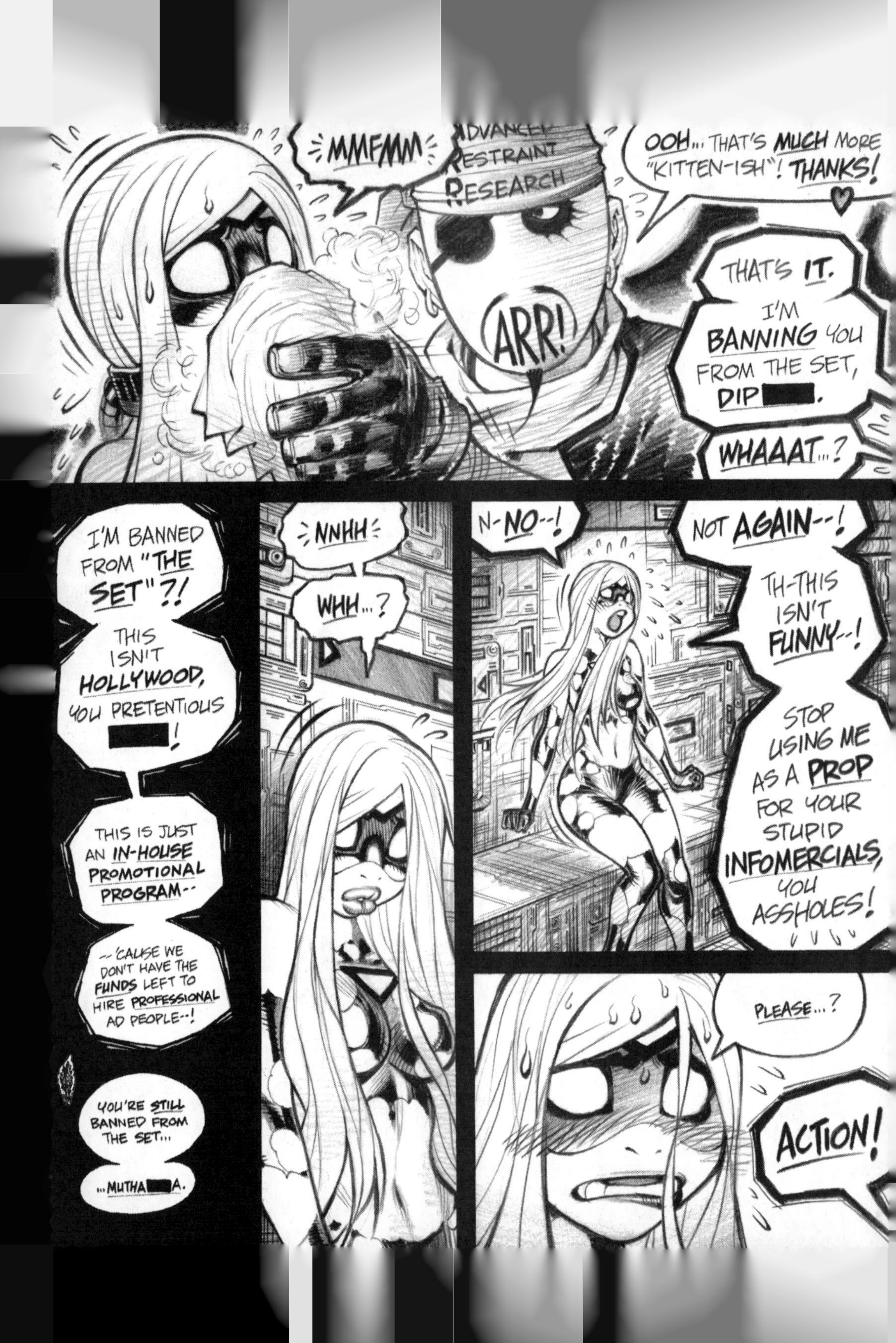
MMFMM
RESTRAINT RESEARCH
ARR!
OOH... THAT'S MUCH MORE "KITTEN-ISH"! THANKS!
THAT'S IT.
I'M BANNING YOU FROM THE SET, DIP[redacted].
WHAAAT...?
I'M BANNED FROM "THE SET"?!
THIS ISN'T HOLLYWOOD, YOU PRETENTIOUS [redacted]!
THIS IS JUST AN IN-HOUSE PROMOTIONAL PROGRAM--
--'CAUSE WE DON'T HAVE THE FUNDS LEFT TO HIRE PROFESSIONAL AD PEOPLE--!
YOU'RE STILL BANNED FROM THE SET...
...MUTHA[redacted]A.
NNHH
WHH...?
N-NO--!
NOT AGAIN--!
TH-THIS ISN'T FUNNY--!
STOP USING ME AS A PROP FOR YOUR STUPID INFOMERCIALS, YOU ASSHOLES!
PLEASE...?
ACTION!

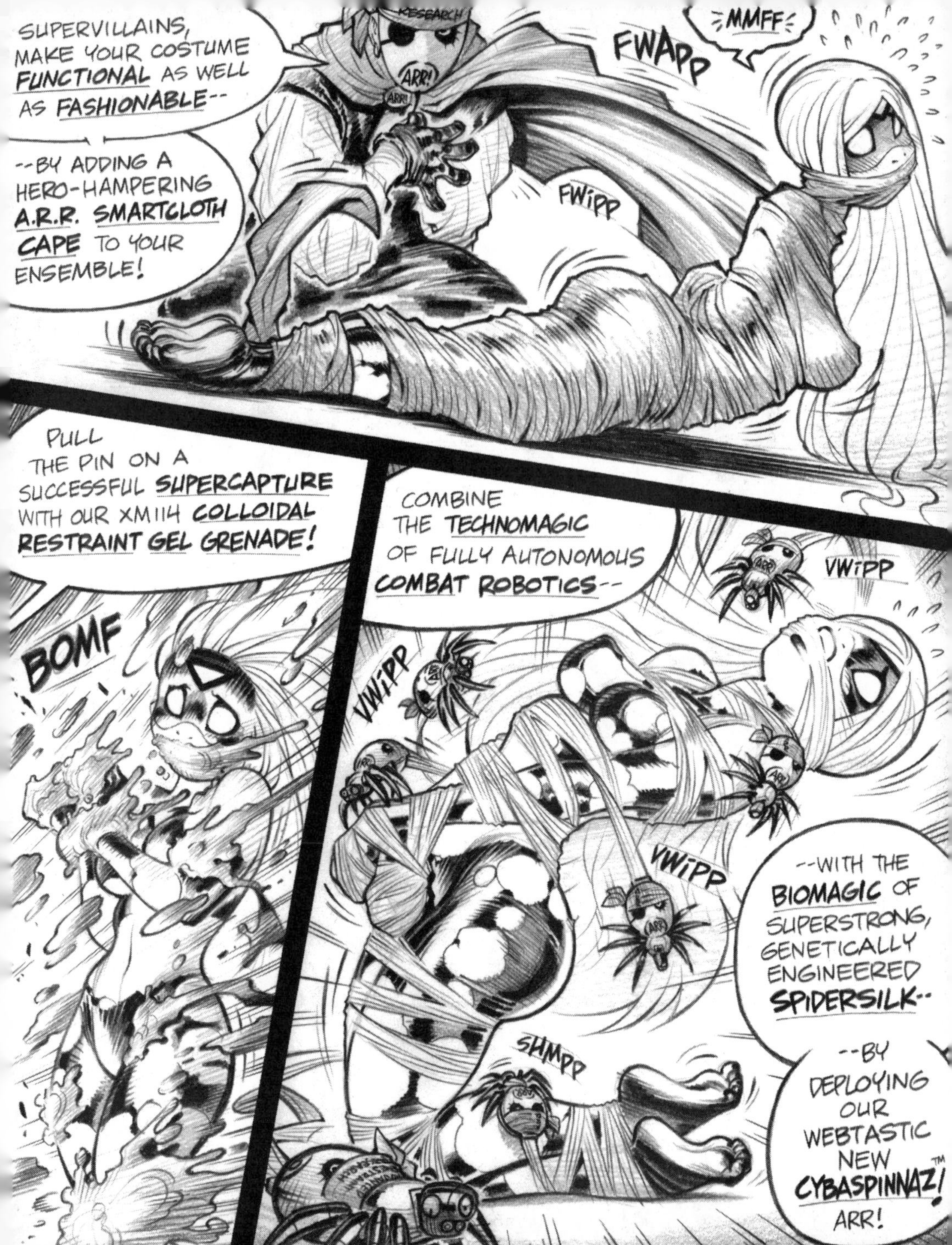
KESEARCH
SUPERVILLAINS, MAKE YOUR COSTUME FUNCTIONAL AS WELL AS FASHIONABLE--
--BY ADDING A HERO-HAMPERING A.R.R. SMARTCLOTH CAPE TO YOUR ENSEMBLE!
ARR!
ARR!
FWAPP
MMFF
FWiPP
PULL THE PIN ON A SUCCESSFUL SUPERCAPTURE WITH OUR XM114 COLLOIDAL RESTRAINT GEL GRENADE!
BOMF
COMBINE THE TECHNOMAGIC OF FULLY AUTONOMOUS COMBAT ROBOTICS--
VWiPP
VWiPP
VWiPP
--WITH THE BIOMAGIC OF SUPERSTRONG, GENETICALLY ENGINEERED SPIDERSILK--
SHMPP
--BY DEPLOYING OUR WEBTASTIC NEW CYBASPINNAZ!™ ARR!

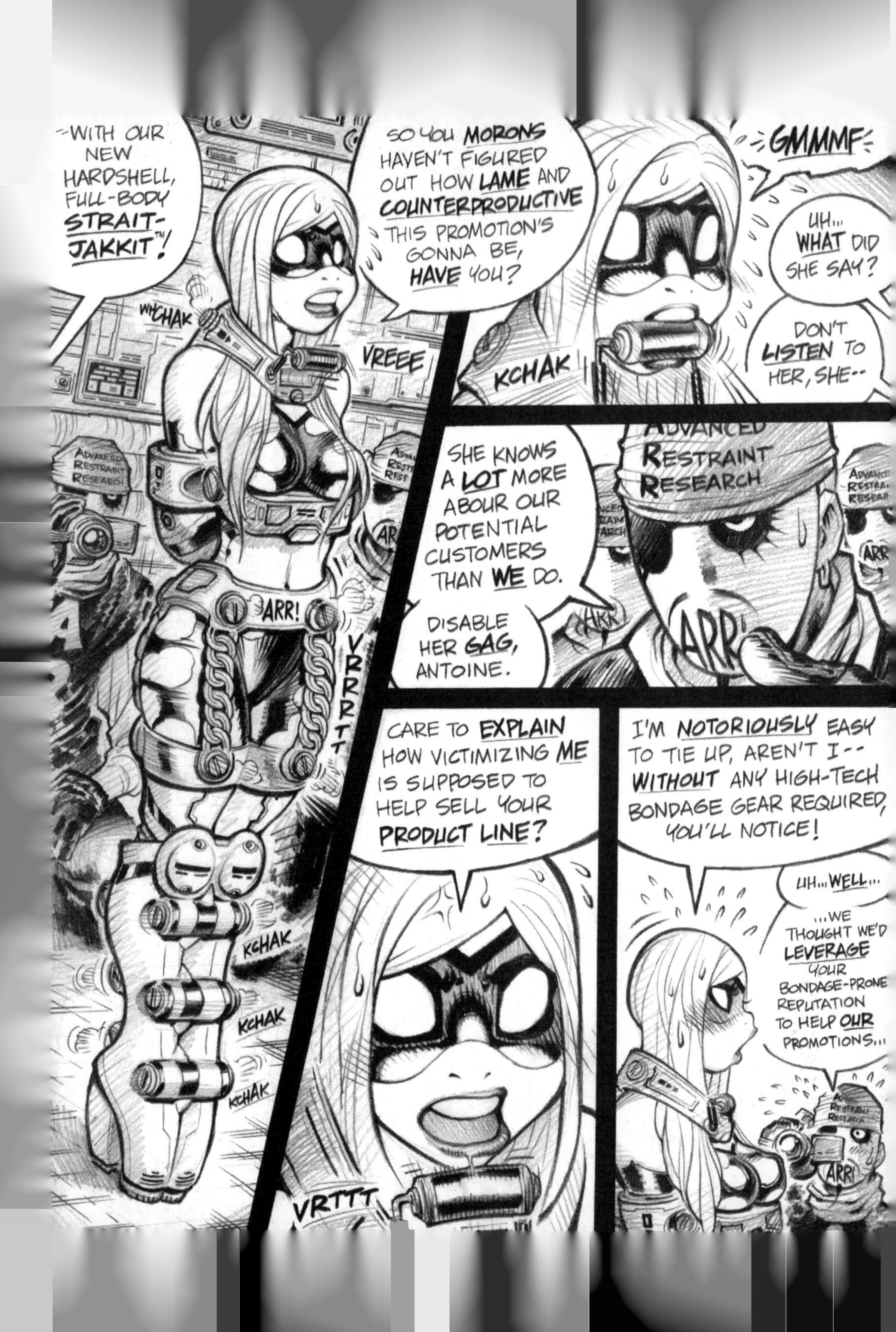
-WITH OUR NEW HARDSHELL, FULL-BODY STRAIT-JAKKIT™!
SO YOU MORONS HAVEN'T FIGURED OUT HOW LAME AND COUNTERPRODUCTIVE THIS PROMOTION'S GONNA BE, HAVE YOU?
VREEE
ARR!
VRRRTTT
KCHAK
KCHAK
KCHAK
GMMMF
KCHAK
UH... WHAT DID SHE SAY?
DON'T LISTEN TO HER, SHE--
ADVANCED RESTRAINT RESEARCH
SHE KNOWS A LOT MORE ABOUR OUR POTENTIAL CUSTOMERS THAN WE DO.
DISABLE HER GAG, ANTOINE.
ARR!
CARE TO EXPLAIN HOW VICTIMIZING ME IS SUPPOSED TO HELP SELL YOUR PRODUCT LINE?
VRTTT
I'M NOTORIOUSLY EASY TO TIE UP, AREN'T I-- WITHOUT ANY HIGH-TECH BONDAGE GEAR REQUIRED, YOU'LL NOTICE!
UH... WELL...
...WE THOUGHT WE'D LEVERAGE YOUR BONDAGE-PRONE REPUTATION TO HELP OUR PROMOTIONS...
ARR!

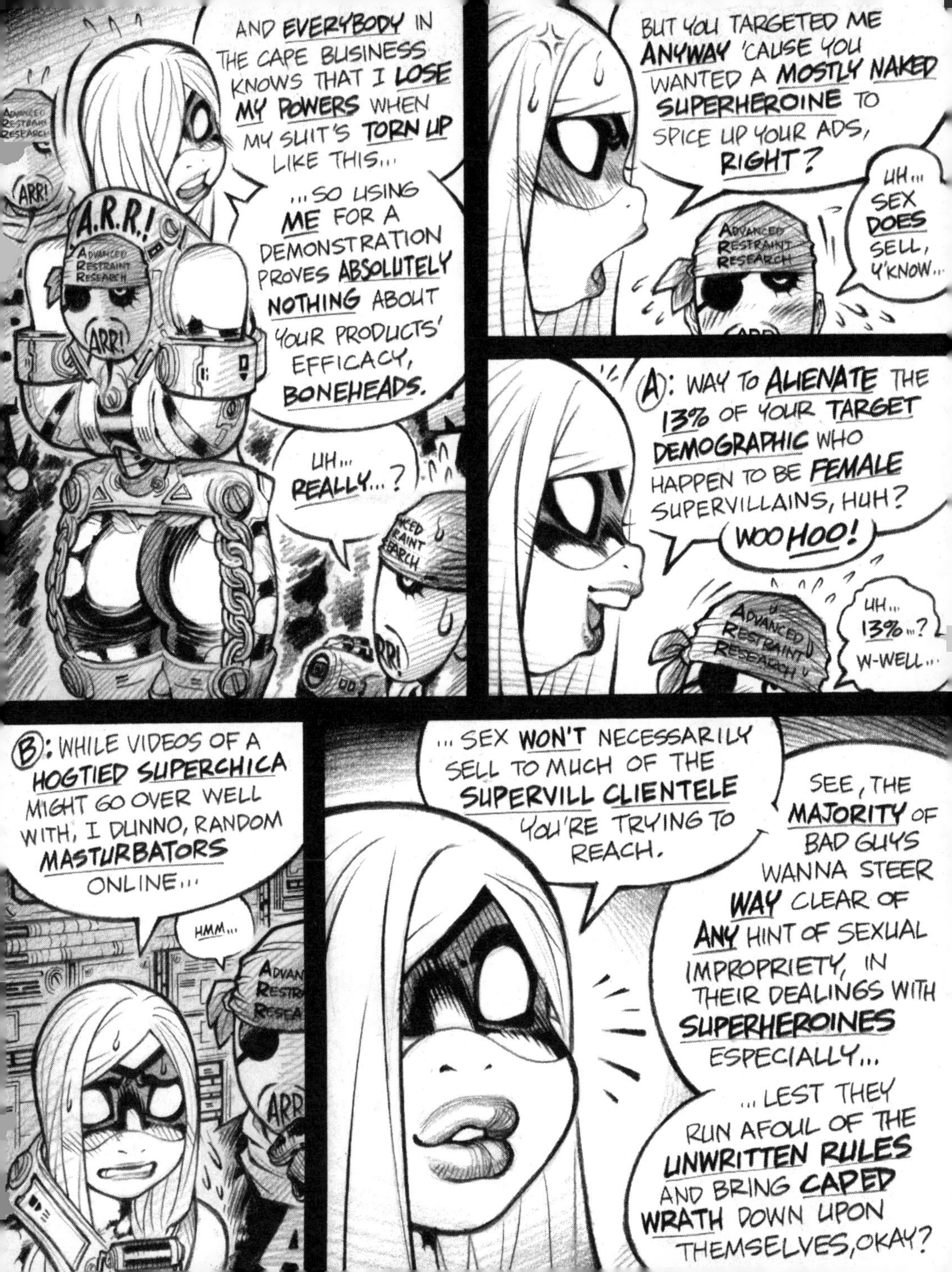
AND EVERYBODY IN THE CAPE BUSINESS KNOWS THAT I LOSE MY POWERS WHEN MY SUIT'S TORN UP LIKE THIS...
...SO USING ME FOR A DEMONSTRATION PROVES ABSOLUTELY NOTHING ABOUT YOUR PRODUCTS' EFFICACY, BONEHEADS.
A.R.R.!
ADVANCED RESTRAINT RESEARCH
ARR!
UH... REALLY...?
BUT YOU TARGETED ME ANYWAY 'CAUSE YOU WANTED A MOSTLY NAKED SUPERHEROINE TO SPICE UP YOUR ADS, RIGHT?
UH... SEX DOES SELL, Y'KNOW...
ADVANCED RESTRAINT RESEARCH
A: WAY TO ALIENATE THE 13% OF YOUR TARGET DEMOGRAPHIC WHO HAPPEN TO BE FEMALE SUPERVILLAINS, HUH?
WOO HOO!
ADVANCED RESTRAINT RESEARCH
UH... 13%...? W-WELL...
B: WHILE VIDEOS OF A HOGTIED SUPERCHICA MIGHT GO OVER WELL WITH, I DUNNO, RANDOM MASTURBATORS ONLINE...
HMM...
...SEX WON'T NECESSARILY SELL TO MUCH OF THE SUPERVILL CLIENTELE YOU'RE TRYING TO REACH.
SEE, THE MAJORITY OF BAD GUYS WANNA STEER WAY CLEAR OF ANY HINT OF SEXUAL IMPROPRIETY, IN THEIR DEALINGS WITH SUPERHEROINES ESPECIALLY...
...LEST THEY RUN AFOUL OF THE UNWRITTEN RULES AND BRING CAPED WRATH DOWN UPON THEMSELVES, OKAY?

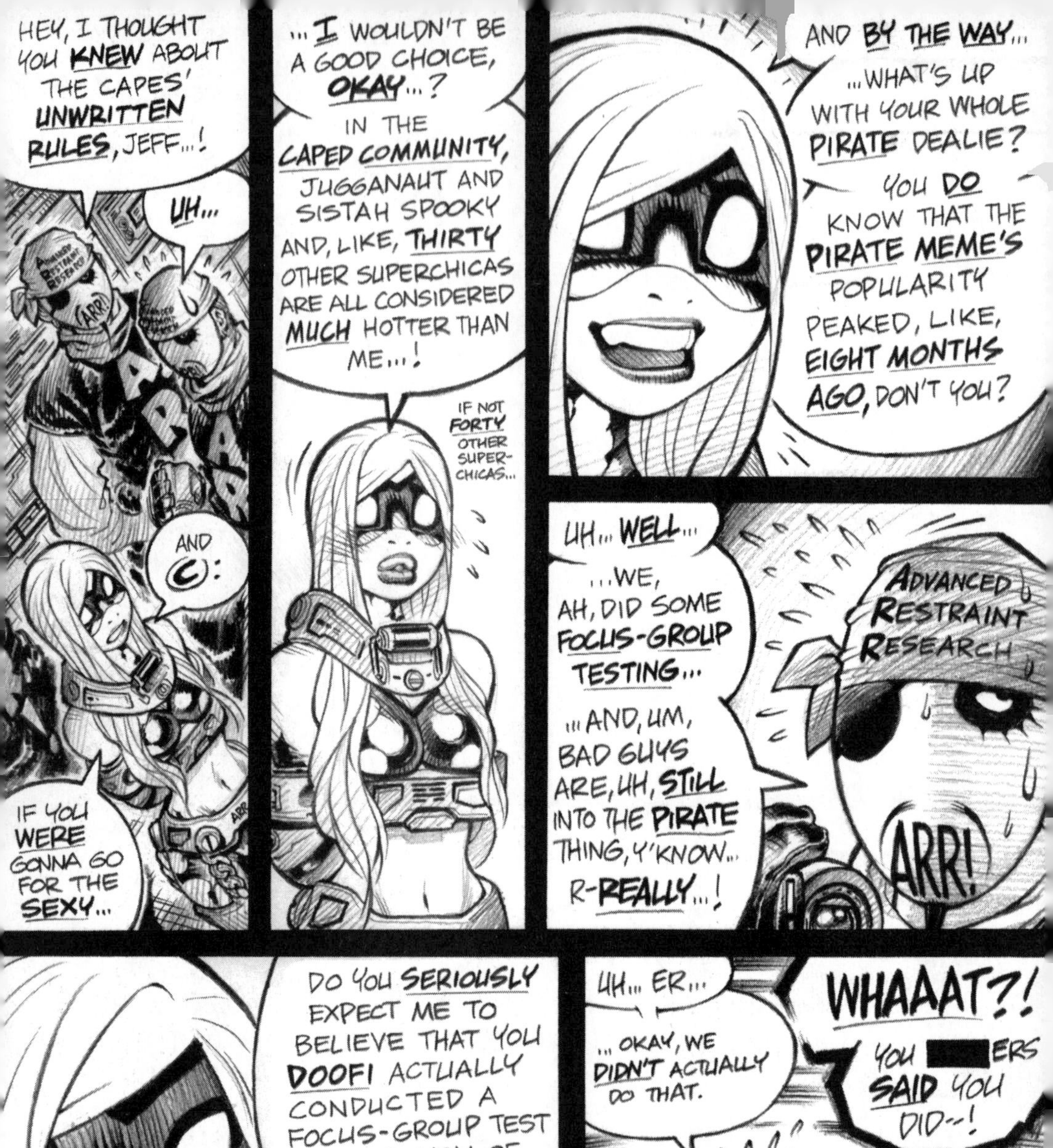
HEY, I THOUGHT YOU KNEW ABOUT THE CAPES' UNWRITTEN RULES, JEFF...!
UH...
ARR!
AND ©:
IF YOU WERE GONNA GO FOR THE SEXY...
...I WOULDN'T BE A GOOD CHOICE, OKAY...?
IN THE CAPED COMMUNITY, JUGGANAUT AND SISTAH SPOOKY AND, LIKE, THIRTY OTHER SUPERCHICAS ARE ALL CONSIDERED MUCH HOTTER THAN ME...!
IF NOT FORTY OTHER SUPER-CHICAS...
AND BY THE WAY...
...WHAT'S UP WITH YOUR WHOLE PIRATE DEALIE?
YOU DO KNOW THAT THE PIRATE MEME'S POPULARITY PEAKED, LIKE, EIGHT MONTHS AGO, DON'T YOU?
UH... WELL...
...WE, AH, DID SOME FOCUS-GROUP TESTING...
...AND, UM, BAD GUYS ARE, UH, STILL INTO THE PIRATE THING, Y'KNOW... R-REALLY...!
ADVANCED RESTRAINT RESEARCH
ARR!
DO YOU SERIOUSLY EXPECT ME TO BELIEVE THAT YOU DOOFI ACTUALLY CONDUCTED A FOCUS-GROUP TEST ON A BUNCH OF SUPERVILLAINS...?
HOW MANY OF YOUR PEOPLE DIED HORRIBLY IN THE PROCESS?
UH... ER...
...OKAY, WE DIDN'T ACTUALLY DO THAT.
WHAAAT?!
YOU [redacted]ERS SAID YOU DID--!
ADVANCED RESTRAINT RESEARCH
ARR

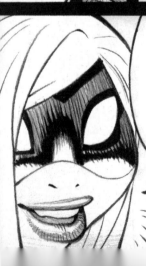

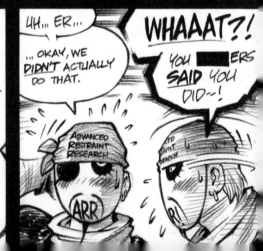

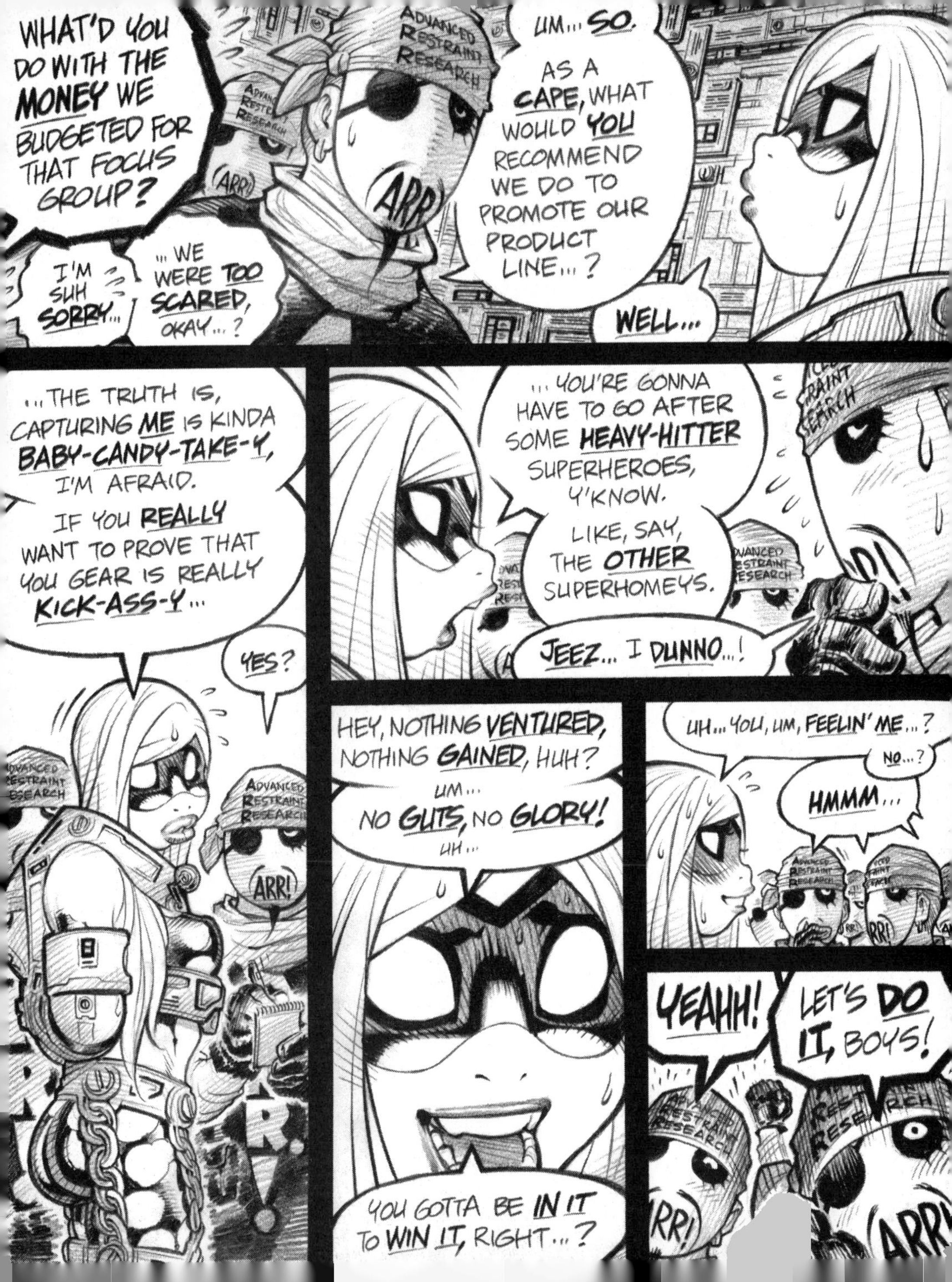
WHAT'D YOU DO WITH THE MONEY WE BUDGETED FOR THAT FOCUS GROUP?
ADVANCED RESTRAINT RESEARCH
ARR
I'M SUH SORRY...
...WE WERE TOO SCARED, OKAY...?
UM... SO.
AS A CAPE, WHAT WOULD YOU RECOMMEND WE DO TO PROMOTE OUR PRODUCT LINE...?
WELL...
...THE TRUTH IS, CAPTURING ME IS KINDA BABY-CANDY-TAKE-Y, I'M AFRAID.
IF YOU REALLY WANT TO PROVE THAT YOU GEAR IS REALLY KICK-ASS-Y...
YES?
ARR!
...YOU'RE GONNA HAVE TO GO AFTER SOME HEAVY-HITTER SUPERHEROES, Y'KNOW.
LIKE, SAY, THE OTHER SUPERHOMEYS.
JEEZ... I DUNNO...!
HEY, NOTHING VENTURED, NOTHING GAINED, HUH?
UM...
NO GUTS, NO GLORY!
UH...
YOU GOTTA BE IN IT TO WIN IT, RIGHT...?
UH... YOU, UM, FEELIN' ME...?
NO...?
HMMM...
YEAHH!
LET'S DO IT, BOYS!
ARR!

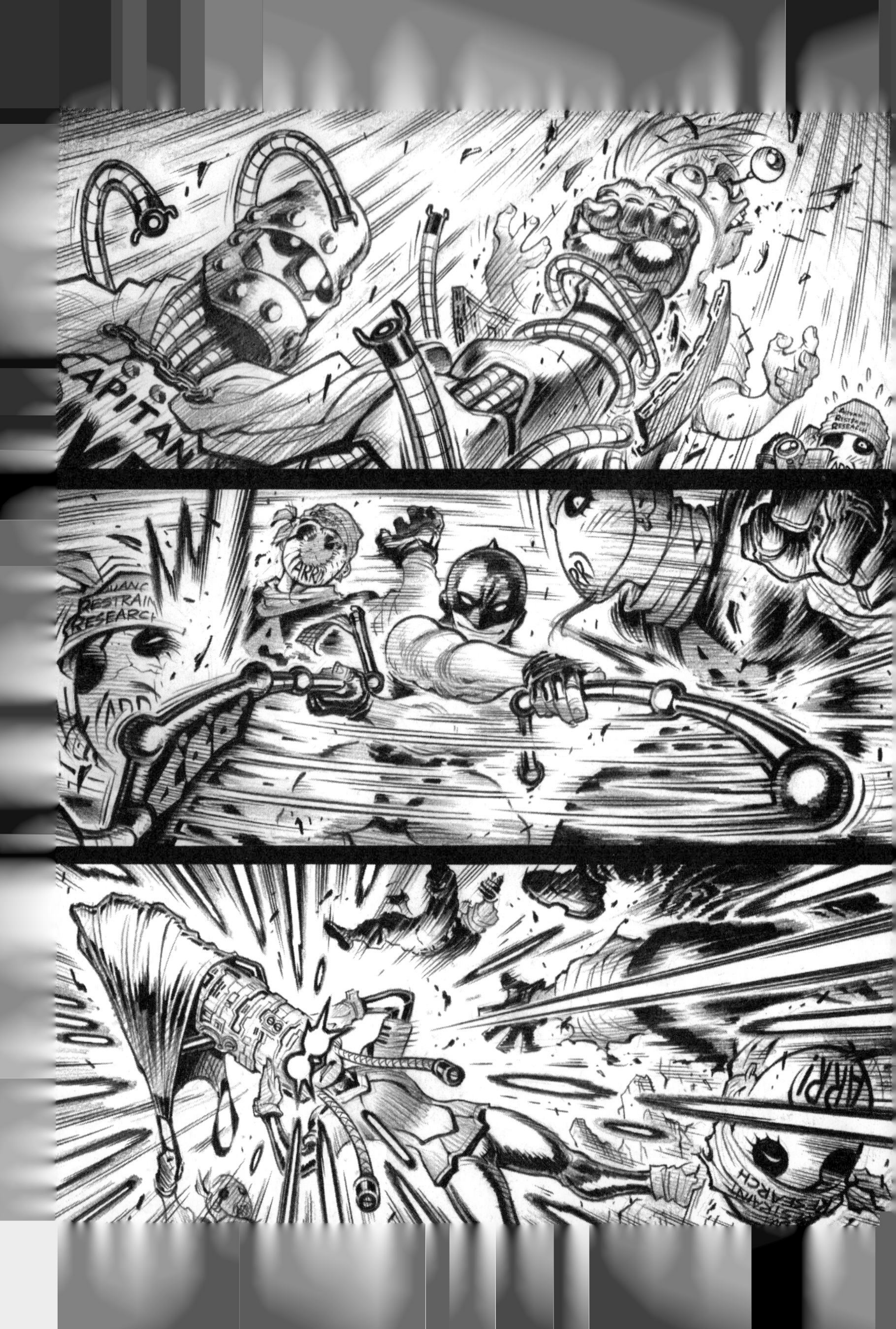

CAPITAN
ARRP
RESTRAIN
RESEARCH
ARRP!
RESEARCH

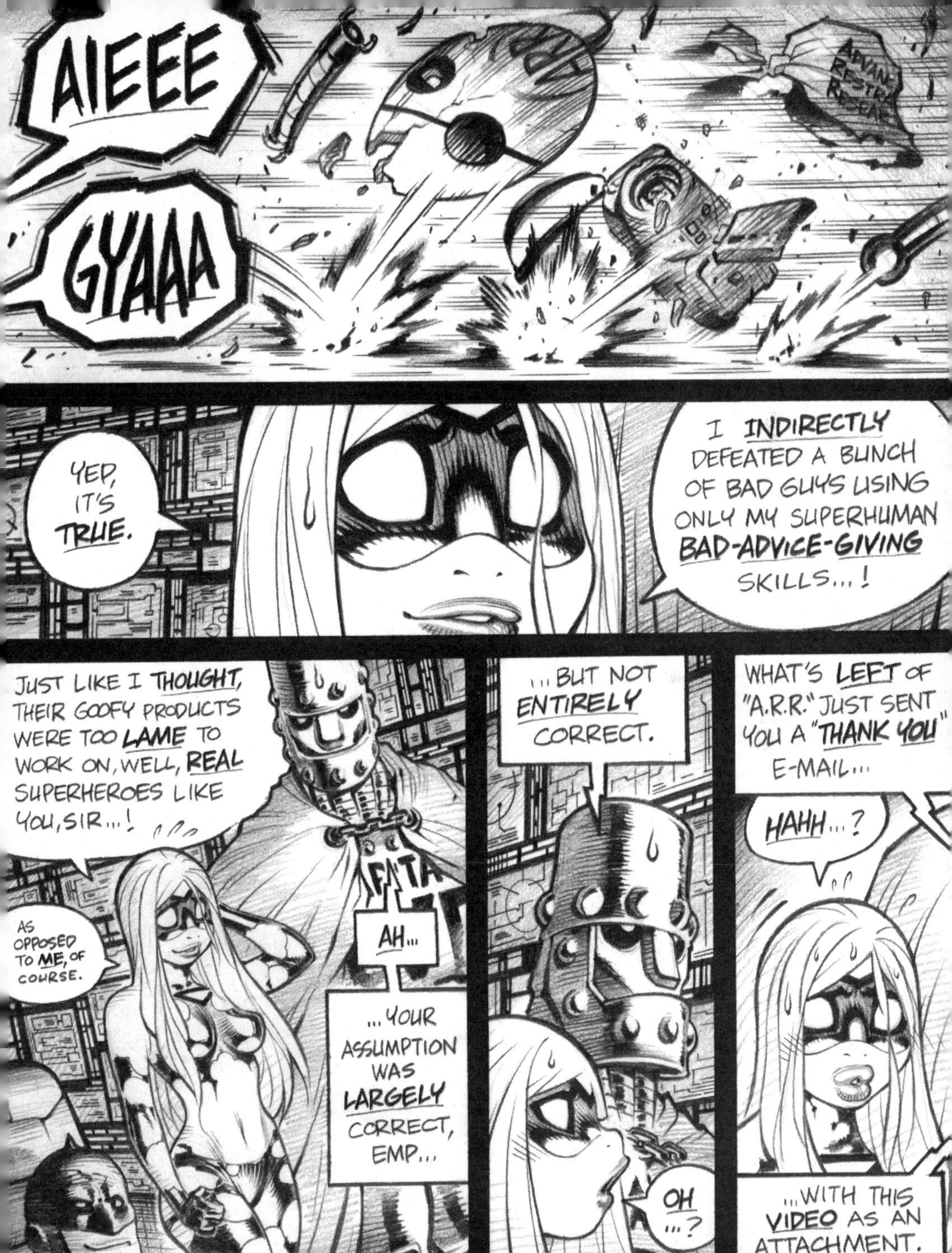
AIEEE
GYAAA
YEP, IT'S TRUE.
I INDIRECTLY DEFEATED A BUNCH OF BAD GUYS USING ONLY MY SUPERHUMAN BAD-ADVICE-GIVING SKILLS...!
JUST LIKE I THOUGHT, THEIR GOOFY PRODUCTS WERE TOO LAME TO WORK ON, WELL, REAL SUPERHEROES LIKE YOU, SIR...!
AS OPPOSED TO ME, OF COURSE.
AH...
...YOUR ASSUMPTION WAS LARGELY CORRECT, EMP...
...BUT NOT ENTIRELY CORRECT.
OH ...?
WHAT'S LEFT OF "A.R.R." JUST SENT YOU A "THANK YOU" E-MAIL...
HAHH...?
...WITH THIS VIDEO AS AN ATTACHMENT.

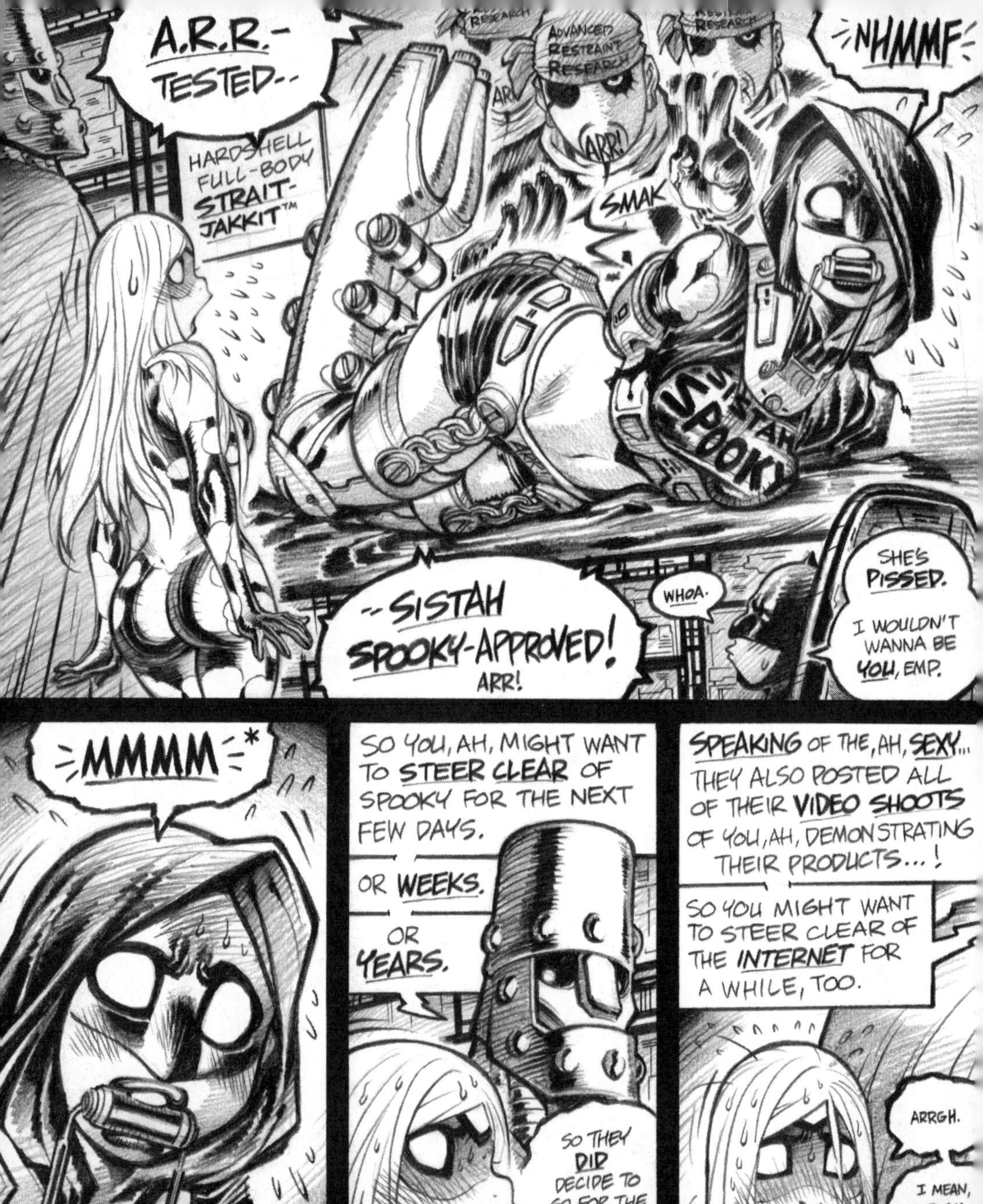
A.R.R.-TESTED--
HARDSHELL FULL-BODY STRAIT-JAKKIT™
ADVANCED RESTRAINT RESEARCH
ARR!
NHMMF
SMAK
SISTAH SPOOKY
--SISTAH SPOOKY-APPROVED! ARR!
WHOA.
SHE'S PISSED.
I WOULDN'T WANNA BE YOU, EMP.
MMMM*
* TRANSLATION: "YOU ARE SO VERY [redacted]ING DEAD, EMP."
SO YOU, AH, MIGHT WANT TO STEER CLEAR OF SPOOKY FOR THE NEXT FEW DAYS.
OR WEEKS.
OR YEARS.
SO THEY DID DECIDE TO GO FOR THE SEXY, AFTER ALL.
GREAT.
SPEAKING OF THE, AH, SEXY... THEY ALSO POSTED ALL OF THEIR VIDEO SHOOTS OF YOU, AH, DEMONSTRATING THEIR PRODUCTS...!
SO YOU MIGHT WANT TO STEER CLEAR OF THE INTERNET FOR A WHILE, TOO.
ARRGH.
I MEAN, A.R.R.GH.

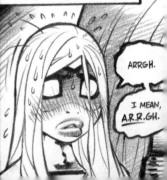

Empowered™

Mysterious Dumbass

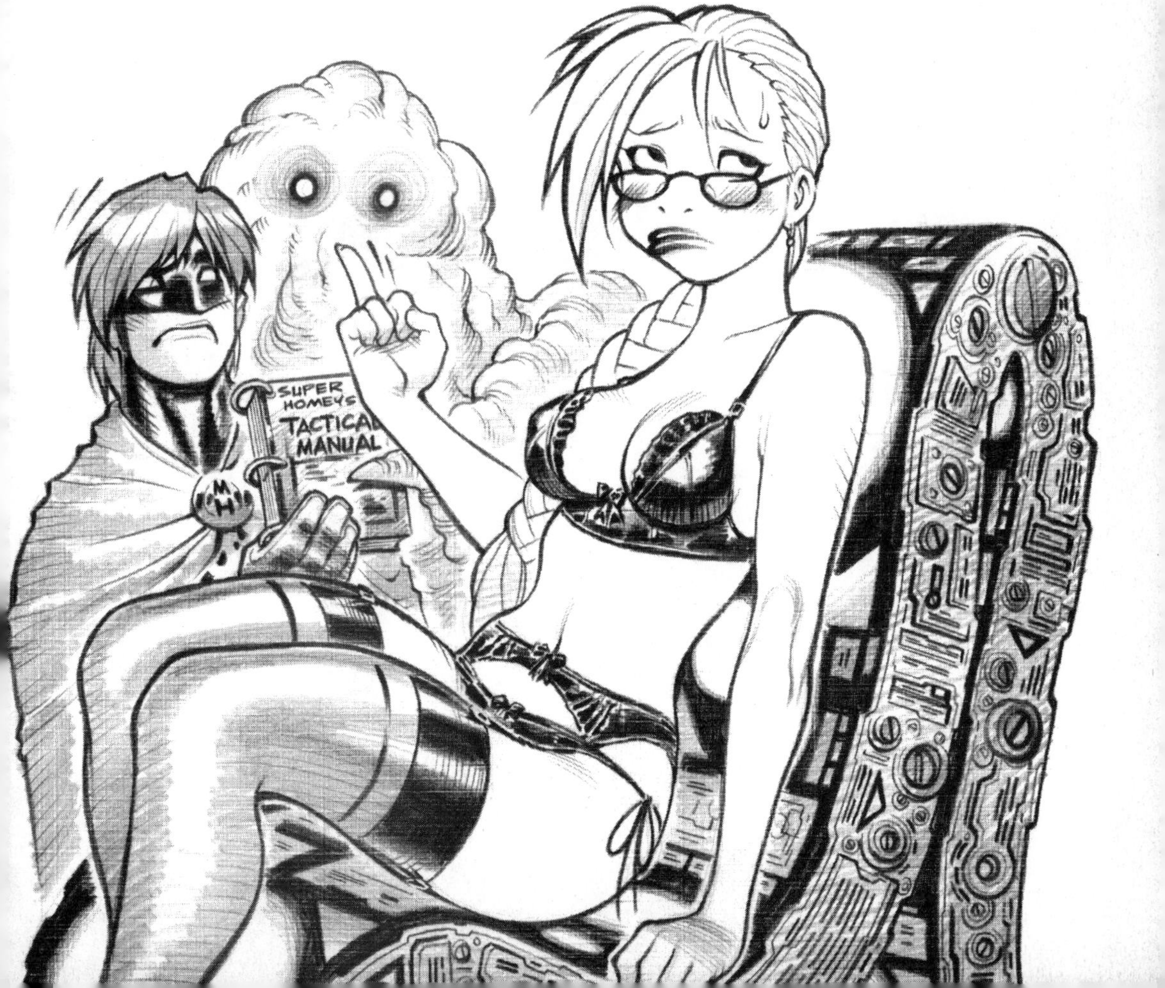
SUPER HOMEYS
TACTICA
MANUAL

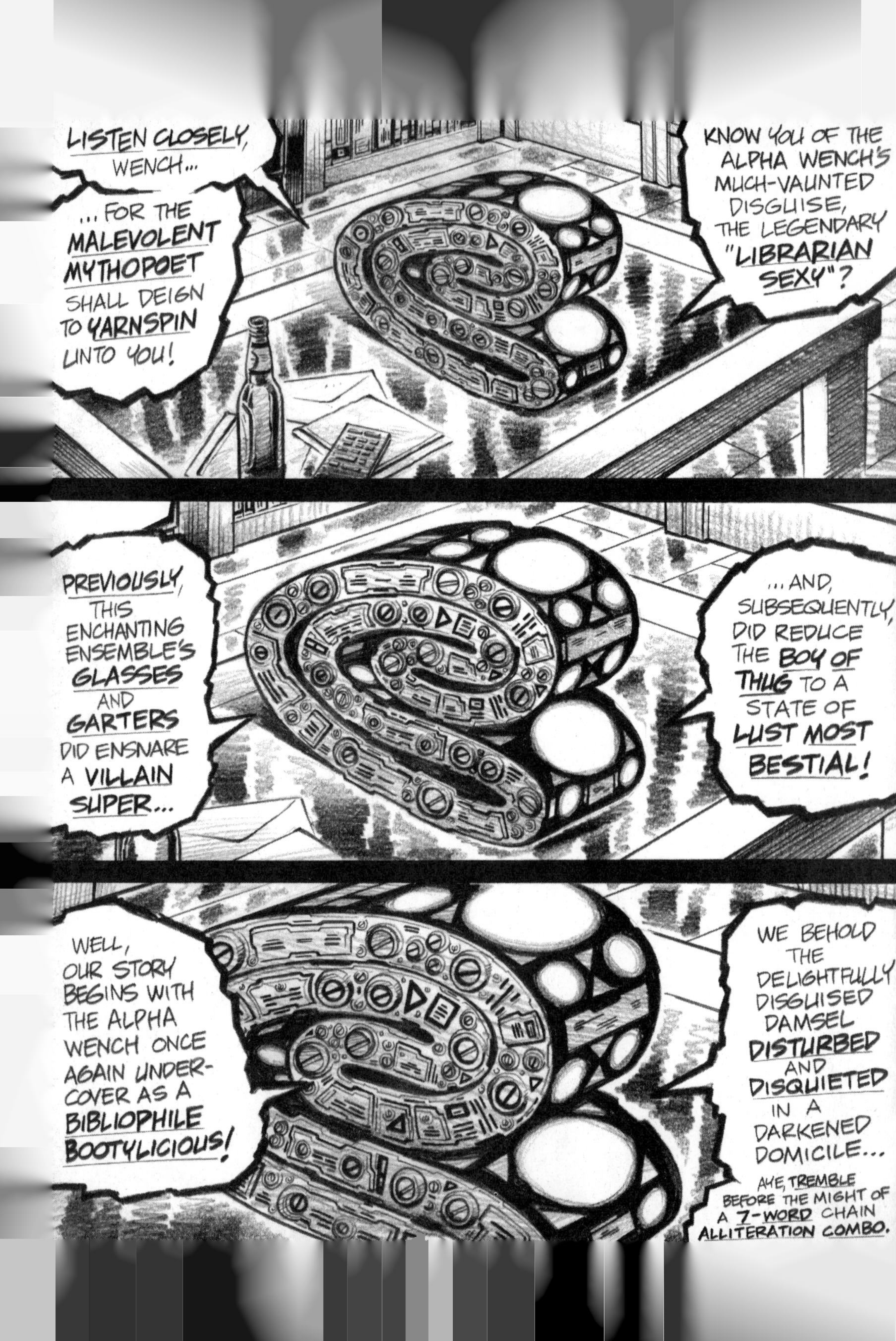
LISTEN CLOSELY, WENCH...
...FOR THE MALEVOLENT MYTHOPOET SHALL DEIGN TO YARNSPIN UNTO YOU!
KNOW YOU OF THE ALPHA WENCH'S MUCH-VAUNTED DISGUISE, THE LEGENDARY "LIBRARIAN SEXY"?
PREVIOUSLY, THIS ENCHANTING ENSEMBLE'S GLASSES AND GARTERS DID ENSNARE A VILLAIN SUPER...
...AND, SUBSEQUENTLY, DID REDUCE THE BOY OF THUG TO A STATE OF LUST MOST BESTIAL!
WELL, OUR STORY BEGINS WITH THE ALPHA WENCH ONCE AGAIN UNDER-COVER AS A BIBLIOPHILE BOOTYLICIOUS!
WE BEHOLD THE DELIGHTFULLY DISGUISED DAMSEL DISTURBED AND DISQUIETED IN A DARKENED DOMICILE...
AYE, TREMBLE BEFORE THE MIGHT OF A 7-WORD CHAIN ALLITERATION COMBO.

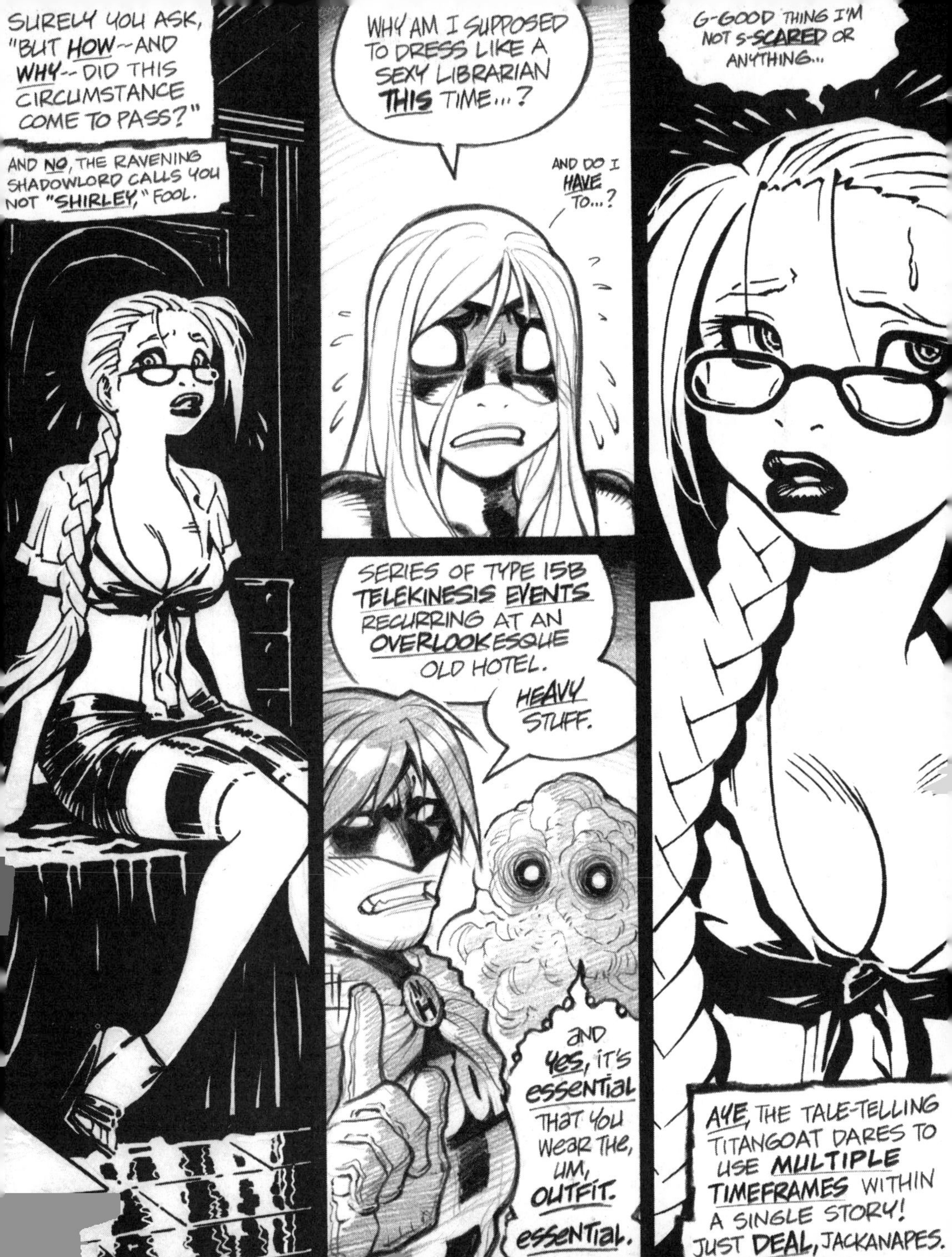
SURELY YOU ASK, "BUT HOW--AND WHY--DID THIS CIRCUMSTANCE COME TO PASS?"
AND NO, THE RAVENING SHADOWLORD CALLS YOU NOT "SHIRLEY," FOOL.
WHY AM I SUPPOSED TO DRESS LIKE A SEXY LIBRARIAN THIS TIME...?
AND DO I HAVE TO...?
SERIES OF TYPE 15B TELEKINESIS EVENTS RECURRING AT AN OVERLOOKESQUE OLD HOTEL.
HEAVY STUFF.
and yes, it's essential that you wear the, um, OUTFIT.
essential.
G-GOOD THING I'M NOT S-SCARED OR ANYTHING...
AYE, THE TALE-TELLING TITANGOAT DARES TO USE MULTIPLE TIMEFRAMES WITHIN A SINGLE STORY! JUST DEAL, JACKANAPES.

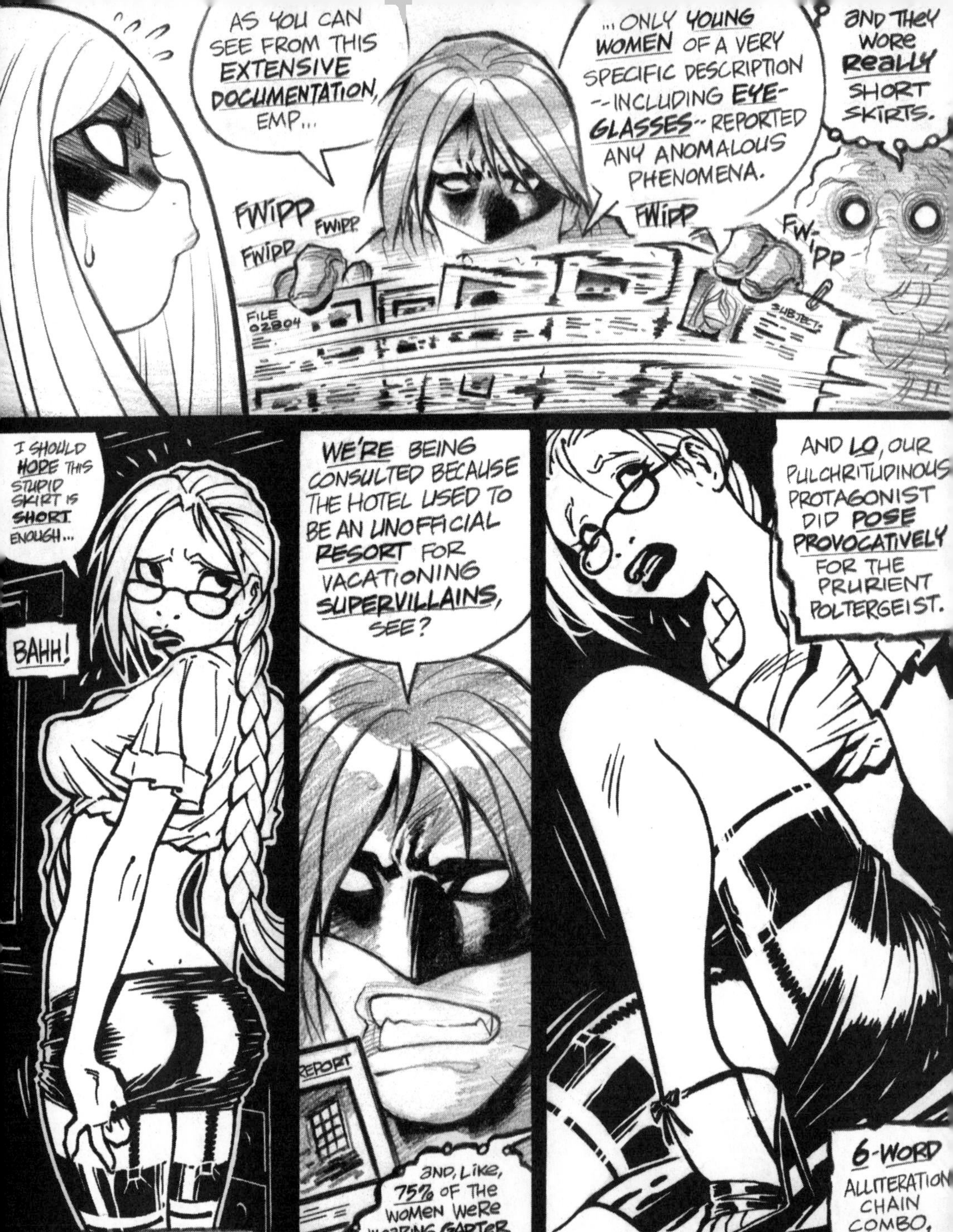
AS YOU CAN SEE FROM THIS EXTENSIVE DOCUMENTATION, EMP...
FWIPP FWIPP FWIPP
...ONLY YOUNG WOMEN OF A VERY SPECIFIC DESCRIPTION --INCLUDING EYE-GLASSES-- REPORTED ANY ANOMALOUS PHENOMENA.
FWIPP
AND THEY WORE REALLY SHORT SKIRTS.
FW-IPP
FILE 02804
SUBJECT
I SHOULD HOPE THIS STUPID SKIRT IS SHORT ENOUGH...
BAHH!
AS IF, MORTAL PRUDE!
WE'RE BEING CONSULTED BECAUSE THE HOTEL USED TO BE AN UNOFFICIAL RESORT FOR VACATIONING SUPERVILLAINS, SEE?
REPORT
AND, LIKE, 75% OF THE WOMEN WERE WEARING GARTER BELTS AND STOCKINGS.
AND LO, OUR PULCHRITUDINOUS PROTAGONIST DID POSE PROVOCATIVELY FOR THE PRURIENT POLTERGEIST.
6-WORD ALLITERATION CHAIN COMBO, FOOL.

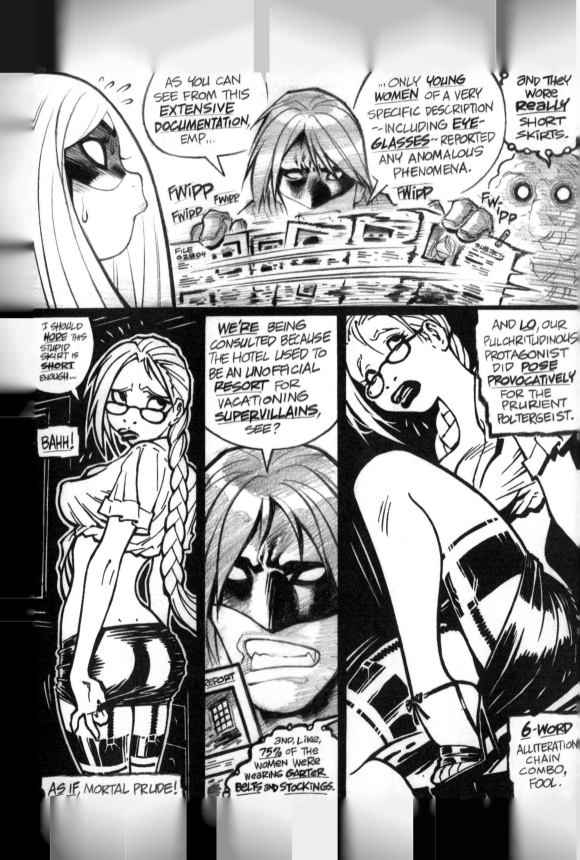

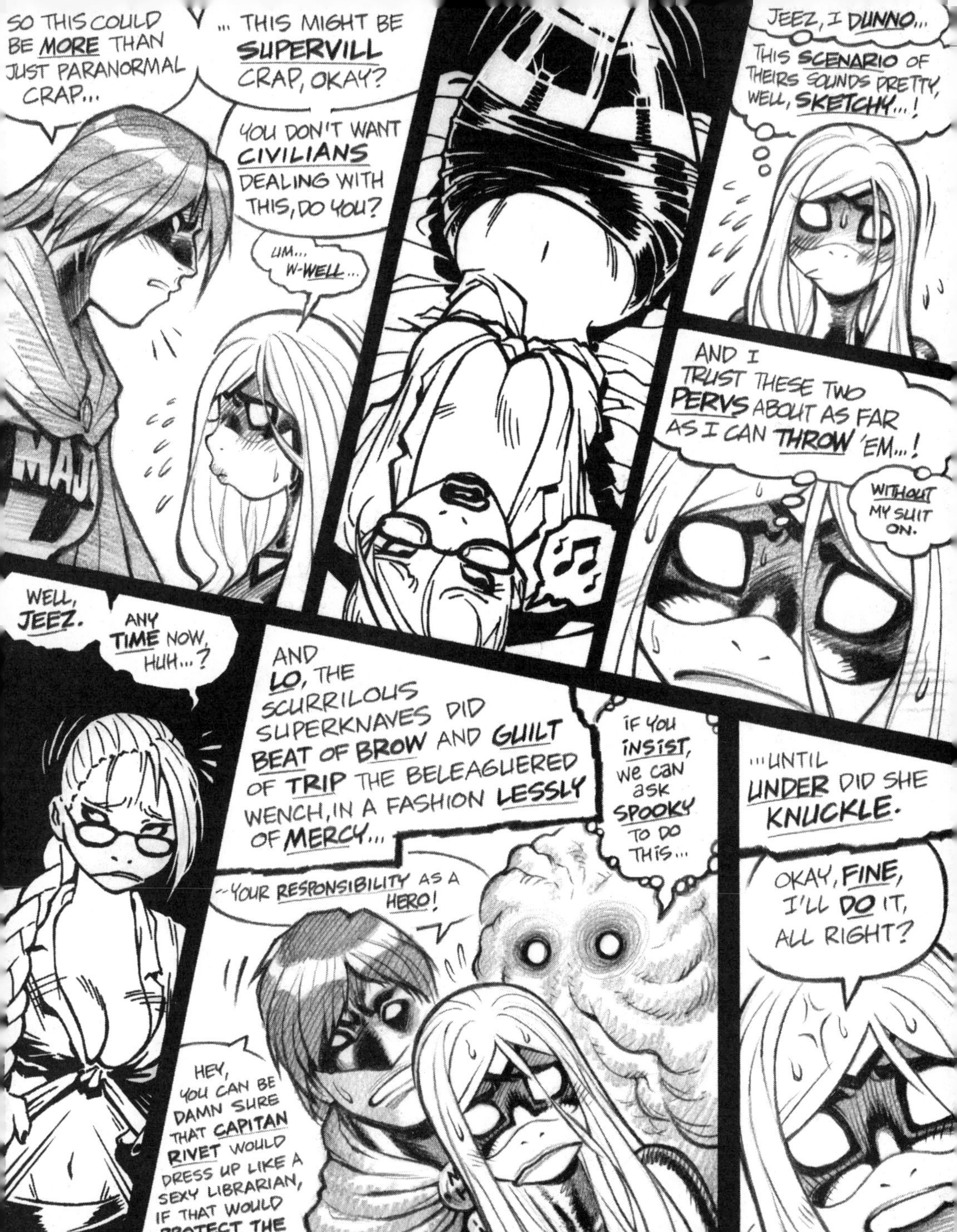
SO THIS COULD BE MORE THAN JUST PARANORMAL CRAP...
... THIS MIGHT BE SUPERVILL CRAP, OKAY?
YOU DON'T WANT CIVILIANS DEALING WITH THIS, DO YOU?
UM... W-WELL...
JEEZ, I DUNNO...
THIS SCENARIO OF THEIRS SOUNDS PRETTY, WELL, SKETCHY...!
AND I TRUST THESE TWO PERVS ABOUT AS FAR AS I CAN THROW 'EM...!
WITHOUT MY SUIT ON.
WELL, JEEZ.
ANY TIME NOW, HUH...?
AND LO, THE SCURRILOUS SUPERKNAVES DID BEAT OF BROW AND GUILT OF TRIP THE BELEAGUERED WENCH, IN A FASHION LESSLY OF MERCY...
if you insist, we can ask SPOOKY to do this...
--YOUR RESPONSIBILITY AS A HERO!
HEY, YOU CAN BE DAMN SURE THAT CAPITAN RIVET WOULD DRESS UP LIKE A SEXY LIBRARIAN, IF THAT WOULD PROTECT THE INNOCENT...!
...UNTIL UNDER DID SHE KNUCKLE.
OKAY, FINE, I'LL DO IT, ALL RIGHT?

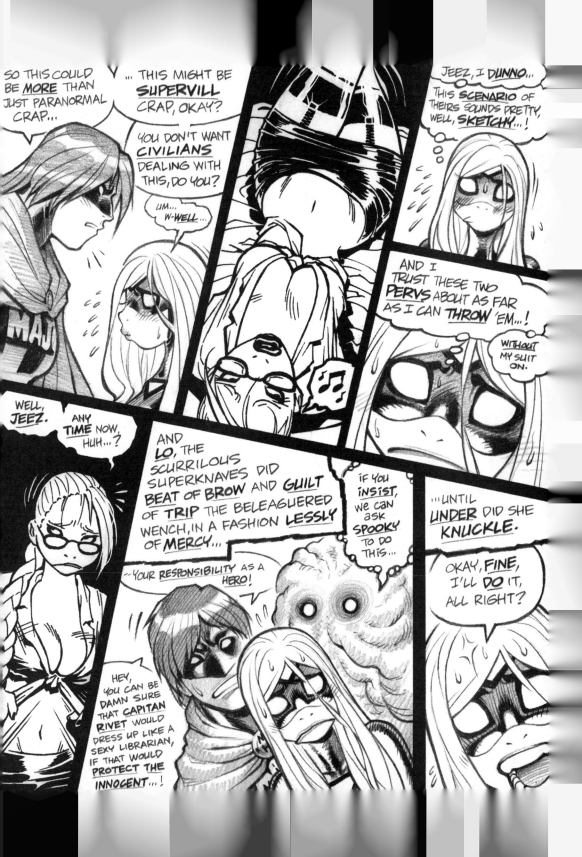

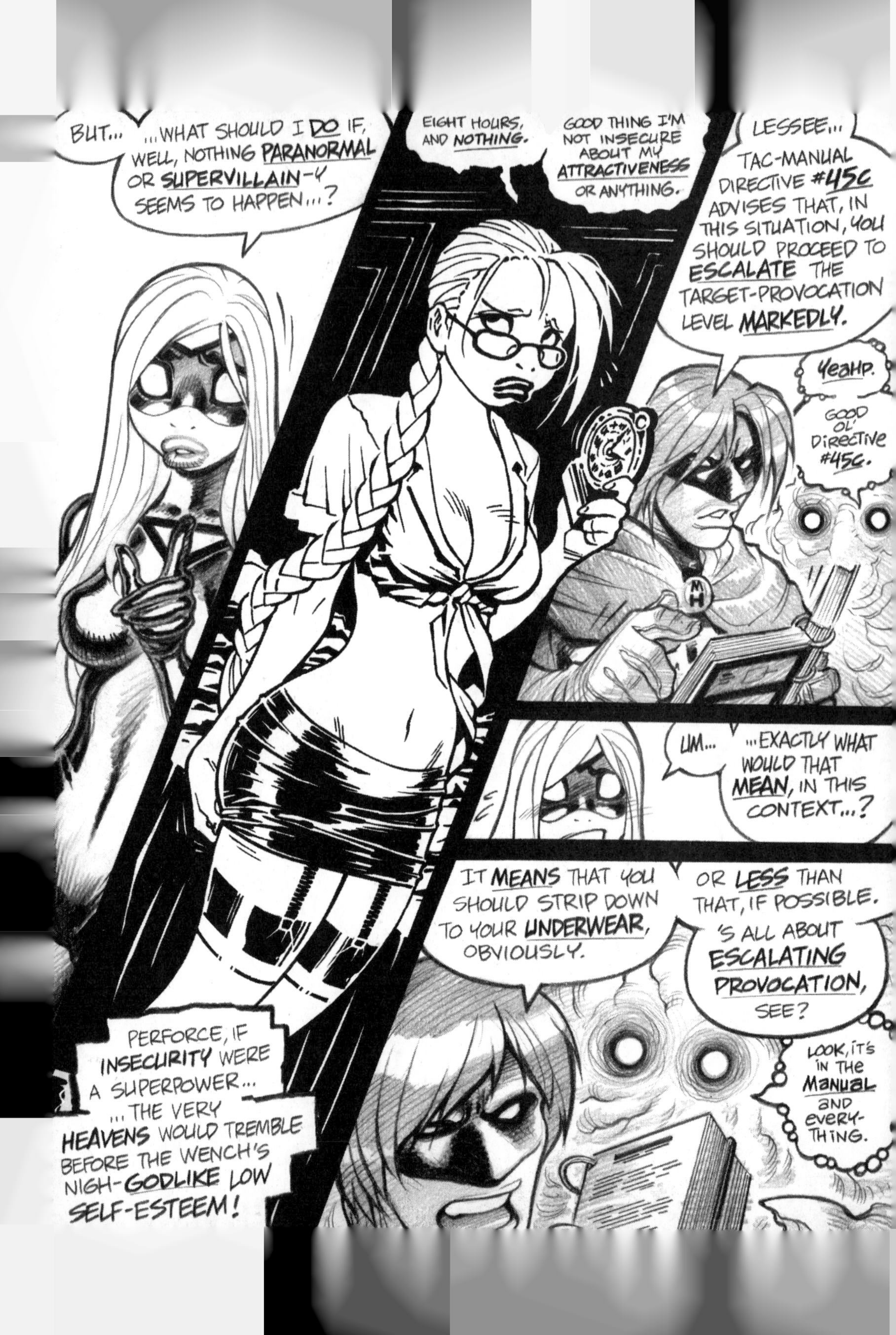

BUT...
...WHAT SHOULD I DO IF, WELL, NOTHING PARANORMAL OR SUPERVILLAIN-Y SEEMS TO HAPPEN...?
EIGHT HOURS, AND NOTHING.
GOOD THING I'M NOT INSECURE ABOUT MY ATTRACTIVENESS OR ANYTHING.
PERFORCE, IF INSECURITY WERE A SUPERPOWER...
...THE VERY HEAVENS WOULD TREMBLE BEFORE THE WENCH'S NIGH-GODLIKE LOW SELF-ESTEEM!
LESSEE...
TAC-MANUAL DIRECTIVE #45C ADVISES THAT, IN THIS SITUATION, YOU SHOULD PROCEED TO ESCALATE THE TARGET-PROVOCATION LEVEL MARKEDLY.
Yeahp.
GOOD OL' DIRECTIVE #45C.
MH
UM...
...EXACTLY WHAT WOULD THAT MEAN, IN THIS CONTEXT...?
IT MEANS THAT YOU SHOULD STRIP DOWN TO YOUR UNDERWEAR, OBVIOUSLY.
OR LESS THAN THAT, IF POSSIBLE.
'S ALL ABOUT ESCALATING PROVOCATION, SEE?
LOOK, IT'S IN THE MANUAL AND EVERY-THING.

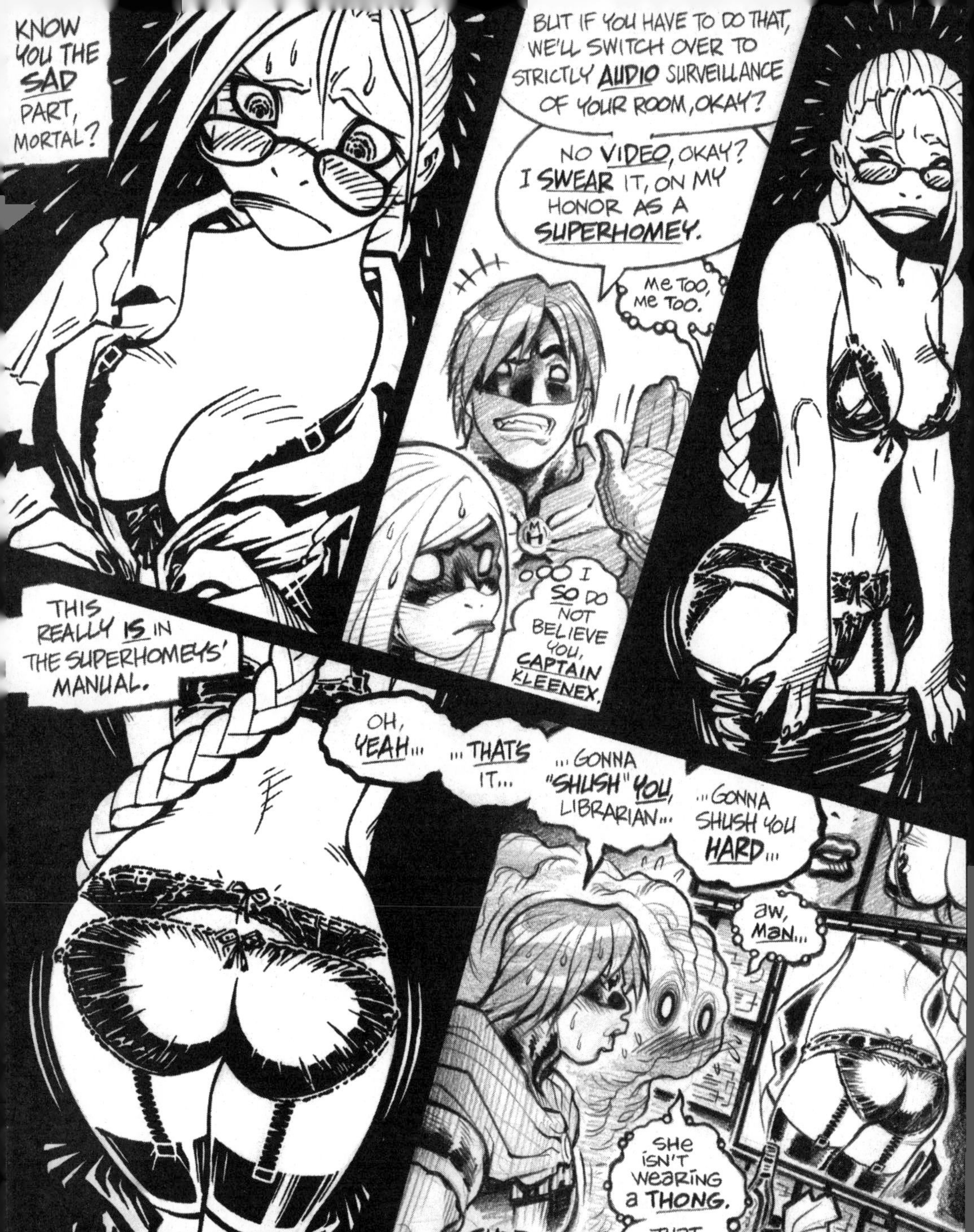
KNOW YOU THE SAD PART, MORTAL?
BUT IF YOU HAVE TO DO THAT, WE'LL SWITCH OVER TO STRICTLY AUDIO SURVEILLANCE OF YOUR ROOM, OKAY?
NO VIDEO, OKAY? I SWEAR IT, ON MY HONOR AS A SUPERHOMEY.
Me TOO, Me TOO.
I SO DO NOT BELIEVE YOU, CAPTAIN KLEENEX.
THIS REALLY IS IN THE SUPERHOMEYS' MANUAL.
OH, YEAH...
...THAT'S IT...
...GONNA "SHUSH" YOU, LIBRARIAN...
...GONNA SHUSH YOU HARD...
aw, Man...
SHe isn't wearing a THONG.
THAT SUCKS.
SHPP SHPP SHPP

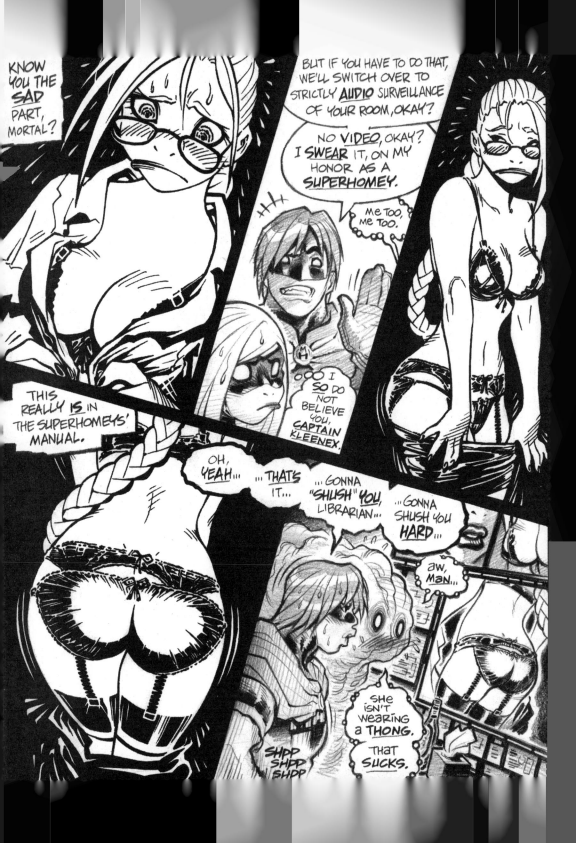

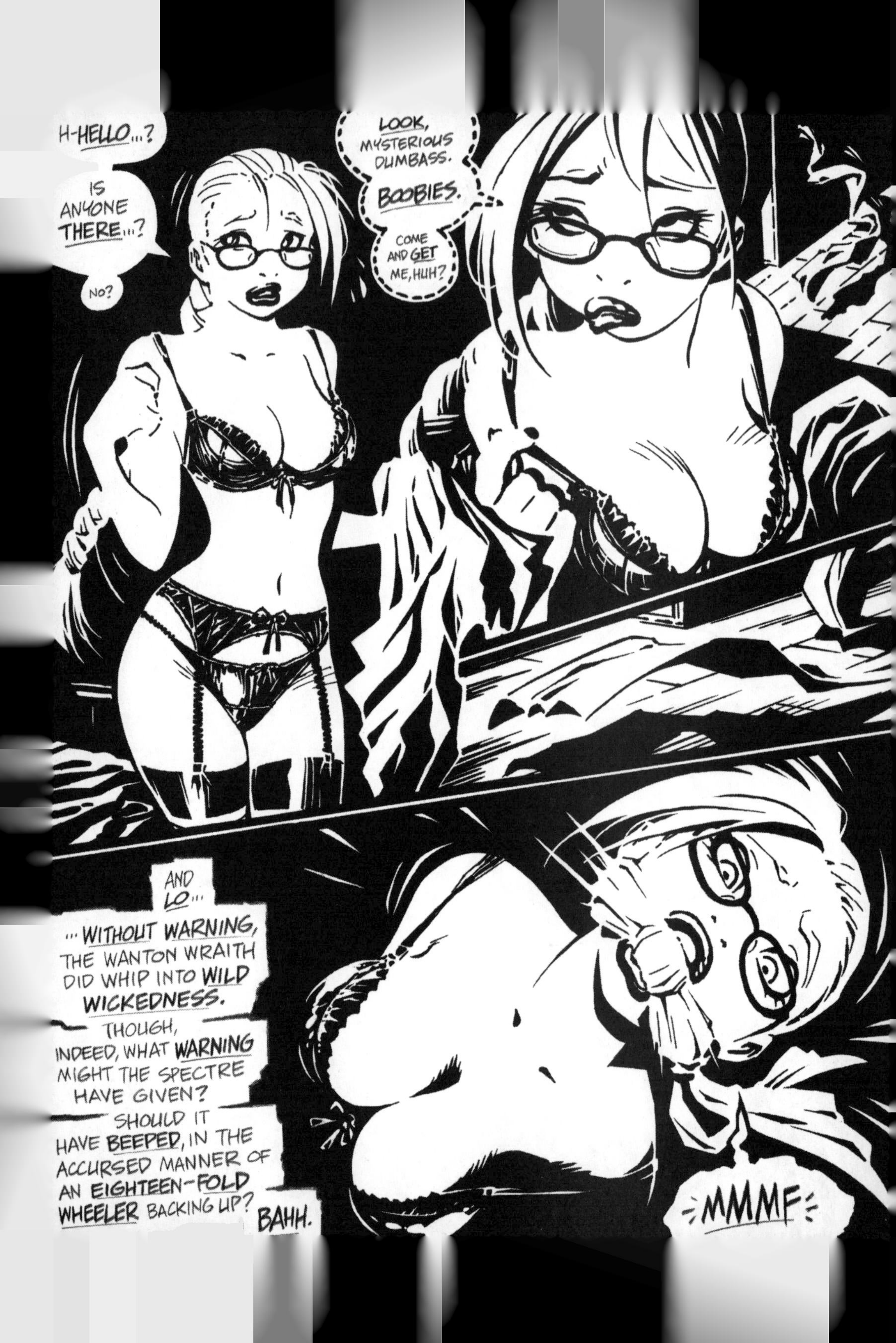
H-HELLO...?
IS ANYONE THERE...?
NO?
LOOK, MYSTERIOUS DUMBASS. BOOBIES. COME AND GET ME, HUH?
AND LO...
...WITHOUT WARNING, THE WANTON WRAITH DID WHIP INTO WILD WICKEDNESS.
THOUGH, INDEED, WHAT WARNING MIGHT THE SPECTRE HAVE GIVEN?
SHOULD IT HAVE BEEPED, IN THE ACCURSED MANNER OF AN EIGHTEEN-FOLD WHEELER BACKING UP?
BAHH.
MMMF

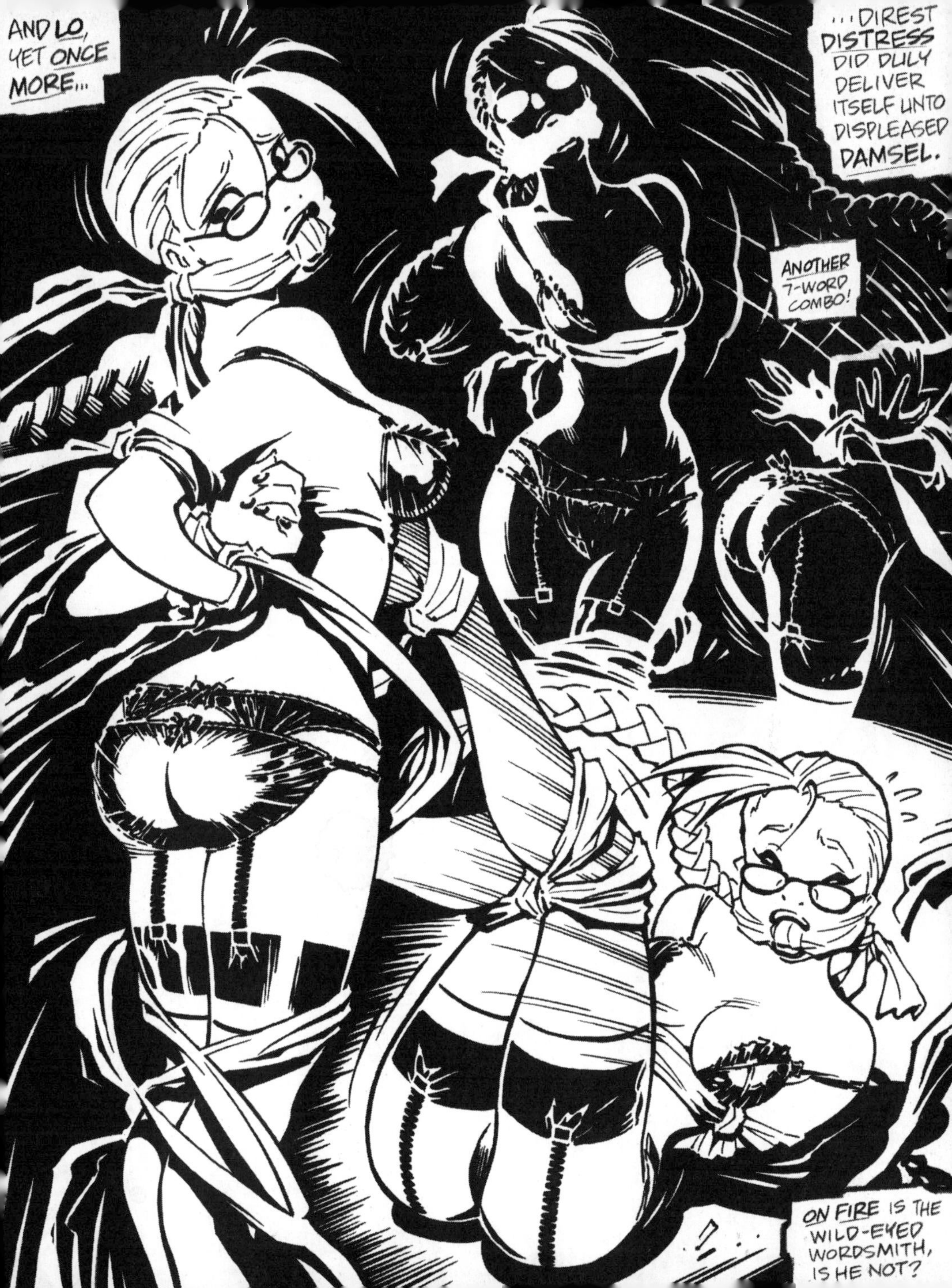
AND LO, YET ONCE MORE...
...DIREST DISTRESS DID DULY DELIVER ITSELF UNTO DISPLEASED DAMSEL.
ANOTHER 7-WORD COMBO!
!
ON FIRE IS THE WILD-EYED WORDSMITH, IS HE NOT?

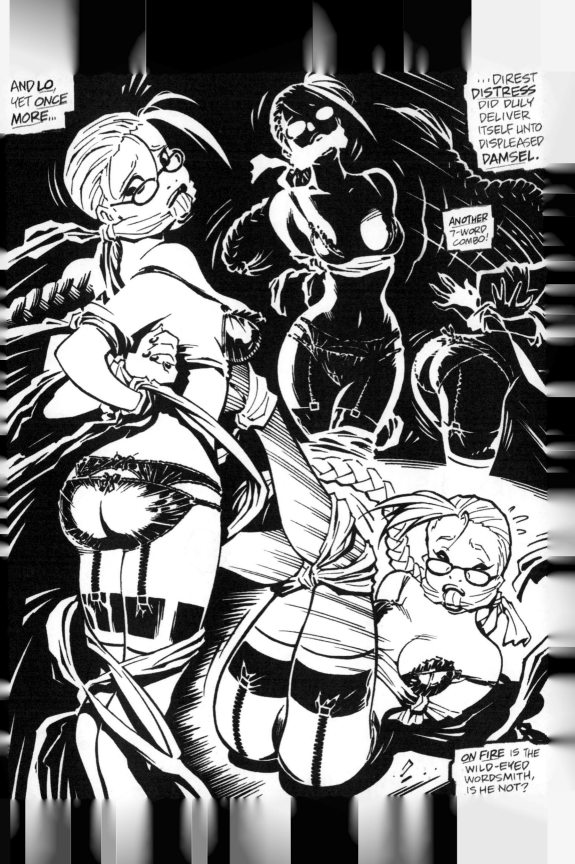

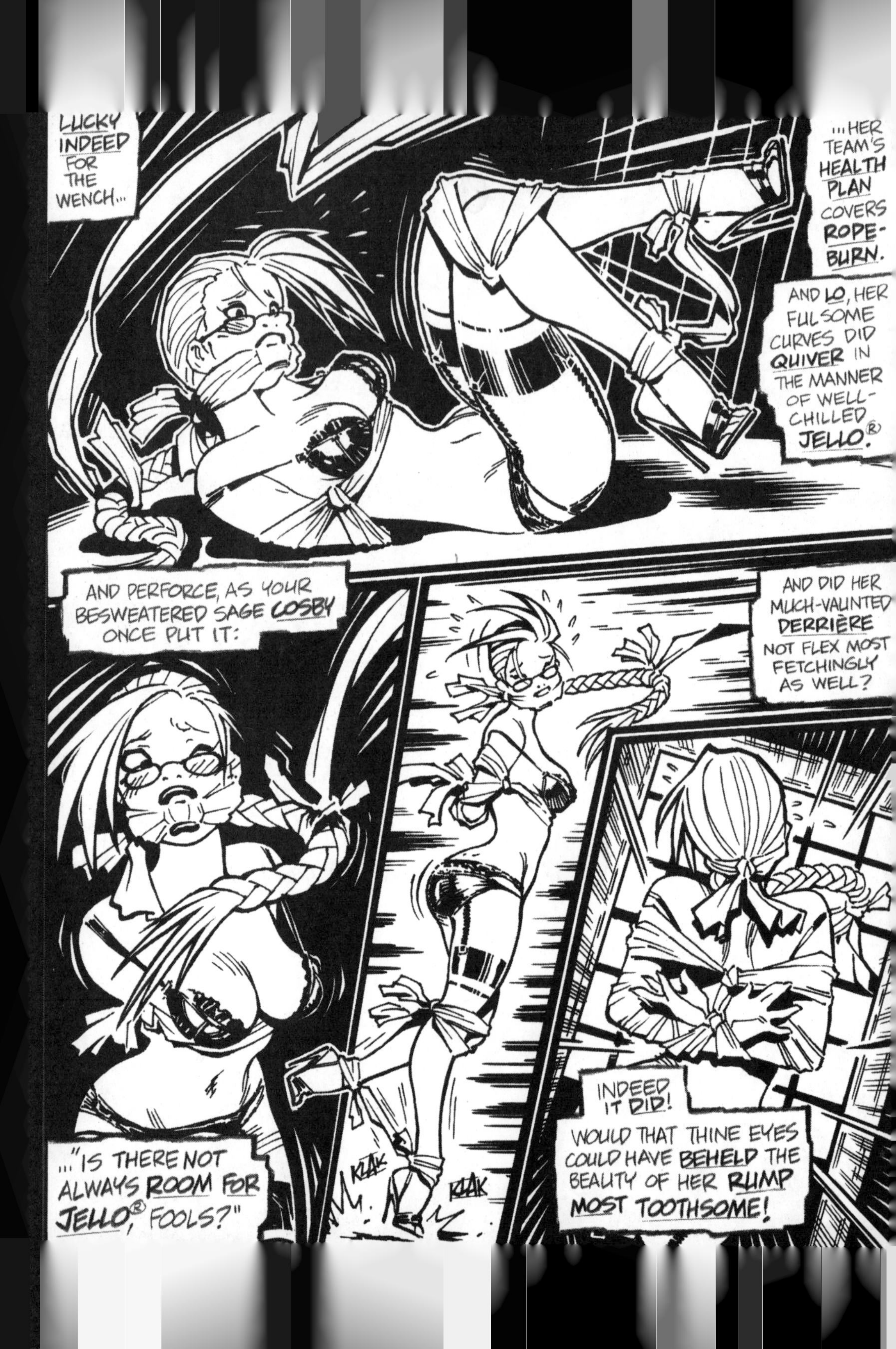
LUCKY INDEED FOR THE WENCH...
...HER TEAM'S HEALTH PLAN COVERS ROPE-BURN.
AND LO, HER FULSOME CURVES DID QUIVER IN THE MANNER OF WELL-CHILLED JELLO.®
AND PERFORCE, AS YOUR BESWEATERED SAGE COSBY ONCE PUT IT:
..."IS THERE NOT ALWAYS ROOM FOR JELLO,® FOOLS?"
AND DID HER MUCH-VAUNTED DERRIÈRE NOT FLEX MOST FETCHINGLY AS WELL?
KLAK
KLAK
INDEED IT DID!
WOULD THAT THINE EYES COULD HAVE BEHELD THE BEAUTY OF HER RUMP MOST TOOTHSOME!

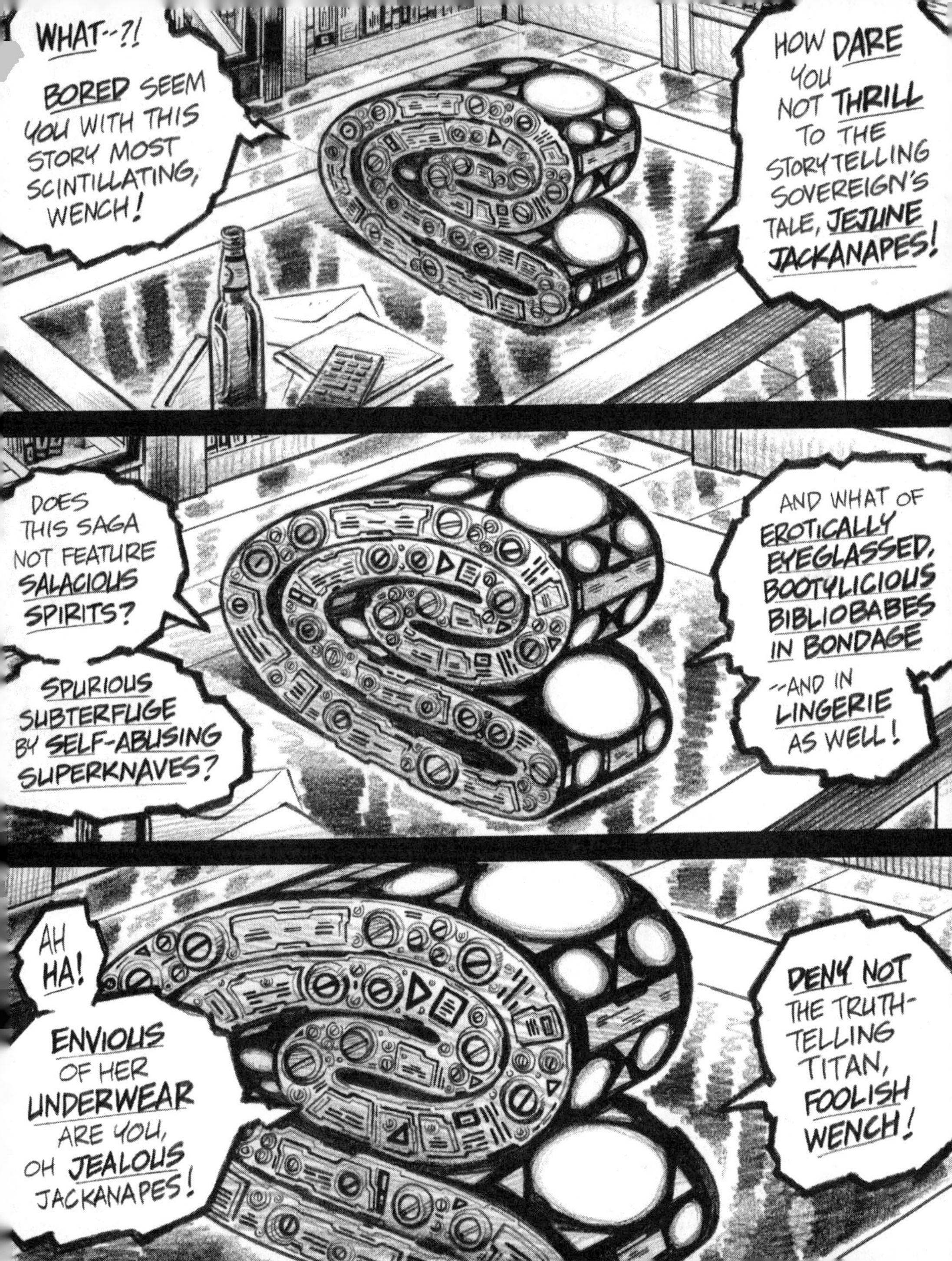
WHAT--?! BORED SEEM YOU WITH THIS STORY MOST SCINTILLATING, WENCH!
HOW DARE YOU NOT THRILL TO THE STORYTELLING SOVEREIGN'S TALE, JEJUNE JACKANAPES!
DOES THIS SAGA NOT FEATURE SALACIOUS SPIRITS?
SPURIOUS SUBTERFUGE BY SELF-ABUSING SUPERKNAVES?
AND WHAT OF EROTICALLY EYEGLASSED, BOOTYLICIOUS BIBLIOBABES IN BONDAGE
--AND IN LINGERIE AS WELL!
AH HA!
ENVIOUS OF HER UNDERWEAR ARE YOU, OH JEALOUS JACKANAPES!
DENY NOT THE TRUTH-TELLING TITAN, FOOLISH WENCH!

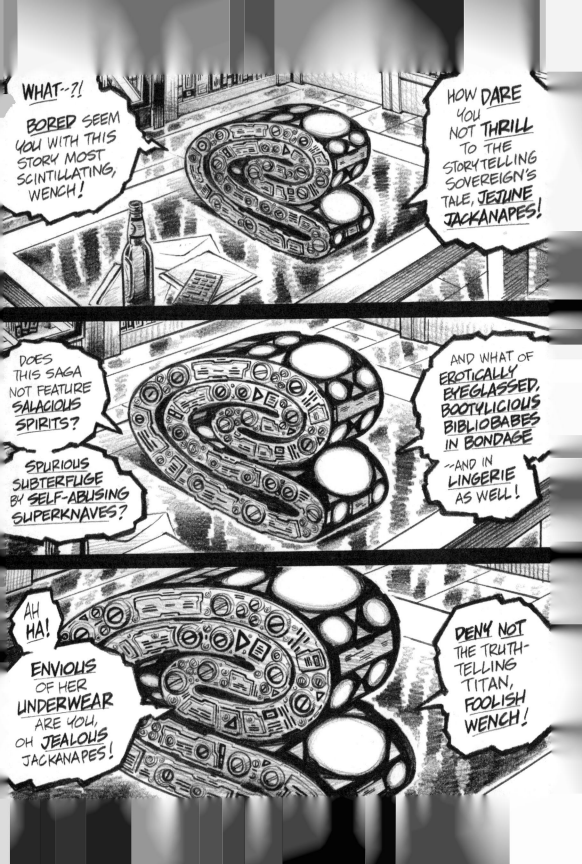

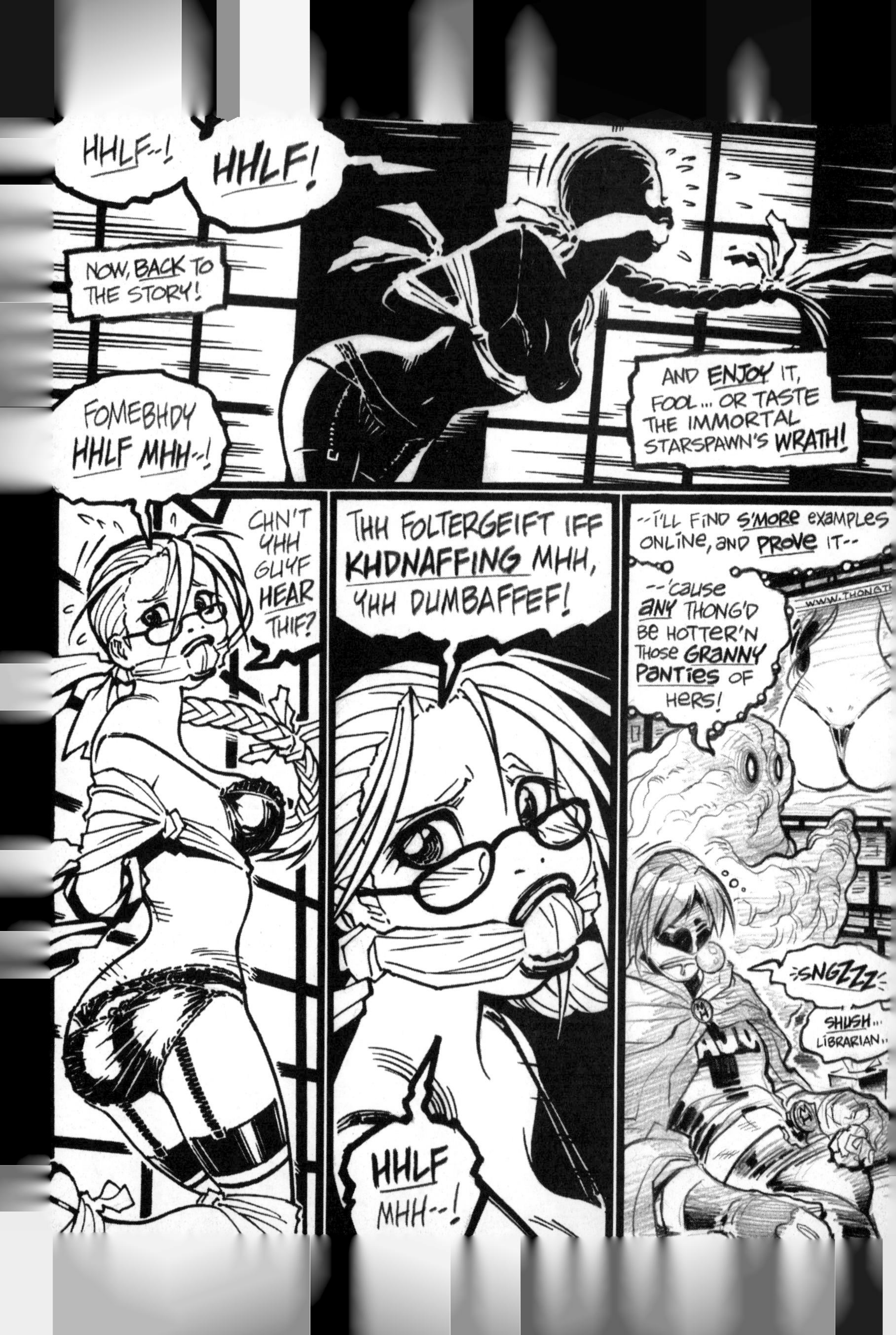
HHLF--!
HHLF!
NOW, BACK TO THE STORY!
FOMEBHDY HHLF MHH--!
AND ENJOY IT, FOOL... OR TASTE THE IMMORTAL STARSPAWN'S WRATH!
CHN'T YHH GUYF HEAR THIF?
THH FOLTERGEIFT IFF KHDNAFFING MHH, YHH DUMBAFFEF!
HHLF MHH--!
--I'LL FIND S'MORE examples ONLINE, and PROVE IT--
--'cause ANY THONG'D Be HOTTER'N THOSE GRANNY PANTIES OF HERS!
SNGZZZ
SHUSH... LIBRARIAN...

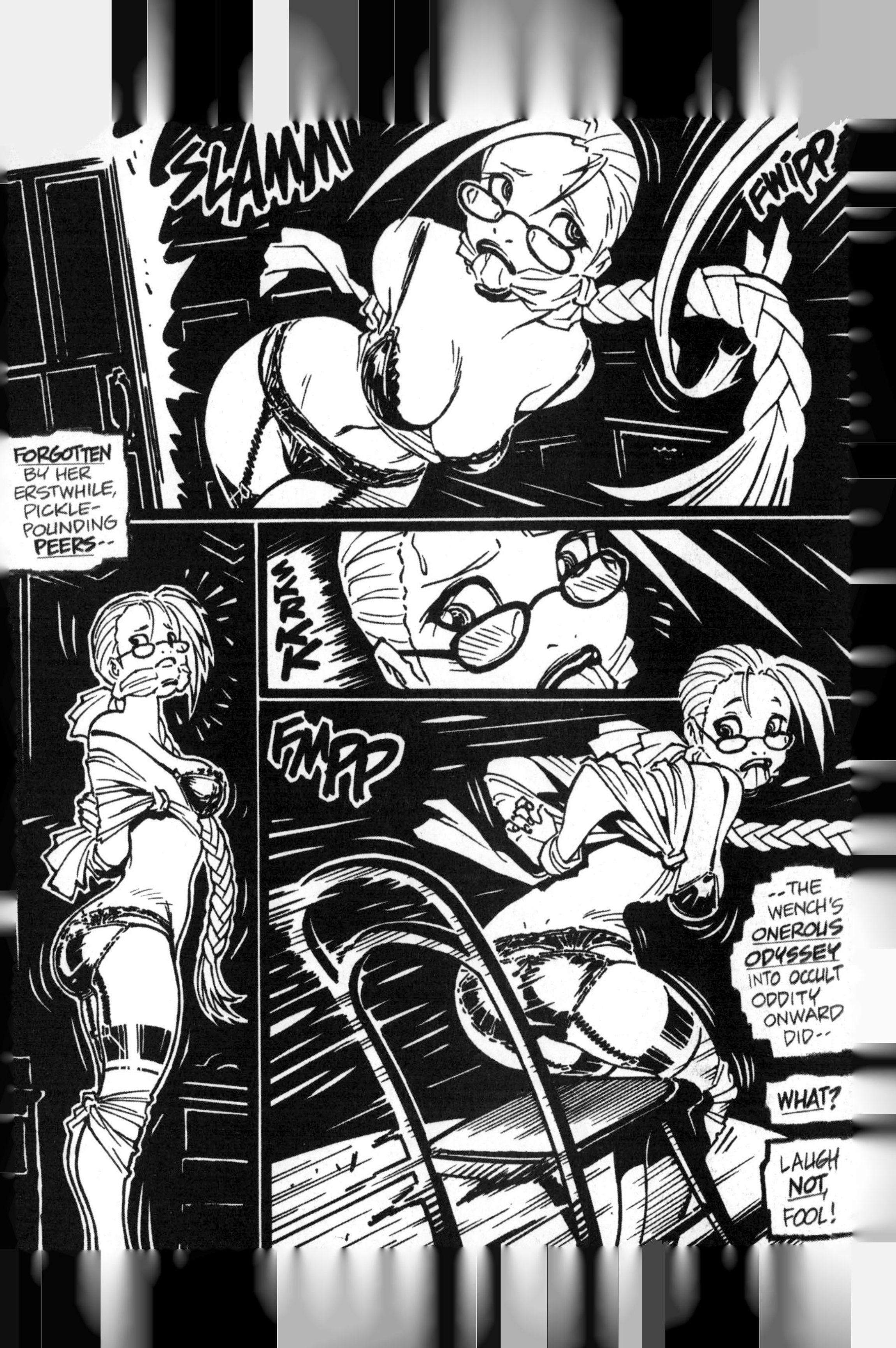
SLAMM
FWIPP
FORGOTTEN BY HER ERSTWHILE, PICKLE-POUNDING PEERS--
FMPP
--THE WENCH'S ONEROUS ODYSSEY INTO OCCULT ODDITY ONWARD DID--
WHAT?
LAUGH NOT, FOOL!

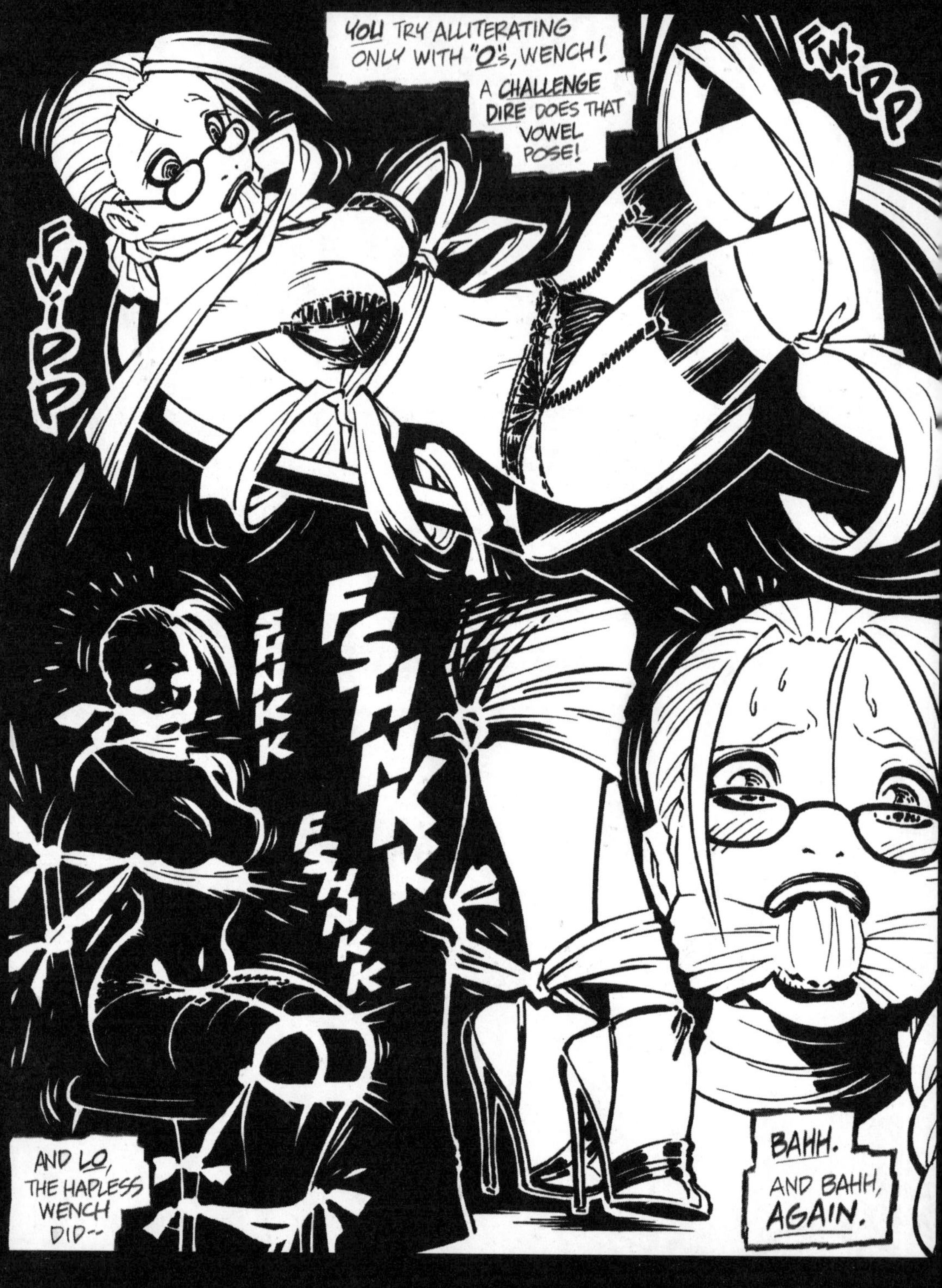
YOU! TRY ALLITERATING ONLY WITH "O"s, WENCH!
A CHALLENGE DIRE DOES THAT VOWEL POSE!
FWIPP
FWIPP
SHNKK
FSHNKK
FSHNKK
AND LO, THE HAPLESS WENCH DID--
BAHH. AND BAHH, AGAIN.

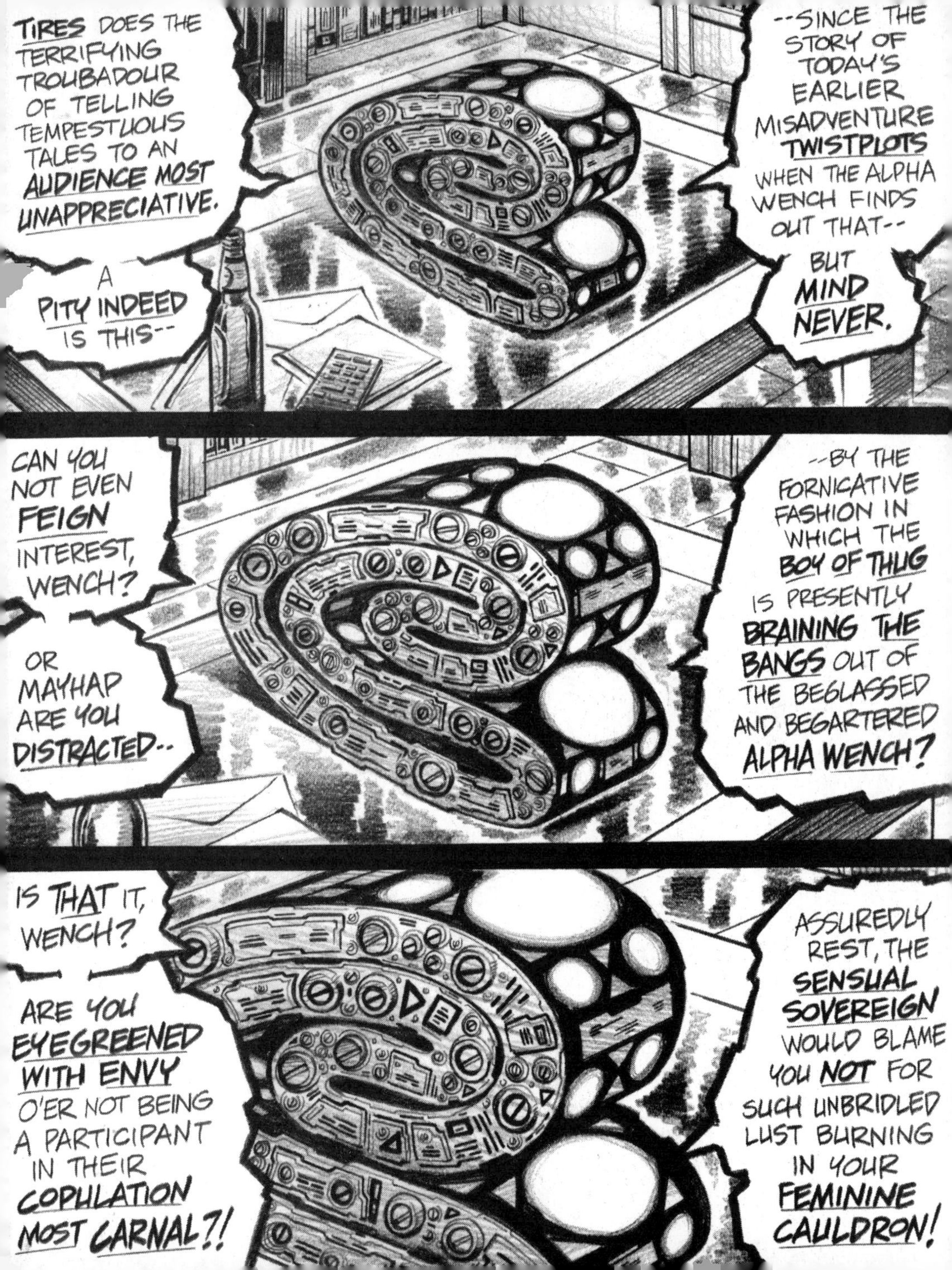
TIRES DOES THE TERRIFYING TROUBADOUR OF TELLING TEMPESTUOUS TALES TO AN AUDIENCE MOST UNAPPRECIATIVE.
A PITY INDEED IS THIS--
--SINCE THE STORY OF TODAY'S EARLIER MISADVENTURE TWISTPLOTS WHEN THE ALPHA WENCH FINDS OUT THAT--
BUT MIND NEVER.
CAN YOU NOT EVEN FEIGN INTEREST, WENCH?
OR MAYHAP ARE YOU DISTRACTED..
--BY THE FORNICATIVE FASHION IN WHICH THE BOY OF THUG IS PRESENTLY BRAINING THE BANGS OUT OF THE BEGLASSED AND BEGARTERED ALPHA WENCH?
IS THAT IT, WENCH?
ARE YOU EYEGREENED WITH ENVY O'ER NOT BEING A PARTICIPANT IN THEIR COPULATION MOST CARNAL?!
ASSUREDLY REST, THE SENSUAL SOVEREIGN WOULD BLAME YOU NOT FOR SUCH UNBRIDLED LUST BURNING IN YOUR FEMININE CAULDRON!

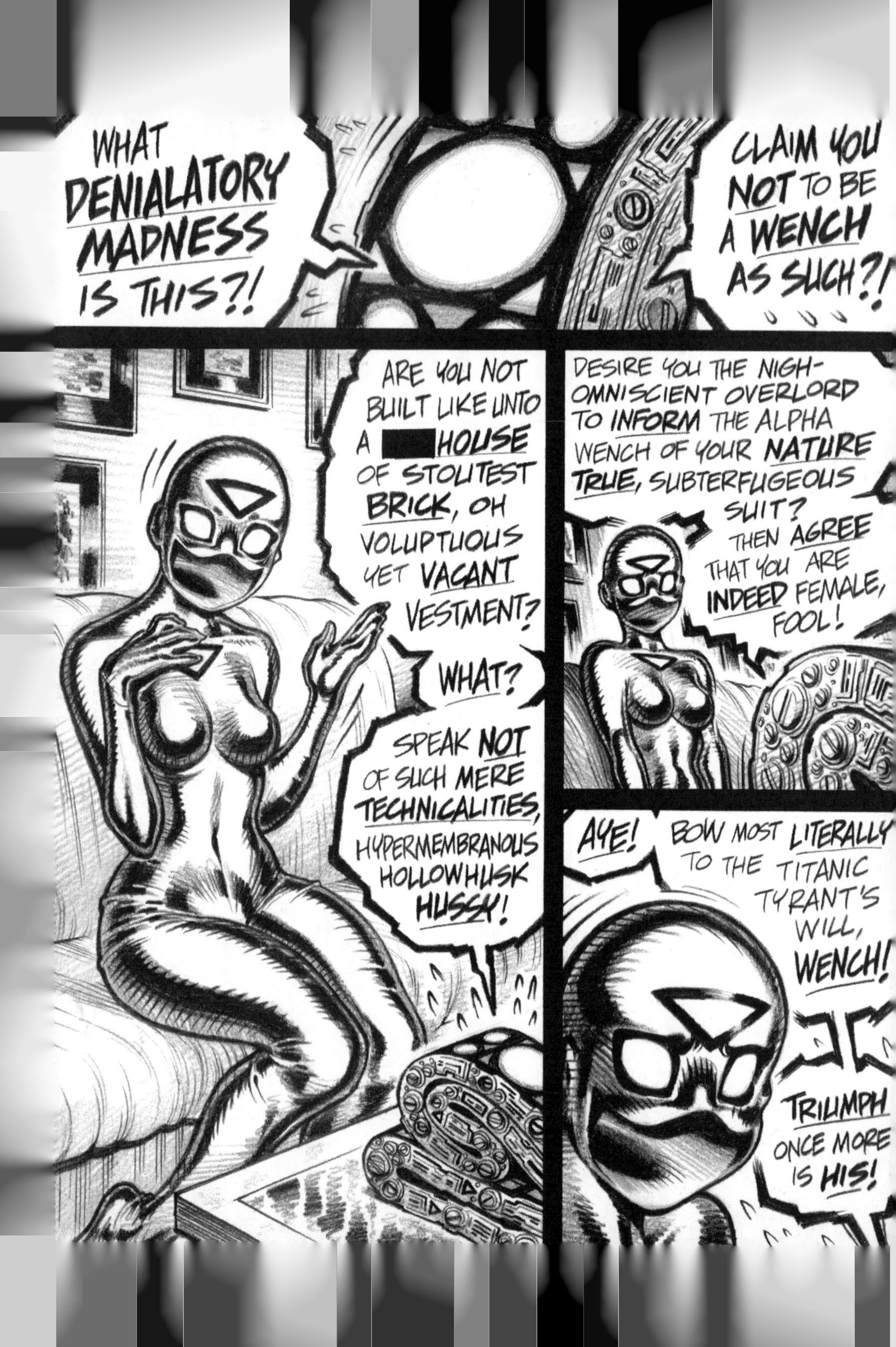
WHAT DENIALATORY MADNESS IS THIS?!
CLAIM YOU NOT TO BE A WENCH AS SUCH?!
ARE YOU NOT BUILT LIKE UNTO A [redacted] HOUSE OF STOUTEST BRICK, OH VOLUPTUOUS YET VACANT VESTMENT?
WHAT?
SPEAK NOT OF SUCH MERE TECHNICALITIES, HYPERMEMBRANOUS HOLLOWHUSK HUSSY!
DESIRE YOU THE NIGH-OMNISCIENT OVERLORD TO INFORM THE ALPHA WENCH OF YOUR NATURE TRUE, SUBTERFUGEOUS SUIT?
THEN AGREE THAT YOU ARE INDEED FEMALE, FOOL!
AYE!
BOW MOST LITERALLY TO THE TITANIC TYRANT'S WILL, WENCH!
TRIUMPH ONCE MORE IS HIS!

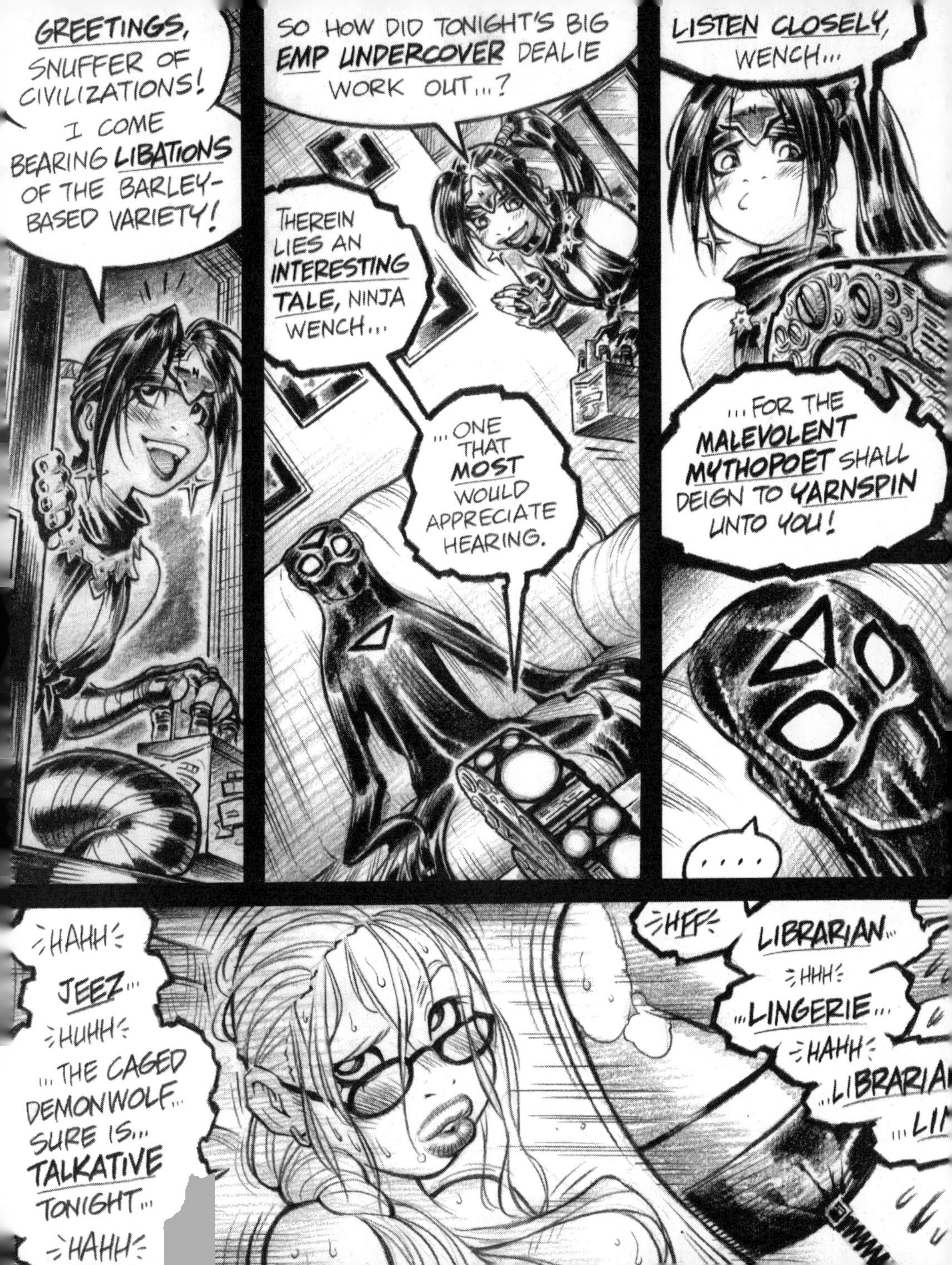
GREETINGS, SNUFFER OF CIVILIZATIONS!
I COME BEARING LIBATIONS OF THE BARLEY-BASED VARIETY!
SO HOW DID TONIGHT'S BIG EMP UNDERCOVER DEALIE WORK OUT...?
THEREIN LIES AN INTERESTING TALE, NINJA WENCH...
...ONE THAT MOST WOULD APPRECIATE HEARING.
LISTEN CLOSELY, WENCH...
...FOR THE MALEVOLENT MYTHOPOET SHALL DEIGN TO YARNSPIN UNTO YOU!
....
HAHH
JEEZ...
HUHH
...THE CAGED DEMONWOLF... SURE IS... TALKATIVE TONIGHT...
HAHH
HFF
LIBRARIAN...
HHH
...LINGERIE...
HAHH
...LIBRARIA
...LI

eMpoWered™

Witless Minions 4-Eva

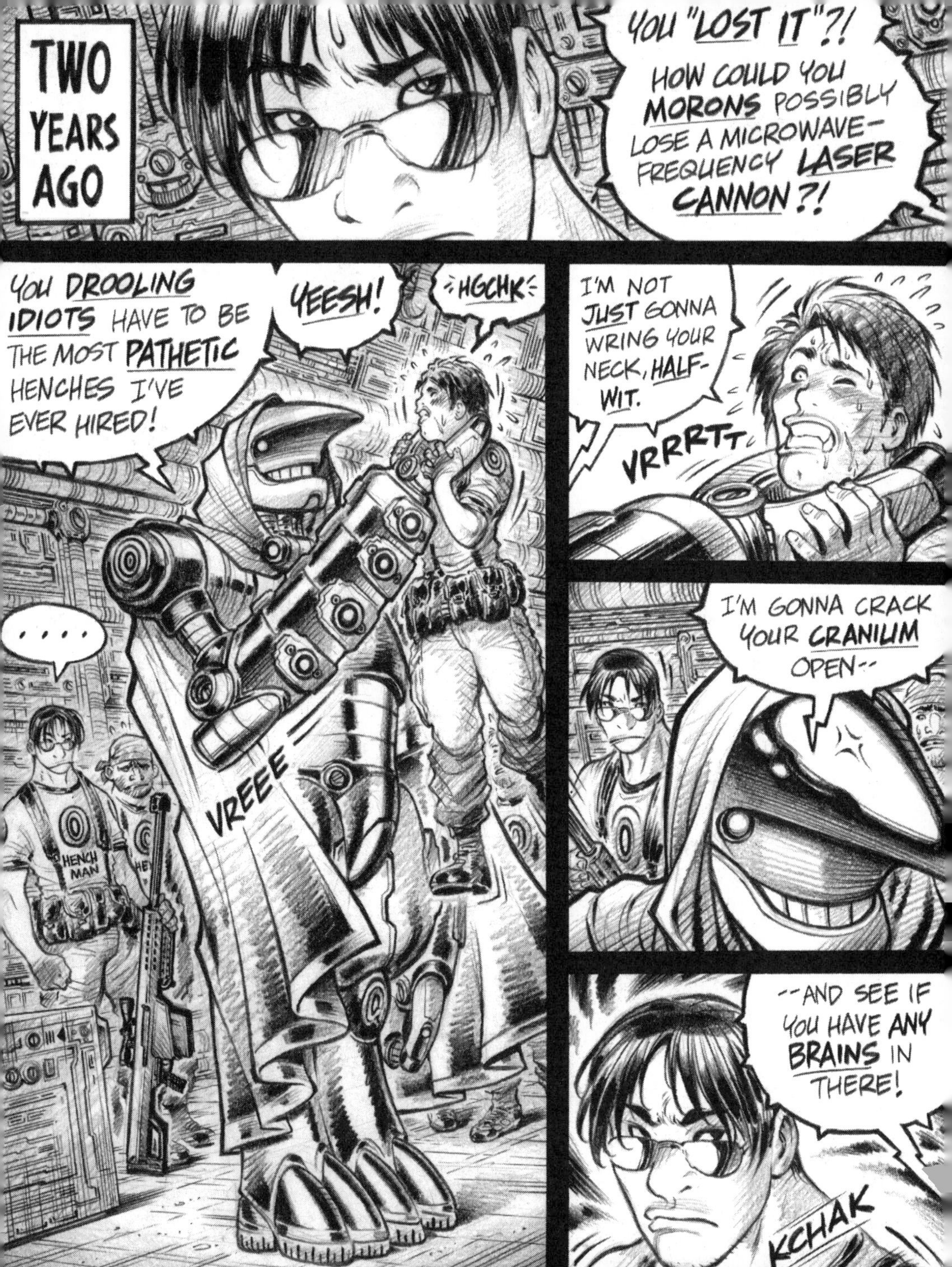
TWO YEARS AGO
YOU "LOST IT"?! HOW COULD YOU MORONS POSSIBLY LOSE A MICROWAVE-FREQUENCY LASER CANNON?!
YOU DROOLING IDIOTS HAVE TO BE THE MOST PATHETIC HENCHES I'VE EVER HIRED!
YEESH!
HGCHK
....
VREEE
HENCH MAN
I'M NOT JUST GONNA WRING YOUR NECK, HALF-WIT.
VRRRTTT
I'M GONNA CRACK YOUR CRANIUM OPEN--
--AND SEE IF YOU HAVE ANY BRAINS IN THERE!
KCHAK

BKOOM
?!
PRETTY CLEVER IDEA, HIDING YOUR SUIT'S COOLING VENTS UNDER THAT CAPE...
HENCH MAN
SKREEEK
WHAT--?!
N-NO--!
BKOOM
...BUT NOT BOTHERING TO UPARMOR THOSE VENTS? NOT SO CLEVER.
OH, [redacted]--!
[redacted]!
SKREEEE

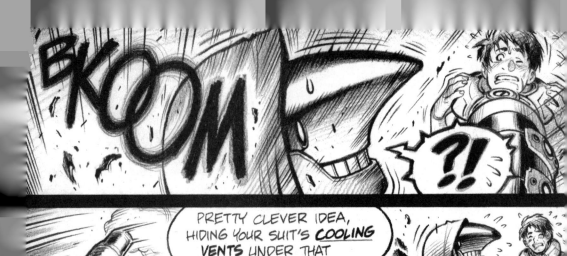

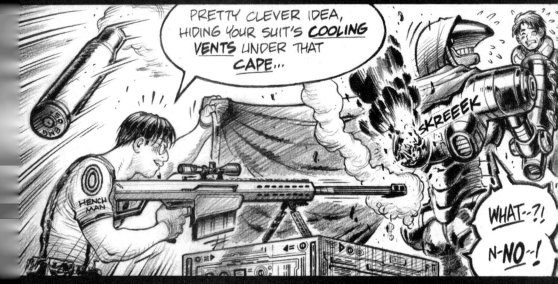

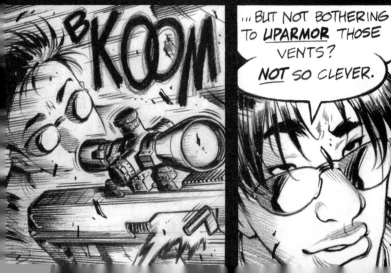

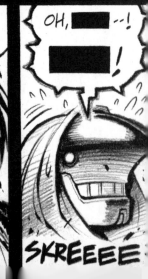

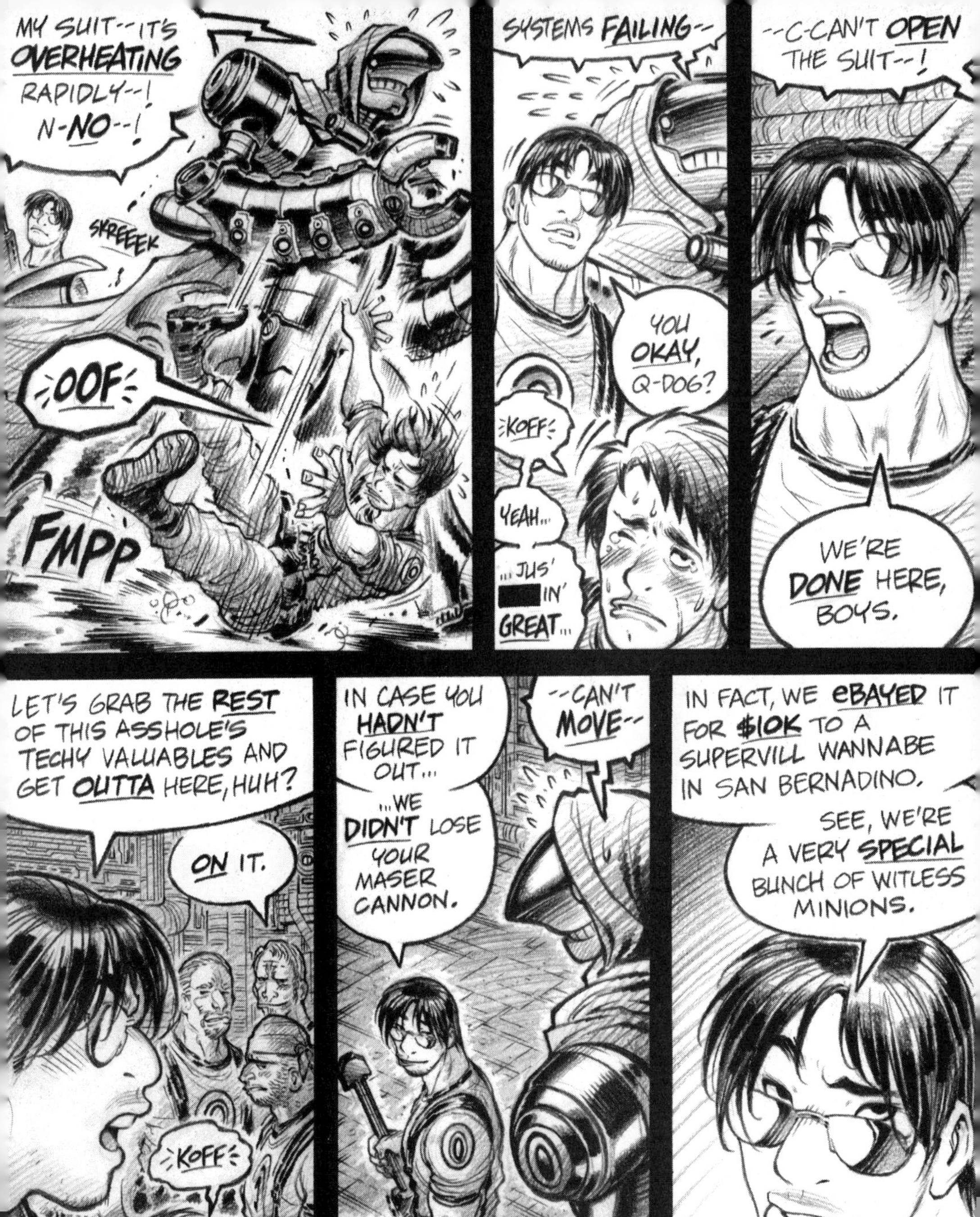

MY SUIT--IT'S OVERHEATING RAPIDLY--! N-NO--!
SKREEEEK
OOF
FMPP
SYSTEMS FAILING--
YOU OKAY, Q-DOG?
KOFF
YEAH...
...JUS' [redacted] IN' GREAT...
--C-CAN'T OPEN THE SUIT--!
WE'RE DONE HERE, BOYS.
LET'S GRAB THE REST OF THIS ASSHOLE'S TECHY VALUABLES AND GET OUTTA HERE, HUH?
ON IT.
KOFF
IN CASE YOU HADN'T FIGURED IT OUT...
...WE DIDN'T LOSE YOUR MASER CANNON.
--CAN'T MOVE--
IN FACT, WE eBAYED IT FOR $10K TO A SUPERVILL WANNABE IN SAN BERNADINO.
SEE, WE'RE A VERY SPECIAL BUNCH OF WITLESS MINIONS.

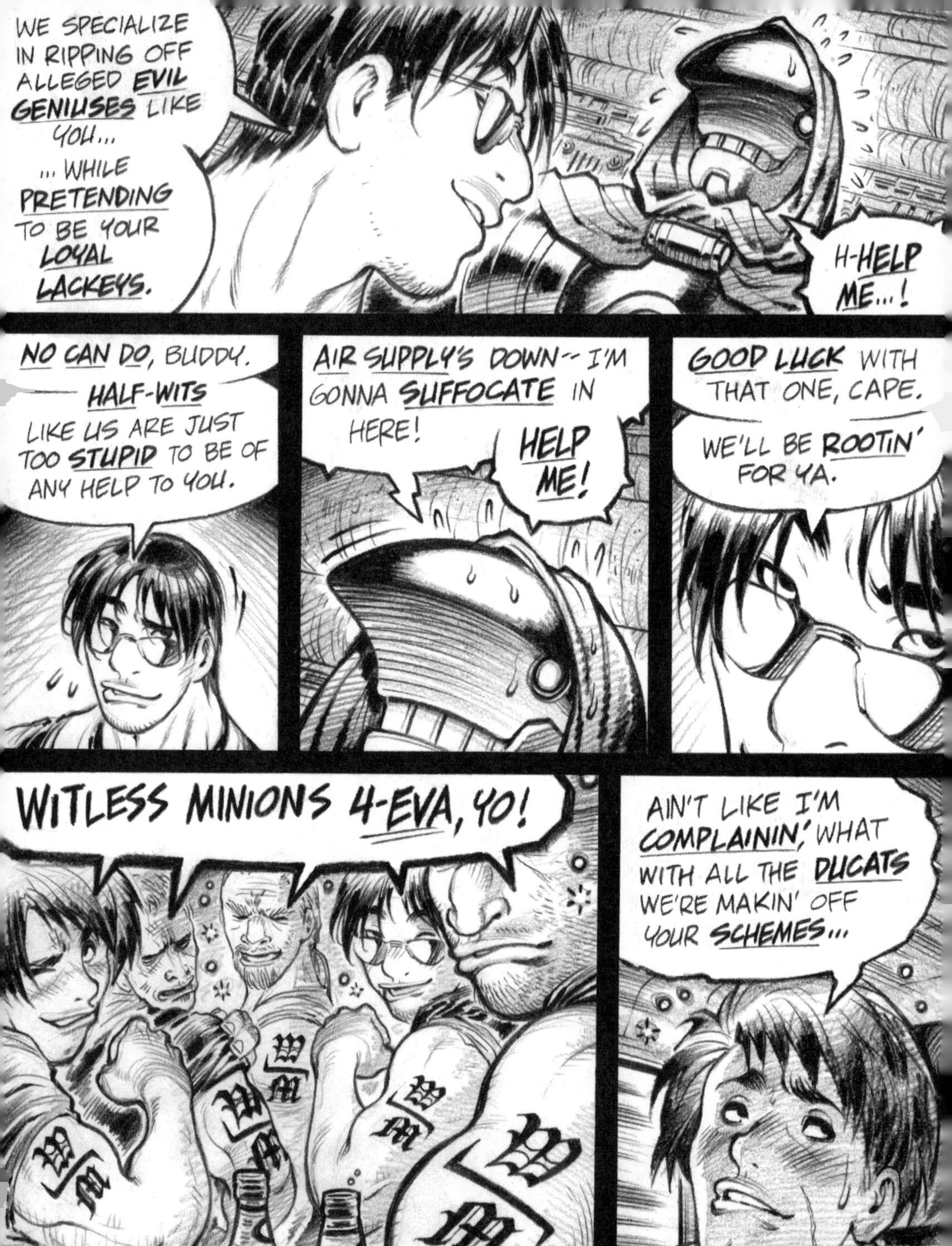
WE SPECIALIZE IN RIPPING OFF ALLEGED EVIL GENIUSES LIKE YOU...
... WHILE PRETENDING TO BE YOUR LOYAL LACKEYS.
H-HELP ME...!
NO CAN DO, BUDDY.
HALF-WITS LIKE US ARE JUST TOO STUPID TO BE OF ANY HELP TO YOU.
AIR SUPPLY'S DOWN-- I'M GONNA SUFFOCATE IN HERE!
HELP ME!
GOOD LUCK WITH THAT ONE, CAPE.
WE'LL BE ROOTIN' FOR YA.
WITLESS MINIONS 4-EVA, YO!
AIN'T LIKE I'M COMPLAININ', WHAT WITH ALL THE DUCATS WE'RE MAKIN' OFF YOUR SCHEMES...

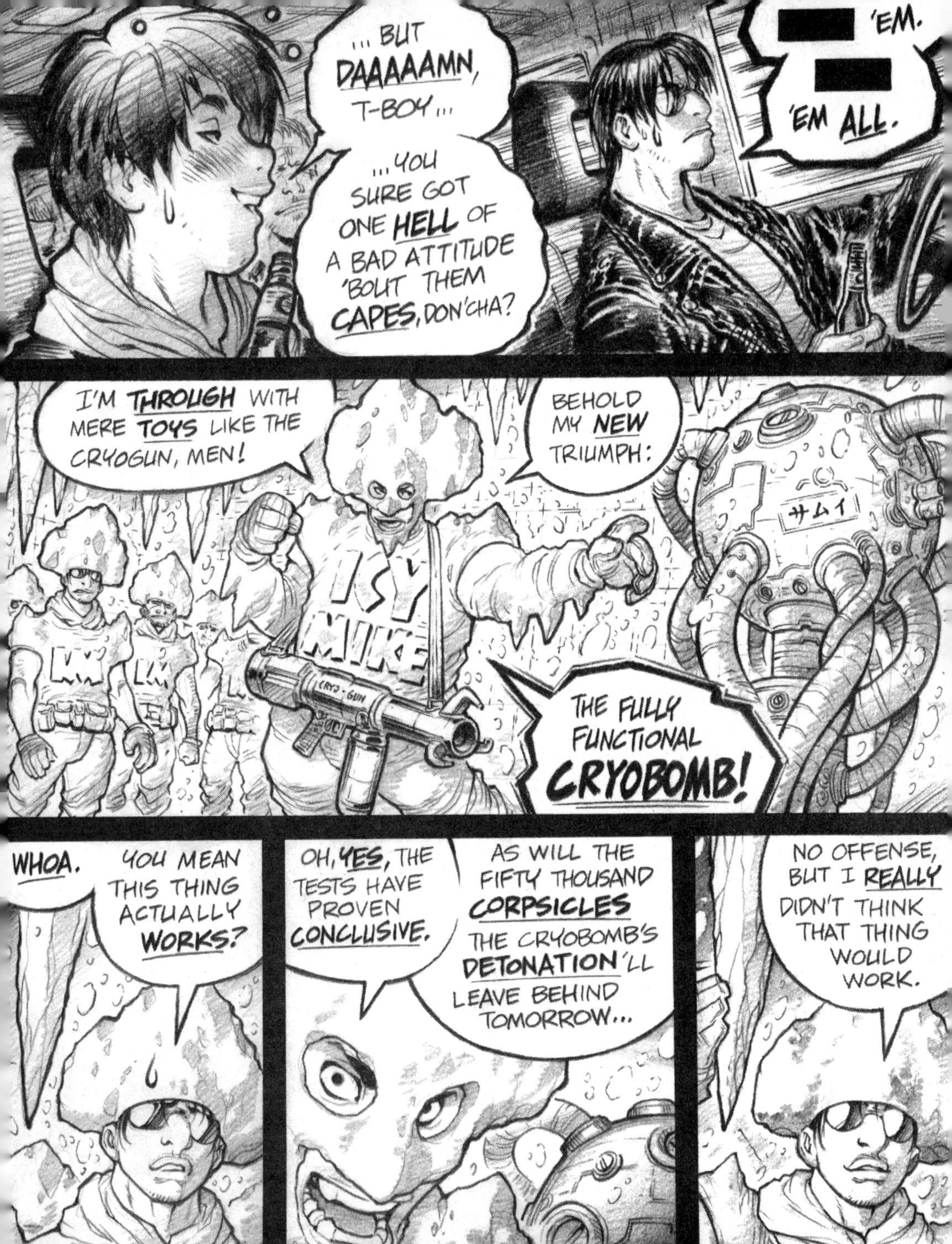

...BUT DAAAAAMN, T-BOY...
...YOU SURE GOT ONE HELL OF A BAD ATTITUDE 'BOUT THEM CAPES, DON'CHA?
[redacted] 'EM. [redacted] 'EM ALL.
I'M THROUGH WITH MERE TOYS LIKE THE CRYOGUN, MEN!
BEHOLD MY NEW TRIUMPH:
サムイ
CRYO-GUN
THE FULLY FUNCTIONAL CRYOBOMB!
WHOA.
YOU MEAN THIS THING ACTUALLY WORKS?
OH, YES, THE TESTS HAVE PROVEN CONCLUSIVE.
AS WILL THE FIFTY THOUSAND CORPSICLES THE CRYOBOMB'S DETONATION'LL LEAVE BEHIND TOMORROW...
NO OFFENSE, BUT I REALLY DIDN'T THINK THAT THING WOULD WORK.

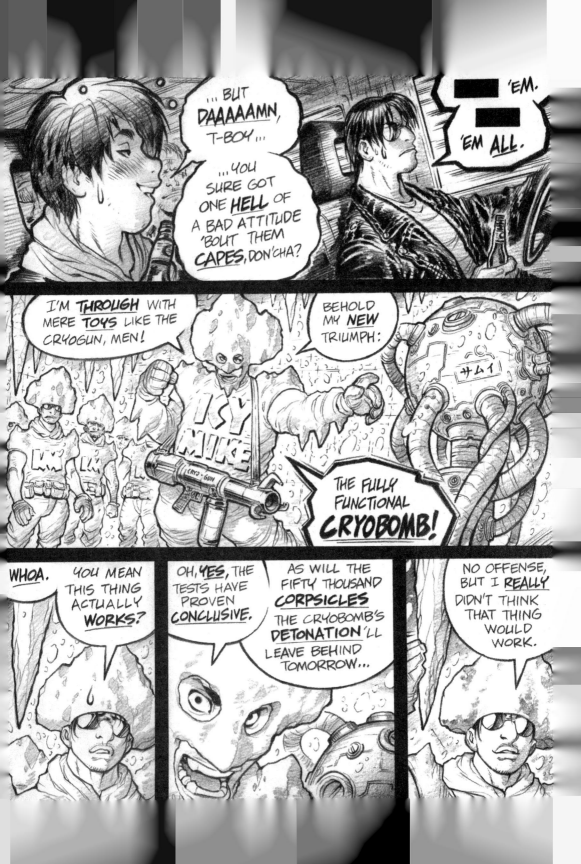

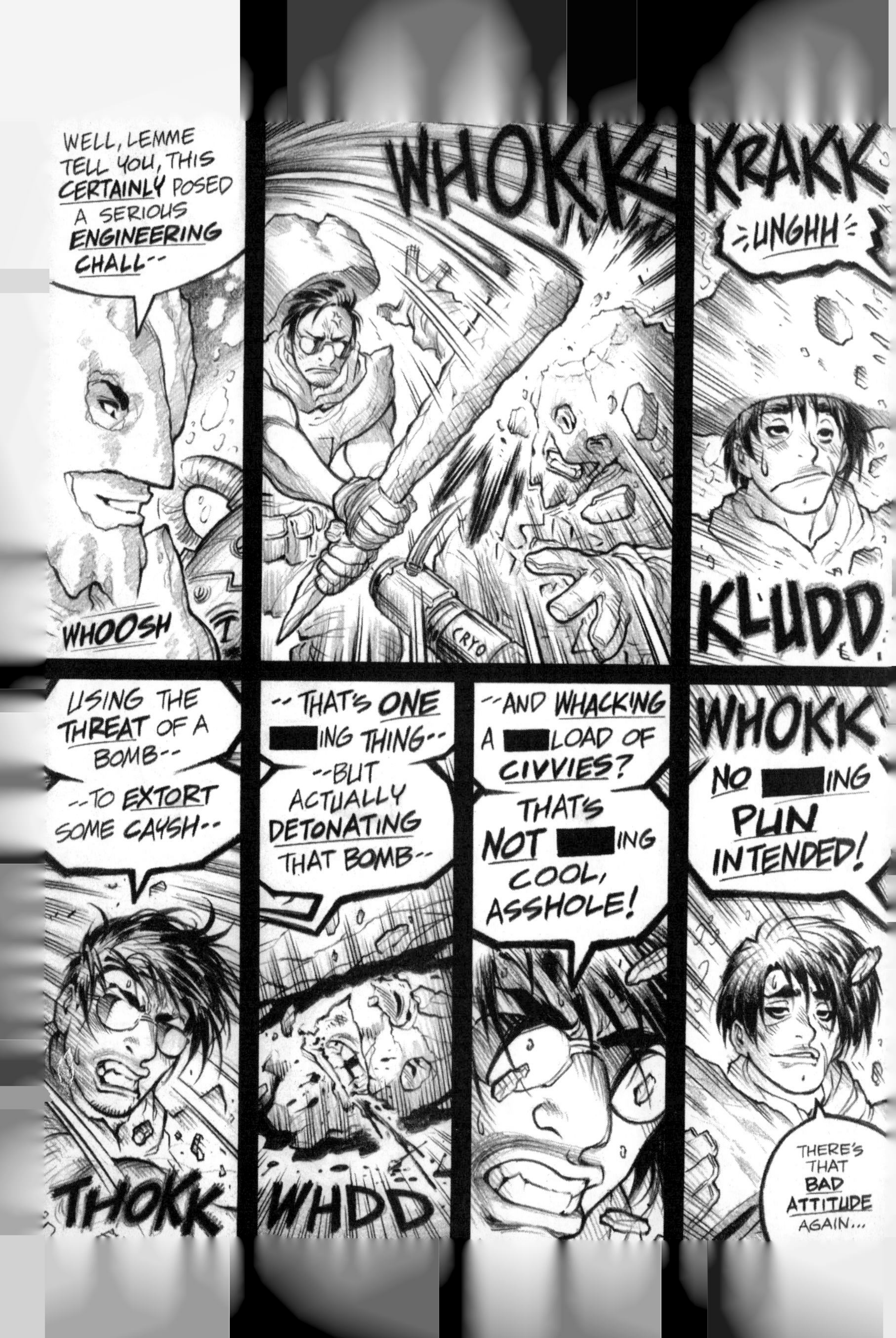
WELL, LEMME TELL YOU, THIS CERTAINLY POSED A SERIOUS ENGINEERING CHALL--
WHOOSH
WHOKK
CRYO
KRAKK
UNGHH
KLUDD
USING THE THREAT OF A BOMB--
--TO EXTORT SOME CAYSH--
THOKK
--THAT'S ONE [redacted]ING THING--
--BUT ACTUALLY DETONATING THAT BOMB--
WHDD
--AND WHACKING A [redacted] LOAD OF CIVVIES?
THAT'S NOT [redacted]ING COOL, ASSHOLE!
WHOKK
NO [redacted]ING PUN INTENDED!
THERE'S THAT BAD ATTITUDE AGAIN...

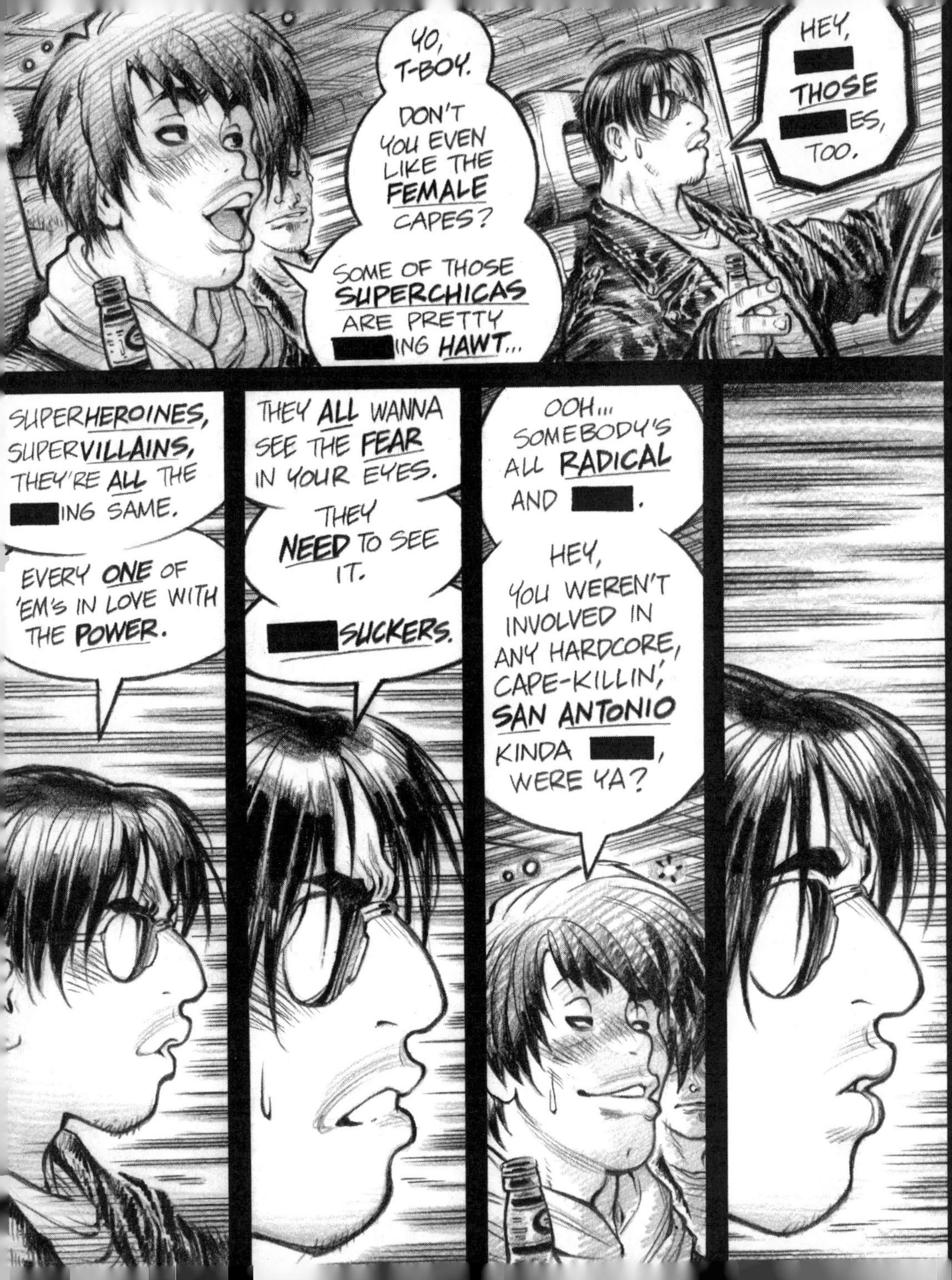

YO, T-BOY.
DON'T YOU EVEN LIKE THE FEMALE CAPES?
SOME OF THOSE SUPERCHICAS ARE PRETTY [redacted]ING HAWT...
HEY, [redacted] THOSE [redacted]ES, TOO.
SUPERHEROINES, SUPERVILLAINS, THEY'RE ALL THE [redacted]ING SAME.
EVERY ONE OF 'EM'S IN LOVE WITH THE POWER.
THEY ALL WANNA SEE THE FEAR IN YOUR EYES.
THEY NEED TO SEE IT.
[redacted]SUCKERS.
OOH... SOMEBODY'S ALL RADICAL AND [redacted].
HEY, YOU WEREN'T INVOLVED IN ANY HARDCORE, CAPE-KILLIN', SAN ANTONIO KINDA [redacted], WERE YA?

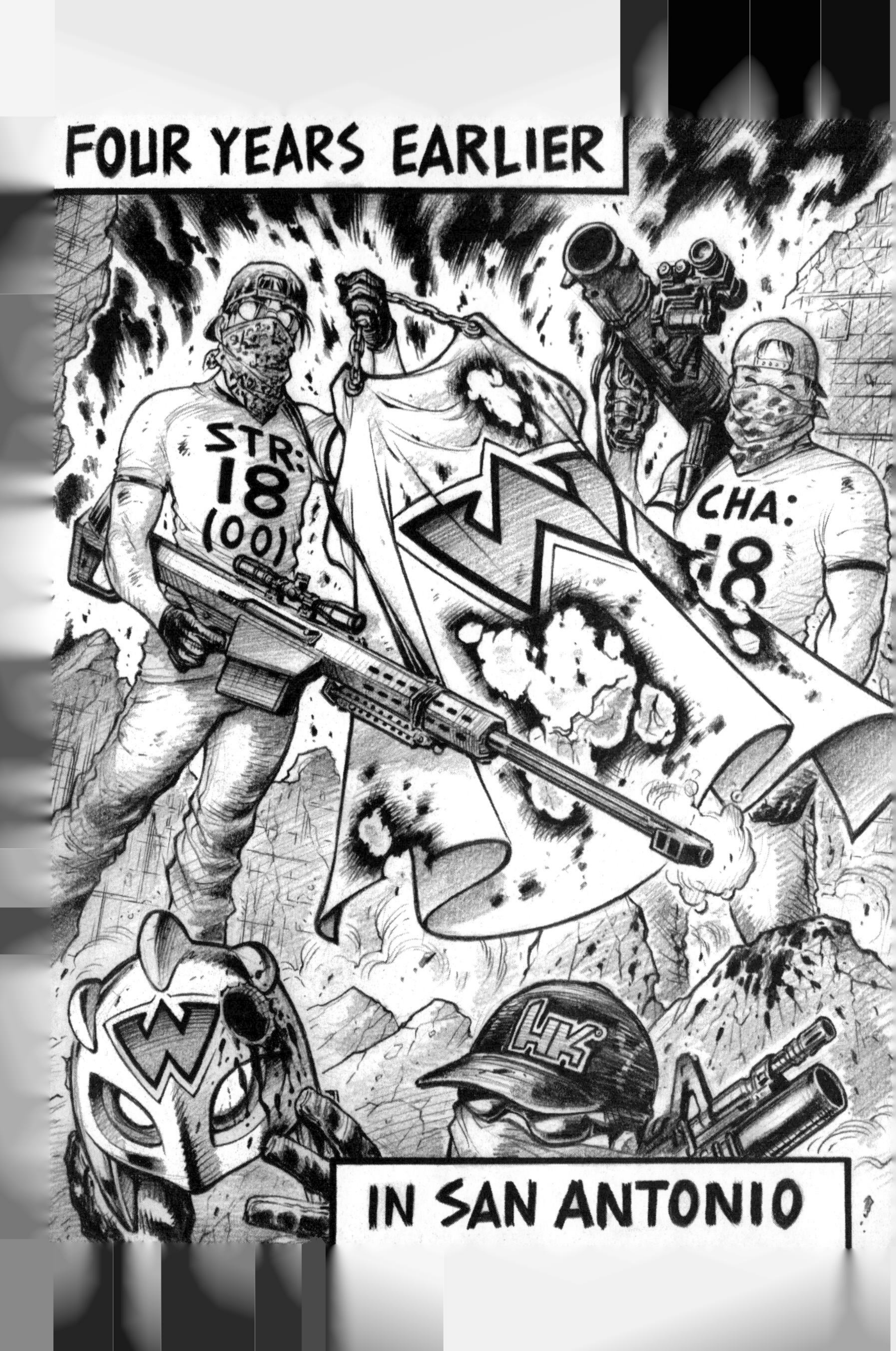
FOUR YEARS EARLIER
STR: 18 (00)
CHA: 18
HK
IN SAN ANTONIO

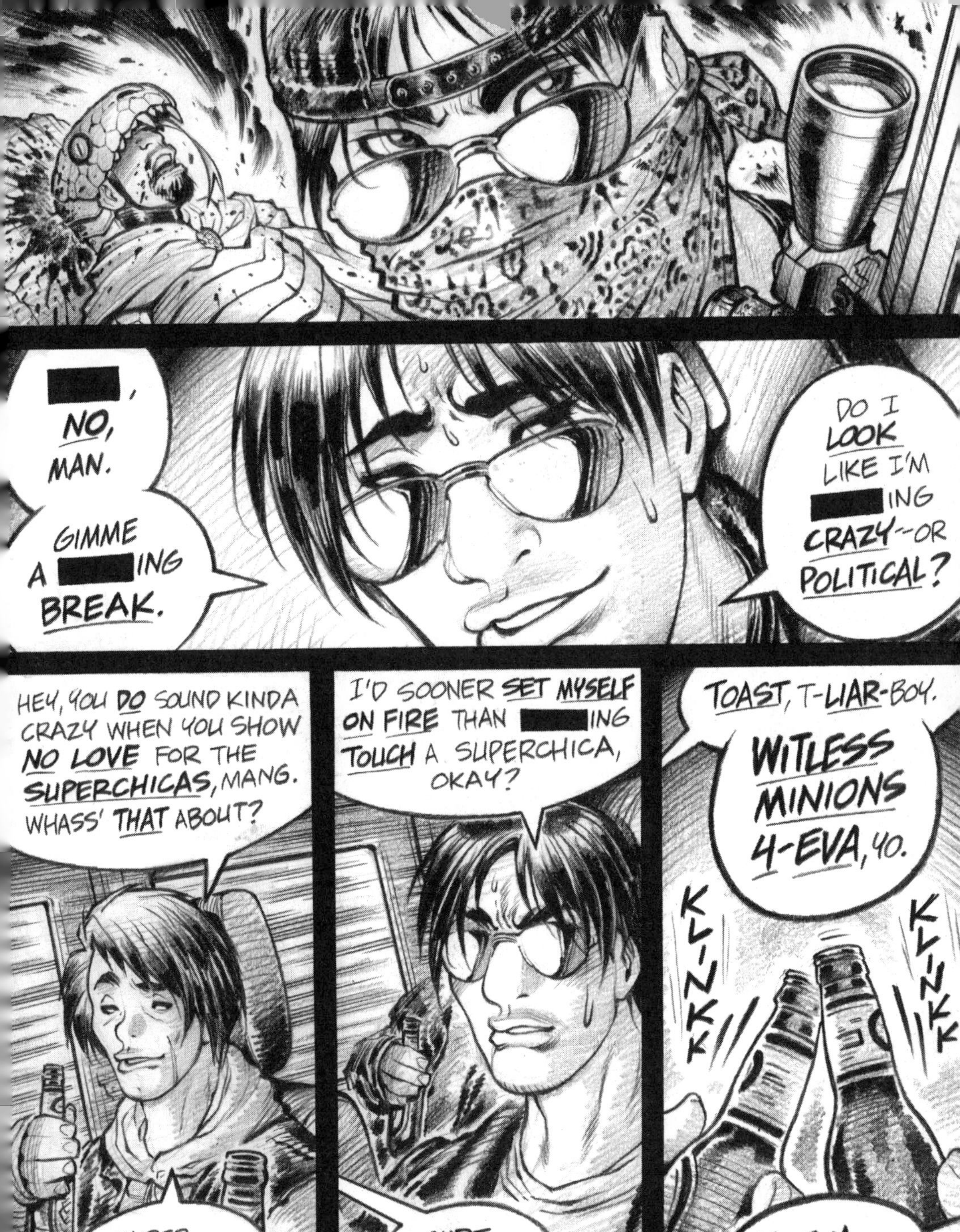
[redacted], NO, MAN.
GIMME A [redacted]ING BREAK.
DO I LOOK LIKE I'M [redacted]ING CRAZY--OR POLITICAL?
HEY, YOU DO SOUND KINDA CRAZY WHEN YOU SHOW NO LOVE FOR THE SUPERCHICAS, MANG. WHASS' THAT ABOUT?
SUPER HAWTNESS, YO.
I'D SOONER SET MYSELF ON FIRE THAN [redacted]ING TOUCH A SUPERCHICA, OKAY?
SURE YOU WOULD.
TOAST, T-LIAR-BOY.
WITLESS MINIONS 4-EVA, YO.
KLINKK
KLINKK
4-EVA, YO.

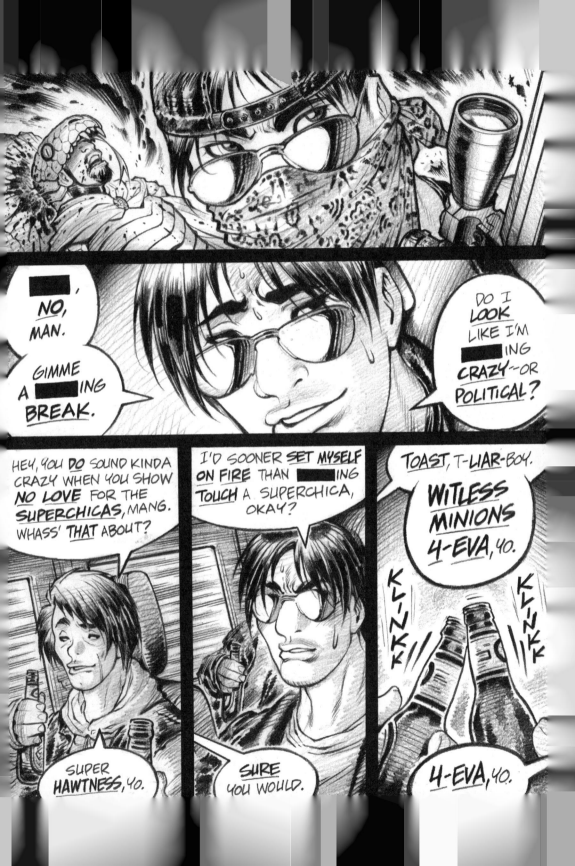

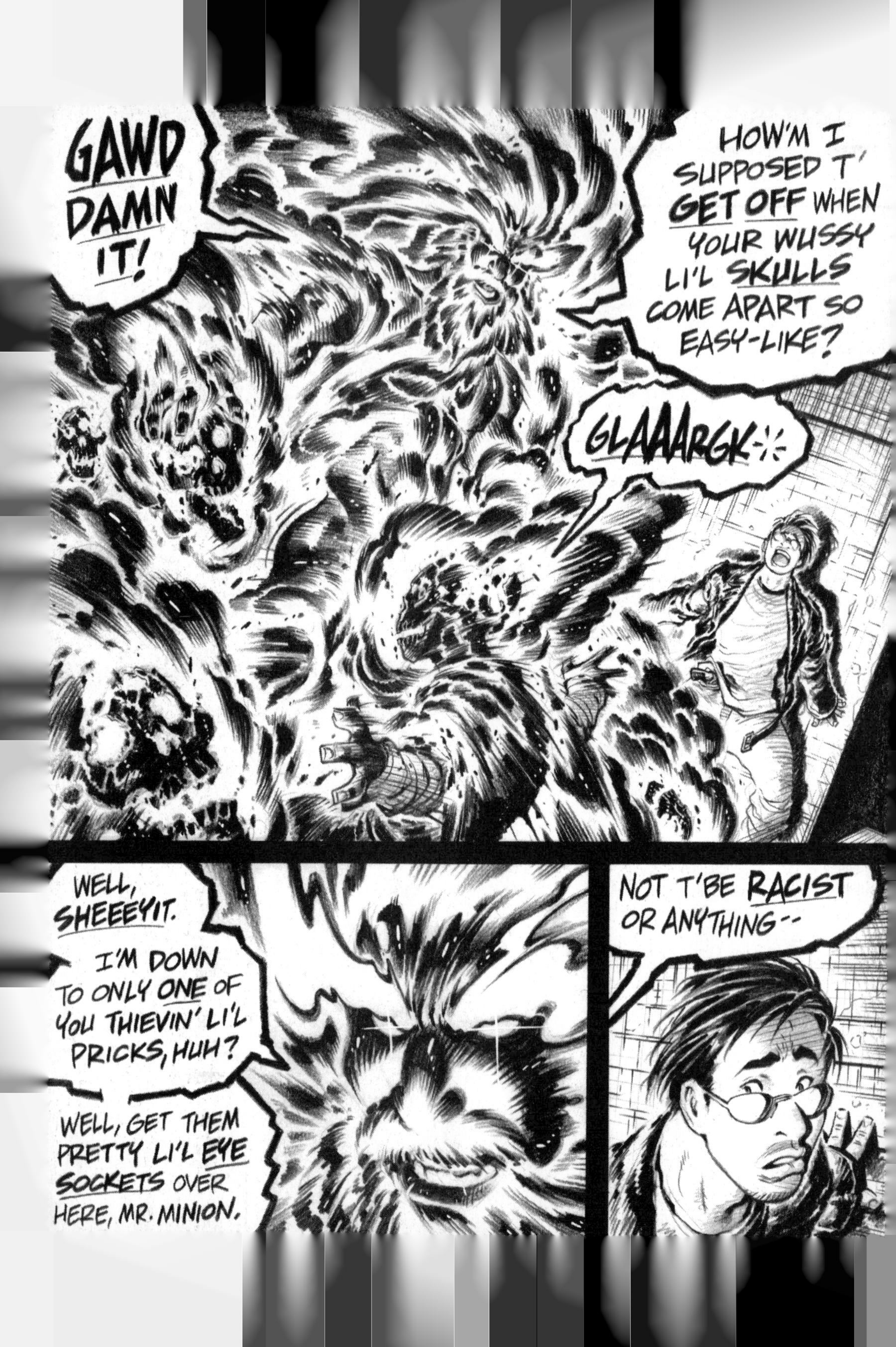
GAWD DAMN IT!
HOW'M I SUPPOSED T' GET OFF WHEN YOUR WUSSY LI'L SKULLS COME APART SO EASY-LIKE?
GLAAAARGK--!
WELL, SHEEEYIT.
I'M DOWN TO ONLY ONE OF YOU THIEVIN' LI'L PRICKS, HUH?
WELL, GET THEM PRETTY LI'L EYE SOCKETS OVER HERE, MR. MINION.
NOT T'BE RACIST OR ANYTHING--

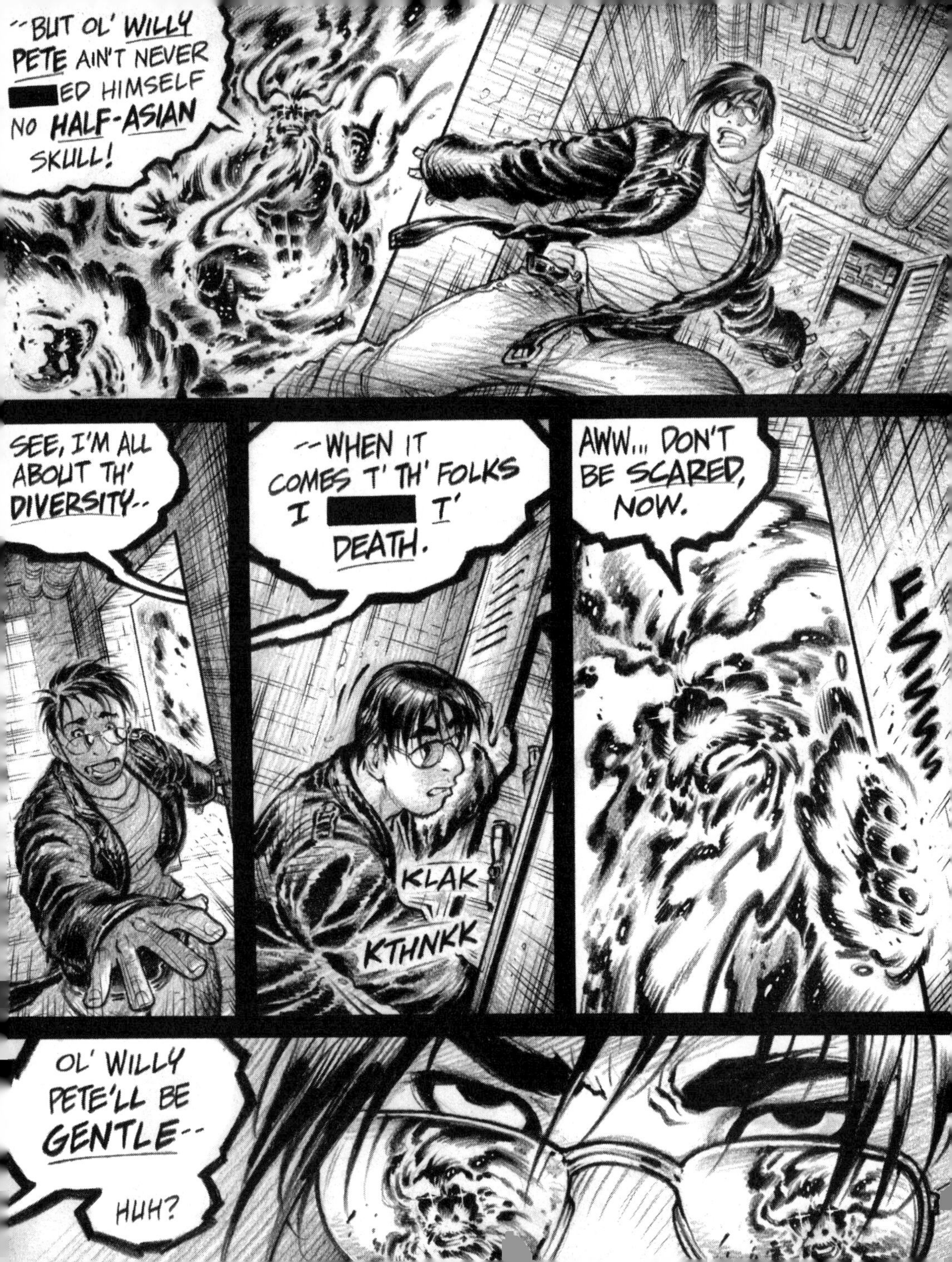
--BUT OL' WILLY PETE AIN'T NEVER [redacted]ED HIMSELF NO HALF-ASIAN SKULL!
SEE, I'M ALL ABOUT TH' DIVERSITY--
--WHEN IT COMES T' TH' FOLKS I [redacted] T' DEATH.
KLAK
KTHNKK
AWW... DON'T BE SCARED, NOW.
FSSSS
OL' WILLY PETE'LL BE GENTLE--
HUH?

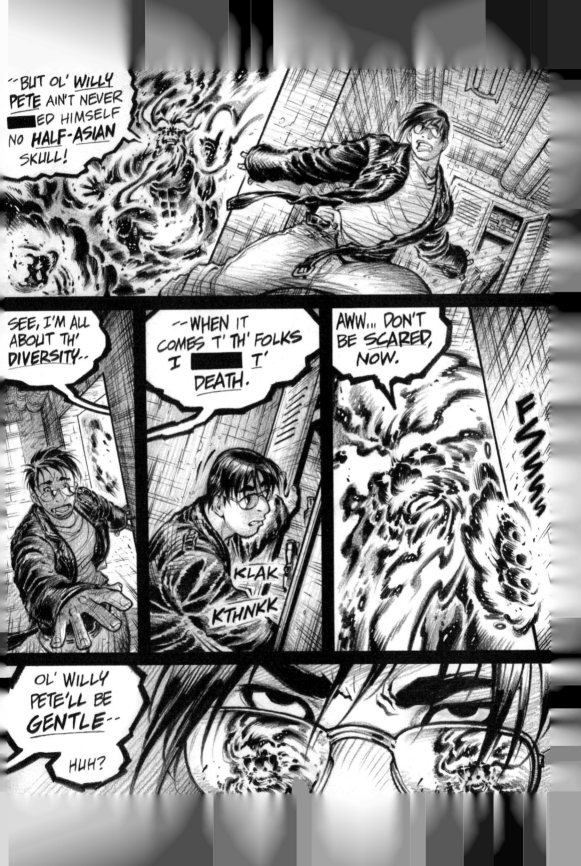

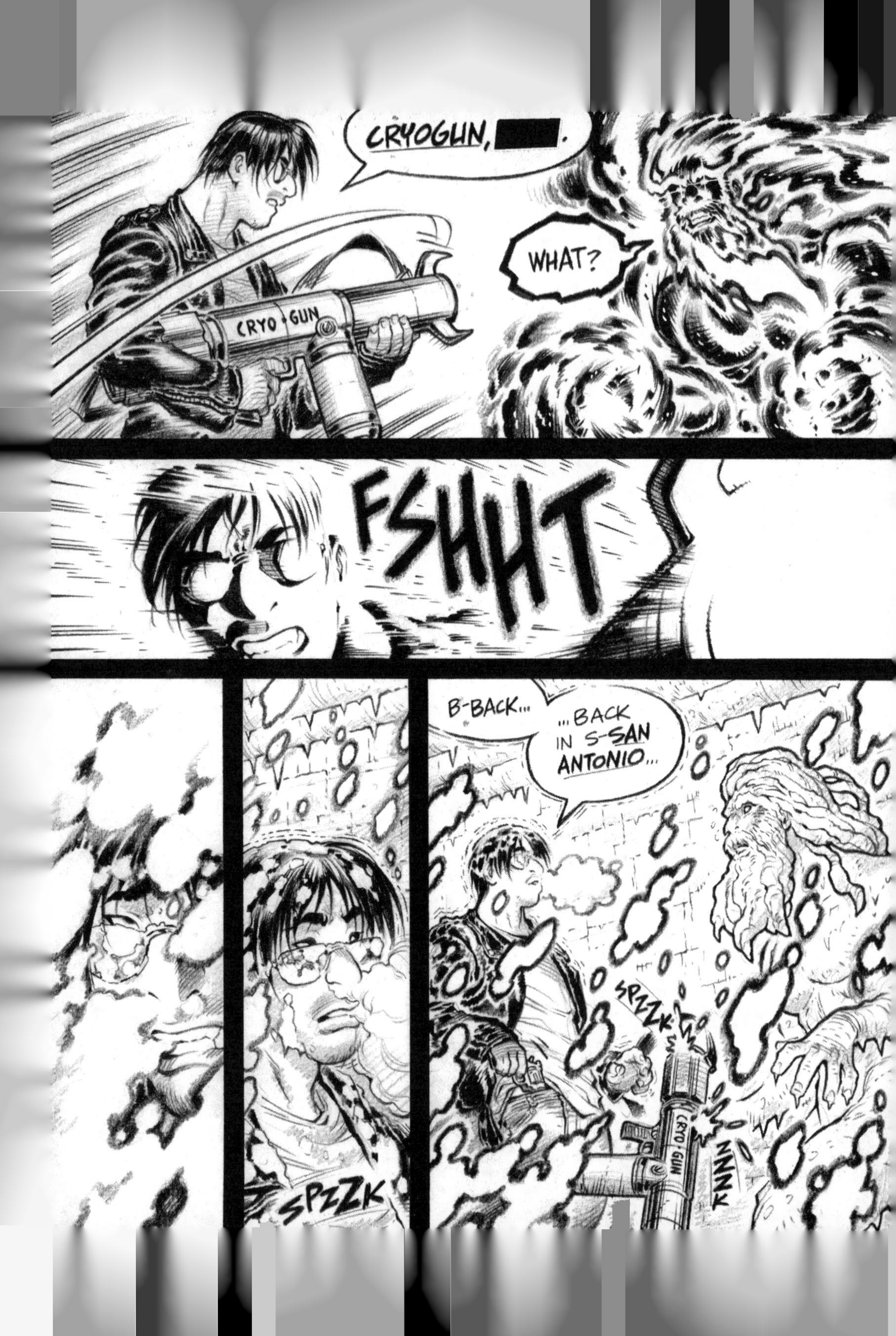
CRYOGUN, [redacted].
CRYO·GUN
WHAT?
FSHHT
SPZZK
B-BACK...
...BACK IN S-SAN ANTONIO...
SPZZK
CRYO·GUN
NNNK

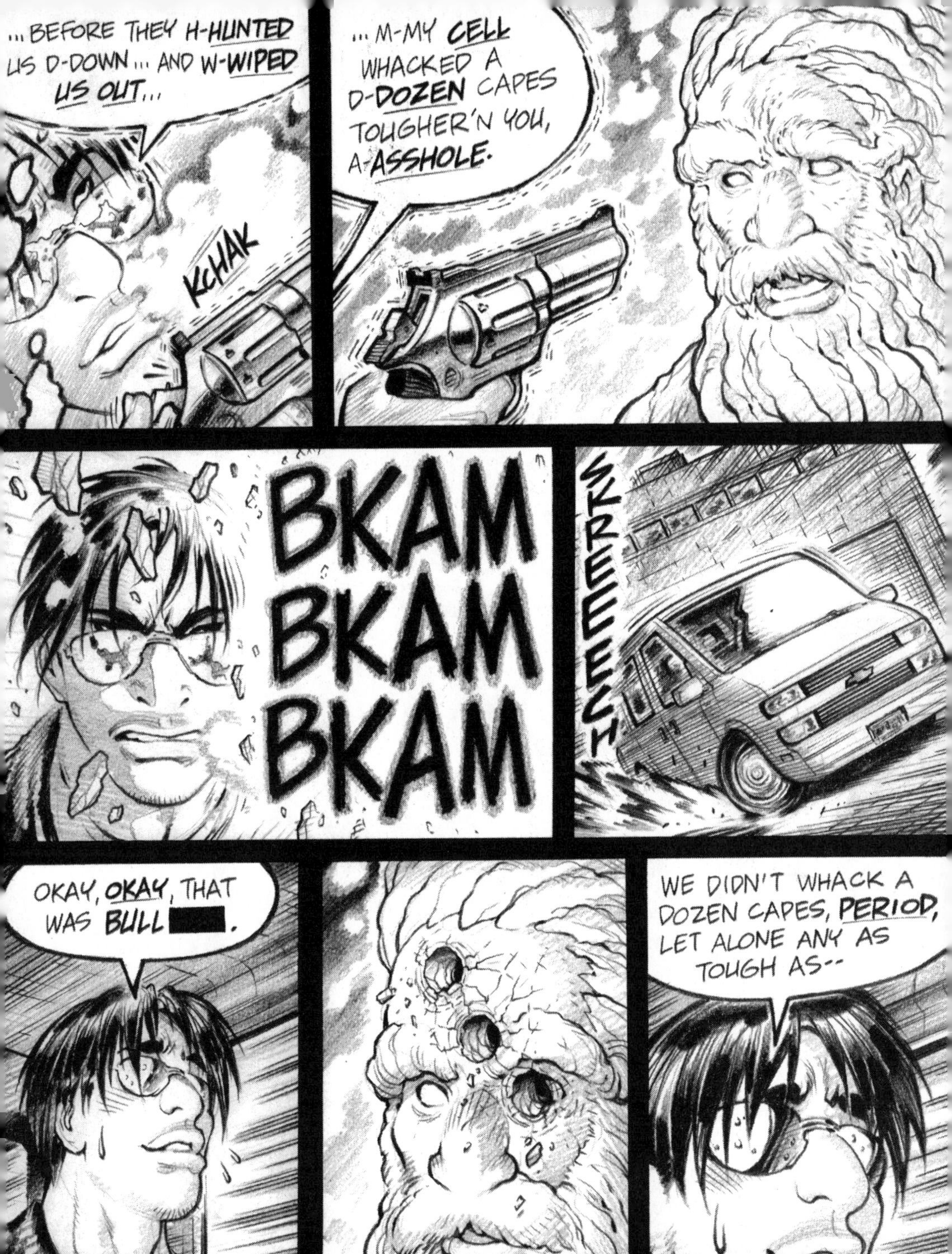
...BEFORE THEY H-HUNTED US D-DOWN... AND W-WIPED US OUT...
KCHAK
...M-MY CELL WHACKED A D-DOZEN CAPES TOUGHER'N YOU, A-ASSHOLE.
BKAM BKAM BKAM
SKREEEECH
OKAY, OKAY, THAT WAS BULL[redacted].
WE DIDN'T WHACK A DOZEN CAPES, PERIOD, LET ALONE ANY AS TOUGH AS--

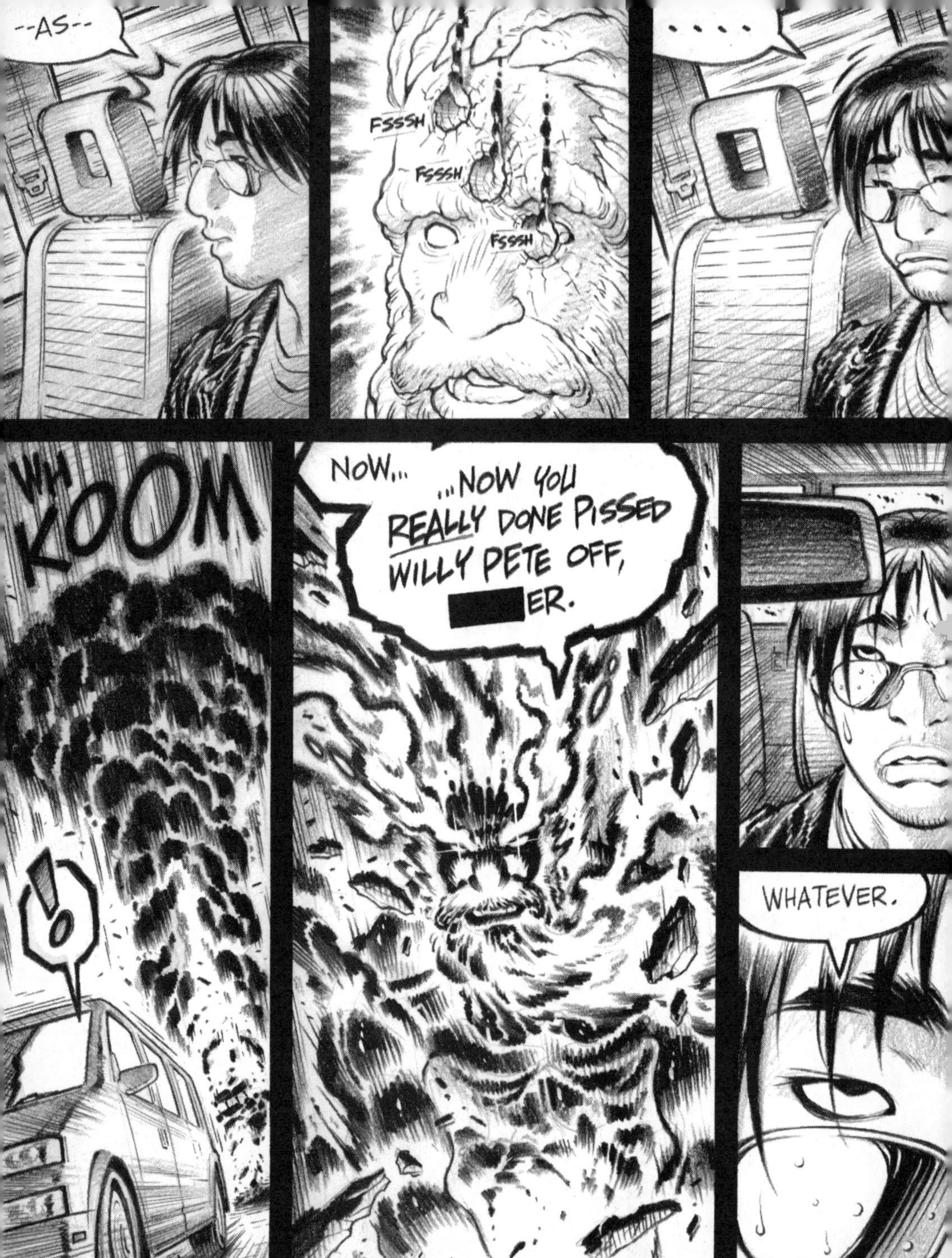
--AS--
FSSSH
FSSSH
FSSSH
. . . .
WH KOOM
!
NOW... ...NOW YOU REALLY DONE PISSED WILLY PETE OFF, [redacted]ER.
WHATEVER.

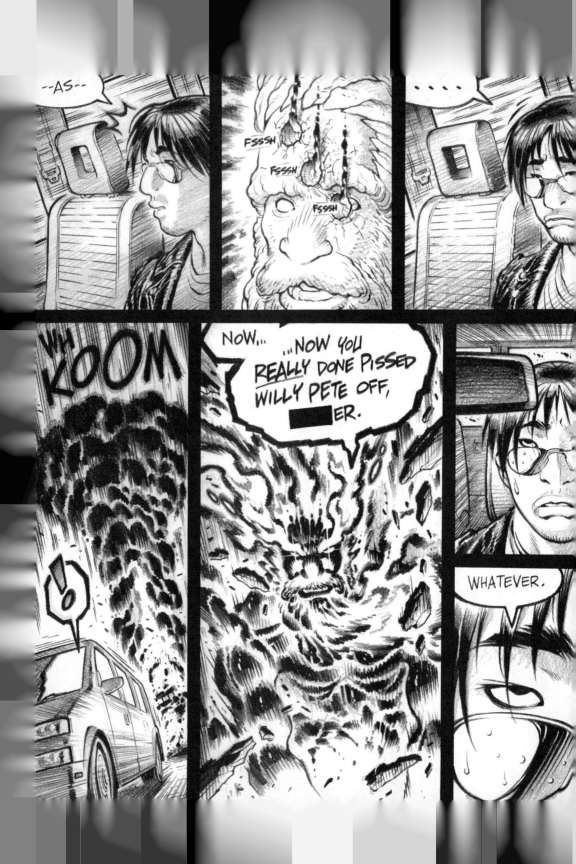

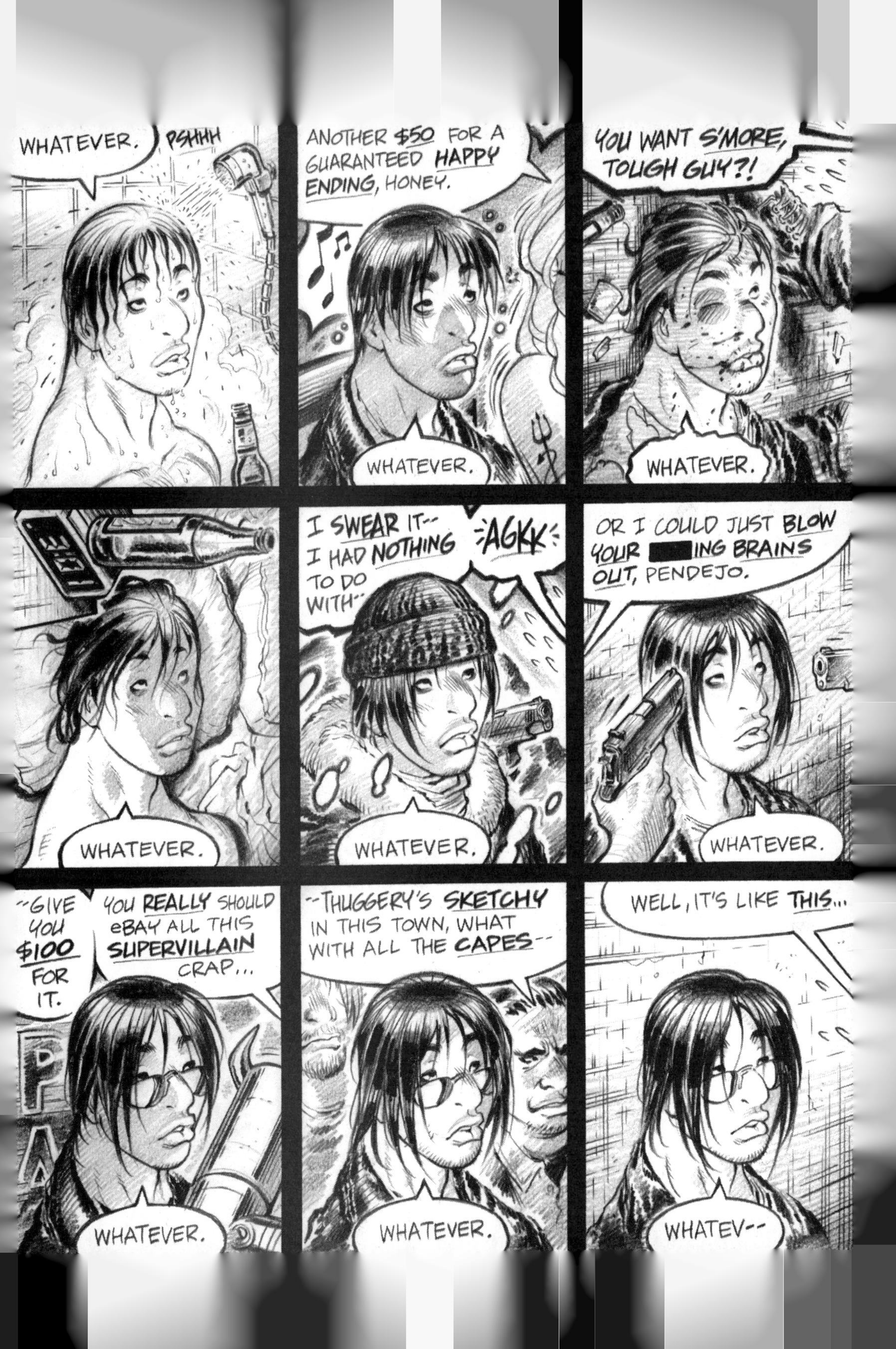
WHATEVER.
PSHHH
ANOTHER $50 FOR A GUARANTEED HAPPY ENDING, HONEY.
WHATEVER.
YOU WANT S'MORE, TOUGH GUY?!
WHATEVER.
WHATEVER.
I SWEAR IT-- I HAD NOTHING TO DO WITH--
AGKK
WHATEVER.
OR I COULD JUST BLOW YOUR [redacted]ING BRAINS OUT, PENDEJO.
WHATEVER.
--GIVE YOU $100 FOR IT.
YOU REALLY SHOULD eBAY ALL THIS SUPERVILLAIN CRAP...
WHATEVER.
--THUGGERY'S SKETCHY IN THIS TOWN, WHAT WITH ALL THE CAPES--
WHATEVER.
WELL, IT'S LIKE THIS...
WHATEV--

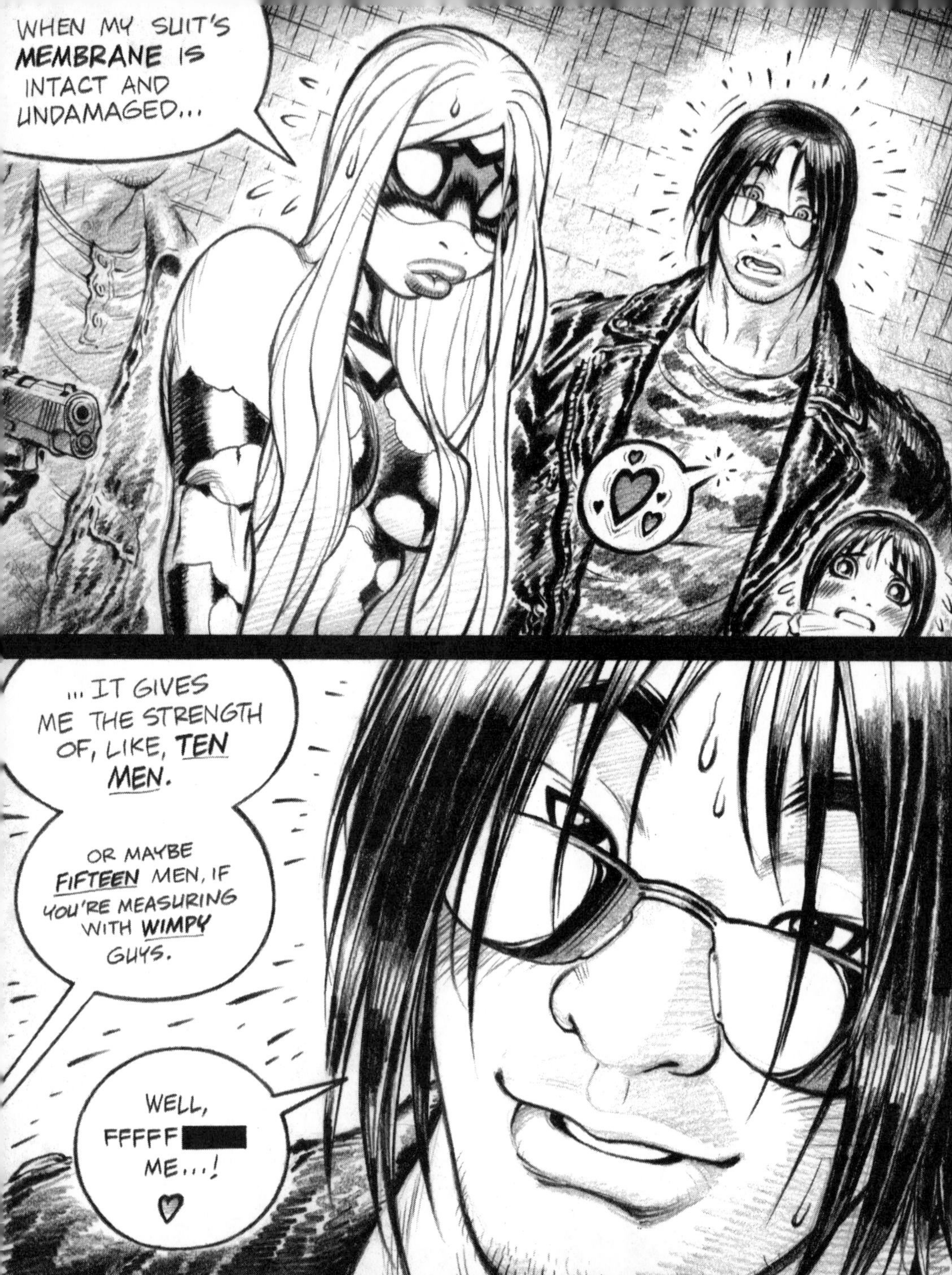
WHEN MY SUIT'S MEMBRANE IS INTACT AND UNDAMAGED...
...IT GIVES ME THE STRENGTH OF, LIKE, TEN MEN.
OR MAYBE FIFTEEN MEN, IF YOU'RE MEASURING WITH WIMPY GUYS.
WELL, FFFFF[redacted] ME...! ♡

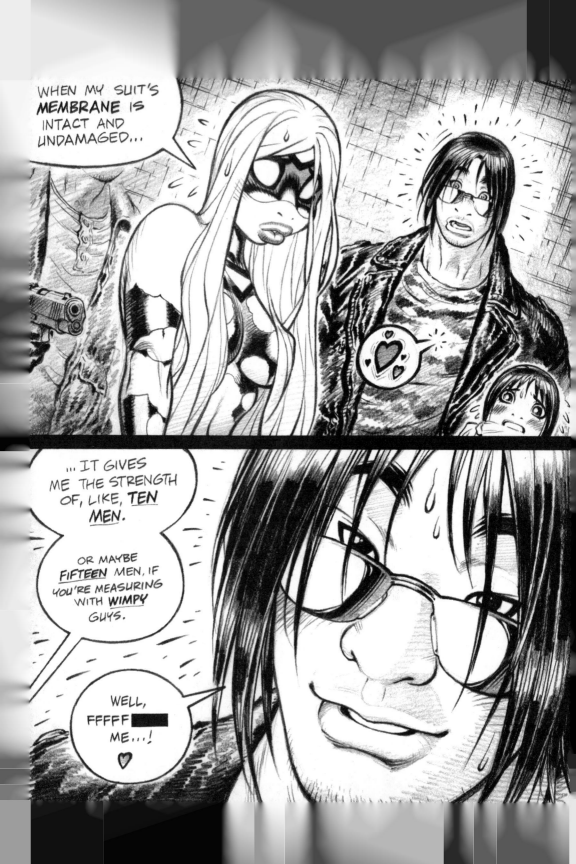

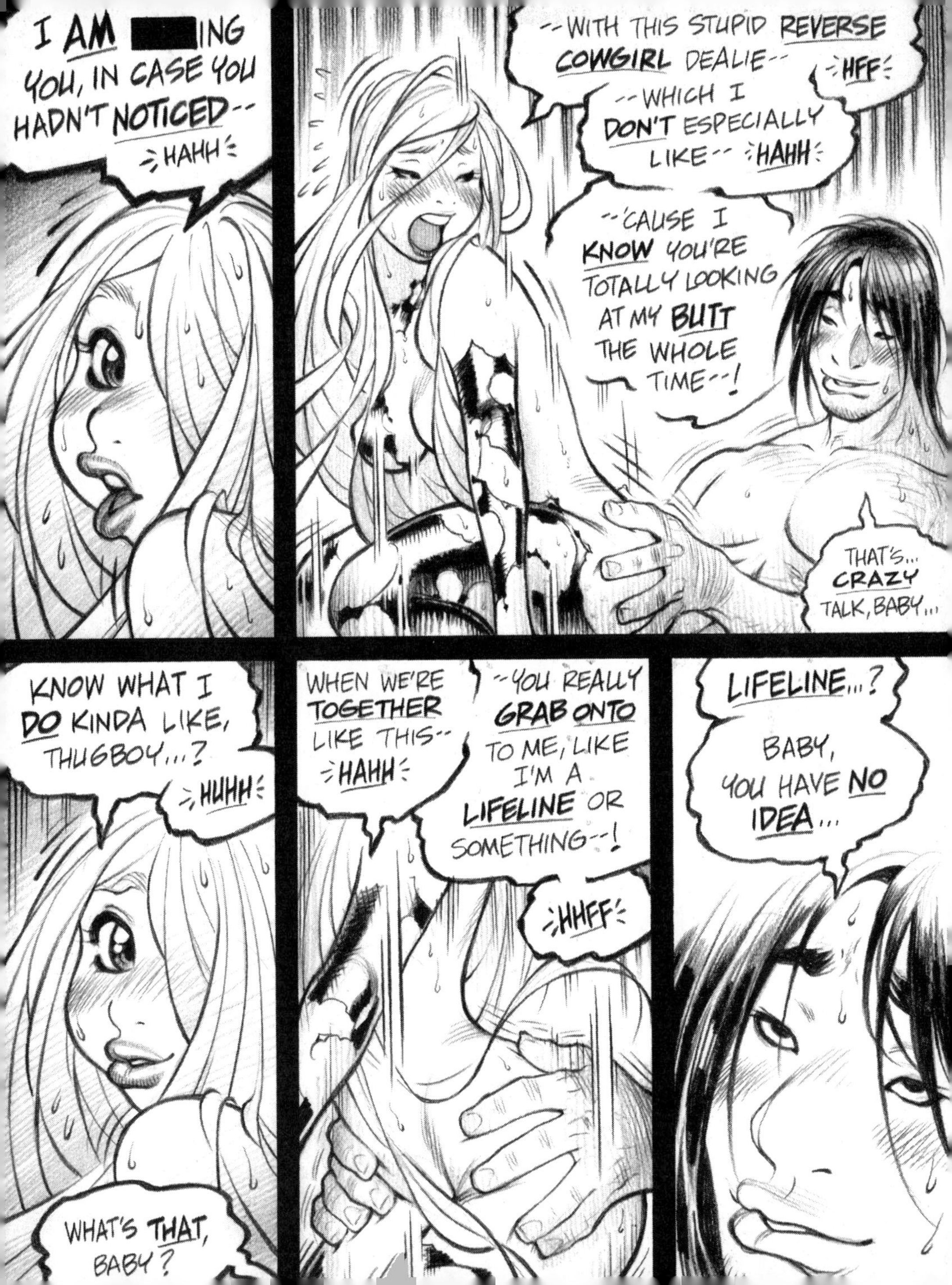
I AM [redacted]ING YOU, IN CASE YOU HADN'T NOTICED--
HAHH
--WITH THIS STUPID REVERSE COWGIRL DEALIE--
HFF
--WHICH I DON'T ESPECIALLY LIKE--
HAHH
--'CAUSE I KNOW YOU'RE TOTALLY LOOKING AT MY BUTT THE WHOLE TIME--!
THAT'S... CRAZY TALK, BABY...
KNOW WHAT I DO KINDA LIKE, THUGBOY...?
HUHH
WHAT'S THAT, BABY?
WHEN WE'RE TOGETHER LIKE THIS--
HAHH
--YOU REALLY GRAB ONTO TO ME, LIKE I'M A LIFELINE OR SOMETHING--!
HHFF
LIFELINE...?
BABY, YOU HAVE NO IDEA...

Empowered™

With Great Hotness . . .

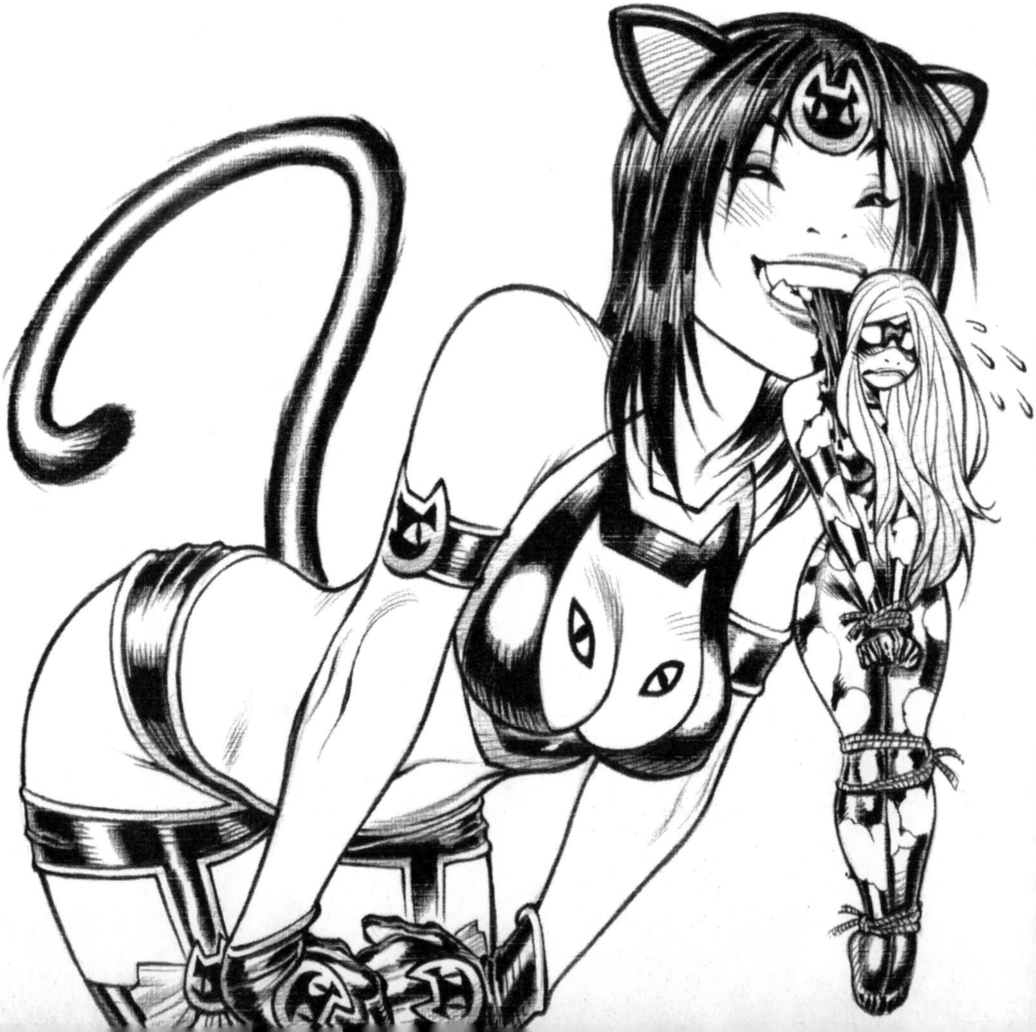

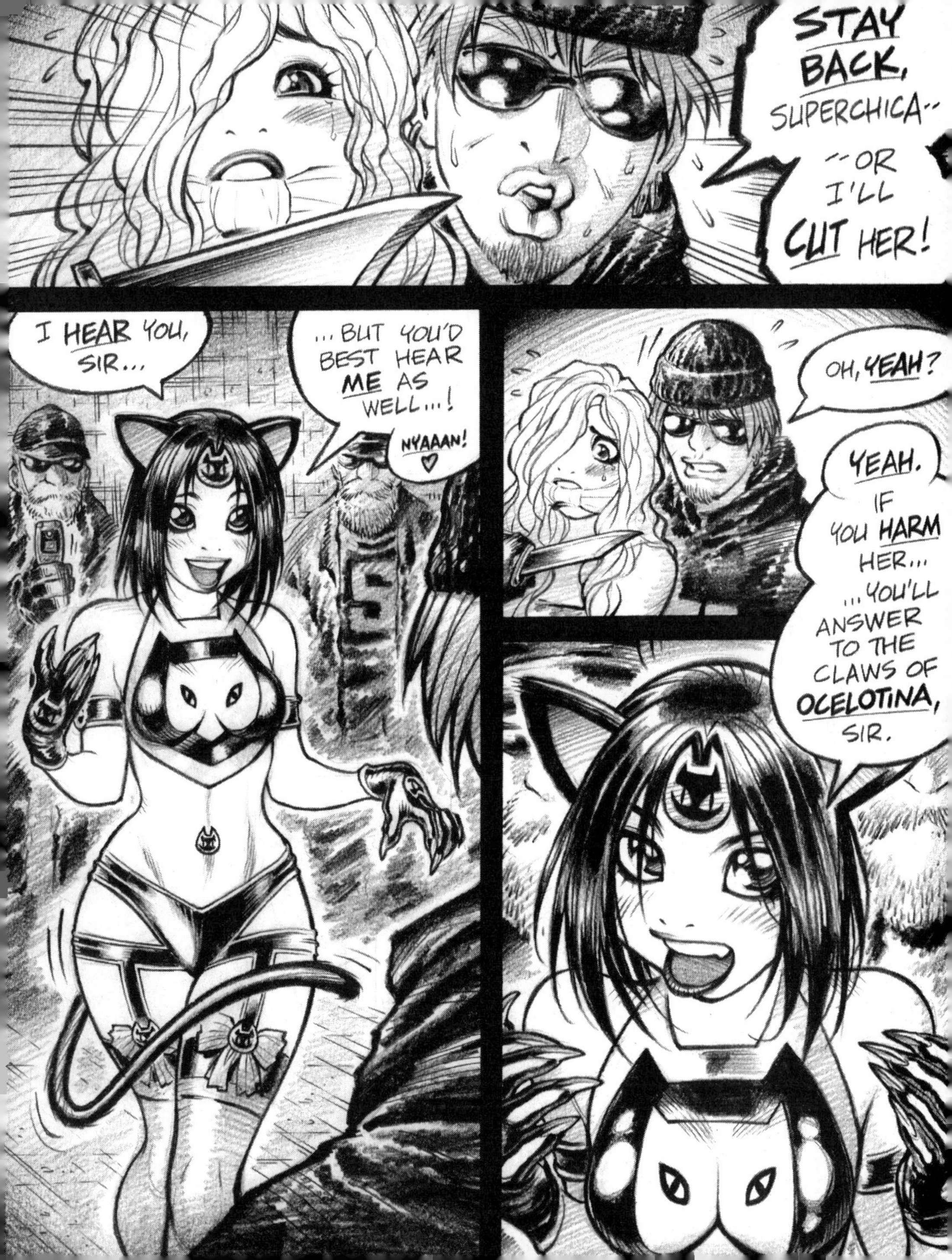
STAY BACK, SUPERCHICA--
--OR I'LL CUT HER!
I HEAR YOU, SIR...
...BUT YOU'D BEST HEAR ME AS WELL...!
NYAAAN!
OH, YEAH?
YEAH.
IF YOU HARM HER...
...YOU'LL ANSWER TO THE CLAWS OF OCELOTINA, SIR.

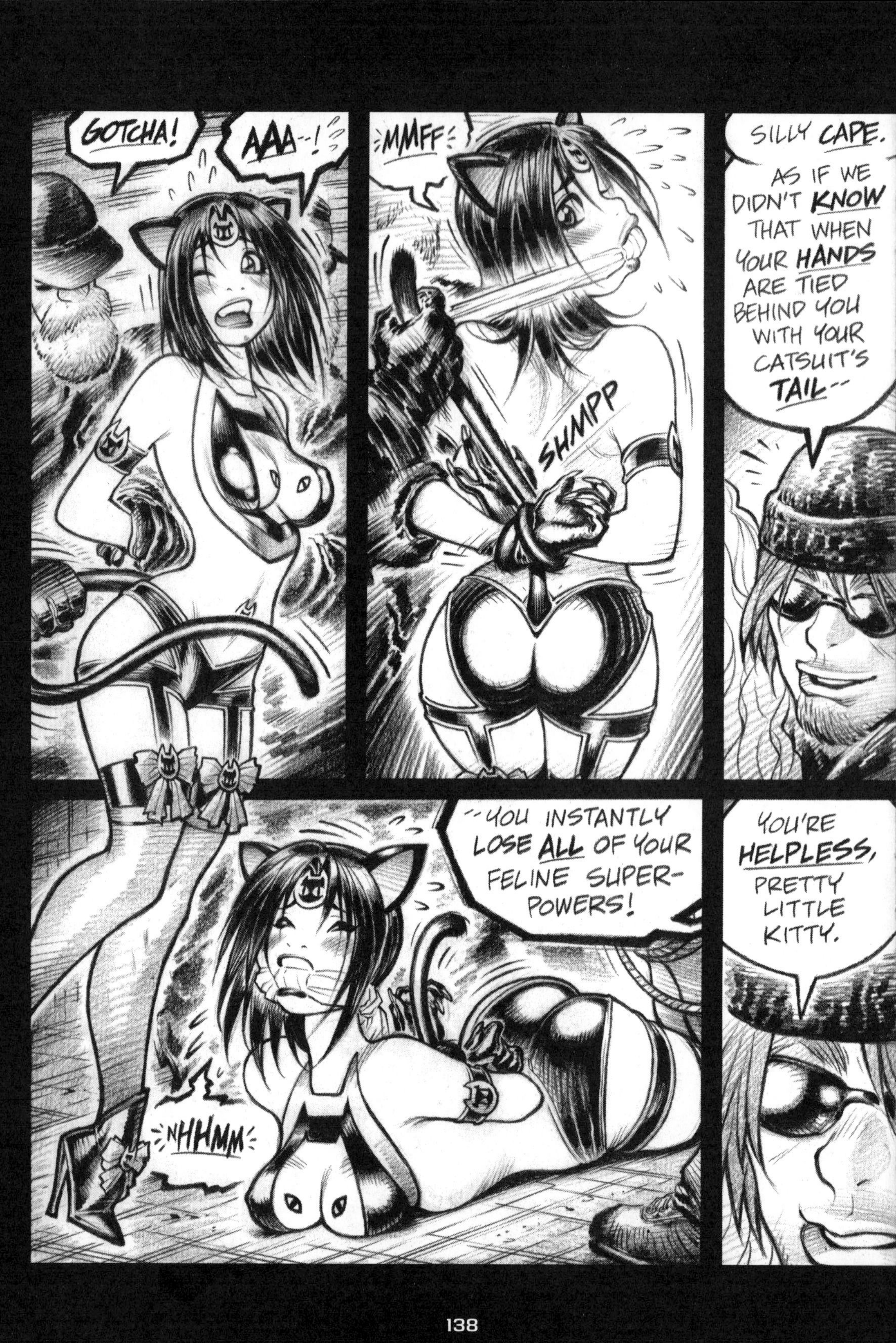
GOTCHA!
AAA--!
MMFF
SHMPP
SILLY CAPE.
AS IF WE DIDN'T KNOW THAT WHEN YOUR HANDS ARE TIED BEHIND YOU WITH YOUR CATSUIT'S TAIL--
--YOU INSTANTLY LOSE ALL OF YOUR FELINE SUPER-POWERS!
NHHMM
YOU'RE HELPLESS, PRETTY LITTLE KITTY.

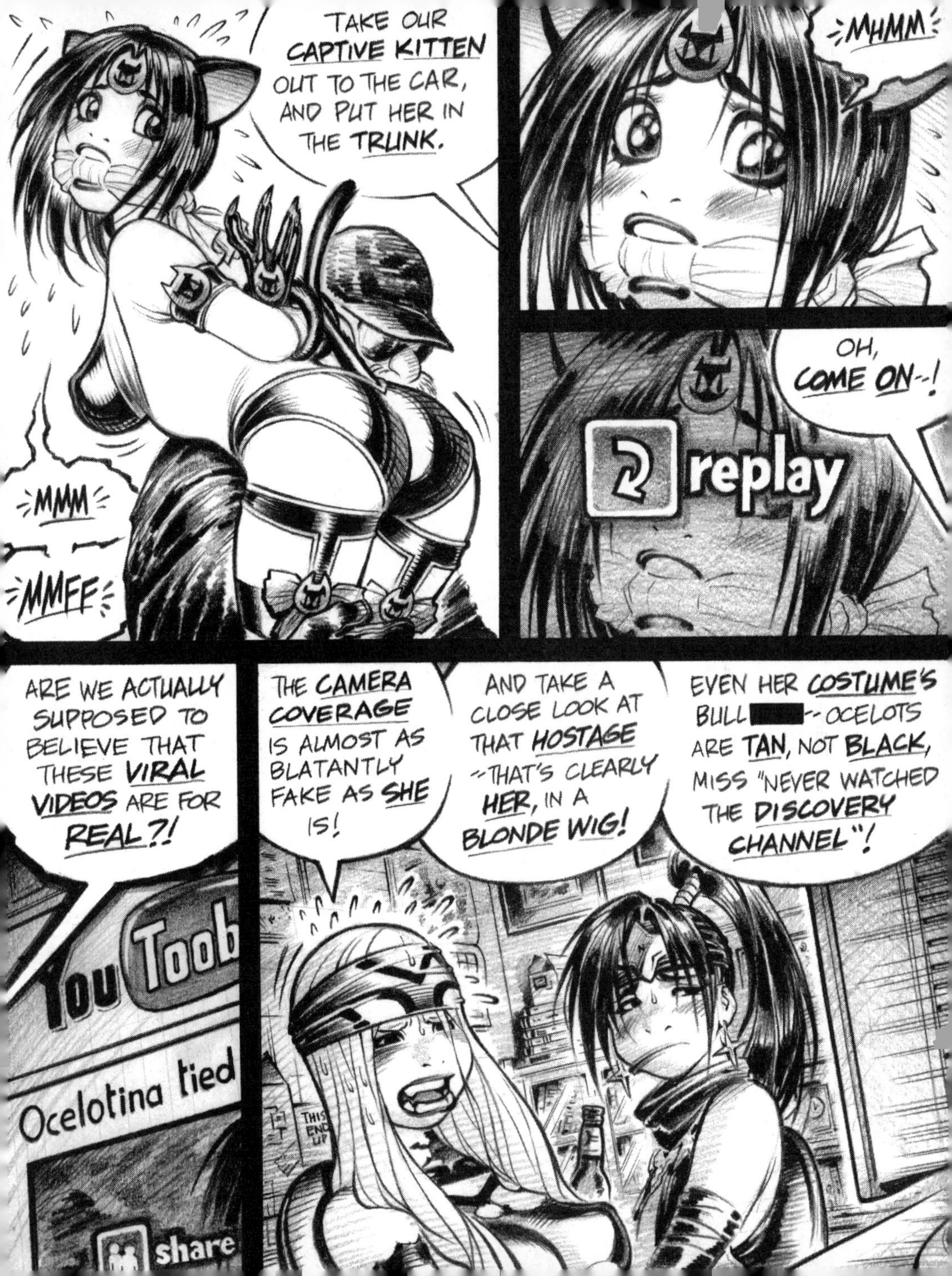
TAKE OUR CAPTIVE KITTEN OUT TO THE CAR, AND PUT HER IN THE TRUNK.
MMM
MMFF
MHMM
replay
OH, COME ON--!
ARE WE ACTUALLY SUPPOSED TO BELIEVE THAT THESE VIRAL VIDEOS ARE FOR REAL?!
YouToob
Ocelotina tied
share
THE CAMERA COVERAGE IS ALMOST AS BLATANTLY FAKE AS SHE IS!
AND TAKE A CLOSE LOOK AT THAT HOSTAGE --THAT'S CLEARLY HER, IN A BLONDE WIG!
EVEN HER COSTUME'S BULL[redacted]--OCELOTS ARE TAN, NOT BLACK, MISS "NEVER WATCHED THE DISCOVERY CHANNEL"!
THIS END UP

AND EXACTLY WHAT ARE HER "**FELINE SUPERPOWERS**" SUPPOSED TO BE?

NO **HINT** OF 'EM IN THESE VIDEOS, OTHER THAN THE ABILITY TO **FLAUNT HERSELF** IN A SKIMPY LITTLE **CATSUIT**!

AND DOES HER "**INSTANT LOSS OF POWERS**" DEALIE --AS **NONEXISTENT** AS THOSE POWERS MIGHT BE--

--DOES THAT SOUND JUST A LITTLE BIT **FAMILIAR**?

SPEAKING OF **FAMILIAR**-- BEFORE SHE BECAME AN INEPT, WANNABE **FAUX SUPERHERO**--

--SHE AND **GOATEE BOY**, THERE, WERE INEPT, WANNABE **CRIMINALS**--

MMMAYBE.

--WHO **FAILED** IN AN ATTEMPT TO **KIDNAP** AND **RANSOM ME**, JUST LIKE IN **THIS** BUNCH OF FAKE VIDEOS--

--EXCEPT THAT THE **REAL-LIFE** INCIDENT WAS EVEN **MORE** HUMILIATING THAN THIS, **OF COURSE**.

BUT NOW SHE'S **SUCCEEDED** IN KIDNAPPING MY **CRAPPY REPUTATION** AS A LAME SUPERHERO--

--AND SHE'S **MAGICALLY TRANSFORMED** IT INTO A WAY TO **MAKE MONEY**, THE ███.

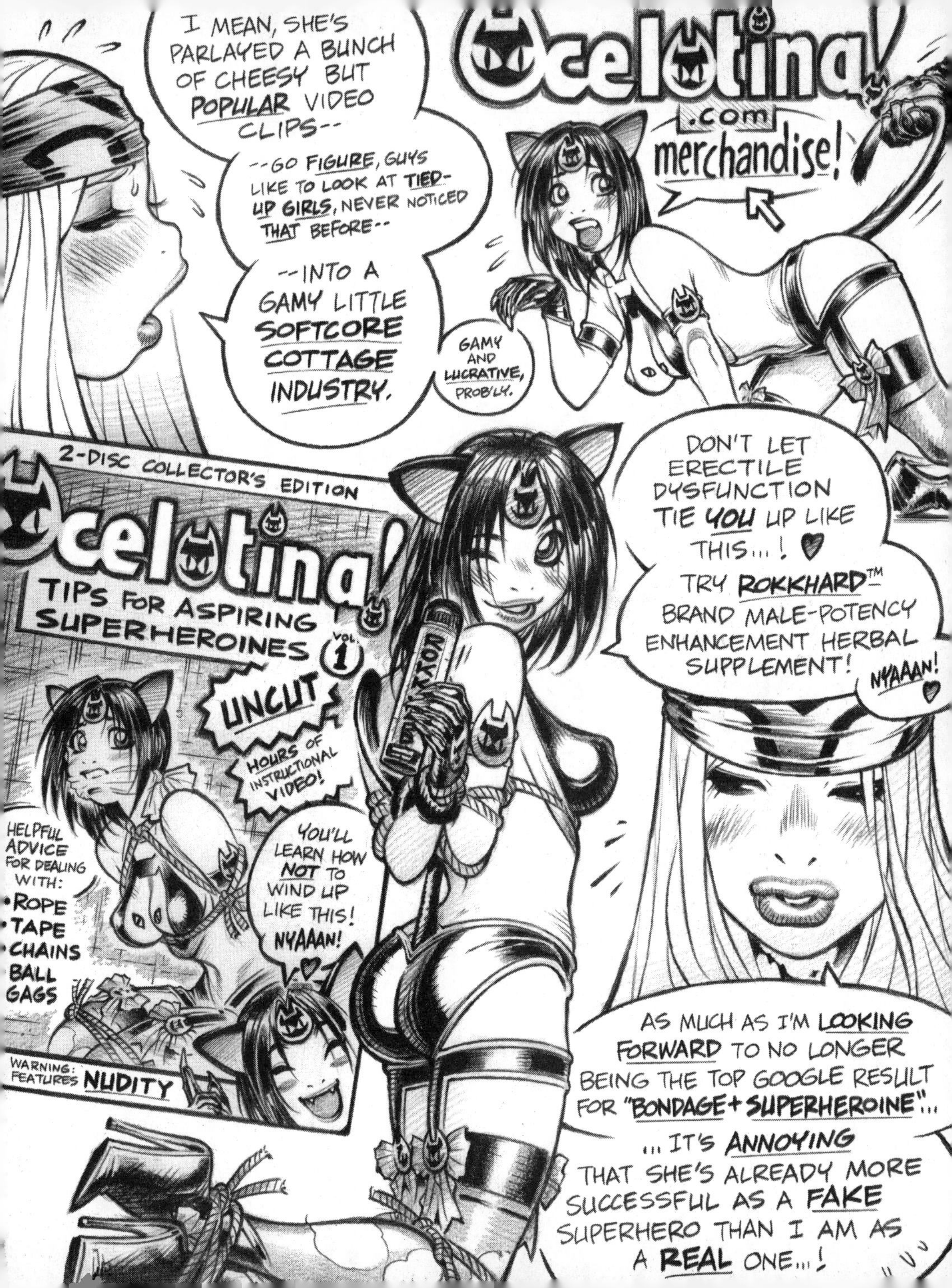
I MEAN, SHE'S PARLAYED A BUNCH OF CHEESY BUT POPULAR VIDEO CLIPS--
--GO FIGURE, GUYS LIKE TO LOOK AT TIED-UP GIRLS, NEVER NOTICED THAT BEFORE--
--INTO A GAMY LITTLE SOFTCORE COTTAGE INDUSTRY.
GAMY AND LUCRATIVE, PROB'LY.
Ocelotina! .com
merchandise!
2-DISC COLLECTOR'S EDITION
Ocelotina!
TIPS FOR ASPIRING SUPERHEROINES VOL. 1
UNCUT
HOURS OF INSTRUCTIONAL VIDEO!
HELPFUL ADVICE FOR DEALING WITH:
• ROPE
• TAPE
• CHAINS
BALL GAGS
YOU'LL LEARN HOW NOT TO WIND UP LIKE THIS! NYAAAN! ♥
WARNING: FEATURES NUDITY
DON'T LET ERECTILE DYSFUNCTION TIE YOU UP LIKE THIS...! ♥
TRY ROKKHARD™ BRAND MALE-POTENCY ENHANCEMENT HERBAL SUPPLEMENT!
NYAAAN! ♥
AS MUCH AS I'M LOOKING FORWARD TO NO LONGER BEING THE TOP GOOGLE RESULT FOR "BONDAGE+SUPERHEROINE"...
...IT'S ANNOYING THAT SHE'S ALREADY MORE SUCCESSFUL AS A FAKE SUPERHERO THAN I AM AS A REAL ONE...!

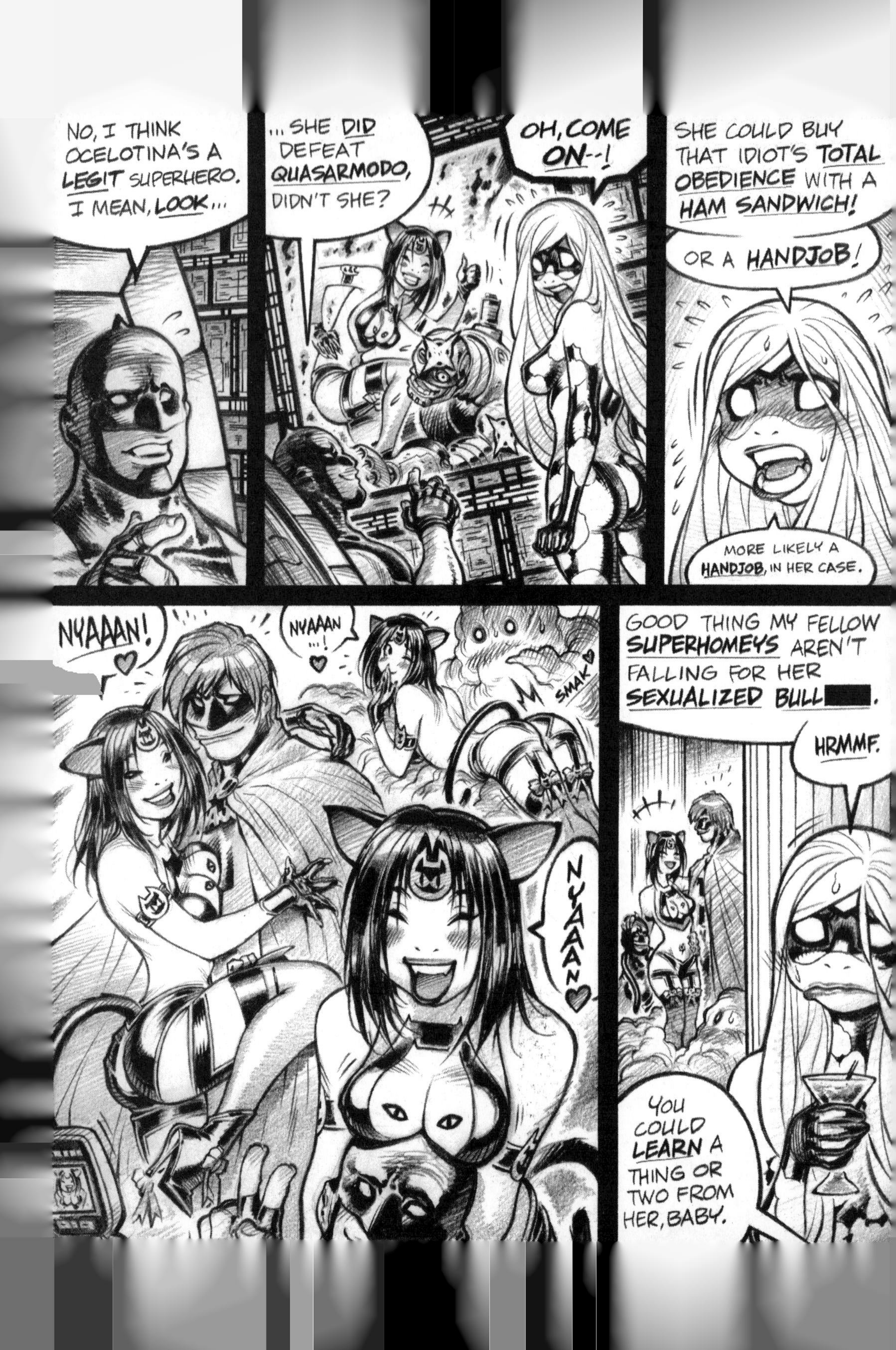

NO, I THINK OCELOTINA'S A LEGIT SUPERHERO. I MEAN, LOOK...
...SHE DID DEFEAT QUASARMODO, DIDN'T SHE?
OH, COME ON--!
SHE COULD BUY THAT IDIOT'S TOTAL OBEDIENCE WITH A HAM SANDWICH!
OR A HANDJOB!
MORE LIKELY A HANDJOB, IN HER CASE.
NYAAAN!
NYAAAN...!
SMAK
NYAAAAN
GOOD THING MY FELLOW SUPERHOMEYS AREN'T FALLING FOR HER SEXUALIZED BULL[redacted].
HRMMF.
YOU COULD LEARN A THING OR TWO FROM HER, BABY.

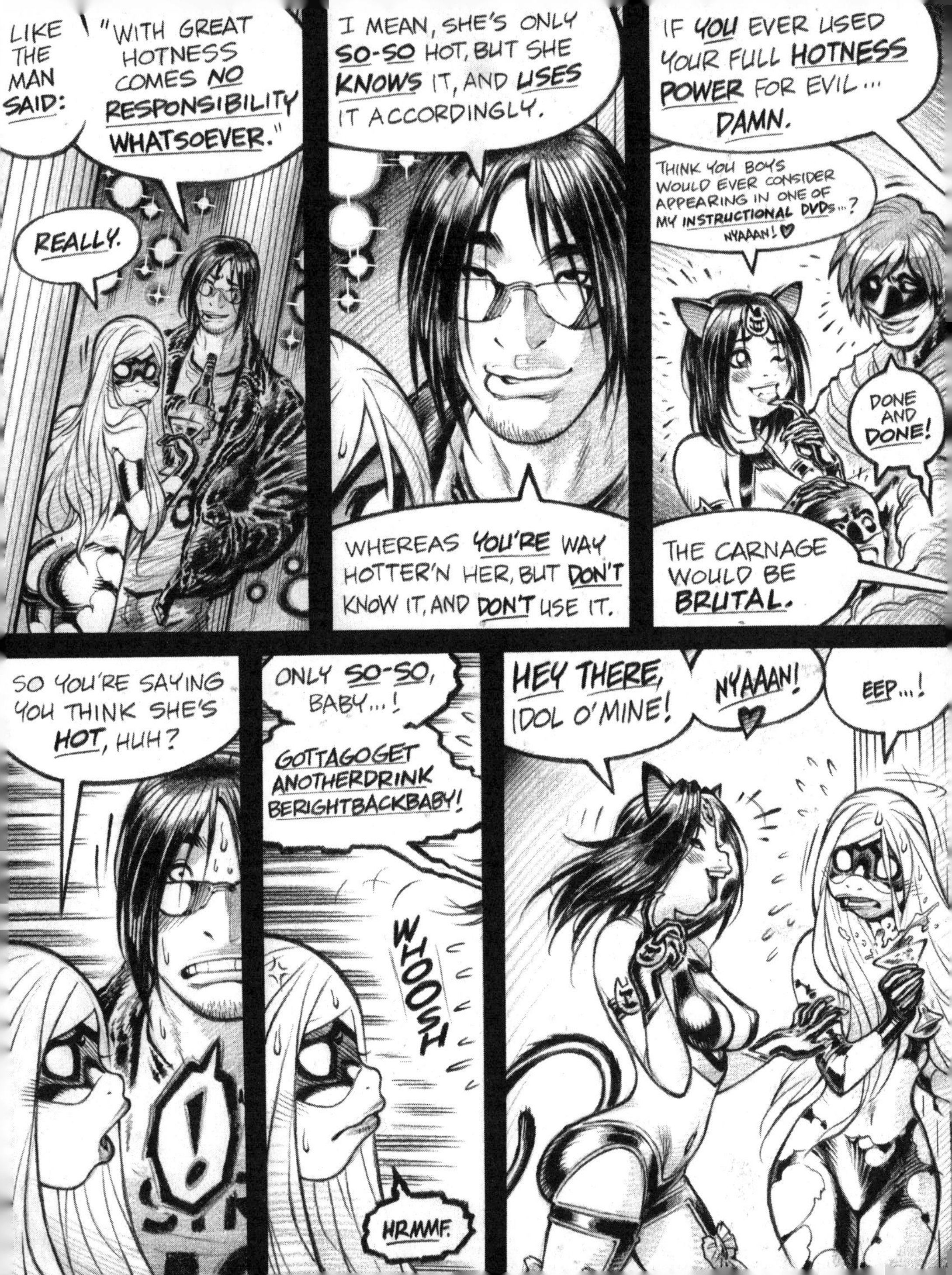
LIKE THE MAN SAID:
"WITH GREAT HOTNESS COMES NO RESPONSIBILITY WHATSOEVER."
REALLY.
I MEAN, SHE'S ONLY SO-SO HOT, BUT SHE KNOWS IT, AND USES IT ACCORDINGLY.
WHEREAS YOU'RE WAY HOTTER'N HER, BUT DON'T KNOW IT, AND DON'T USE IT.
IF YOU EVER USED YOUR FULL HOTNESS POWER FOR EVIL... DAMN.
THINK YOU BOYS WOULD EVER CONSIDER APPEARING IN ONE OF MY INSTRUCTIONAL DVDs...? NYAAAN!
DONE AND DONE!
THE CARNAGE WOULD BE BRUTAL.
SO YOU'RE SAYING YOU THINK SHE'S HOT, HUH?
ONLY SO-SO, BABY...!
GOTTAGOGET ANOTHERDRINK BERIGHTBACKBABY!
WHOOSH
HRMMF.
HEY THERE, IDOL O'MINE!
NYAAAN!
EEP...!

WITHOUT **YOU**, I'D NEVER HAVE THOUGHT OF THE WHOLE **"SEXY, BONDAGE-PRONE SUPERHEROINE"** THING!

WHICH IS A **LICENSE TO PRINT MONEY,** GIRLFRIEND! YOU'RE A **GENIUS!**

"A LICENSE TO PRINT MONEY"...?

SO DOES THIS MEAN I DON'T HAVE TO WORRY ABOUT YOU TRYING TO KIDNAP AND **RANSOM** ME AGAIN...?

OH, HEH... **SORRY** 'BOUT THAT, 'KAY? I **REALLY** DIDN'T HAVE MUCH OF A **BUSINESS PLAN,** BACK THEN...

AND, UM, **FEELING YOU UP** THE WAY I DID... THAT WAS KIND OF A VIOLATION OF THE **"UNWRITTEN RULES,"** WASN'T IT...?

OOPSIE ...!

YES, THAT WAS JUST A **TAD** INAPPROPRIATE, OKAY...?

BUT, **C'MON**... EVERYONE KNOWS THAT THE **RULES** JUST DON'T **APPLY** WHEN IT COMES TO **REALLY CUTE GIRLS** LIKE OURSELVES, RIGHT?

NYAAAN! ♥

TEE HEE!

WHY ARE YOU FLASHING CLEAVAGE AT **ME**...?

...THOUGH THE **"UNWRITTEN RULES"** ARE KINDA **USEFUL** FOR MY BUSINESS, 'CAUSE THEY GIVE SUPERHEROINES SOME EXTRA **FORBIDDEN-FRUITY** APPEAL...!

KEH, KEH, KEH...

OH, HEY, I WANTED TO **ASK YOU**... HOW MUCH DID YOU GET FROM THOSE **ADVANCED RESTRAINT RESEARCH** JACKASSES FOR THOSE **PROMO VIDEOS** YOU SHOT FOR 'EM?

HOW MUCH DID I **GET** ...?

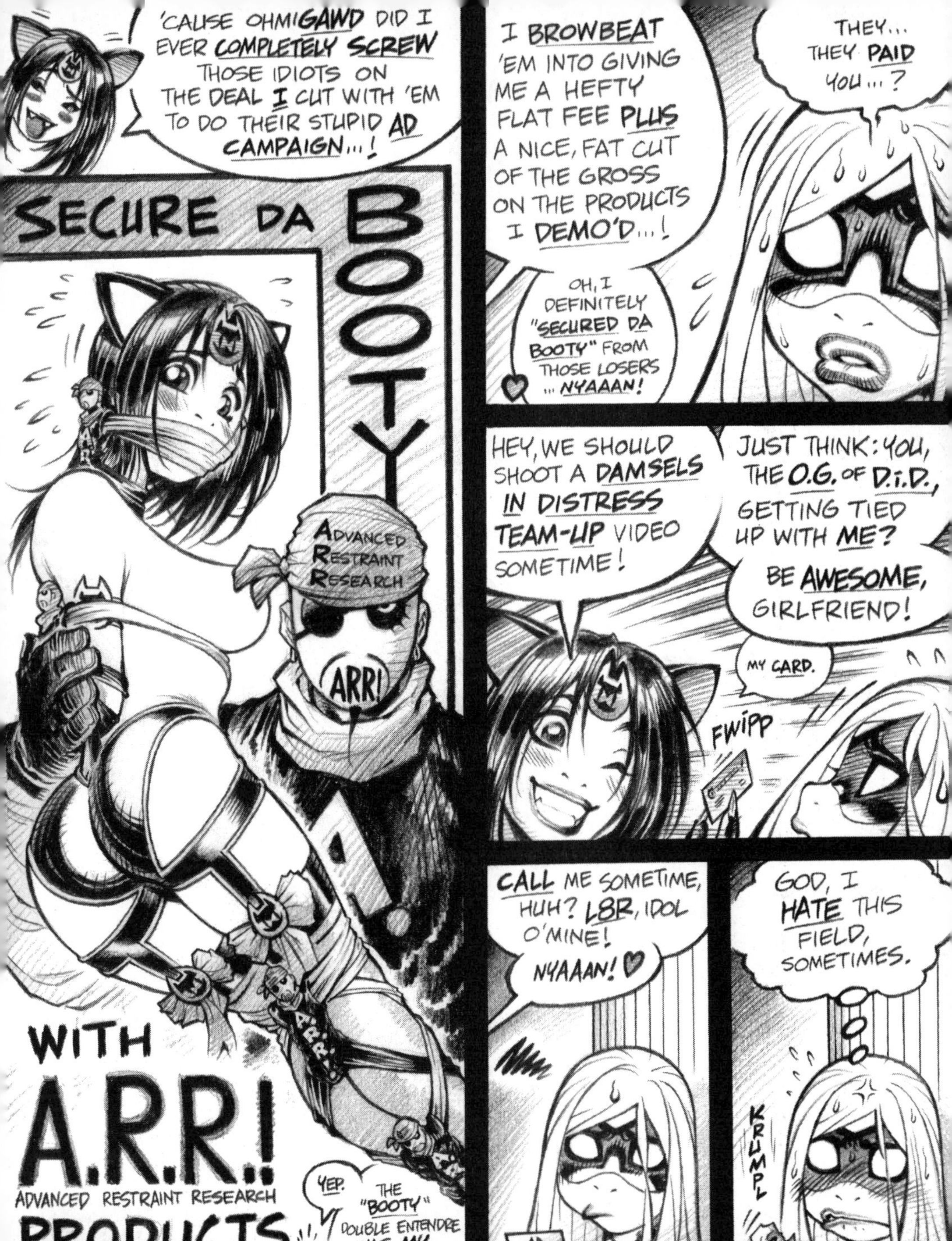
'CAUSE OHMIGAWD DID I EVER COMPLETELY SCREW THOSE IDIOTS ON THE DEAL I CUT WITH 'EM TO DO THEIR STUPID AD CAMPAIGN...!
SECURE DA BOOTY!
ADVANCED RESTRAINT RESEARCH
ARR!
A.R.R.
WITH A.R.R.! ADVANCED RESTRAINT RESEARCH PRODUCTS
YEP.
THE "BOOTY" DOUBLE ENTENDRE WAS MY IDEA! ♡
I BROWBEAT 'EM INTO GIVING ME A HEFTY FLAT FEE PLUS A NICE, FAT CUT OF THE GROSS ON THE PRODUCTS I DEMO'D...!
OH, I DEFINITELY "SECURED DA BOOTY" FROM THOSE LOSERS ...NYAAAN! ♡
THEY... THEY PAID YOU...?
HEY, WE SHOULD SHOOT A DAMSELS IN DISTRESS TEAM-UP VIDEO SOMETIME!
JUST THINK: YOU, THE O.G. OF D.i.D., GETTING TIED UP WITH ME?
BE AWESOME, GIRLFRIEND!
MY CARD.
FWIPP
CALL ME SOMETIME, HUH? L8R, IDOL O'MINE!
NYAAAN! ♡
GOD, I HATE THIS FIELD, SOMETIMES.
KRUMPL

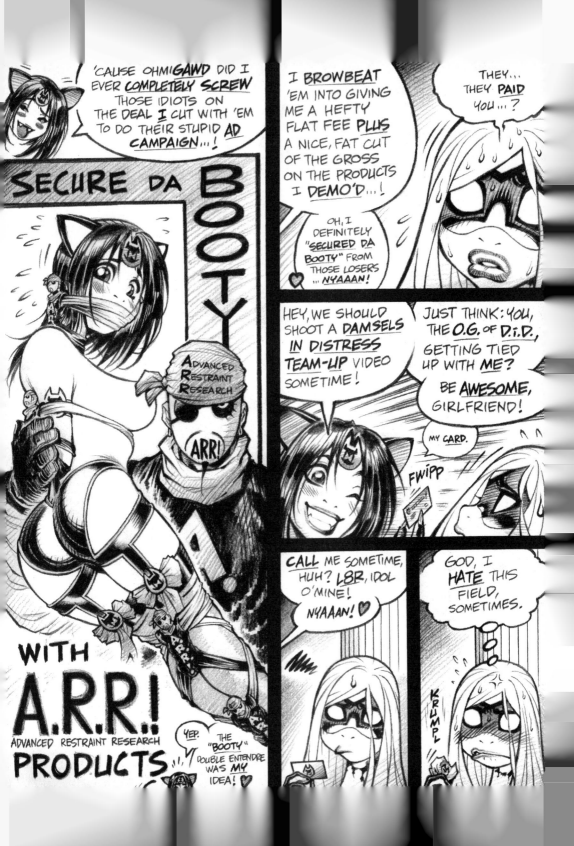

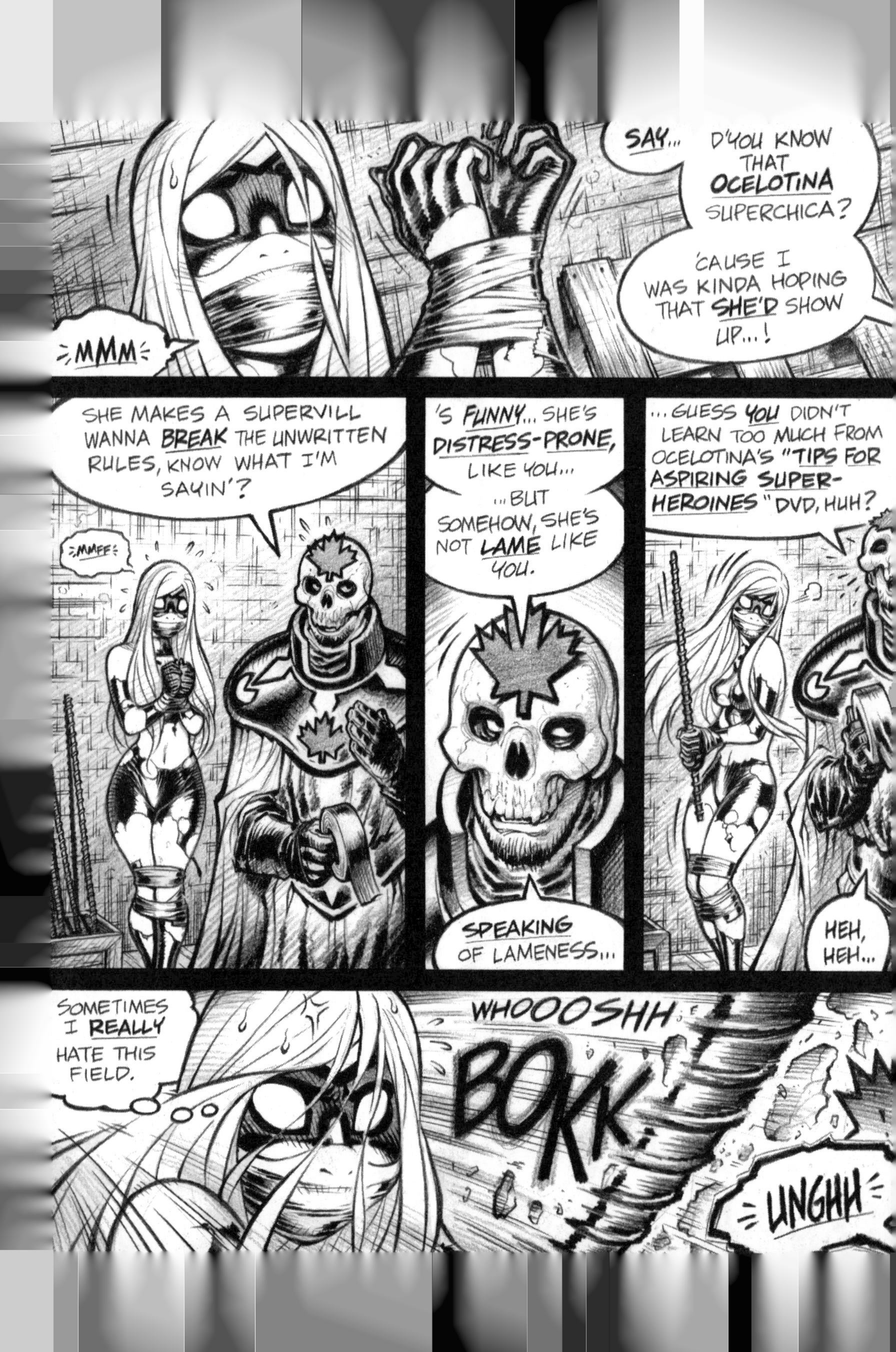
SAY... D'YOU KNOW THAT OCELOTINA SUPERCHICA?
'CAUSE I WAS KINDA HOPING THAT SHE'D SHOW UP...!
MMM
SHE MAKES A SUPERVILL WANNA BREAK THE UNWRITTEN RULES, KNOW WHAT I'M SAYIN'?
MMFF
'S FUNNY... SHE'S DISTRESS-PRONE, LIKE YOU...
...BUT SOMEHOW, SHE'S NOT LAME LIKE YOU.
SPEAKING OF LAMENESS...
...GUESS YOU DIDN'T LEARN TOO MUCH FROM OCELOTINA'S "TIPS FOR ASPIRING SUPER-HEROINES" DVD, HUH?
HEH, HEH...
SOMETIMES I REALLY HATE THIS FIELD.
WHOOOSHH
BOKK
UNGHH

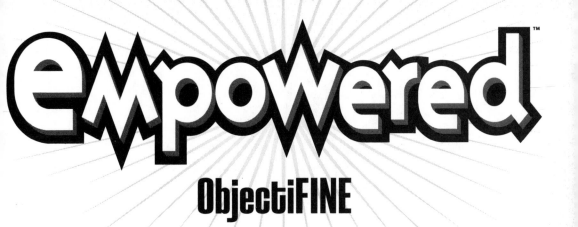

EMPOWERED™

ObjectiFINE

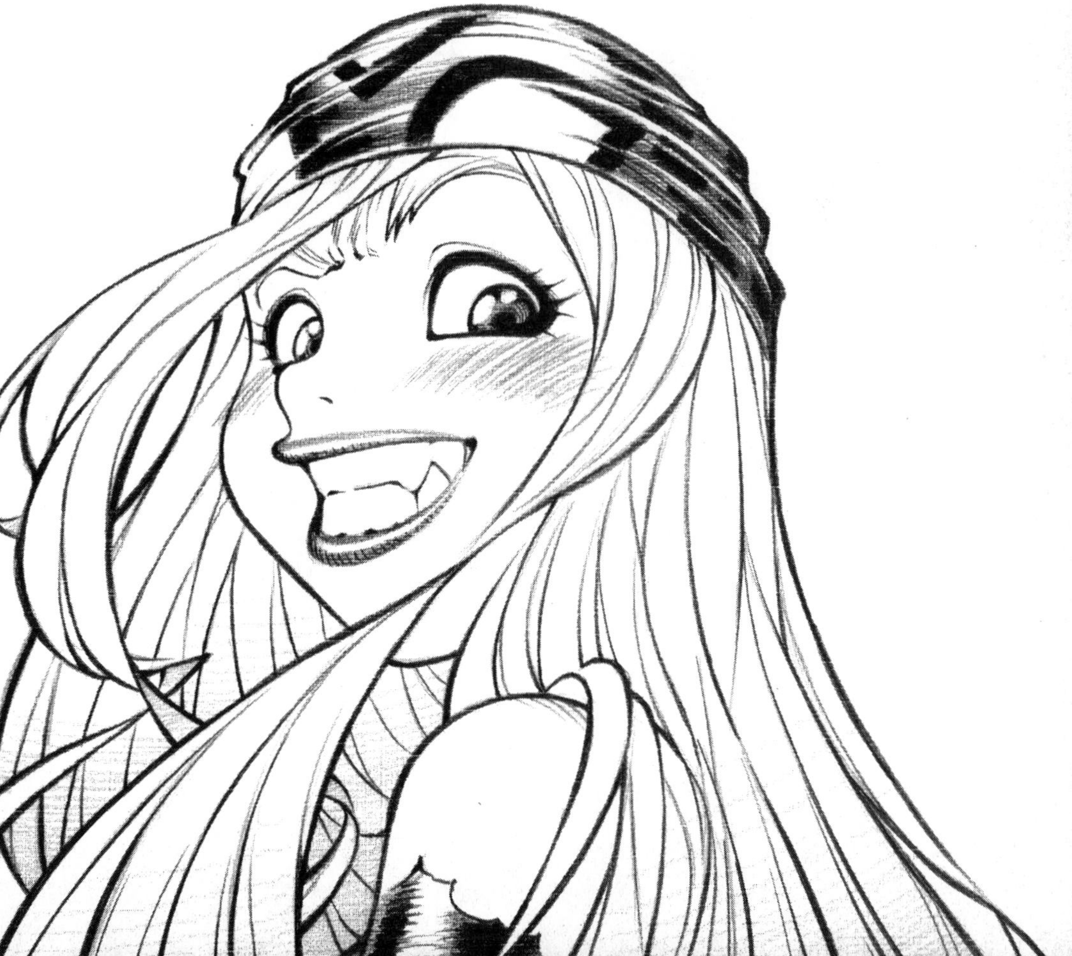

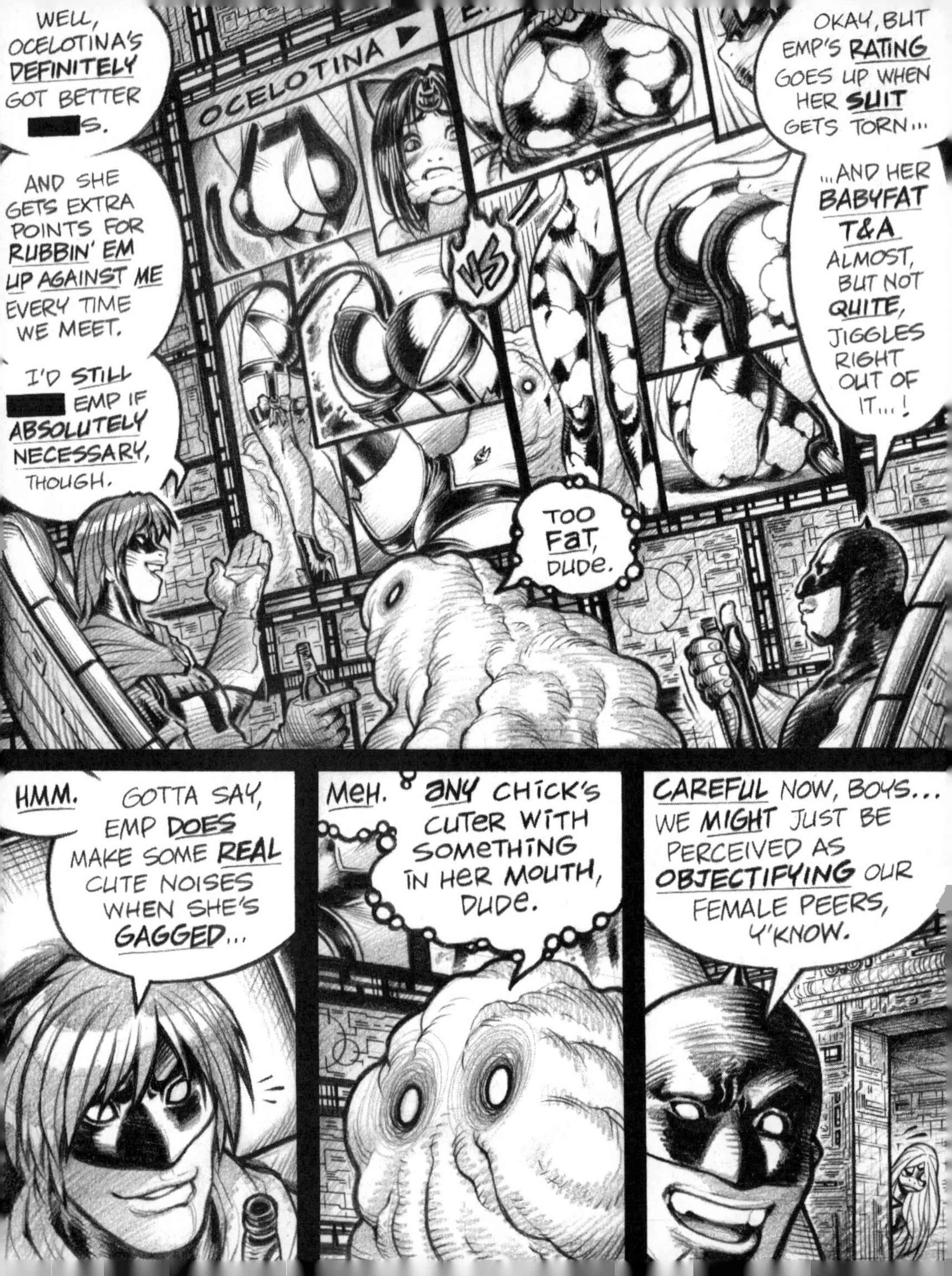
OCELOTINA ▶
OCELOTINA
VS
WELL, OCELOTINA'S DEFINITELY GOT BETTER [redacted]S.
AND SHE GETS EXTRA POINTS FOR RUBBIN' EM UP AGAINST ME EVERY TIME WE MEET.
I'D STILL [redacted] EMP IF ABSOLUTELY NECESSARY, THOUGH.
OKAY, BUT EMP'S RATING GOES UP WHEN HER SUIT GETS TORN...
...AND HER BABYFAT T&A ALMOST, BUT NOT QUITE, JIGGLES RIGHT OUT OF IT...!
TOO FAT, DUDE.
HMM.
GOTTA SAY, EMP DOES MAKE SOME REAL CUTE NOISES WHEN SHE'S GAGGED...
MEH.
ANY CHICK'S CUTER WITH SOMETHING IN HER MOUTH, DUDE.
CAREFUL NOW, BOYS... WE MIGHT JUST BE PERCEIVED AS OBJECTIFYING OUR FEMALE PEERS, Y'KNOW.

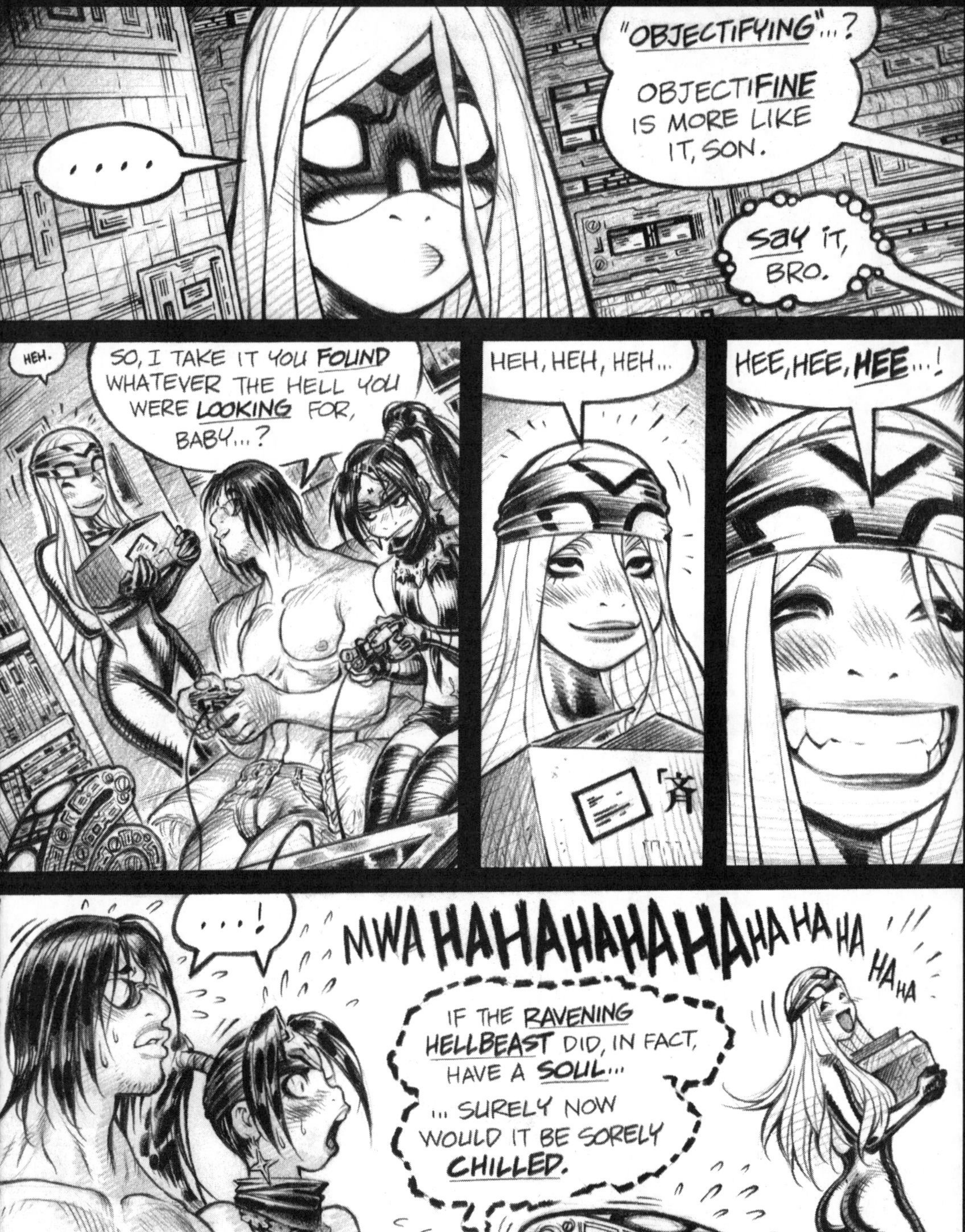
....
"OBJECTIFYING"...?
OBJECTIFINE IS MORE LIKE IT, SON.
SAY IT, BRO.
HEH.
SO, I TAKE IT YOU FOUND WHATEVER THE HELL YOU WERE LOOKING FOR, BABY...?
HEH, HEH, HEH...
「斉
HEE, HEE, HEE...!
...!
MWA HAHAHAHAHAHAHAHA HA HA HA HA HA
IF THE RAVENING HELLBEAST DID, IN FACT, HAVE A SOUL...
... SURELY NOW WOULD IT BE SORELY CHILLED.

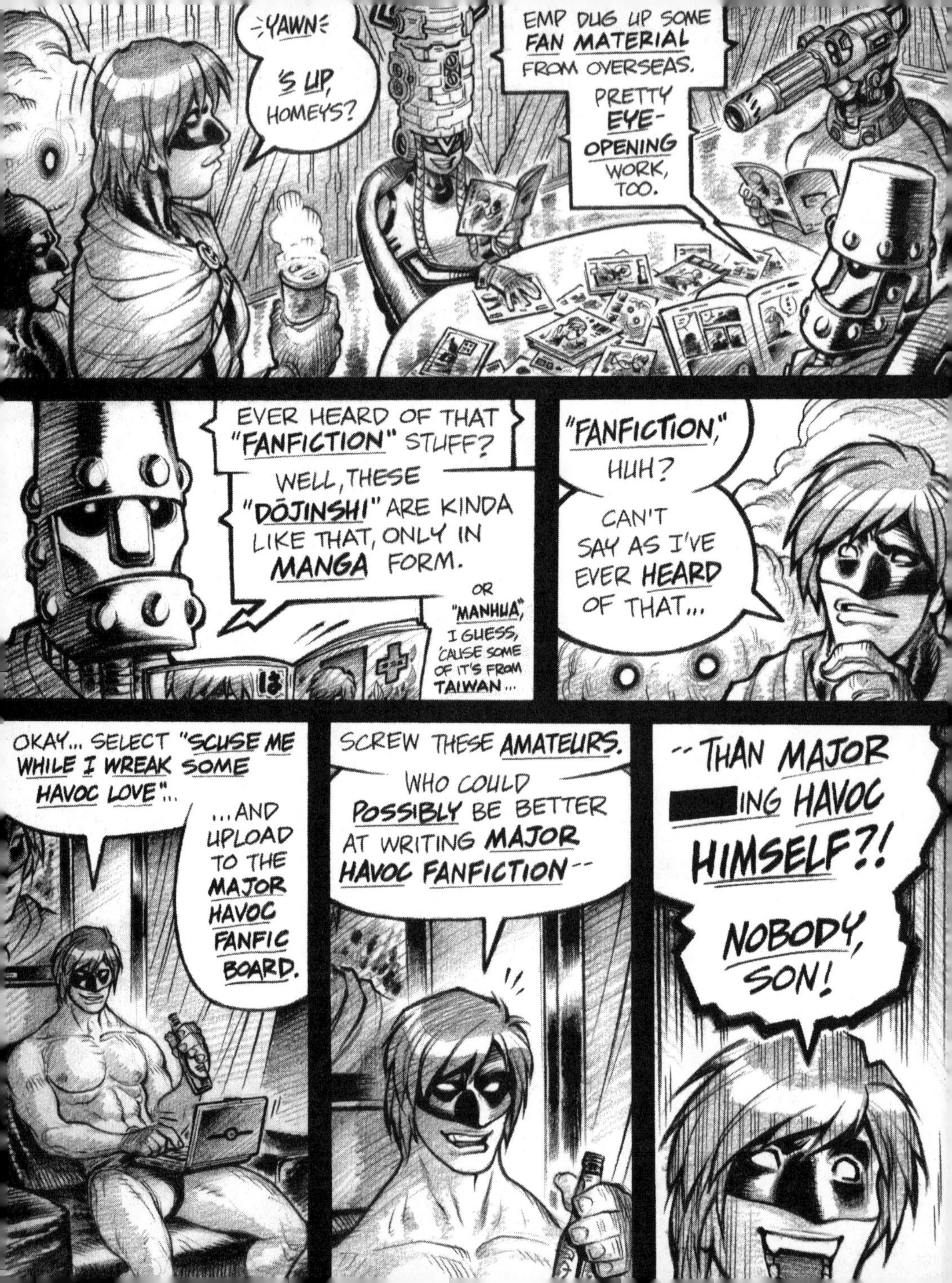
YAWN
'S UP, HOMEYS?
EMP DUG UP SOME FAN MATERIAL FROM OVERSEAS.
PRETTY EYE-OPENING WORK, TOO.
EVER HEARD OF THAT "FANFICTION" STUFF?
WELL, THESE "DŌJINSHI" ARE KINDA LIKE THAT, ONLY IN MANGA FORM.
OR "MANHUA", I GUESS, 'CAUSE SOME OF IT'S FROM TAIWAN...
"FANFICTION," HUH?
CAN'T SAY AS I'VE EVER HEARD OF THAT...
OKAY... SELECT "SCUSE ME WHILE I WREAK SOME HAVOC LOVE"...
...AND UPLOAD TO THE MAJOR HAVOC FANFIC BOARD.
SCREW THESE AMATEURS.
WHO COULD POSSIBLY BE BETTER AT WRITING MAJOR HAVOC FANFICTION--
--THAN MAJOR [redacted]ING HAVOC HIMSELF?!
NOBODY, SON!

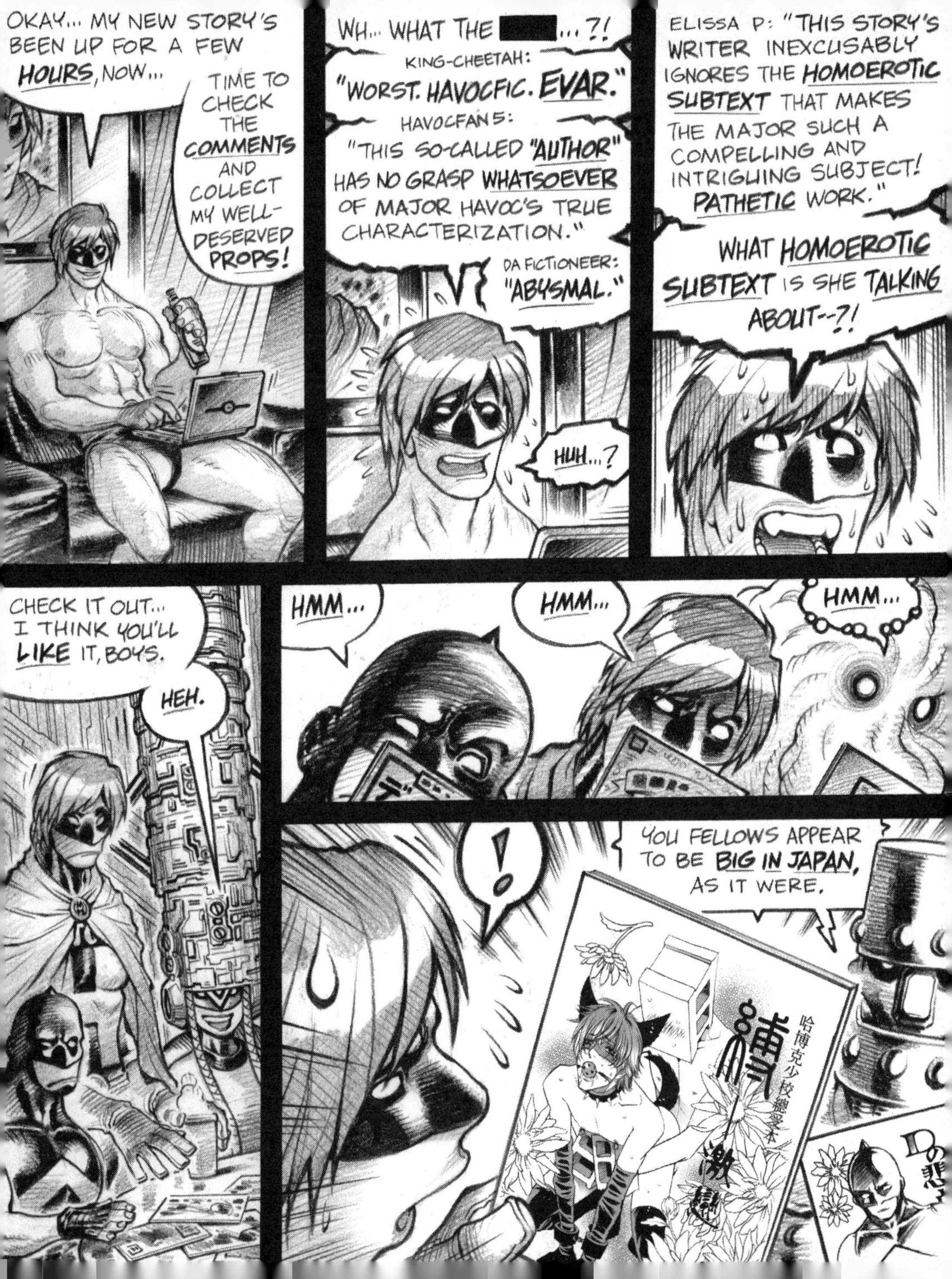
OKAY... MY NEW STORY'S BEEN UP FOR A FEW HOURS, NOW...
TIME TO CHECK THE COMMENTS AND COLLECT MY WELL-DESERVED PROPS!
WH... WHAT THE [redacted]...?!
KING-CHEETAH: "WORST. HAVOCFIC. EVAR."
HAVOCFAN5: "THIS SO-CALLED "AUTHOR" HAS NO GRASP WHATSOEVER OF MAJOR HAVOC'S TRUE CHARACTERIZATION."
DA FICTIONEER: "ABYSMAL."
HUH...?
ELISSA P: "THIS STORY'S WRITER INEXCUSABLY IGNORES THE HOMOEROTIC SUBTEXT THAT MAKES THE MAJOR SUCH A COMPELLING AND INTRIGUING SUBJECT! PATHETIC WORK."
WHAT HOMOEROTIC SUBTEXT IS SHE TALKING ABOUT--?!
CHECK IT OUT... I THINK YOU'LL LIKE IT, BOYS.
HEH.
HMM...
HMM...
HMM...
!
YOU FELLOWS APPEAR TO BE BIG IN JAPAN, AS IT WERE.
哈博克少校總受本
續
Dの

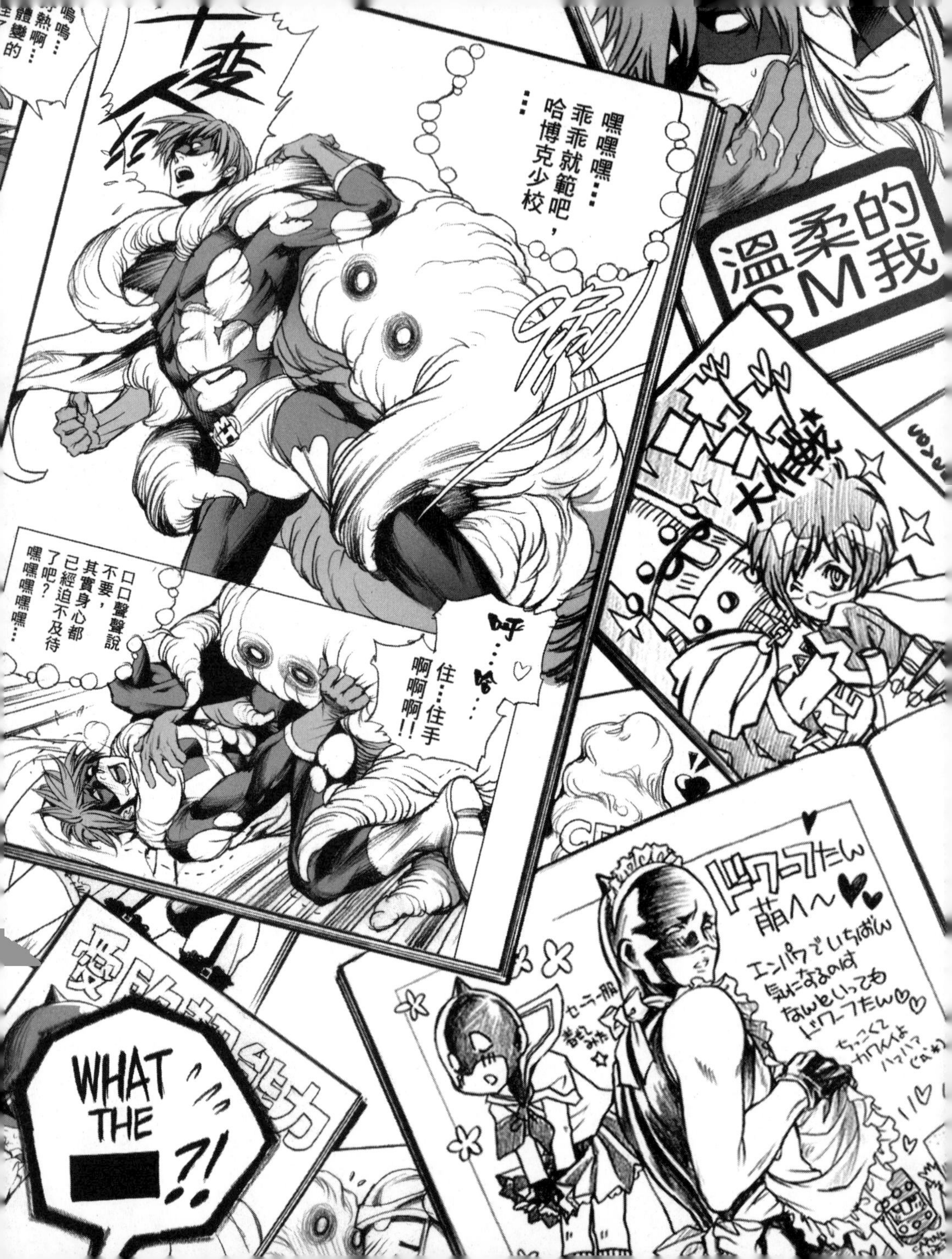

嘿嘿嘿……
乖乖就範吧，
哈博克少校
……
溫柔的我
SM
口口聲聲說
不要，
其實身心都
已經迫不及待
了吧？
嘿嘿嘿嘿嘿……
呼……哈……
住……住手
啊啊啊!!
WHAT THE [redacted] ?!
ドワーフたん
萌へ〜
エンパクでいちばん
気になるのは
なんといっても
ドワーフたん
セーラー服

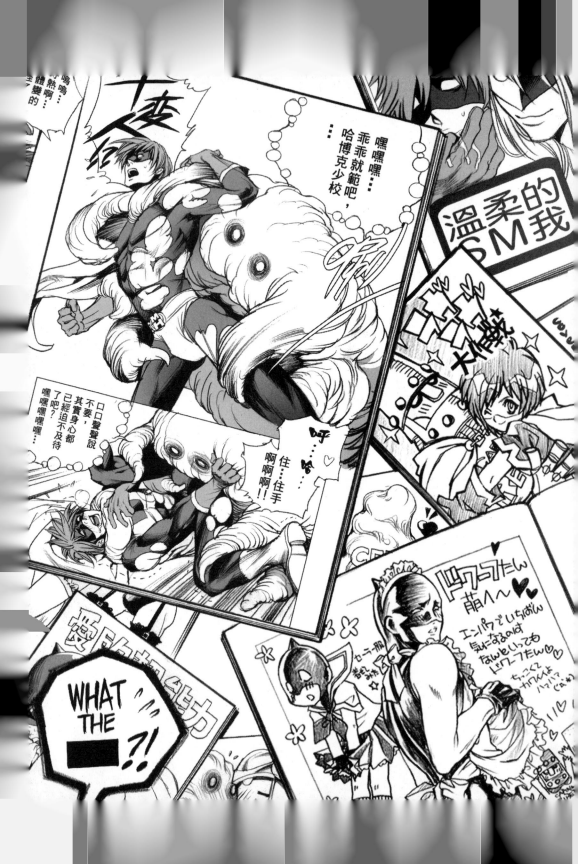

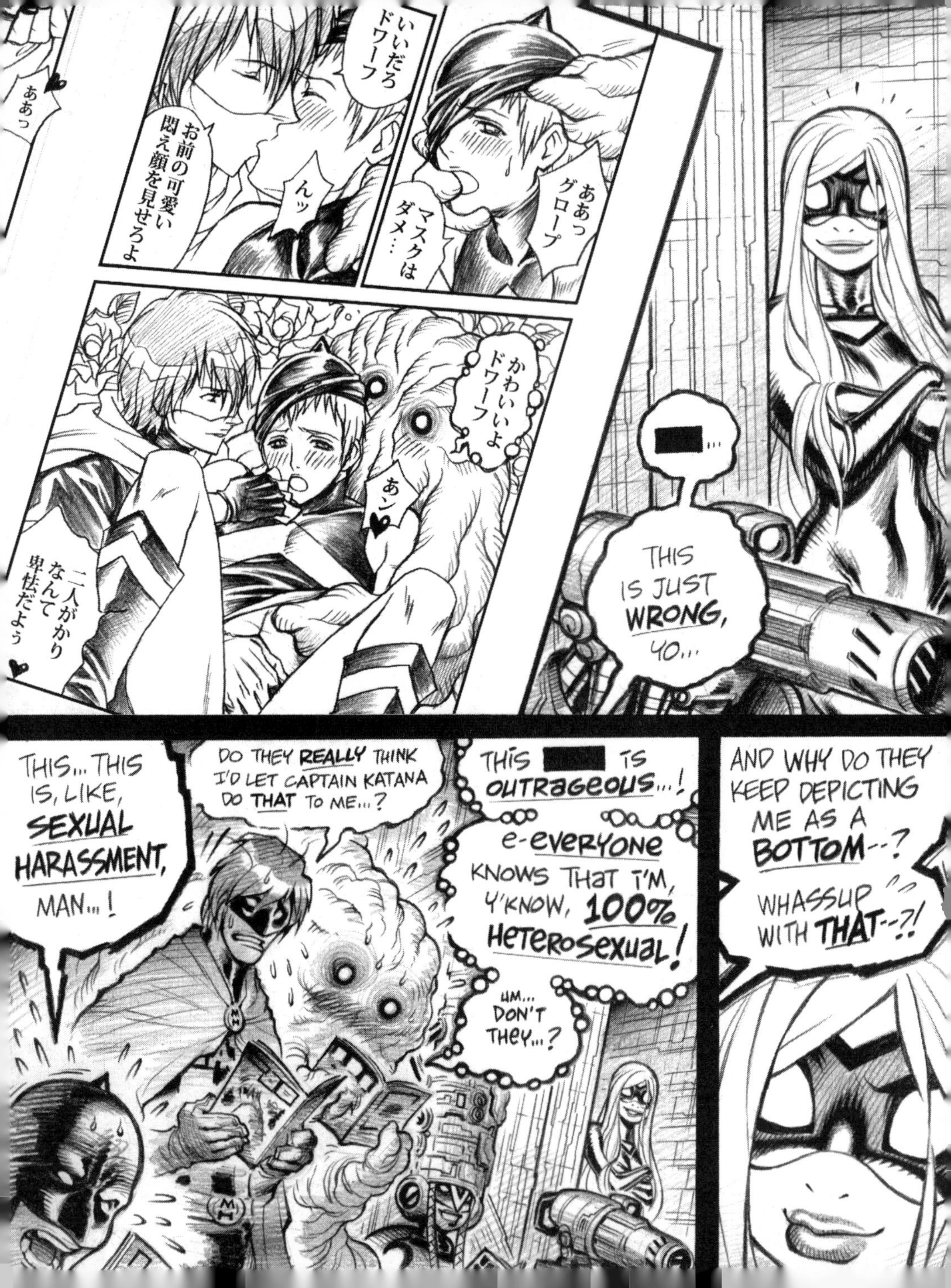

ああっ
いいだろ ドワーフ
お前の可愛い 悶え顔を見せろよ
んッ
ああっ グローブ
マスクは ダメ…
かわいいよ ドワーフ
あン
二人がかり なんて 卑怯だよぅ
[redacted]...
THIS IS JUST WRONG, YO...
THIS... THIS IS, LIKE, SEXUAL HARASSMENT, MAN...!
DO THEY REALLY THINK I'D LET CAPTAIN KATANA DO THAT TO ME...?
THIS [redacted] IS OUTRAGEOUS...!
e-EVERYONE KNOWS THAT I'M, Y'KNOW, 100% HETEROSEXUAL!
UM... DON'T THEY...?
AND WHY DO THEY KEEP DEPICTING ME AS A BOTTOM--?
WHASSUP WITH THAT--?!

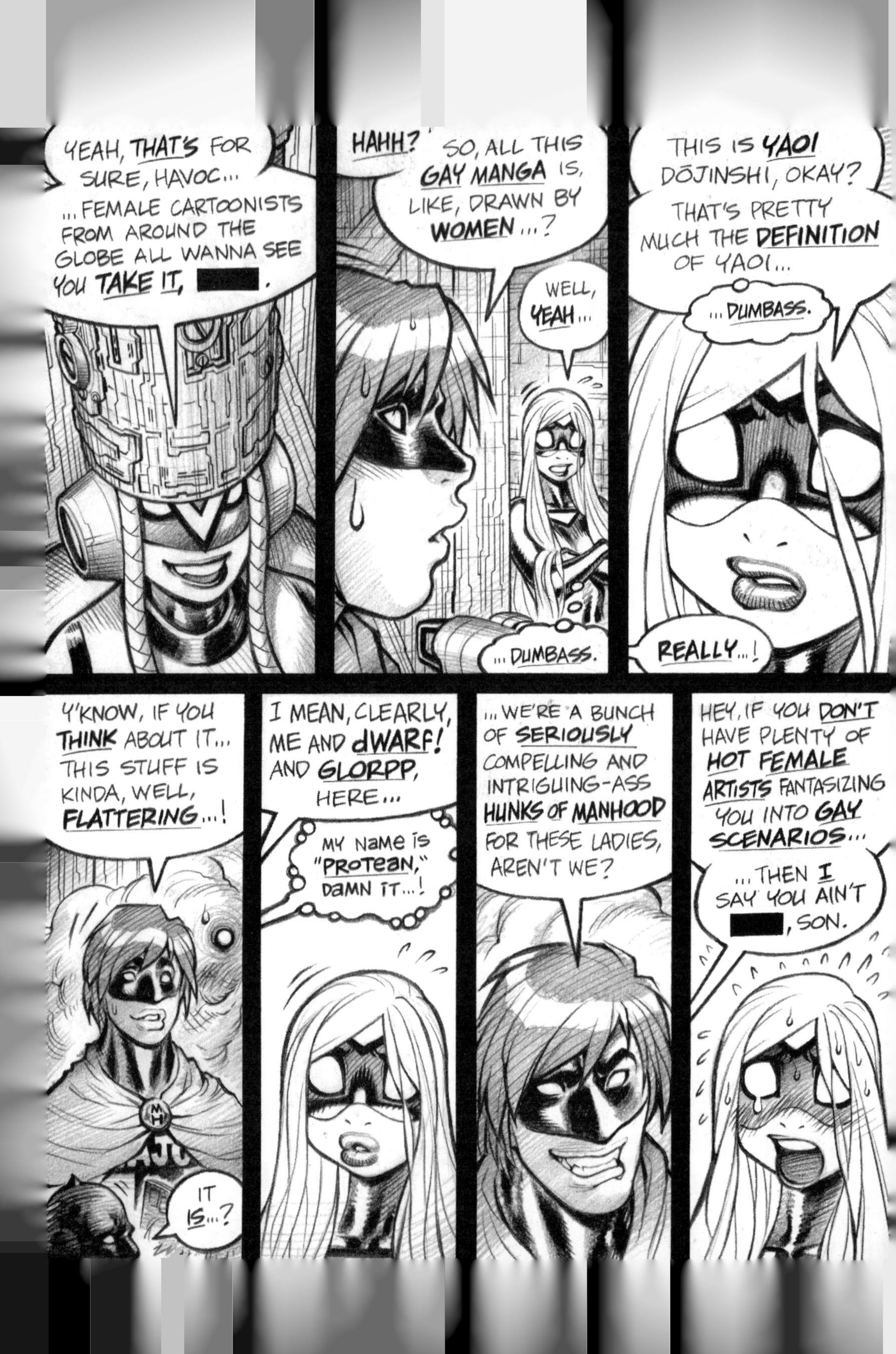
YEAH, THAT'S FOR SURE, HAVOC... ...FEMALE CARTOONISTS FROM AROUND THE GLOBE ALL WANNA SEE YOU TAKE IT, [redacted].
HAHH?
SO, ALL THIS GAY MANGA IS, LIKE, DRAWN BY WOMEN...?
WELL, YEAH...
...DUMBASS.
THIS IS YAOI DŌJINSHI, OKAY? THAT'S PRETTY MUCH THE DEFINITION OF YAOI...
...DUMBASS.
REALLY...!
Y'KNOW, IF YOU THINK ABOUT IT... THIS STUFF IS KINDA, WELL, FLATTERING...!
IT IS...?
I MEAN, CLEARLY, ME AND dWARF! AND GLORPP, HERE...
MY NAME IS "PROTEAN," DAMN IT...!
...WE'RE A BUNCH OF SERIOUSLY COMPELLING AND INTRIGUING-ASS HUNKS OF MANHOOD FOR THESE LADIES, AREN'T WE?
HEY, IF YOU DON'T HAVE PLENTY OF HOT FEMALE ARTISTS FANTASIZING YOU INTO GAY SCENARIOS...
...THEN I SAY YOU AIN'T [redacted], SON.

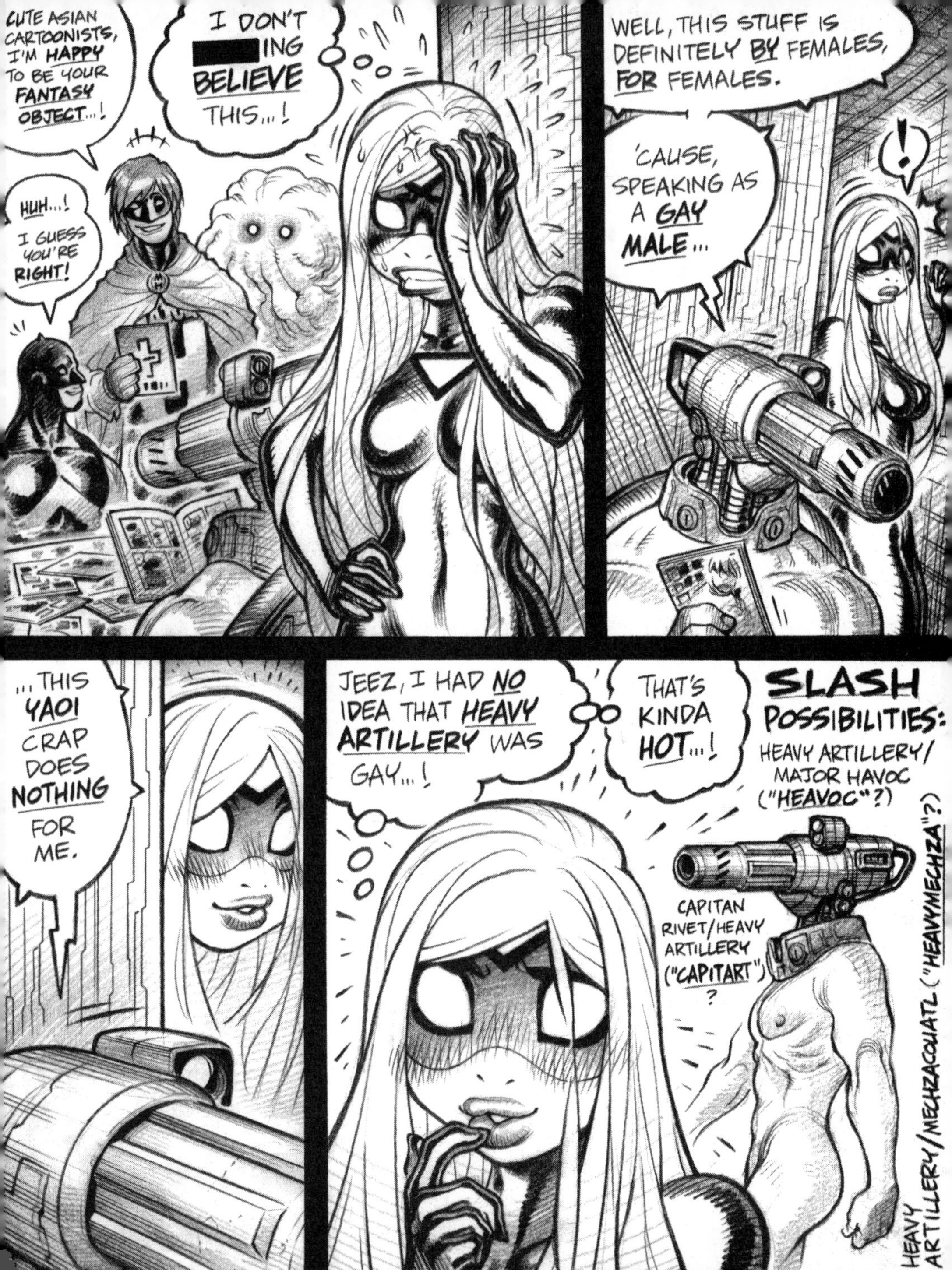
CUTE ASIAN CARTOONISTS, I'M HAPPY TO BE YOUR FANTASY OBJECT...!
I DON'T [redacted]ING BELIEVE THIS...!
HUH...! I GUESS YOU'RE RIGHT!
WELL, THIS STUFF IS DEFINITELY BY FEMALES, FOR FEMALES.
'CAUSE, SPEAKING AS A GAY MALE...
!
...THIS YAOI CRAP DOES NOTHING FOR ME.
JEEZ, I HAD NO IDEA THAT HEAVY ARTILLERY WAS GAY...!
THAT'S KINDA HOT...!
SLASH POSSIBILITIES:
HEAVY ARTILLERY/ MAJOR HAVOC ("HEAVOC"?)
CAPITAN RIVET/HEAVY ARTILLERY ("CAPITART")?
HEAVY ARTILLERY/MECHZACOATL ("HEAVYMECHZA"?)

empowered™

E.M.P. and the Nukenin Princess

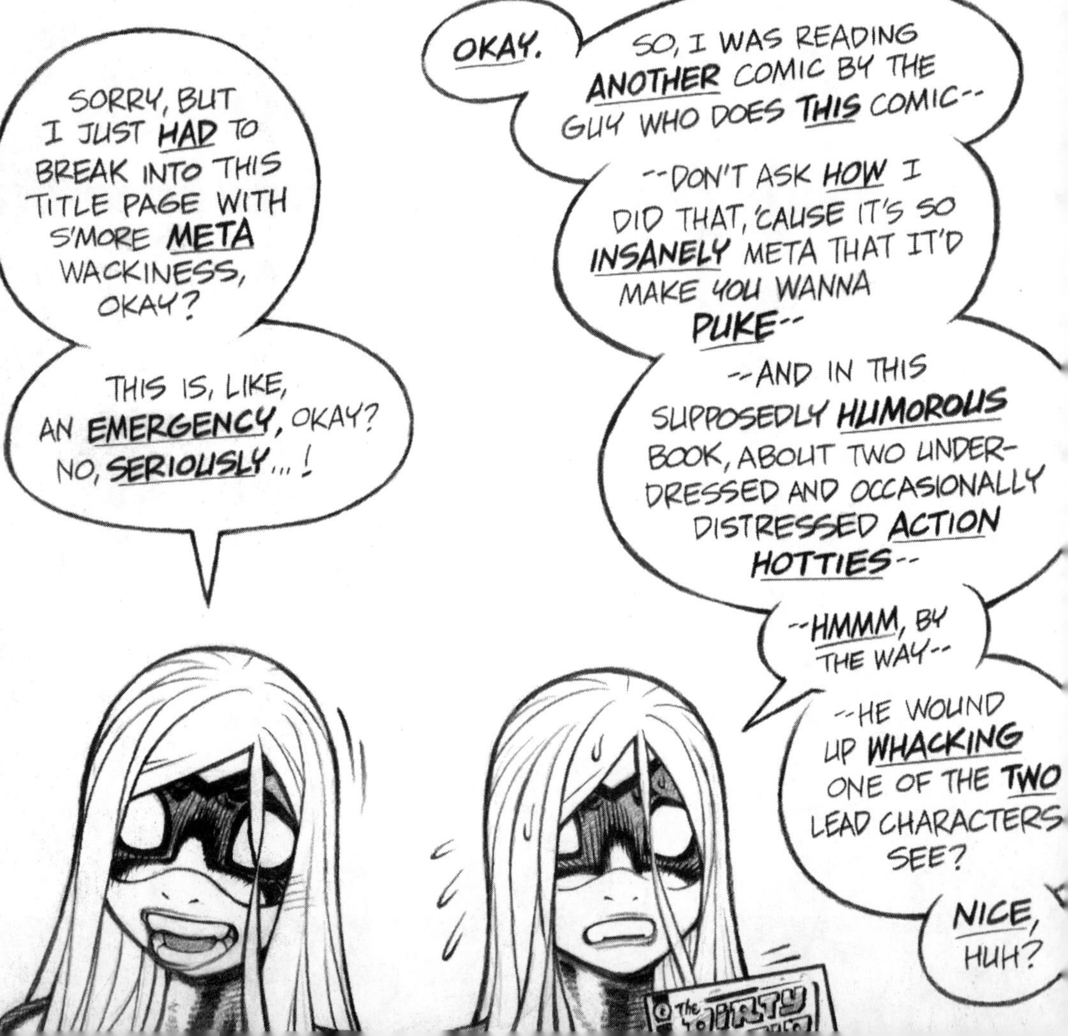
SORRY, BUT I JUST HAD TO BREAK INTO THIS TITLE PAGE WITH S'MORE META WACKINESS, OKAY?
THIS IS, LIKE, AN EMERGENCY, OKAY? NO, SERIOUSLY...!
OKAY.
SO, I WAS READING ANOTHER COMIC BY THE GUY WHO DOES THIS COMIC--
--DON'T ASK HOW I DID THAT, 'CAUSE IT'S SO INSANELY META THAT IT'D MAKE YOU WANNA PUKE--
--AND IN THIS SUPPOSEDLY HUMOROUS BOOK, ABOUT TWO UNDER-DRESSED AND OCCASIONALLY DISTRESSED ACTION HOTTIES--
--HMMM, BY THE WAY--
--HE WOUND UP WHACKING ONE OF THE TWO LEAD CHARACTERS, SEE?
NICE, HUH?

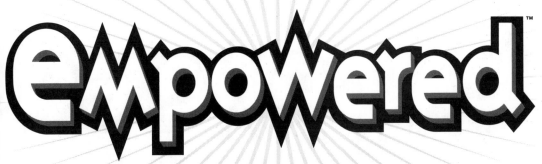

empowered™

E.M.P. and the Nukenin Princess

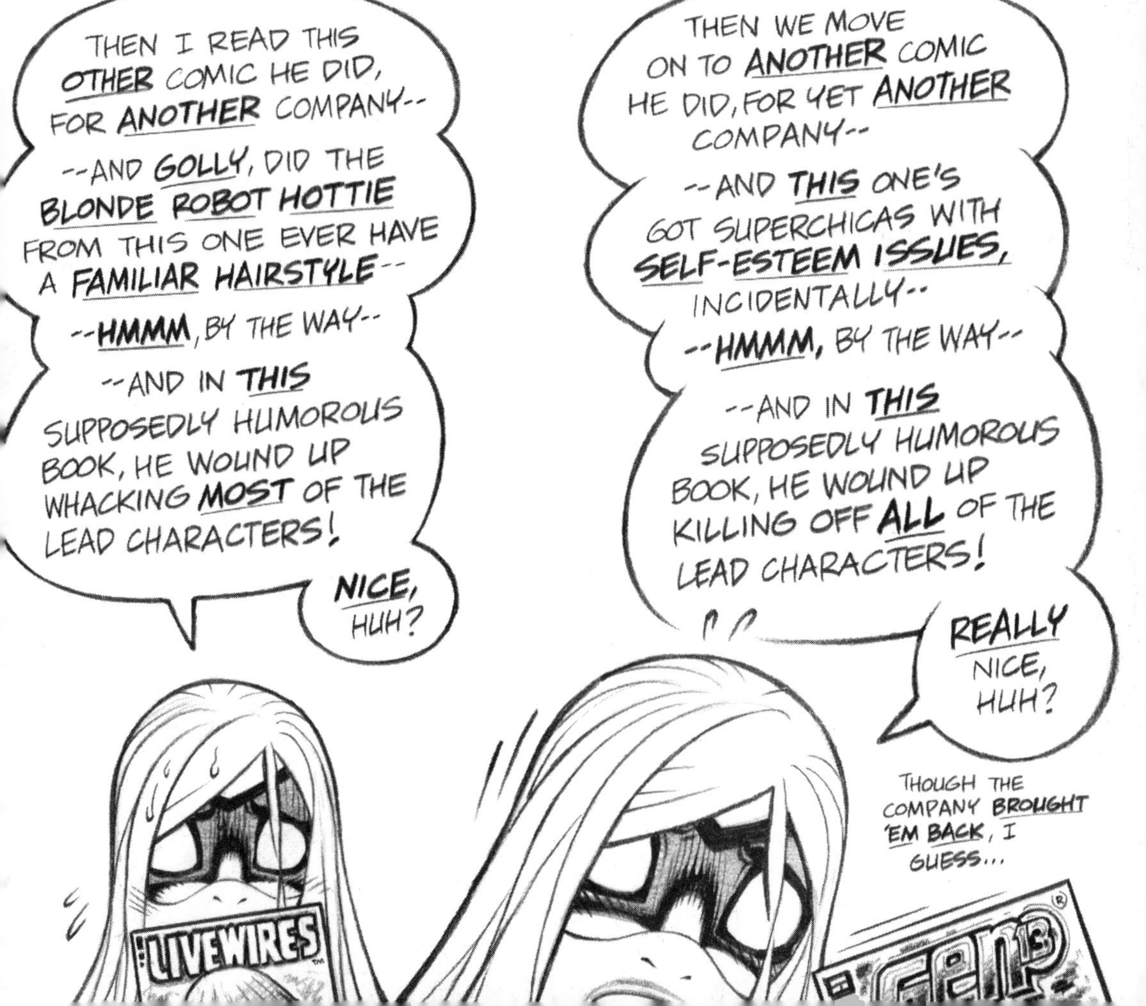
THEN I READ THIS OTHER COMIC HE DID, FOR ANOTHER COMPANY--
--AND GOLLY, DID THE BLONDE ROBOT HOTTIE FROM THIS ONE EVER HAVE A FAMILIAR HAIRSTYLE--
--HMMM, BY THE WAY--
--AND IN THIS SUPPOSEDLY HUMOROUS BOOK, HE WOUND UP WHACKING MOST OF THE LEAD CHARACTERS!
NICE, HUH?
THEN WE MOVE ON TO ANOTHER COMIC HE DID, FOR YET ANOTHER COMPANY--
--AND THIS ONE'S GOT SUPERCHICAS WITH SELF-ESTEEM ISSUES, INCIDENTALLY--
--HMMM, BY THE WAY--
--AND IN THIS SUPPOSEDLY HUMOROUS BOOK, HE WOUND UP KILLING OFF ALL OF THE LEAD CHARACTERS!
REALLY NICE, HUH?
THOUGH THE COMPANY BROUGHT 'EM BACK, I GUESS...
LIVEWIRES

Empowered™

E.M.P. and the Nukenin Princess

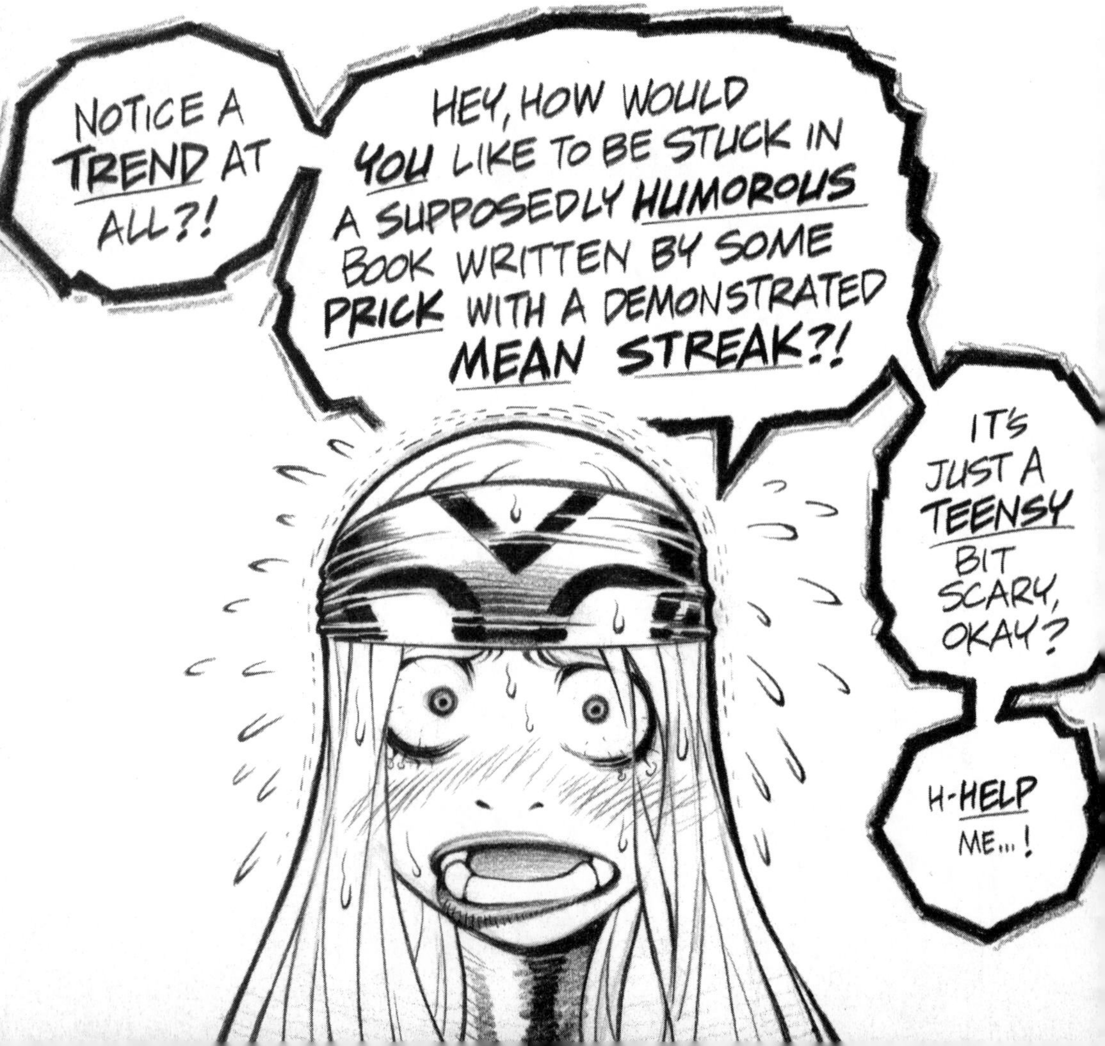

NOTICE A TREND AT ALL?!
HEY, HOW WOULD YOU LIKE TO BE STUCK IN A SUPPOSEDLY HUMOROUS BOOK WRITTEN BY SOME PRICK WITH A DEMONSTRATED MEAN STREAK?!
IT'S JUST A TEENSY BIT SCARY, OKAY?
H-HELP ME...!

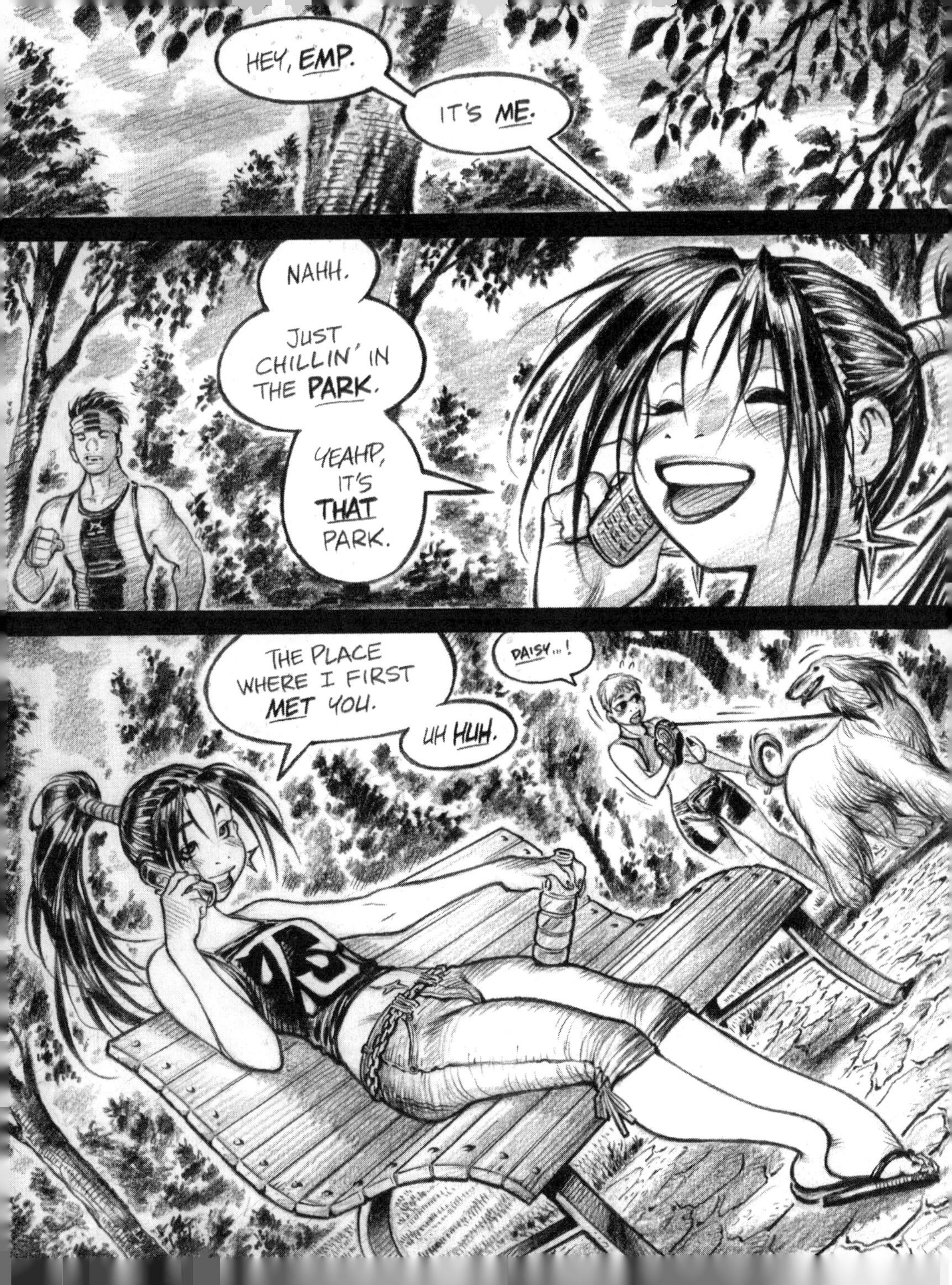
HEY, EMP.
IT'S ME.
NAHH.
JUST CHILLIN' IN THE PARK.
YEAHP, IT'S THAT PARK.
THE PLACE WHERE I FIRST MET YOU.
UH HUH.
DAISY...!

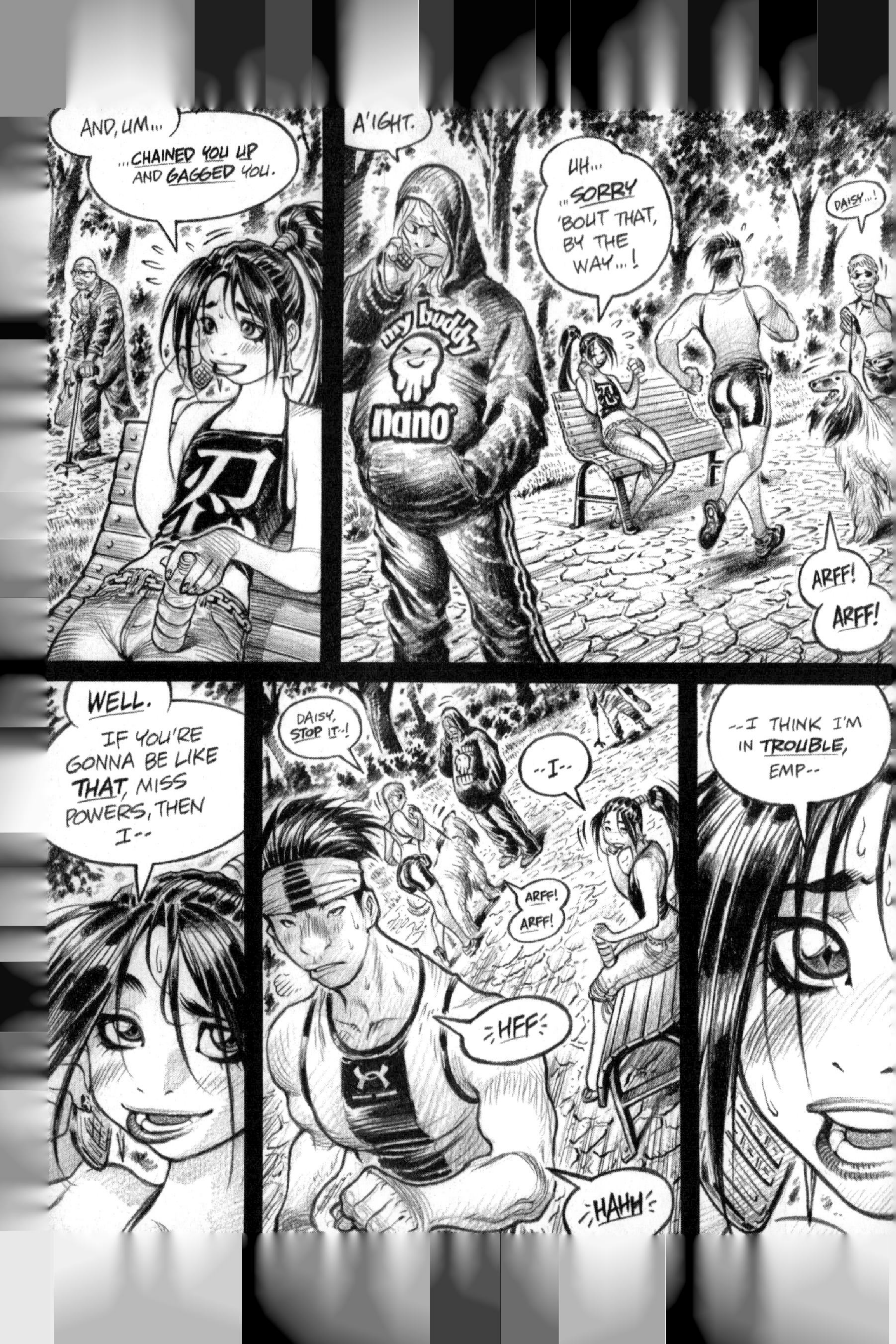
AND, UM...
...CHAINED YOU UP AND GAGGED YOU.
A'IGHT.
UH...
...SORRY 'BOUT THAT, BY THE WAY...!
DAISY...!
ARFF!
ARFF!
WELL.
IF YOU'RE GONNA BE LIKE THAT, MISS POWERS, THEN I--
DAISY, STOP IT--!
--I--
ARFF!
ARFF!
HFF
HAHH
--I THINK I'M IN TROUBLE, EMP--

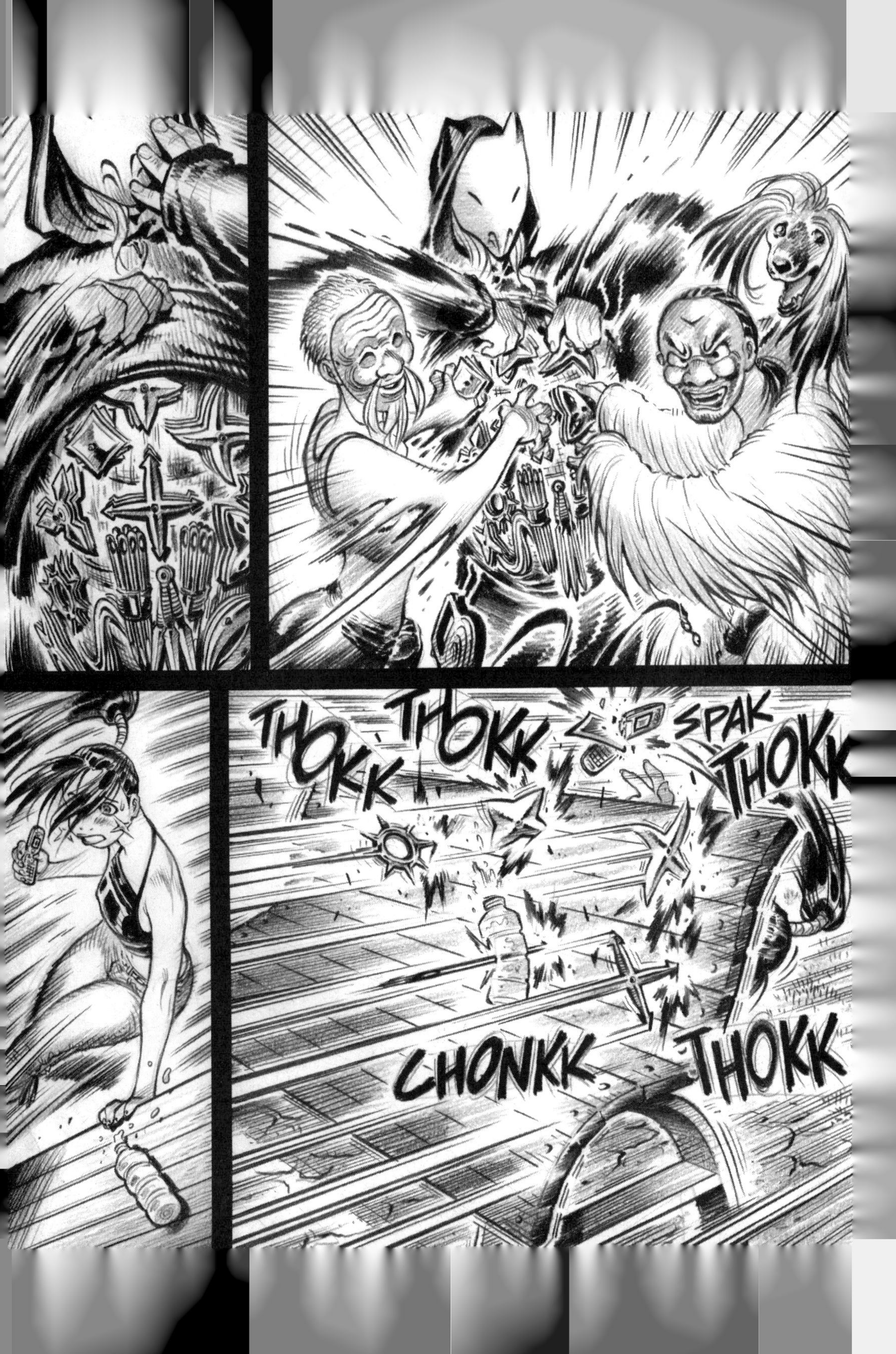
THOKK
THOKK
SPAK
THOKK
CHONKK
THOKK

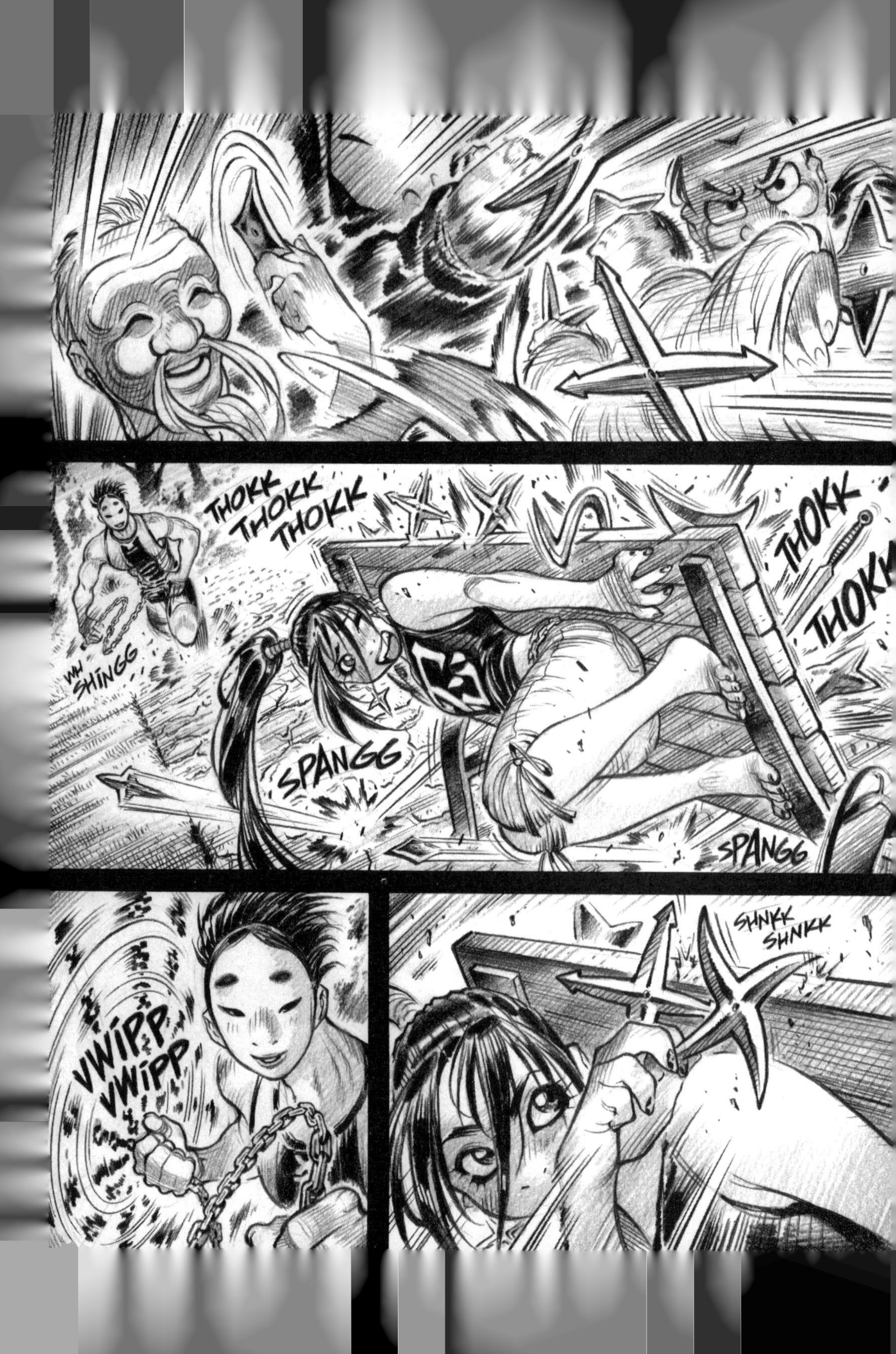
THOKK THOKK THOKK
THOKK
THOKK
WH SHINGG
SPANGG
SPANGG
VWIPP VWIPP
SHNKK SHNKK

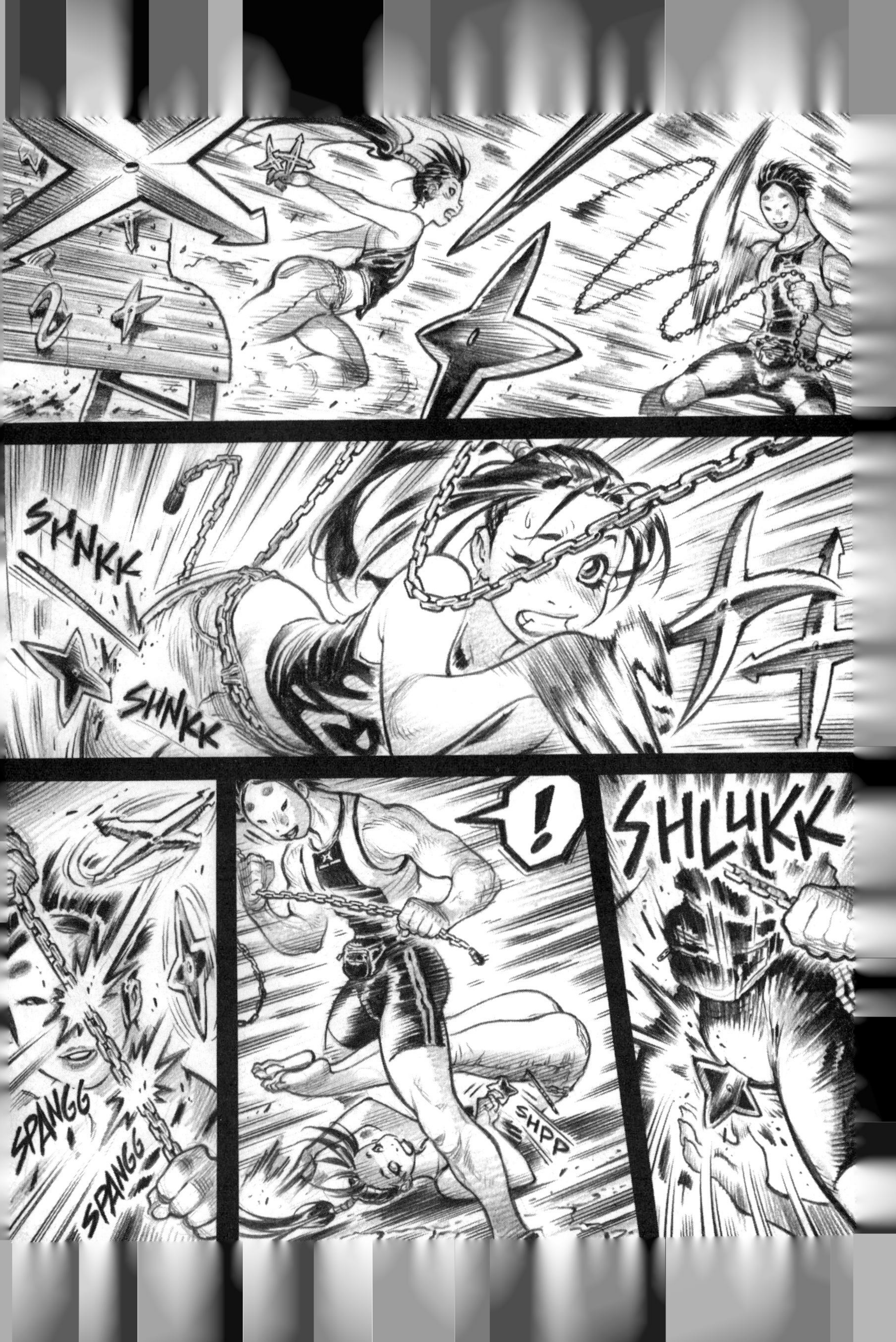
SHNKK
SHNKK
SPANGG
SPANGG
SHPP
!
SHLUKK

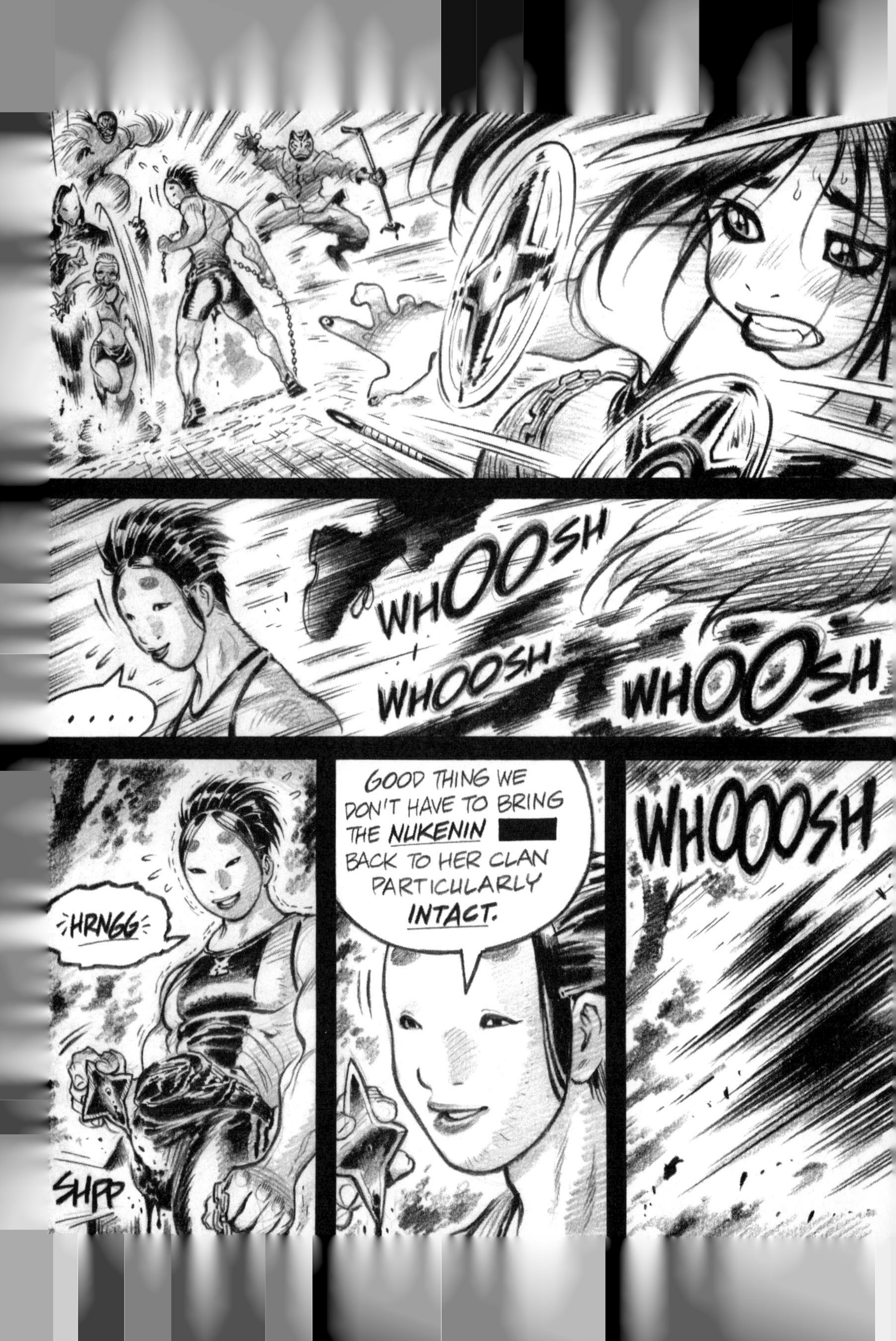
....
WHOOSH
WHOOSH
WHOOSH
HRNGG
SHPP
GOOD THING WE DON'T HAVE TO BRING THE NUKENIN [redacted] BACK TO HER CLAN PARTICULARLY INTACT.
WHOOOSH

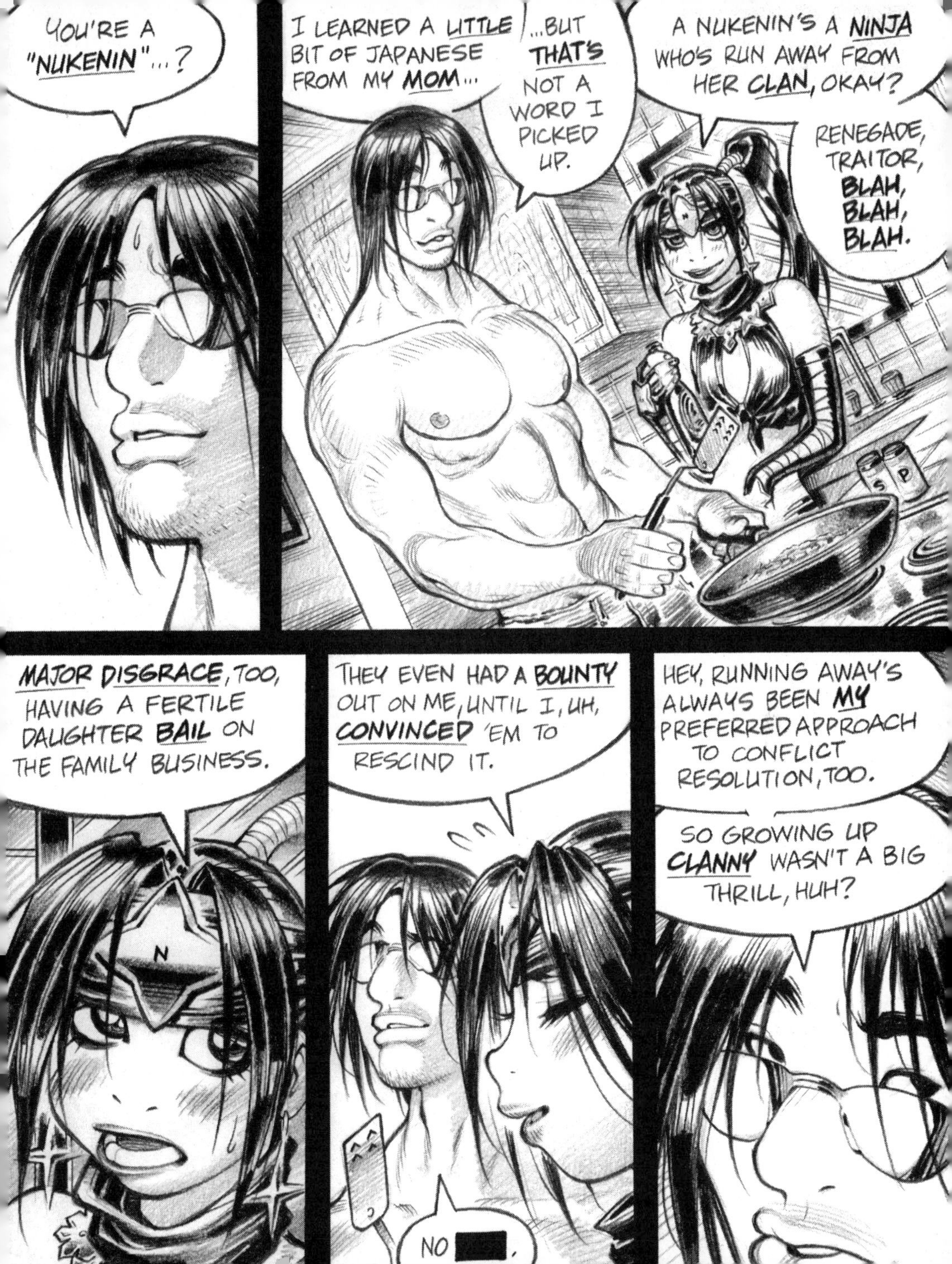
YOU'RE A "NUKENIN"...?
I LEARNED A LITTLE BIT OF JAPANESE FROM MY MOM...
...BUT THAT'S NOT A WORD I PICKED UP.
A NUKENIN'S A NINJA WHO'S RUN AWAY FROM HER CLAN, OKAY?
RENEGADE, TRAITOR, BLAH, BLAH, BLAH.
MAJOR DISGRACE, TOO, HAVING A FERTILE DAUGHTER BAIL ON THE FAMILY BUSINESS.
THEY EVEN HAD A BOUNTY OUT ON ME, UNTIL I, UH, CONVINCED 'EM TO RESCIND IT.
NO [redacted].
HEY, RUNNING AWAY'S ALWAYS BEEN MY PREFERRED APPROACH TO CONFLICT RESOLUTION, TOO.
SO GROWING UP CLANNY WASN'T A BIG THRILL, HUH?

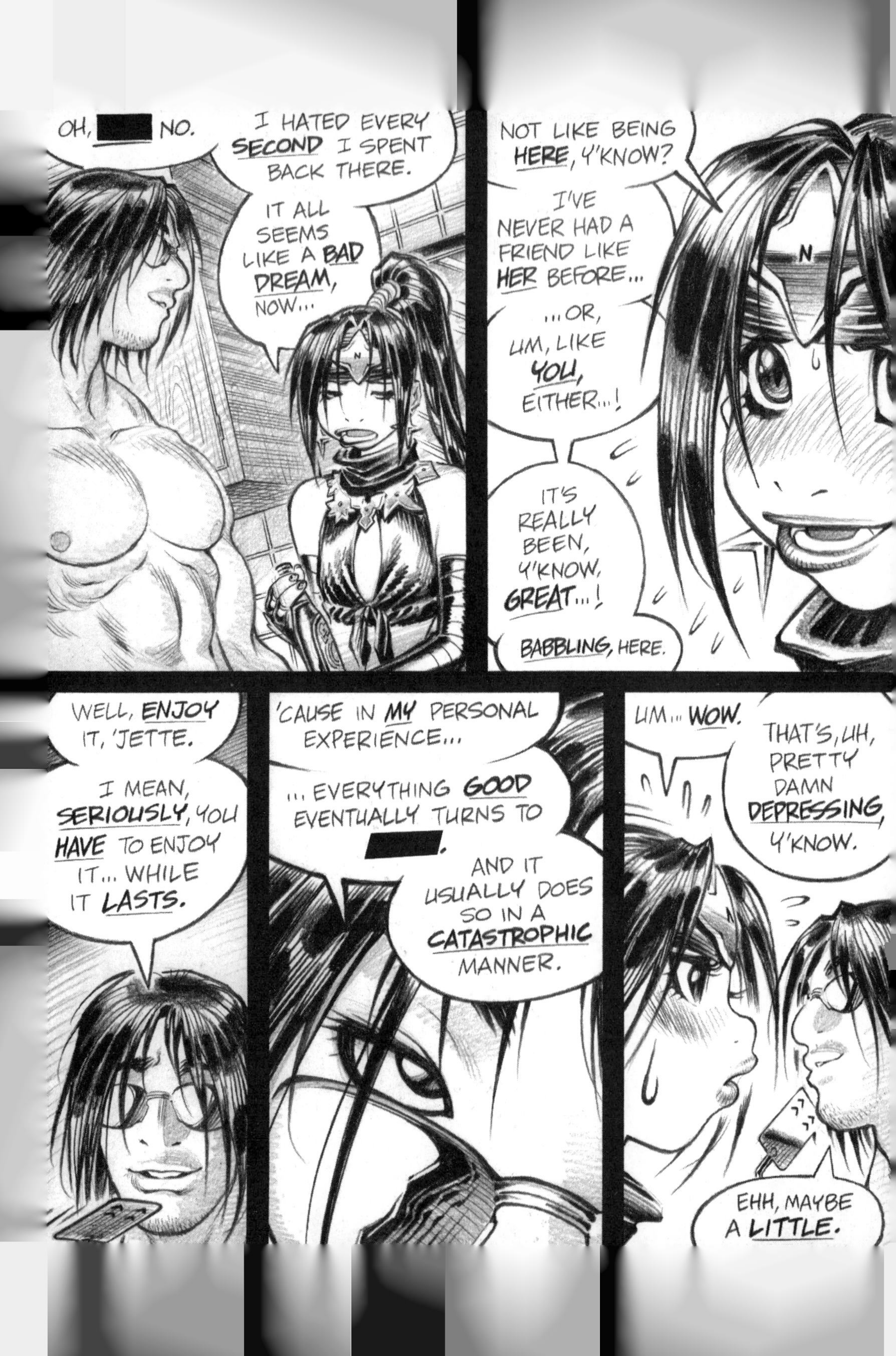

OH, [redacted] NO.
I HATED EVERY SECOND I SPENT BACK THERE.
IT ALL SEEMS LIKE A BAD DREAM, NOW...
NOT LIKE BEING HERE, Y'KNOW?
I'VE NEVER HAD A FRIEND LIKE HER BEFORE...
...OR, UM, LIKE YOU, EITHER...!
IT'S REALLY BEEN, Y'KNOW, GREAT...!
BABBLING, HERE.
WELL, ENJOY IT, 'JETTE.
I MEAN, SERIOUSLY, YOU HAVE TO ENJOY IT... WHILE IT LASTS.
'CAUSE IN MY PERSONAL EXPERIENCE...
...EVERYTHING GOOD EVENTUALLY TURNS TO [redacted].
AND IT USUALLY DOES SO IN A CATASTROPHIC MANNER.
UM... WOW.
THAT'S, UH, PRETTY DAMN DEPRESSING, Y'KNOW.
EHH, MAYBE A LITTLE.

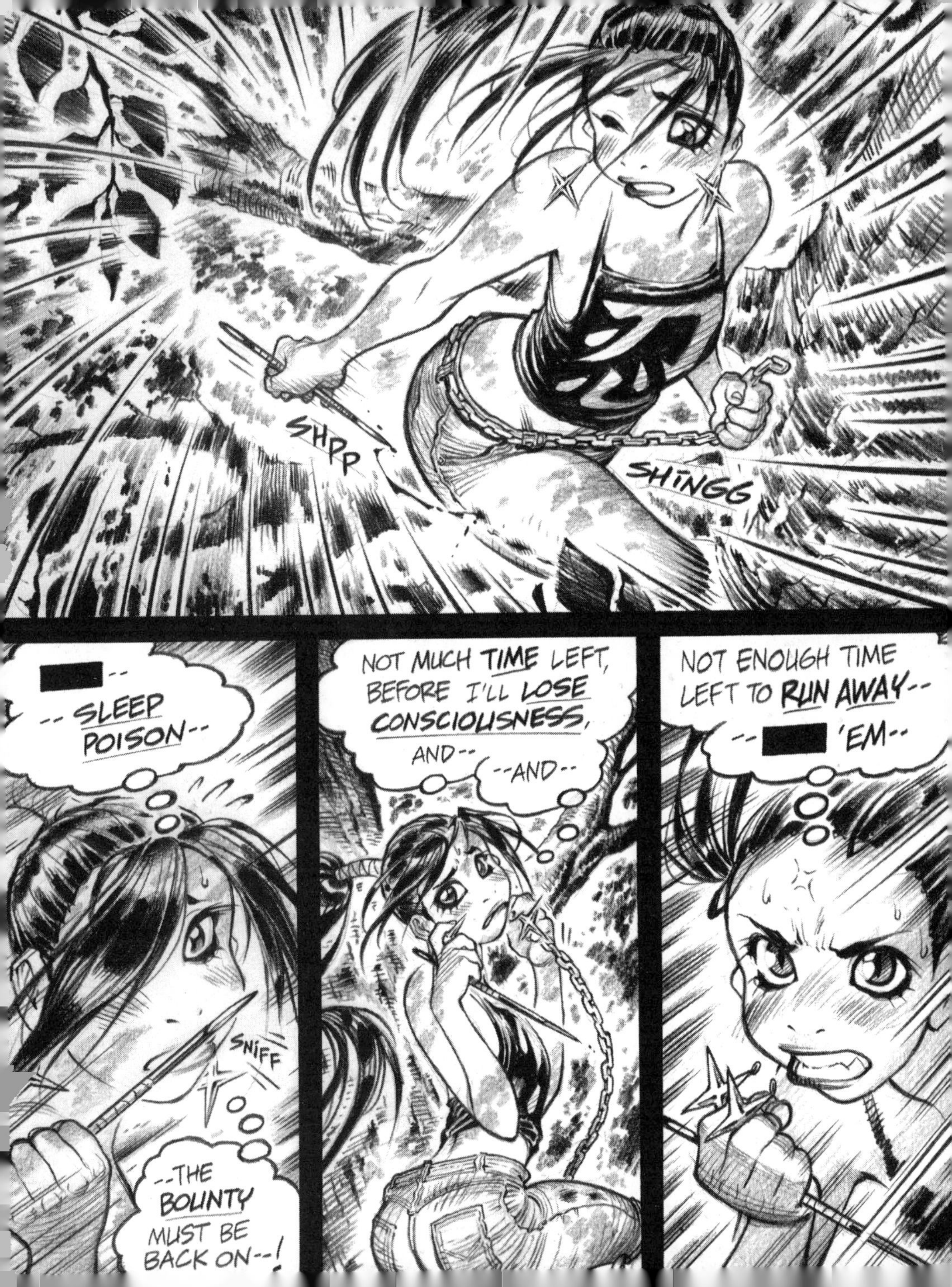
SHPP
SHINGG
[redacted]--
--SLEEP POISON--
SNIFF
--THE BOUNTY MUST BE BACK ON--!
NOT MUCH TIME LEFT, BEFORE I'LL LOSE CONSCIOUSNESS,
AND--
--AND--
NOT ENOUGH TIME LEFT TO RUN AWAY--
--[redacted] 'EM--

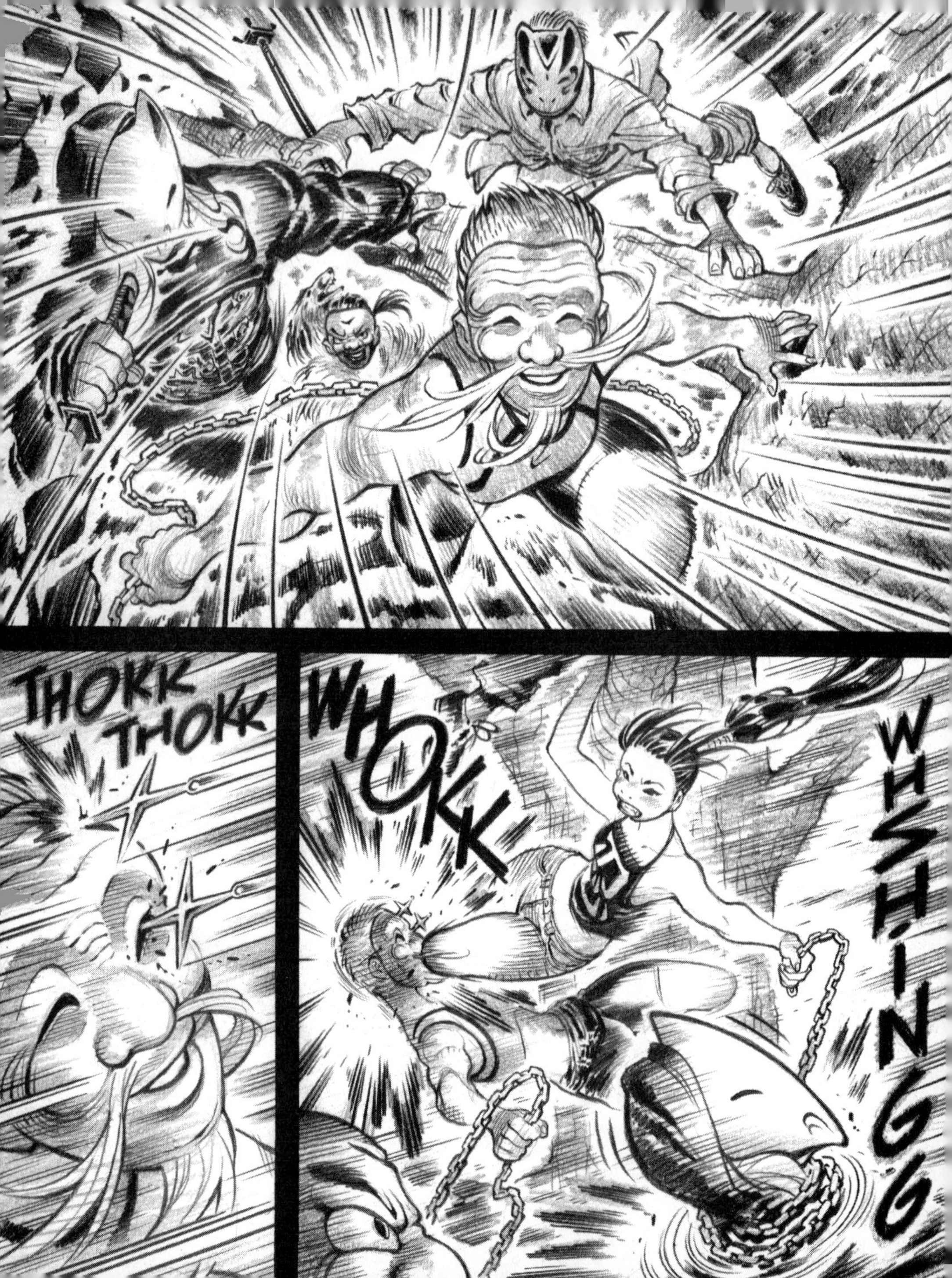
THOKK THOKK
WHOKK
WHSHINGG

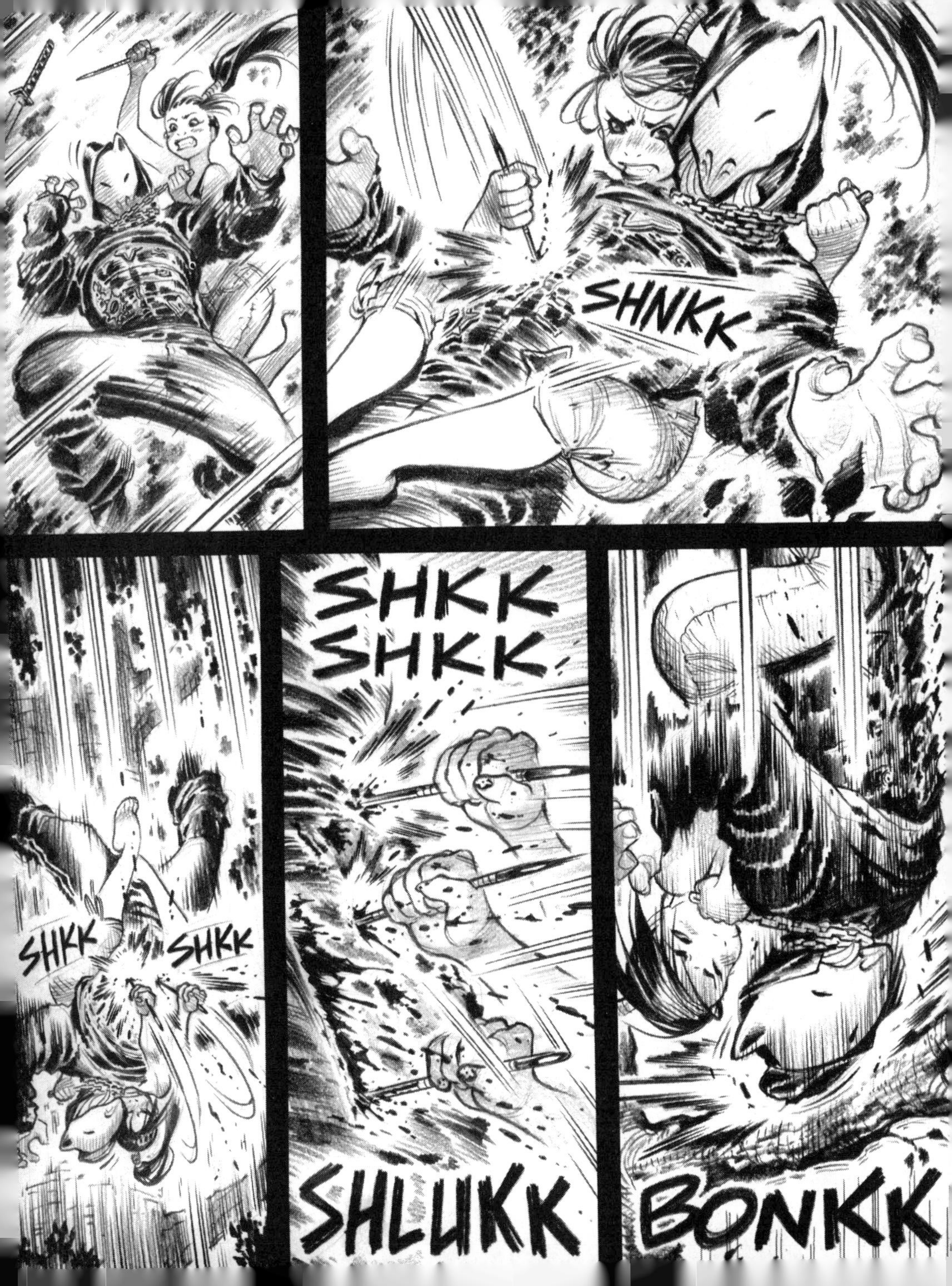
SHNKK
SHKK
SHKK
SHKK
SHKK
SHLUKK
BONKK

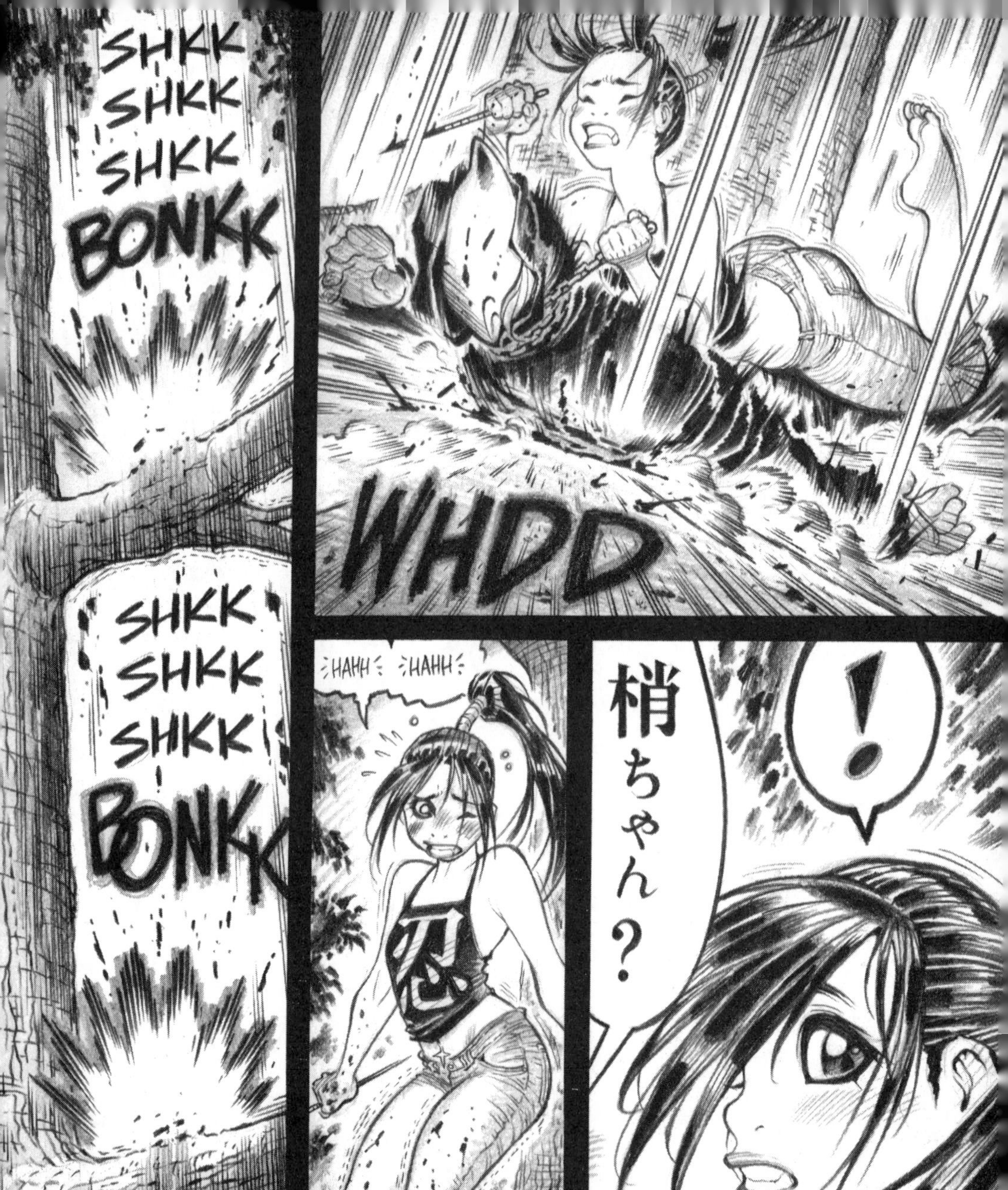
SHKK
SHKK
SHKK
BONKK
SHKK
SHKK
SHKK
BONKK
WHDD
HAHH HAHH
梢ちゃん？
!

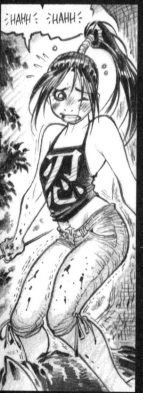

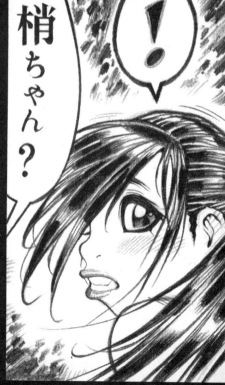

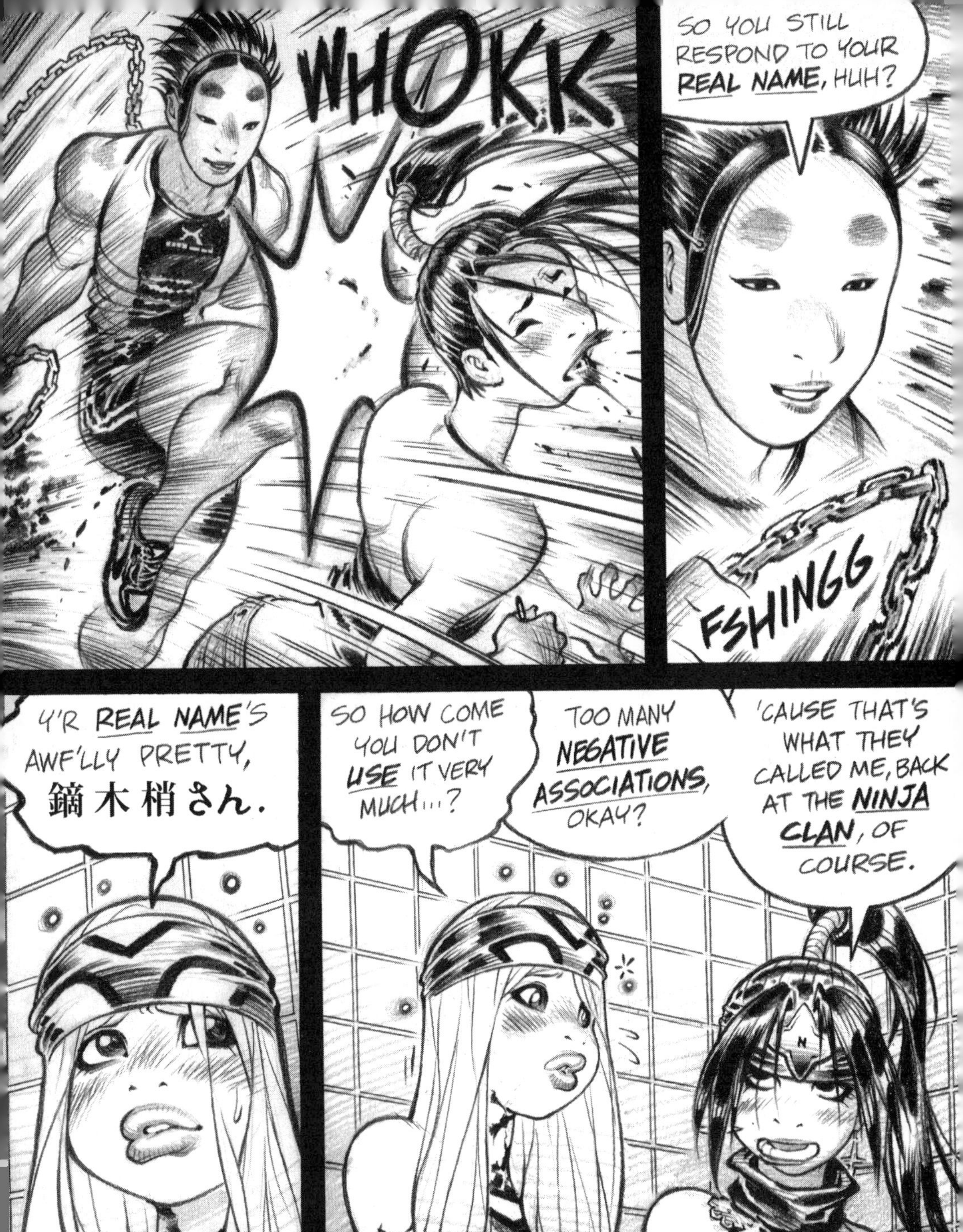
WHOKK
SO YOU STILL RESPOND TO YOUR REAL NAME, HUH?
FSHINGG
Y'R REAL NAME'S AWF'LLY PRETTY, 鏑木梢さん.
SO HOW COME YOU DON'T USE IT VERY MUCH...?
TOO MANY NEGATIVE ASSOCIATIONS, OKAY?
'CAUSE THAT'S WHAT THEY CALLED ME, BACK AT THE NINJA CLAN, OF COURSE.

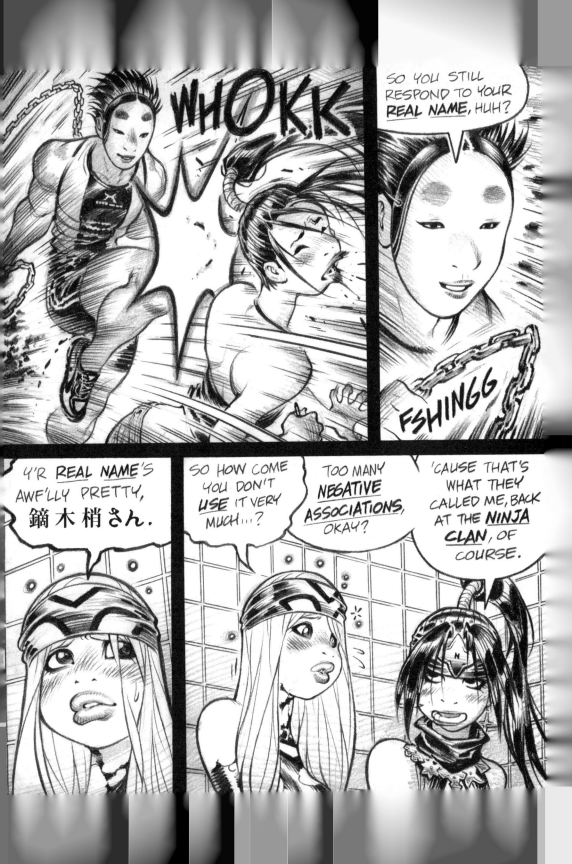

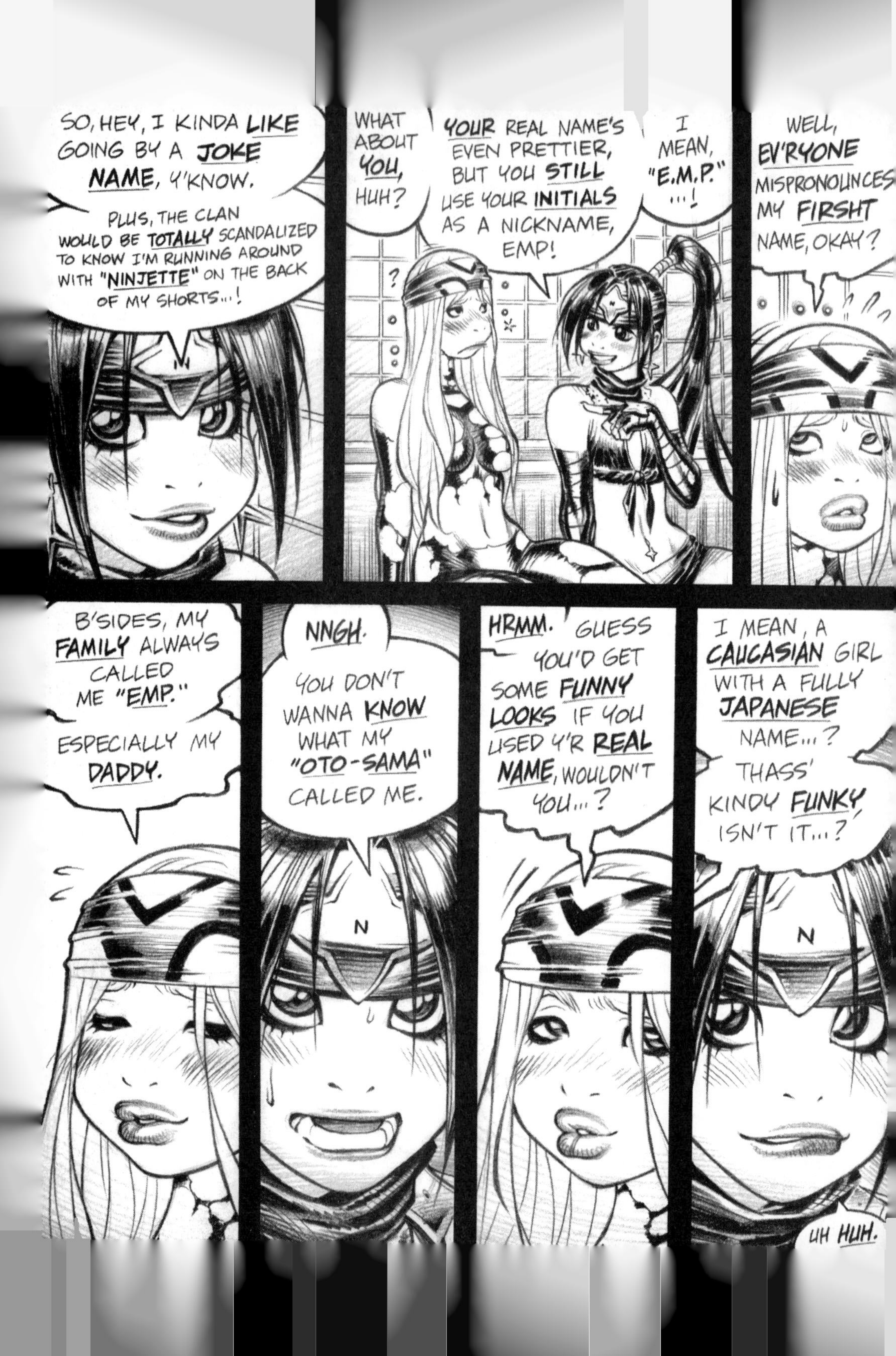
SO, HEY, I KINDA LIKE GOING BY A JOKE NAME, Y'KNOW.
PLUS, THE CLAN WOULD BE TOTALLY SCANDALIZED TO KNOW I'M RUNNING AROUND WITH "NINJETTE" ON THE BACK OF MY SHORTS...!
WHAT ABOUT YOU, HUH?
YOUR REAL NAME'S EVEN PRETTIER, BUT YOU STILL USE YOUR INITIALS AS A NICKNAME, EMP!
I MEAN, "E.M.P." ...!
WELL, EV'RYONE MISPRONOUNCES MY FIRSHT NAME, OKAY?
B'SIDES, MY FAMILY ALWAYS CALLED ME "EMP."
ESPECIALLY MY DADDY.
NNGH.
YOU DON'T WANNA KNOW WHAT MY "OTO-SAMA" CALLED ME.
HRMM. GUESS YOU'D GET SOME FUNNY LOOKS IF YOU USED Y'R REAL NAME, WOULDN'T YOU...?
I MEAN, A CAUCASIAN GIRL WITH A FULLY JAPANESE NAME...?
THASS' KINDY FUNKY, ISN'T IT...?
UH HUH.

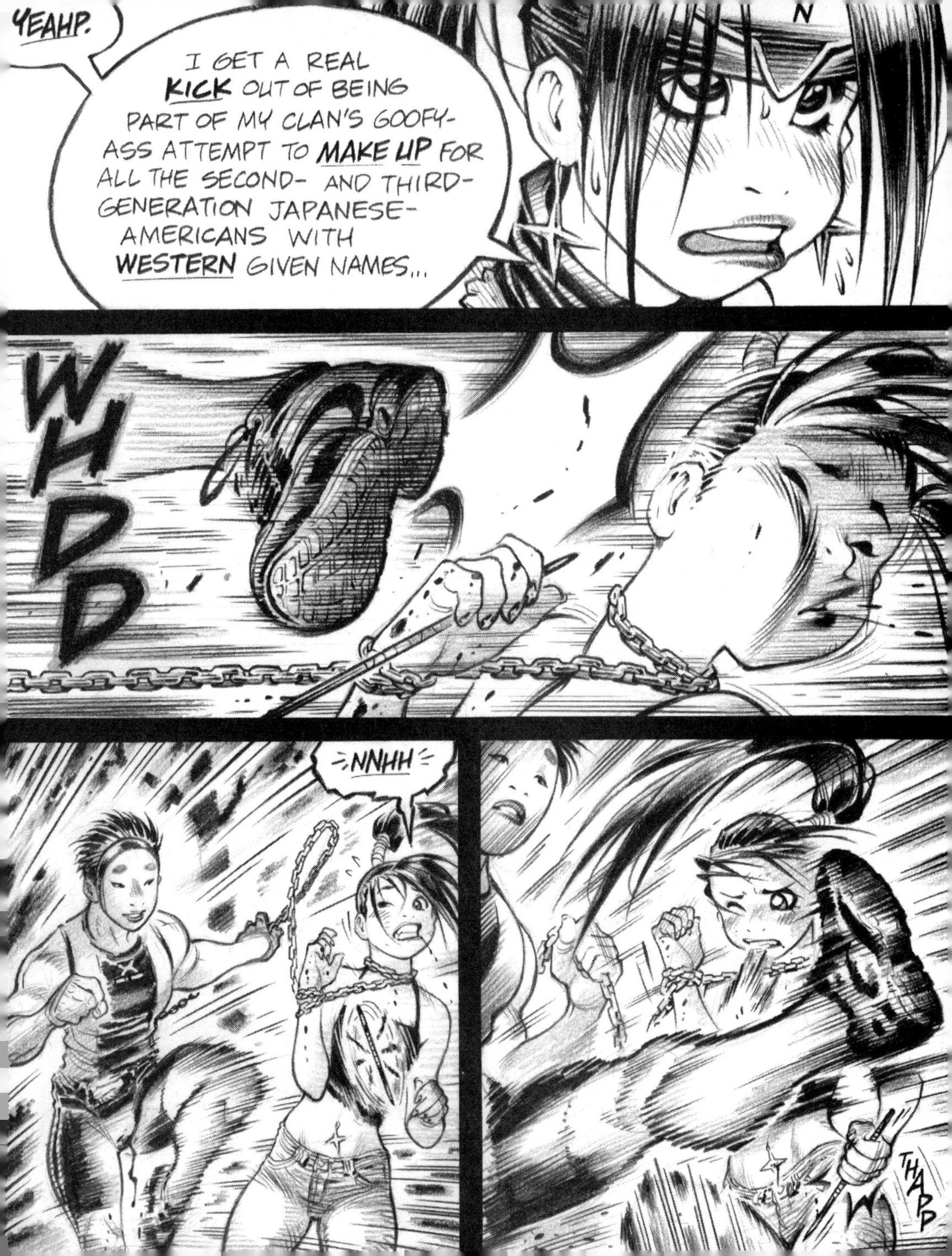
YEAHP.
I GET A REAL KICK OUT OF BEING PART OF MY CLAN'S GOOFY-ASS ATTEMPT TO MAKE UP FOR ALL THE SECOND- AND THIRD-GENERATION JAPANESE-AMERICANS WITH WESTERN GIVEN NAMES...
N
WHDD
NNHH
THAPP

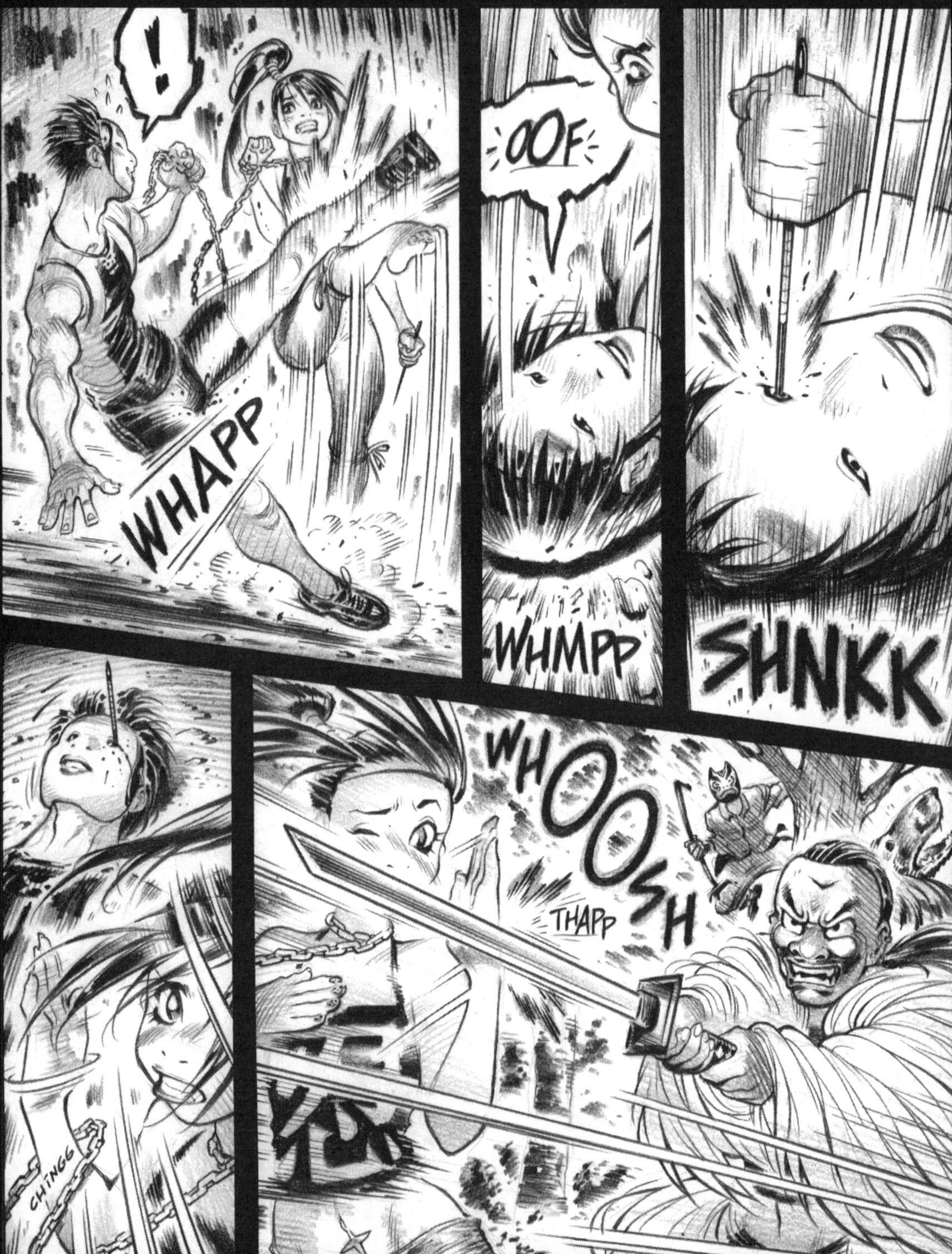
!
WHAPP
OOF
WHMPP
SHNKK
CHINGG
WHOOOSH
THAPP

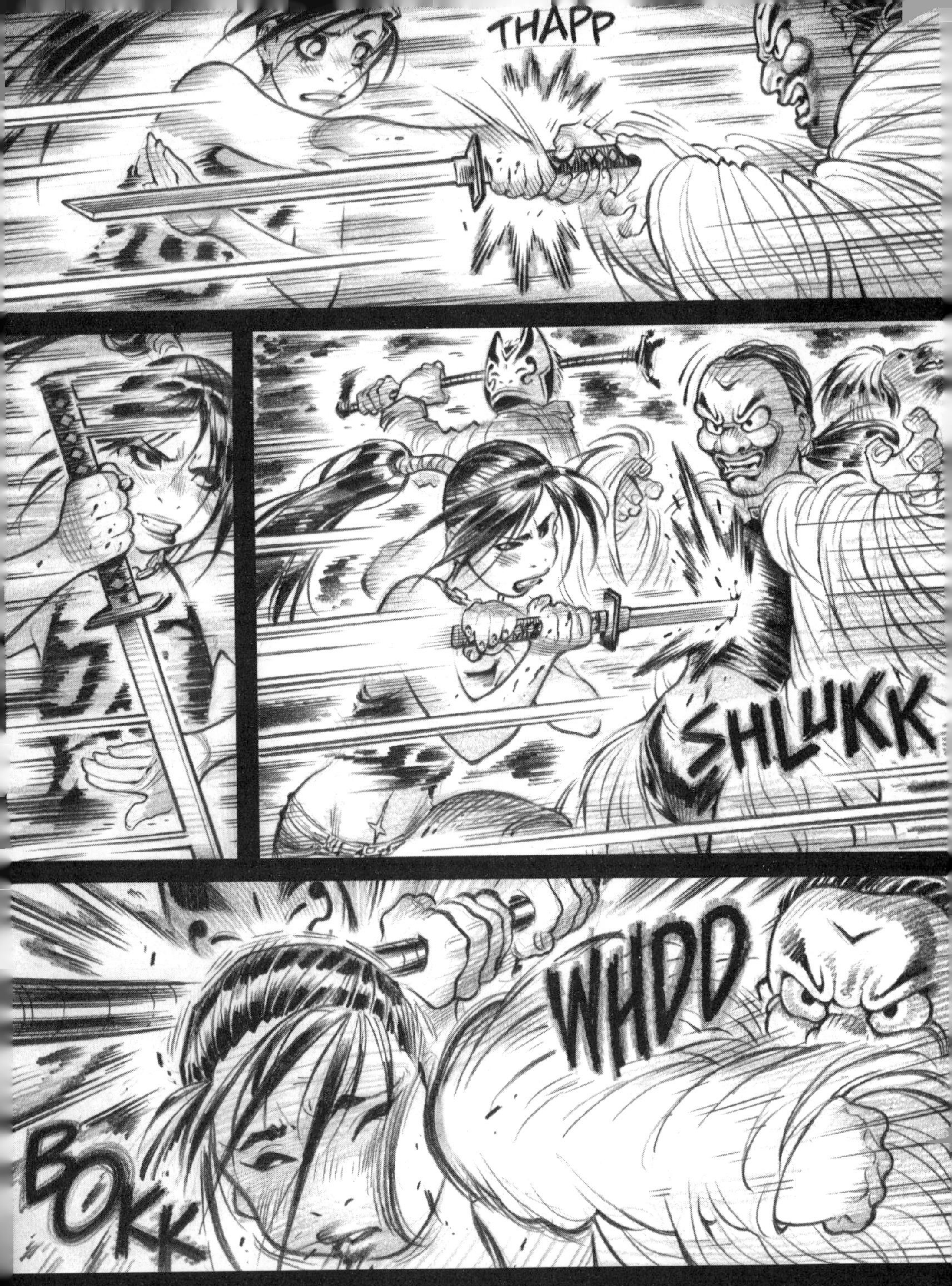
THAPP
SHLUKK
WHDD
BOKK

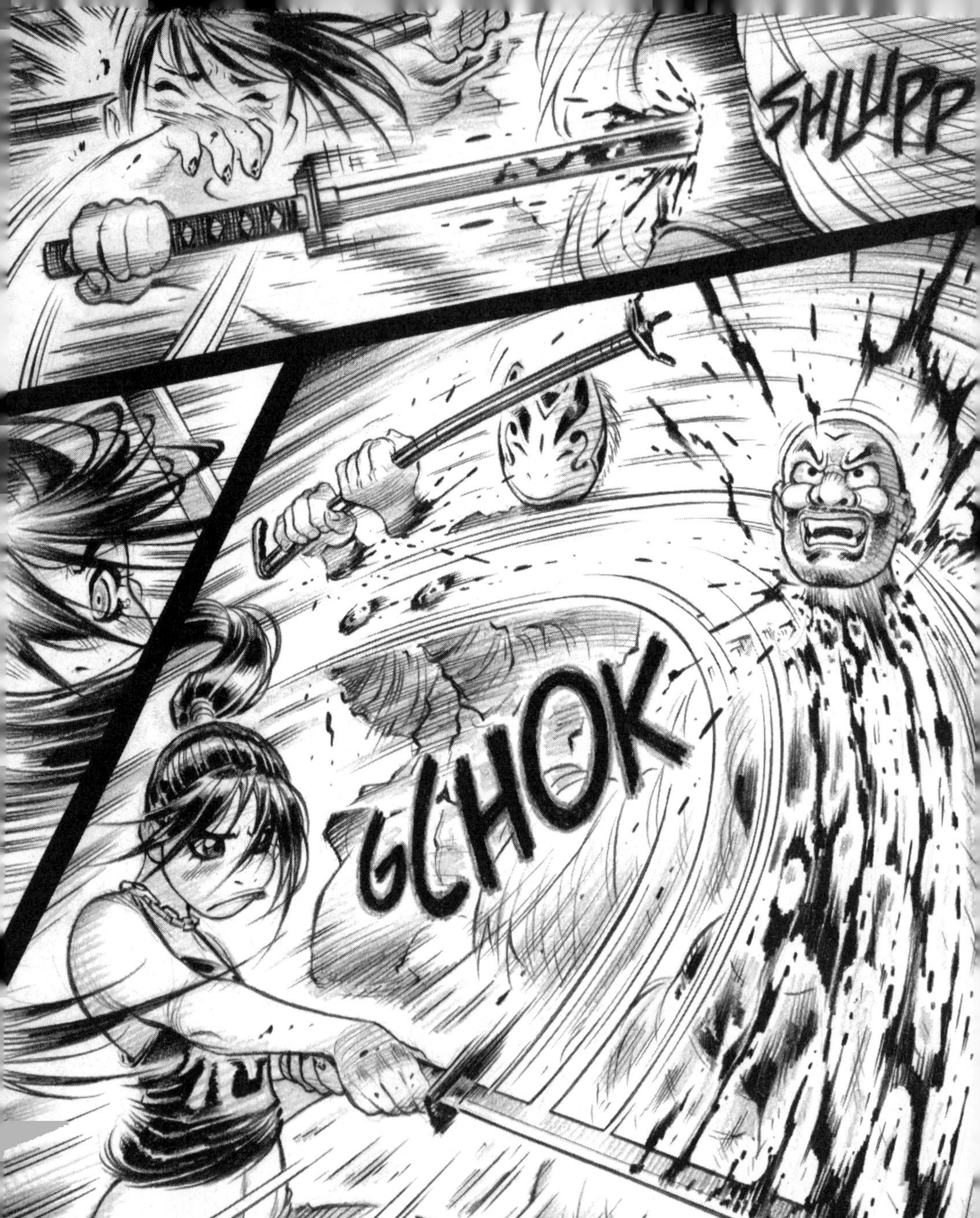
SHLUPP
GCHOK

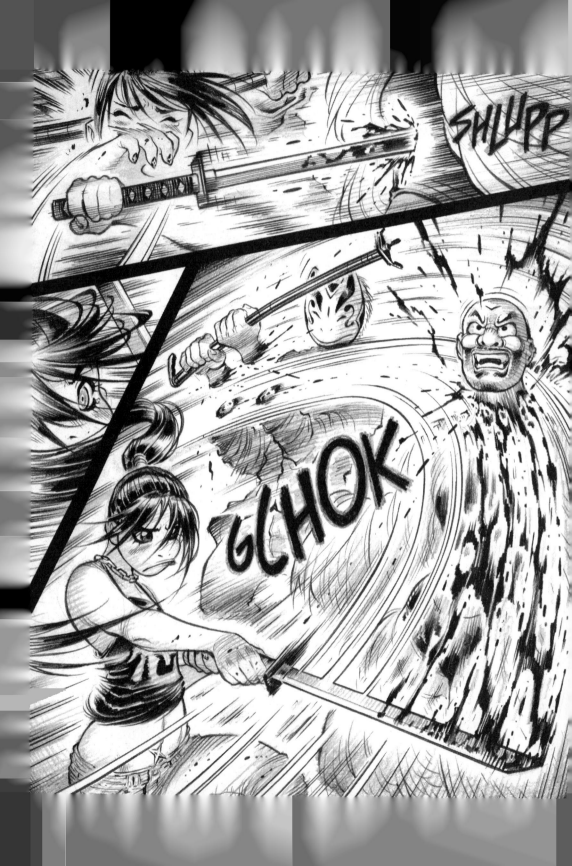

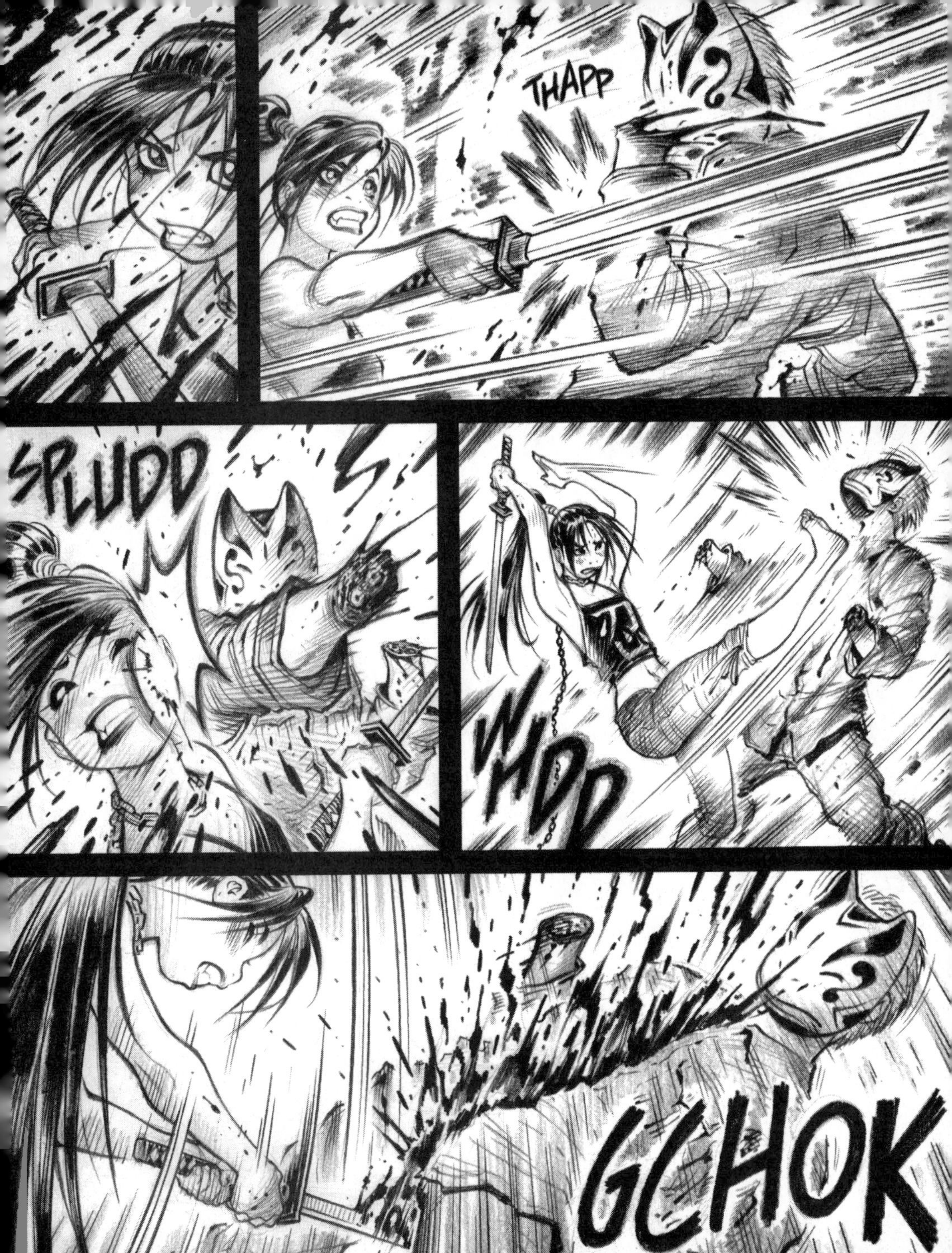
THAPP
SPLUDD
WHDD
GCHOK

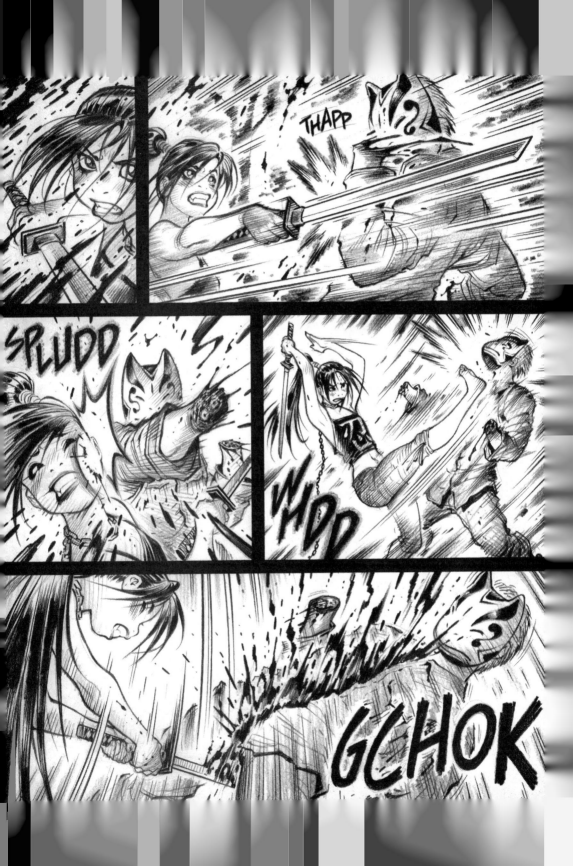

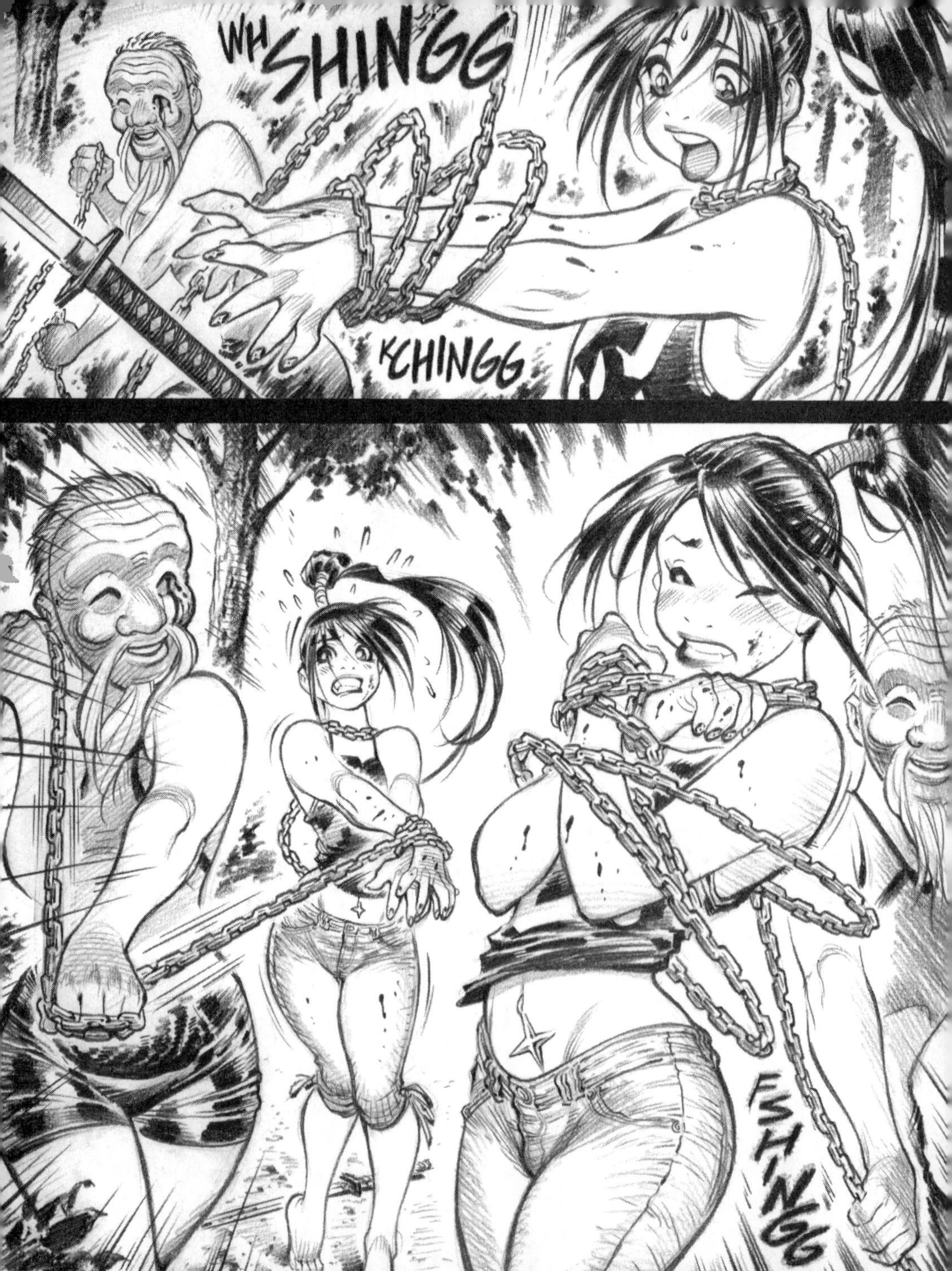
WH SHINGG
KCHINGG
FSHINGG

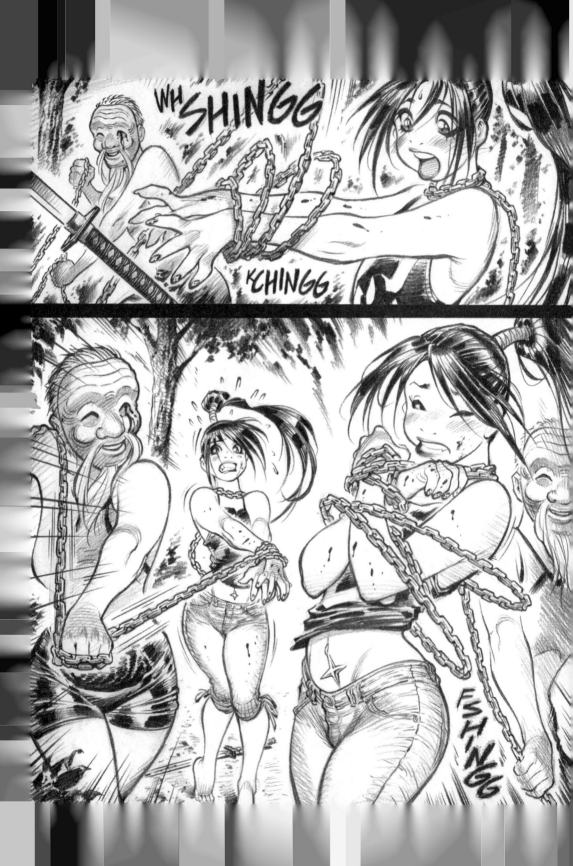

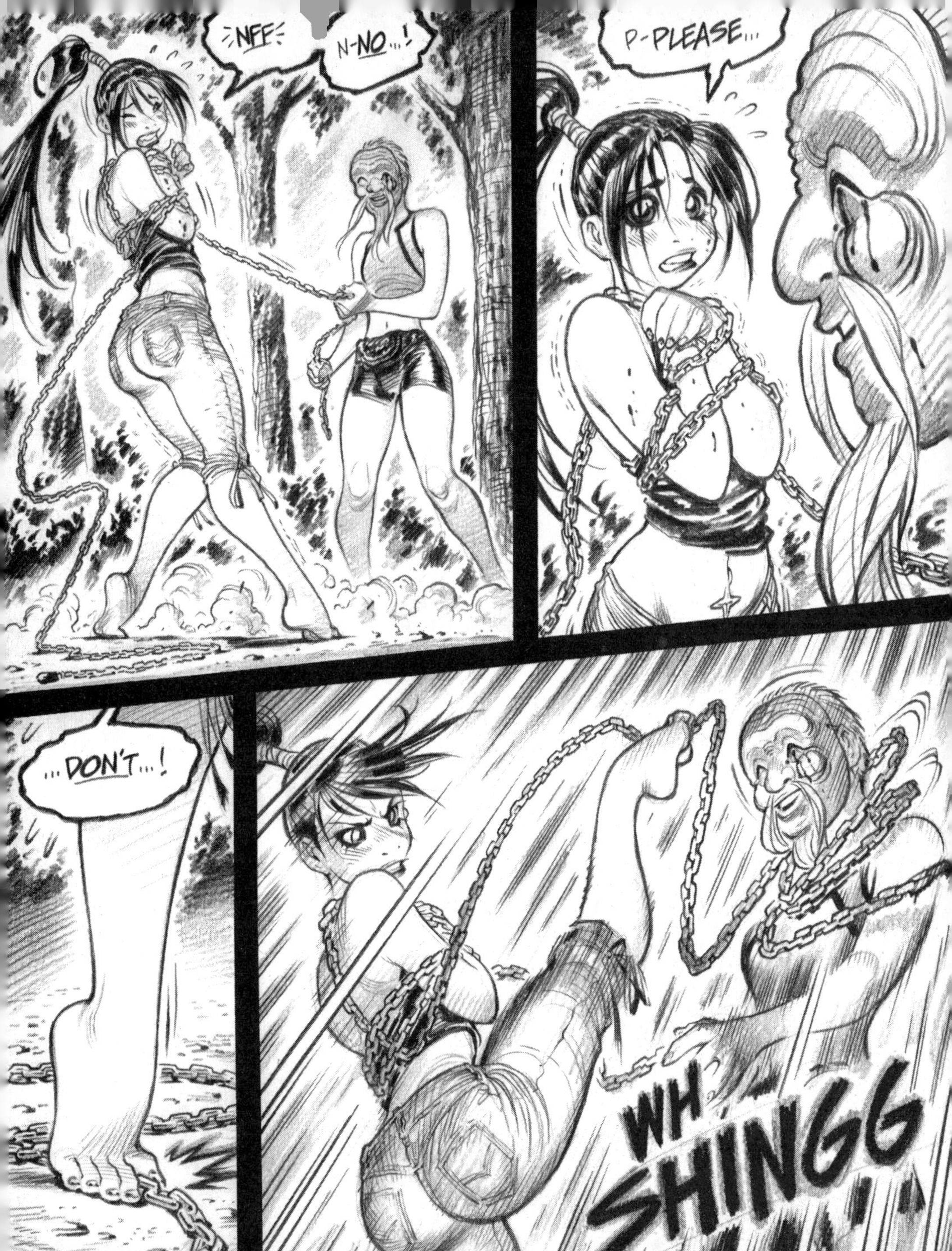
NFF
N-NO...!
P-PLEASE...
...DON'T...!
WH
SHINGG

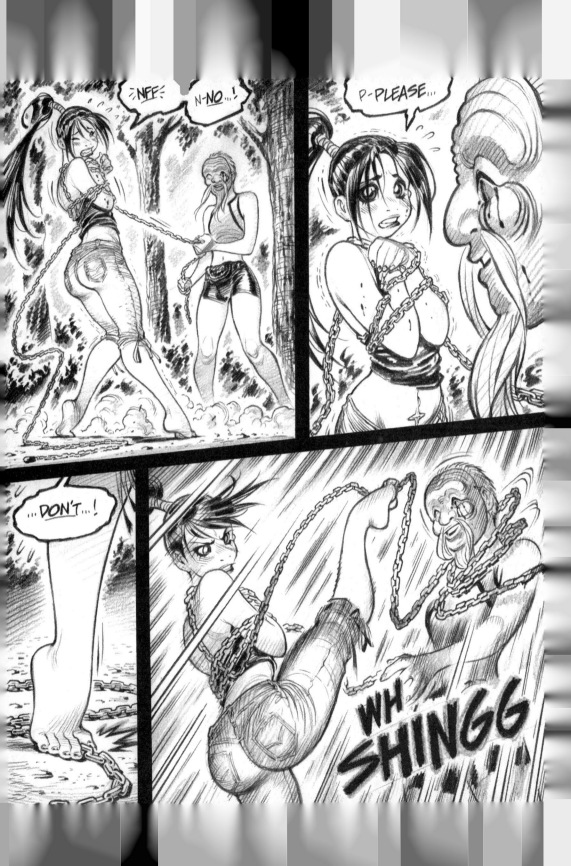

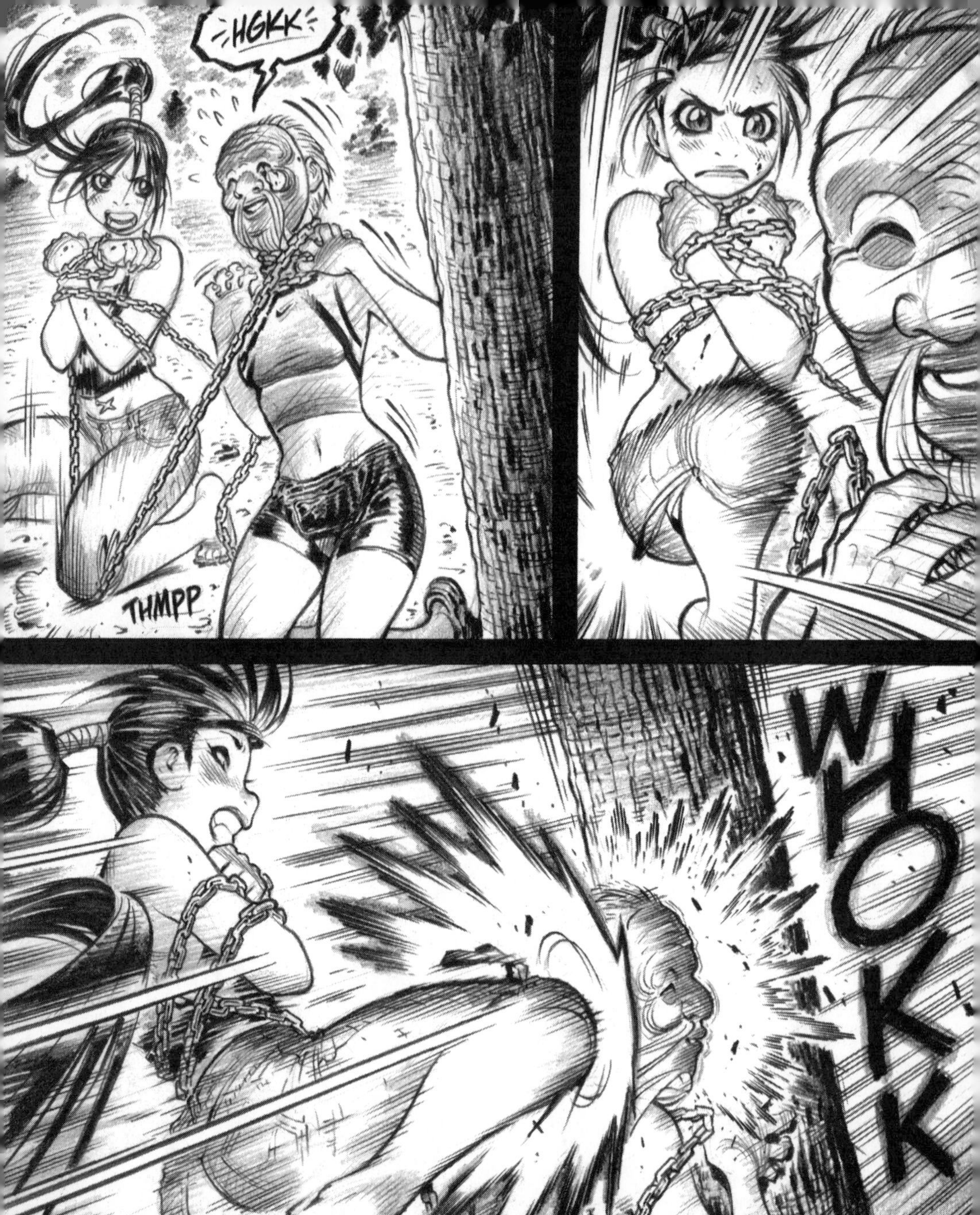
HGKK
THMPP
WHOKK

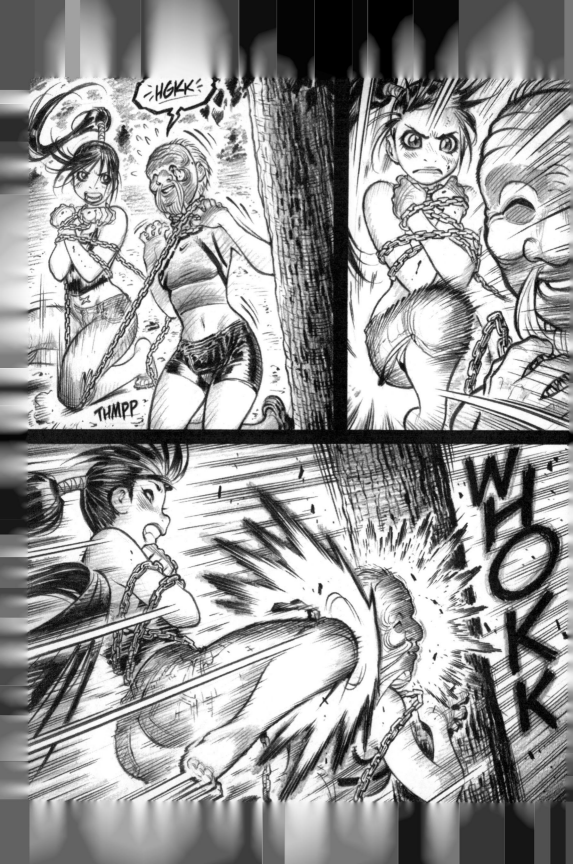

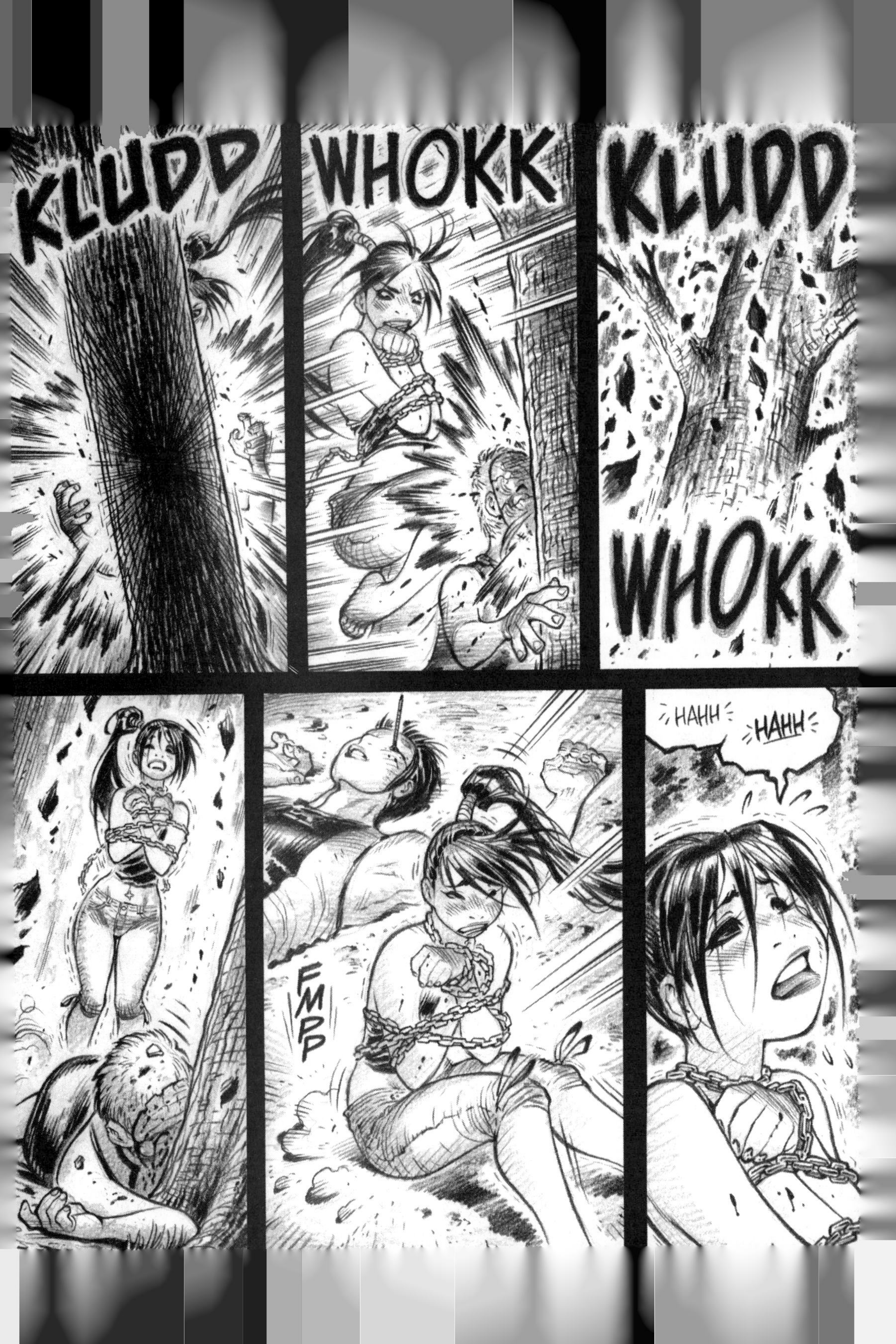
KLUDD
WHOKK
KLUDD
WHOKK
FMPP
HAHH
HAHH

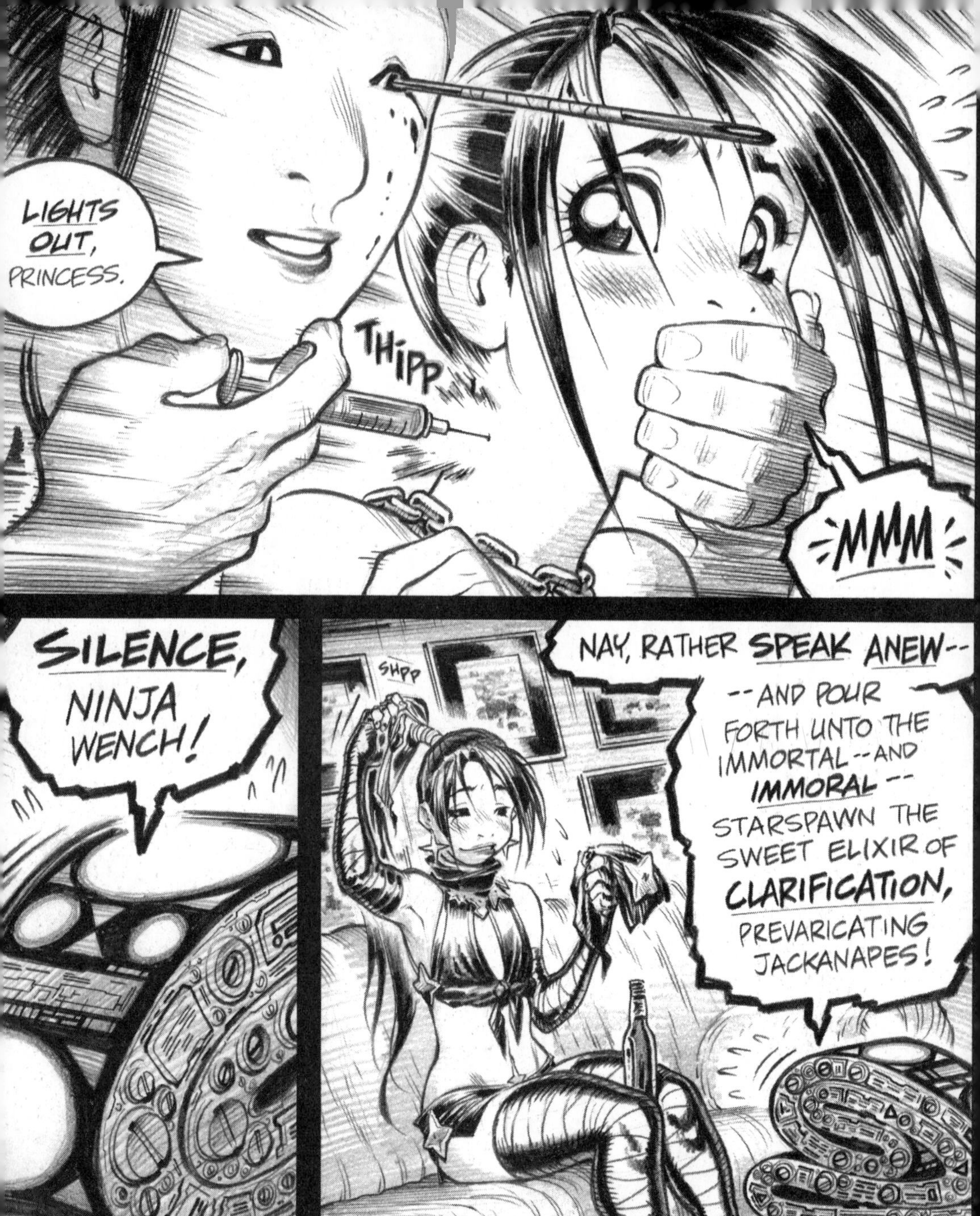
LIGHTS OUT, PRINCESS.
THIPP
MMM
SILENCE, NINJA WENCH!
SHPP
NAY, RATHER SPEAK ANEW--
--AND POUR FORTH UNTO THE IMMORTAL--AND IMMORAL--STARSPAWN THE SWEET ELIXIR OF CLARIFICATION, PREVARICATING JACKANAPES!

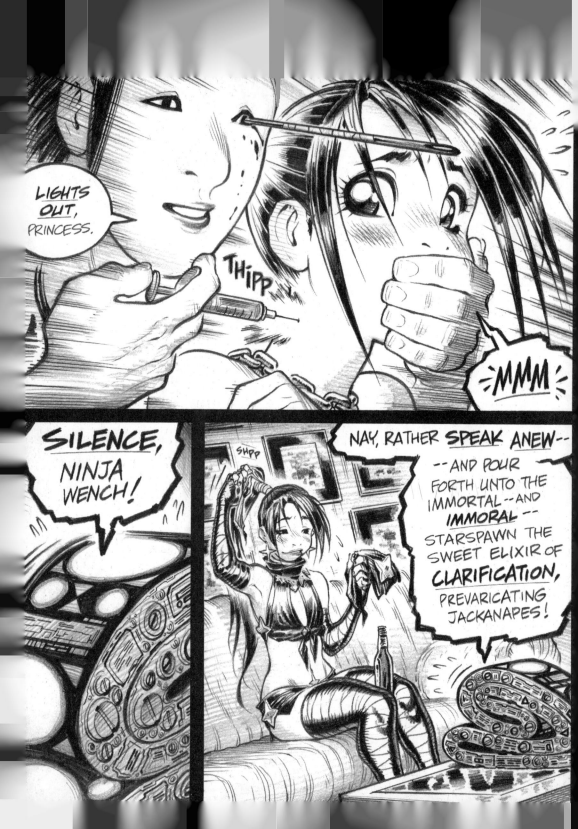

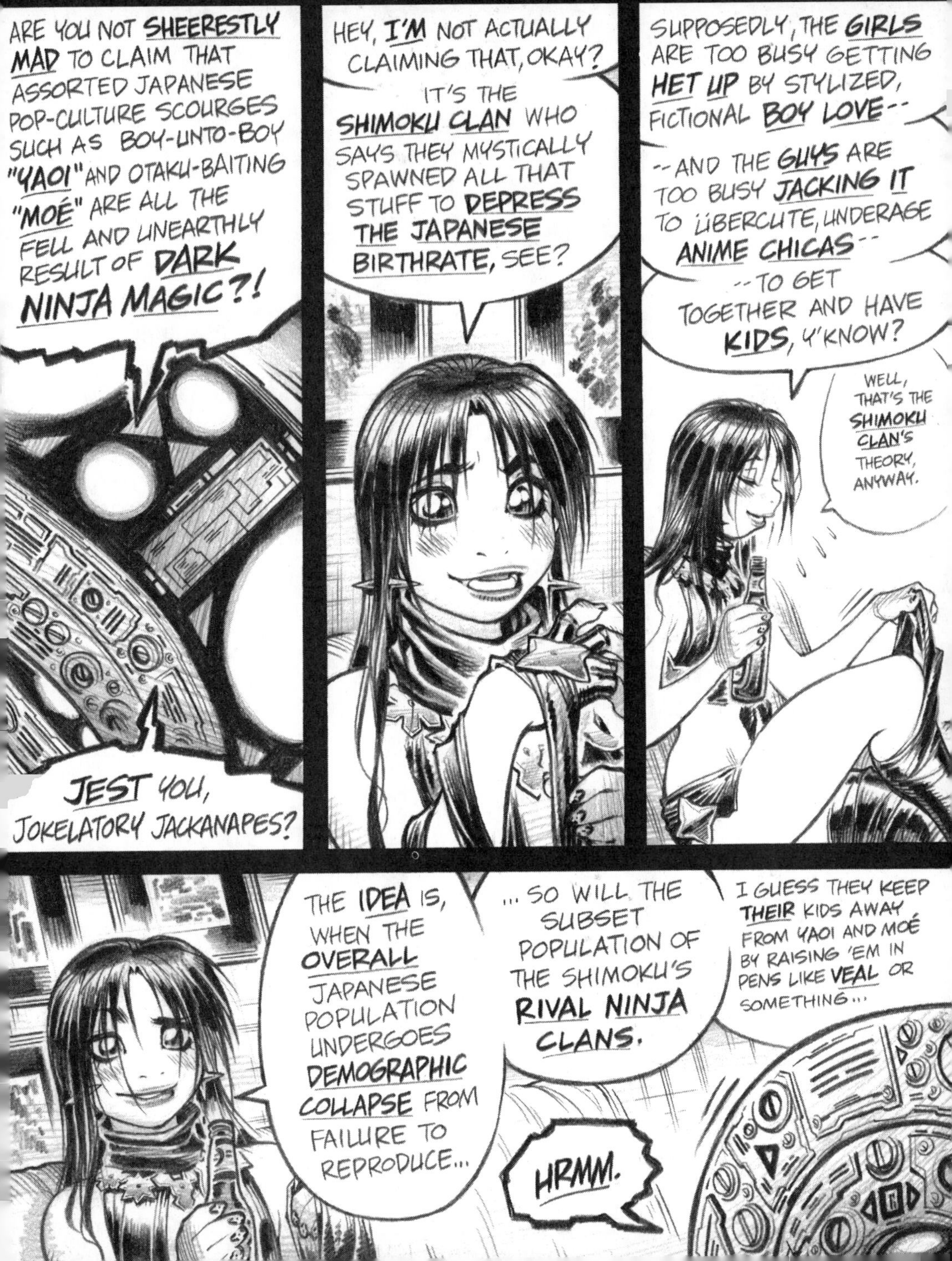
ARE YOU NOT SHEERESTLY MAD TO CLAIM THAT ASSORTED JAPANESE POP-CULTURE SCOURGES SUCH AS BOY-UNTO-BOY "YAOI" AND OTAKU-BAITING "MOÉ" ARE ALL THE FELL AND UNEARTHLY RESULT OF DARK NINJA MAGIC?!
JEST YOU, JOKELATORY JACKANAPES?
HEY, I'M NOT ACTUALLY CLAIMING THAT, OKAY?
IT'S THE SHIMOKU CLAN WHO SAYS THEY MYSTICALLY SPAWNED ALL THAT STUFF TO DEPRESS THE JAPANESE BIRTHRATE, SEE?
SUPPOSEDLY, THE GIRLS ARE TOO BUSY GETTING HET UP BY STYLIZED, FICTIONAL BOY LOVE--
--AND THE GUYS ARE TOO BUSY JACKING IT TO ÜBERCUTE, UNDERAGE ANIME CHICAS--
--TO GET TOGETHER AND HAVE KIDS, Y'KNOW?
WELL, THAT'S THE SHIMOKU CLAN'S THEORY, ANYWAY.
THE IDEA IS, WHEN THE OVERALL JAPANESE POPULATION UNDERGOES DEMOGRAPHIC COLLAPSE FROM FAILURE TO REPRODUCE...
... SO WILL THE SUBSET POPULATION OF THE SHIMOKU'S RIVAL NINJA CLANS.
I GUESS THEY KEEP THEIR KIDS AWAY FROM YAOI AND MOÉ BY RAISING 'EM IN PENS LIKE VEAL OR SOMETHING...
HRMM.

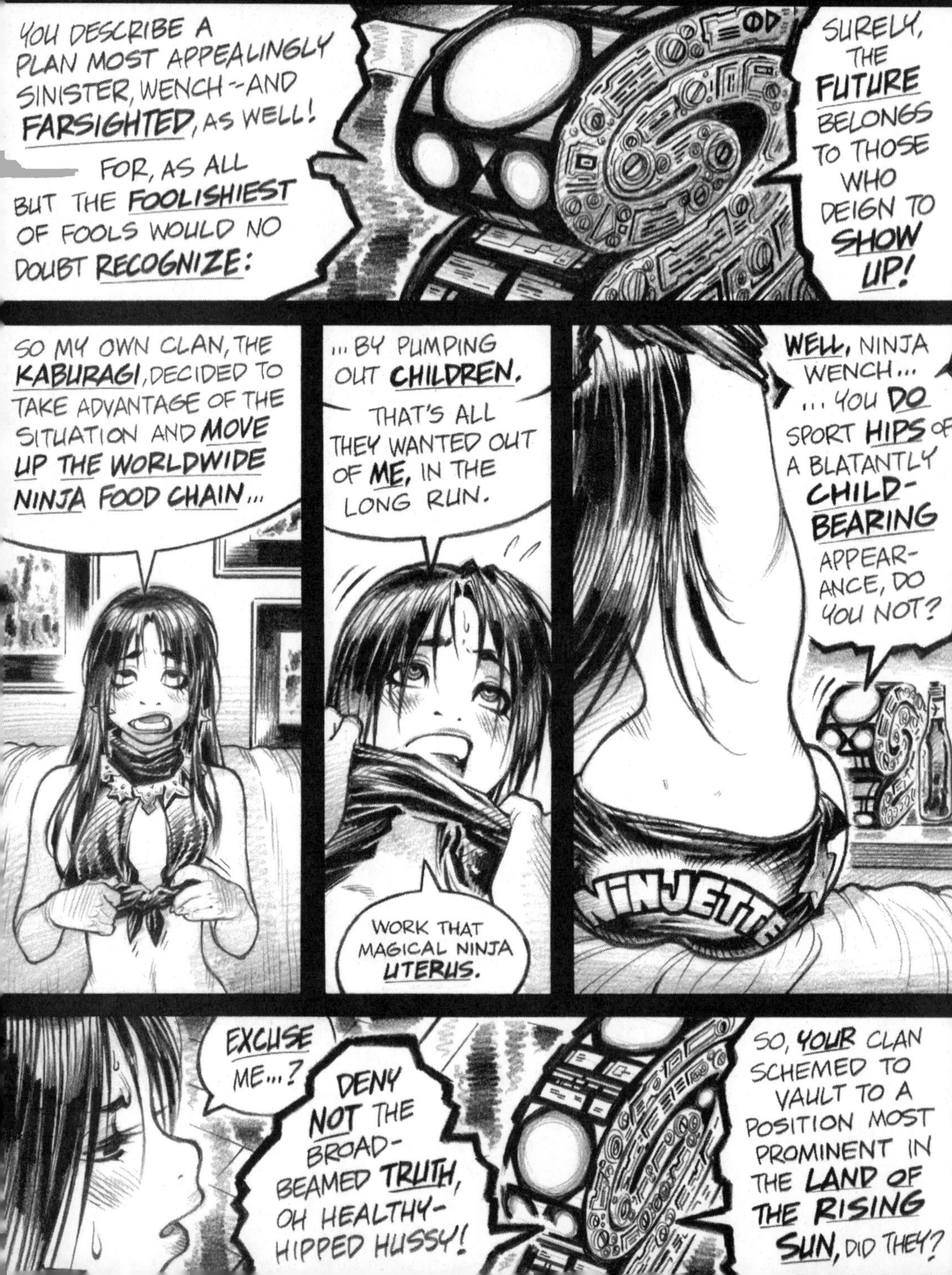
YOU DESCRIBE A PLAN MOST APPEALINGLY SINISTER, WENCH--AND FARSIGHTED, AS WELL!
FOR, AS ALL BUT THE FOOLISHIEST OF FOOLS WOULD NO DOUBT RECOGNIZE:
SURELY, THE FUTURE BELONGS TO THOSE WHO DEIGN TO SHOW UP!
SO MY OWN CLAN, THE KABURAGI, DECIDED TO TAKE ADVANTAGE OF THE SITUATION AND MOVE UP THE WORLDWIDE NINJA FOOD CHAIN...
...BY PUMPING OUT CHILDREN.
THAT'S ALL THEY WANTED OUT OF ME, IN THE LONG RUN.
WORK THAT MAGICAL NINJA UTERUS.
WELL, NINJA WENCH...
...YOU DO SPORT HIPS OF A BLATANTLY CHILD-BEARING APPEAR-ANCE, DO YOU NOT?
NINJETTE
EXCUSE ME...?
DENY NOT THE BROAD-BEAMED TRUTH, OH HEALTHY-HIPPED HUSSY!
SO, YOUR CLAN SCHEMED TO VAULT TO A POSITION MOST PROMINENT IN THE LAND OF THE RISING SUN, DID THEY?

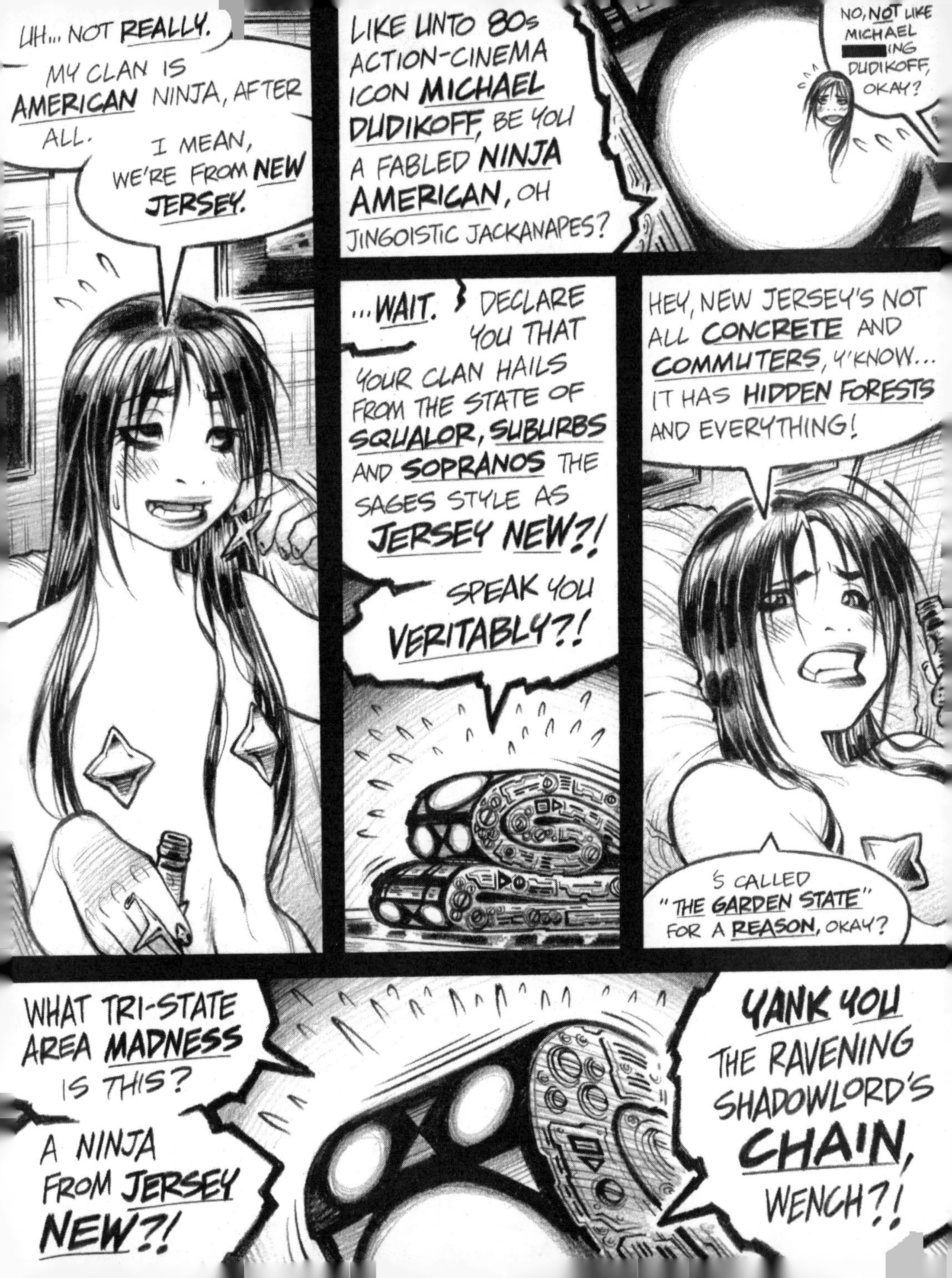
UH... NOT REALLY.
MY CLAN IS AMERICAN NINJA, AFTER ALL.
I MEAN, WE'RE FROM NEW JERSEY.
LIKE UNTO 80s ACTION-CINEMA ICON MICHAEL DUDIKOFF, BE YOU A FABLED NINJA AMERICAN, OH JINGOISTIC JACKANAPES?
NO, NOT LIKE MICHAEL [redacted]ING DUDIKOFF, OKAY?
...WAIT. DECLARE YOU THAT YOUR CLAN HAILS FROM THE STATE OF SQUALOR, SUBURBS AND SOPRANOS THE SAGES STYLE AS JERSEY NEW?!
SPEAK YOU VERITABLY?!
HEY, NEW JERSEY'S NOT ALL CONCRETE AND COMMUTERS, Y'KNOW... IT HAS HIDDEN FORESTS AND EVERYTHING!
'S CALLED "THE GARDEN STATE" FOR A REASON, OKAY?
WHAT TRI-STATE AREA MADNESS IS THIS?
A NINJA FROM JERSEY NEW?!
YANK YOU THE RAVENING SHADOWLORD'S CHAIN, WENCH?!

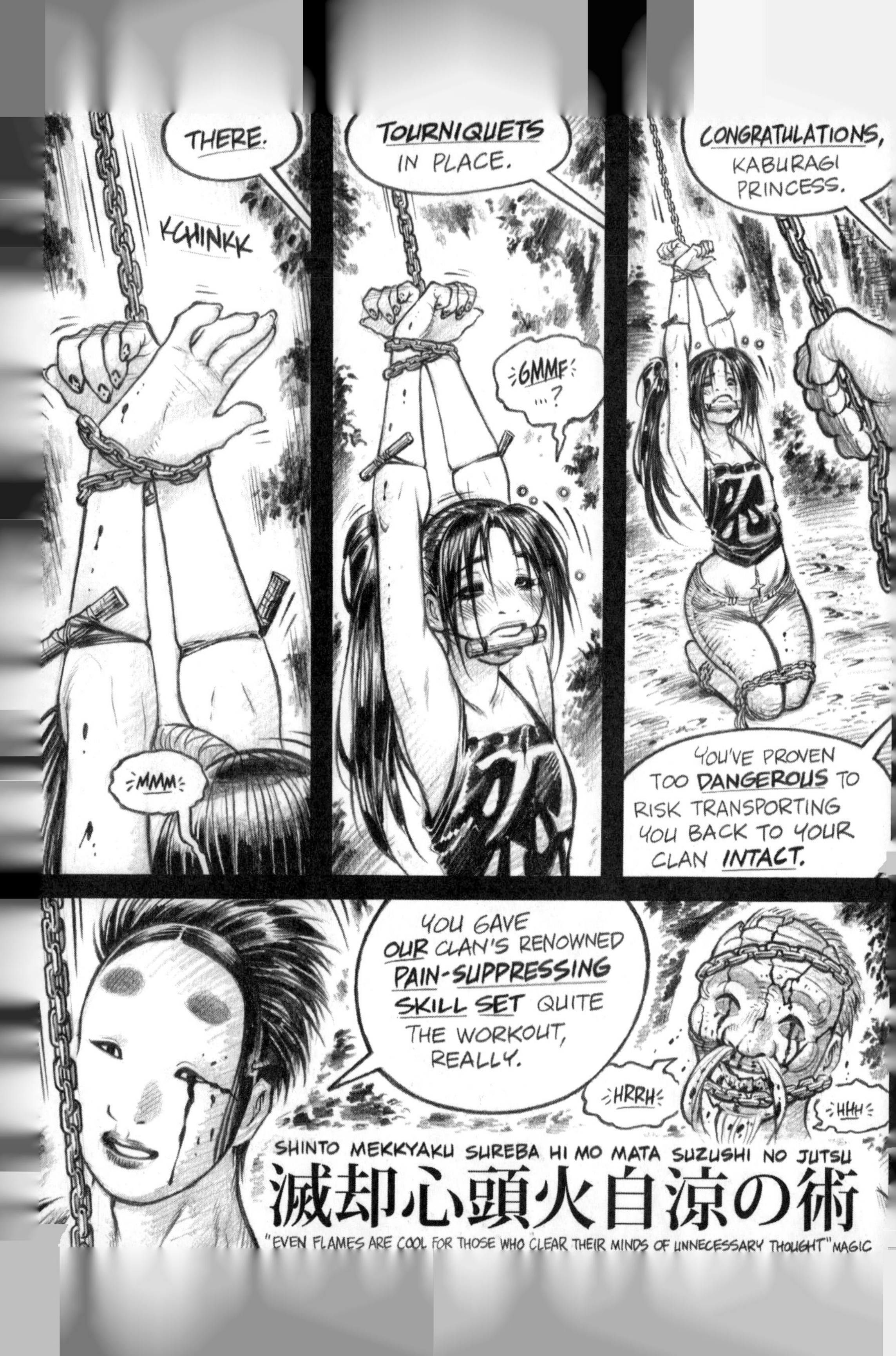
THERE.
KCHINKK
MMM
TOURNIQUETS IN PLACE.
GMMF ...?
CONGRATULATIONS, KABURAGI PRINCESS.
YOU'VE PROVEN TOO DANGEROUS TO RISK TRANSPORTING YOU BACK TO YOUR CLAN INTACT.
YOU GAVE OUR CLAN'S RENOWNED PAIN-SUPPRESSING SKILL SET QUITE THE WORKOUT, REALLY.
HRRH
HHH
SHINTO MEKKYAKU SUREBA HI MO MATA SUZUSHI NO JUTSU
滅却心頭火自涼の術
"EVEN FLAMES ARE COOL FOR THOSE WHO CLEAR THEIR MINDS OF UNNECESSARY THOUGHT" MAGIC

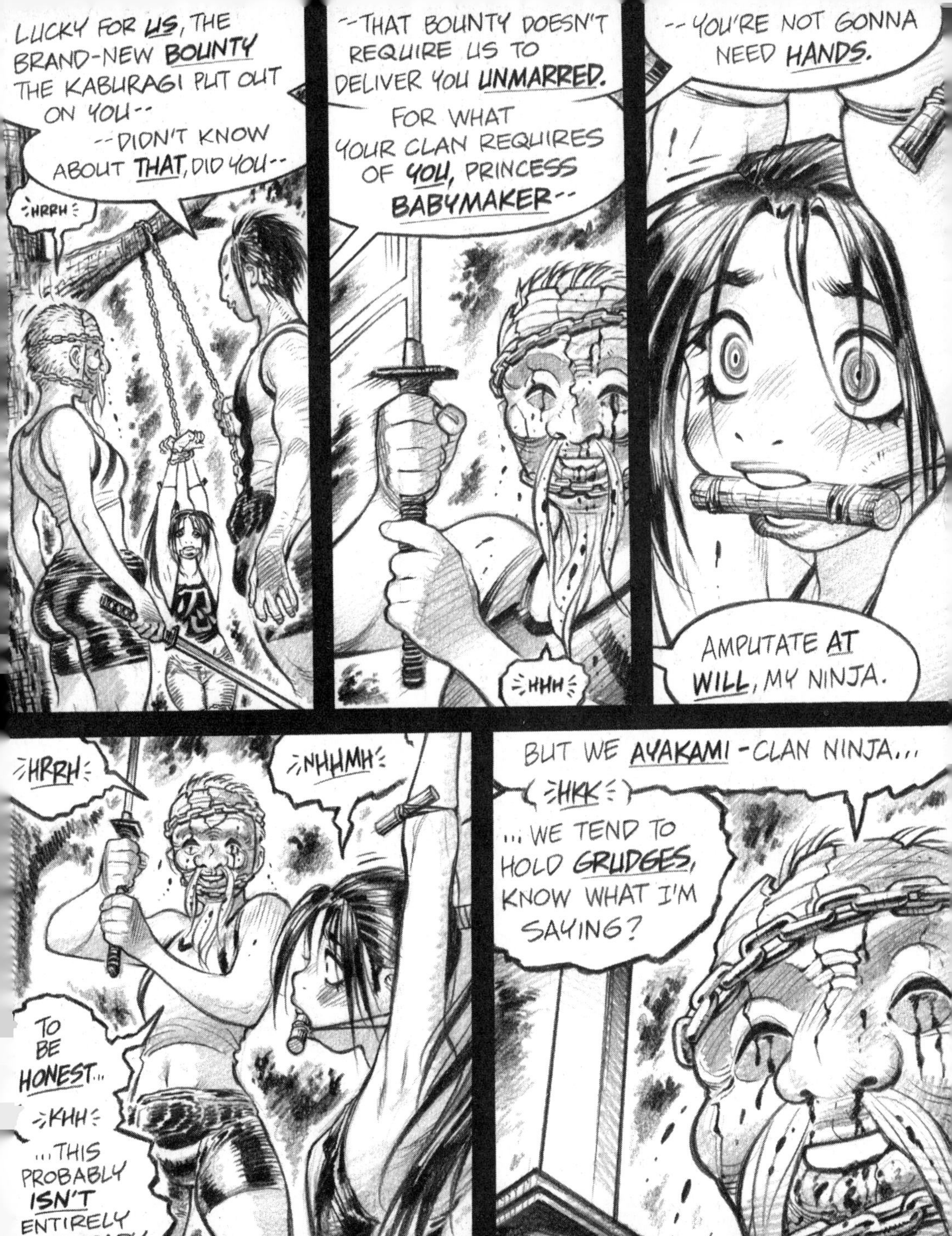
LUCKY FOR US, THE BRAND-NEW BOUNTY THE KABURAGI PUT OUT ON YOU--
--DIDN'T KNOW ABOUT THAT, DID YOU--
HRRH
--THAT BOUNTY DOESN'T REQUIRE US TO DELIVER YOU UNMARRED.
FOR WHAT YOUR CLAN REQUIRES OF YOU, PRINCESS BABYMAKER--
HHH
--YOU'RE NOT GONNA NEED HANDS.
AMPUTATE AT WILL, MY NINJA.
HRRH
NHHMH
TO BE HONEST...
KHH
...THIS PROBABLY ISN'T ENTIRELY NECESSARY.
BUT WE AYAKAMI-CLAN NINJA...
HKK
...WE TEND TO HOLD GRUDGES, KNOW WHAT I'M SAYING?

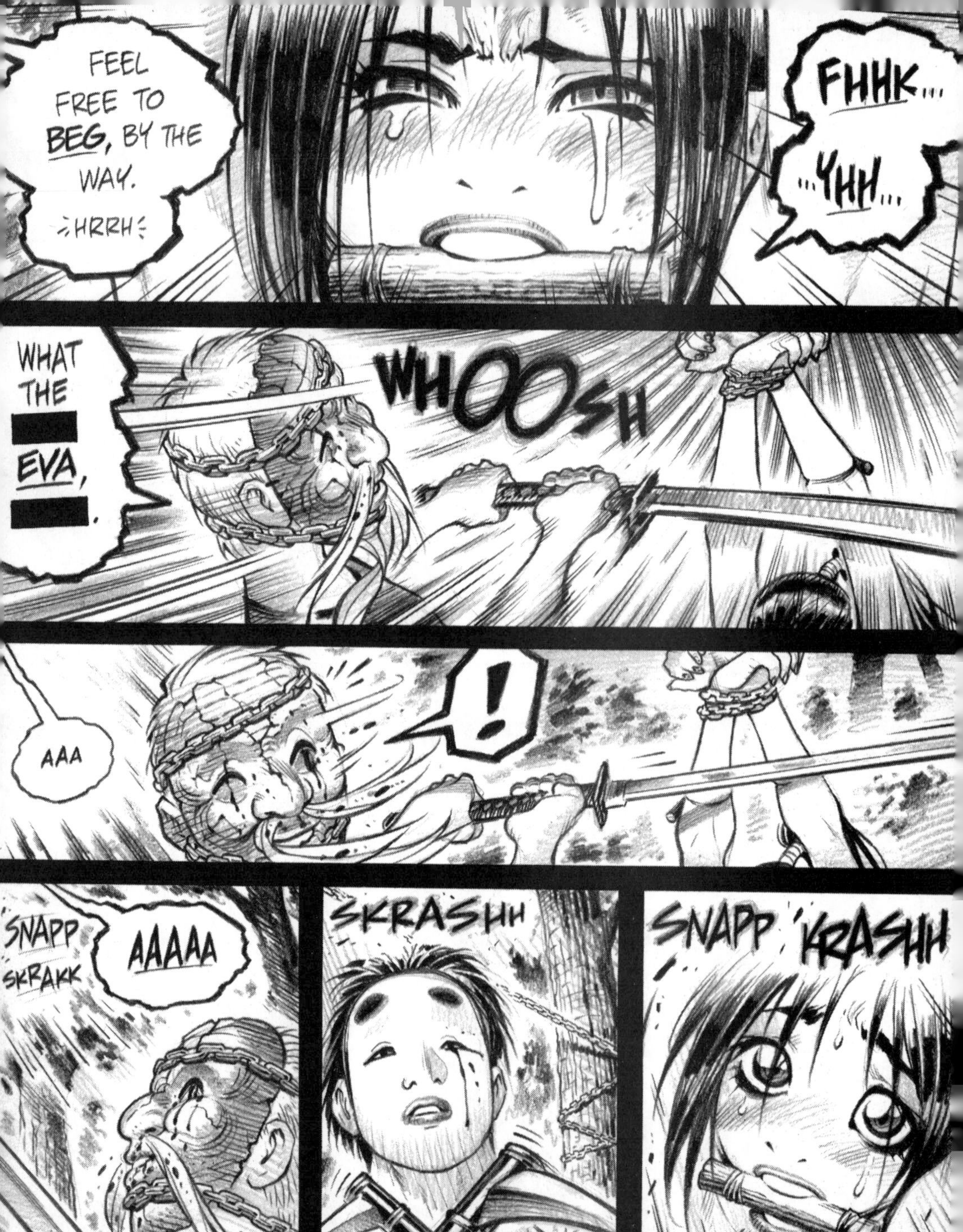
FEEL FREE TO BEG, BY THE WAY.
HRRH
FHHK... ...YHH...
WHAT THE [redacted] EVA, [redacted].
WHOOSH
AAA
!
SNAPP
SKRAKK
AAAAA
SKRASHH
SNAPP
KRASHH

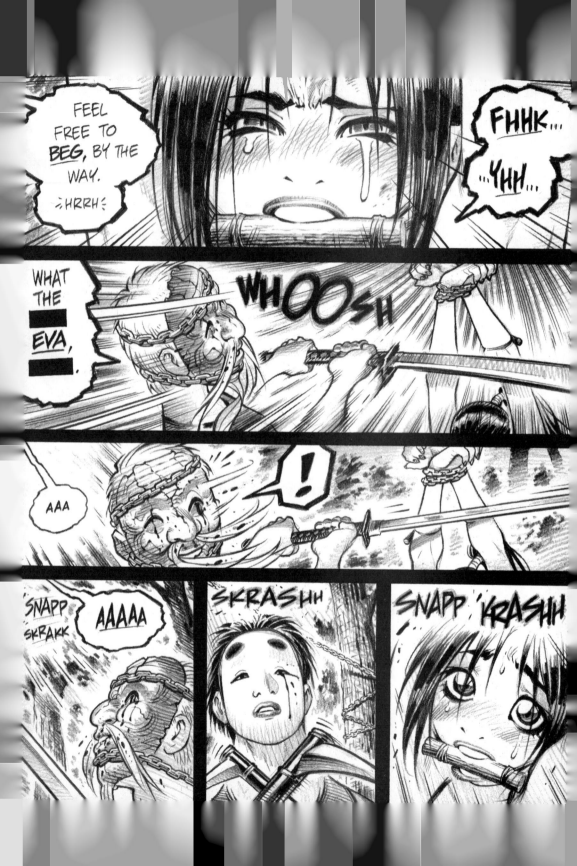

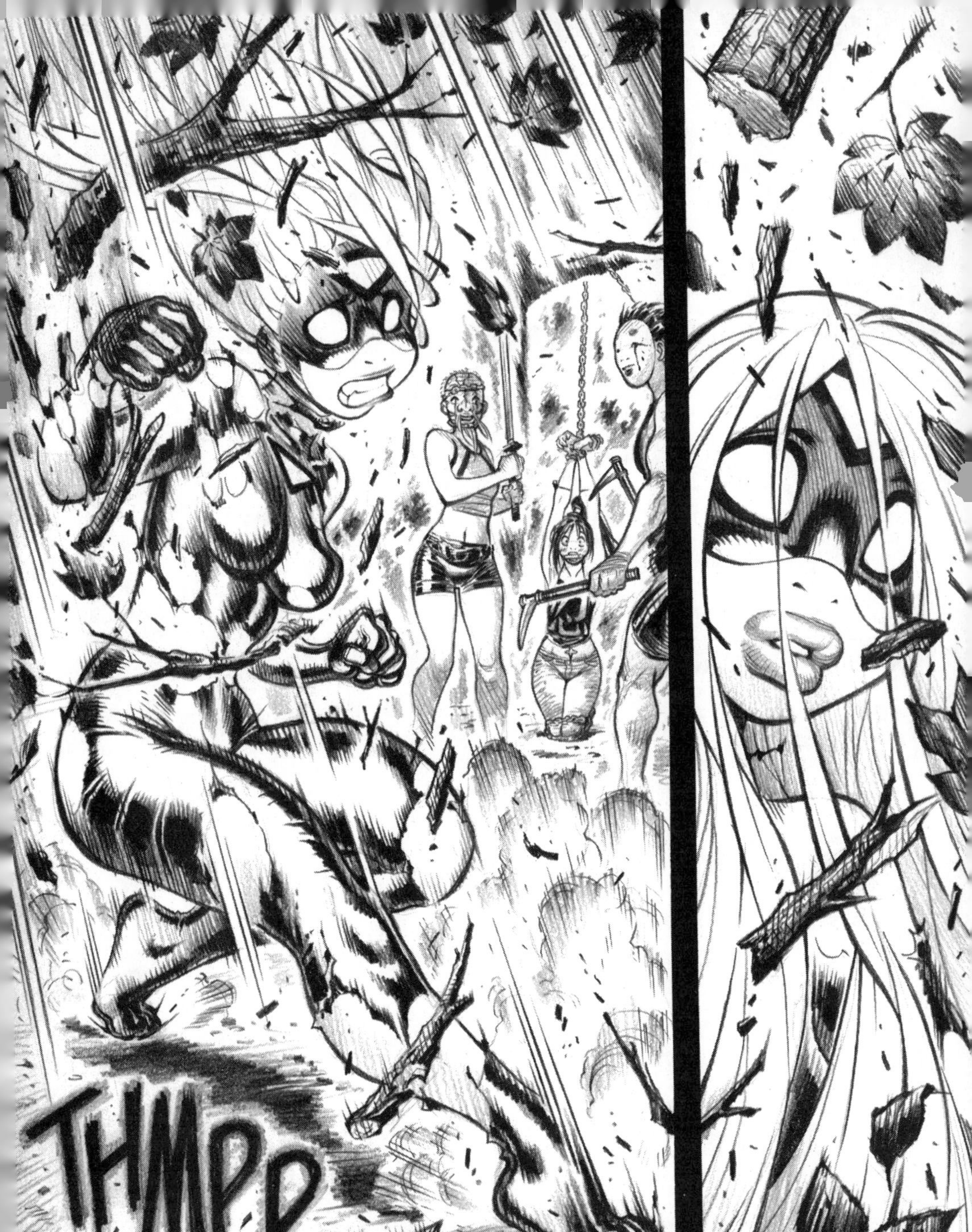
THMPP

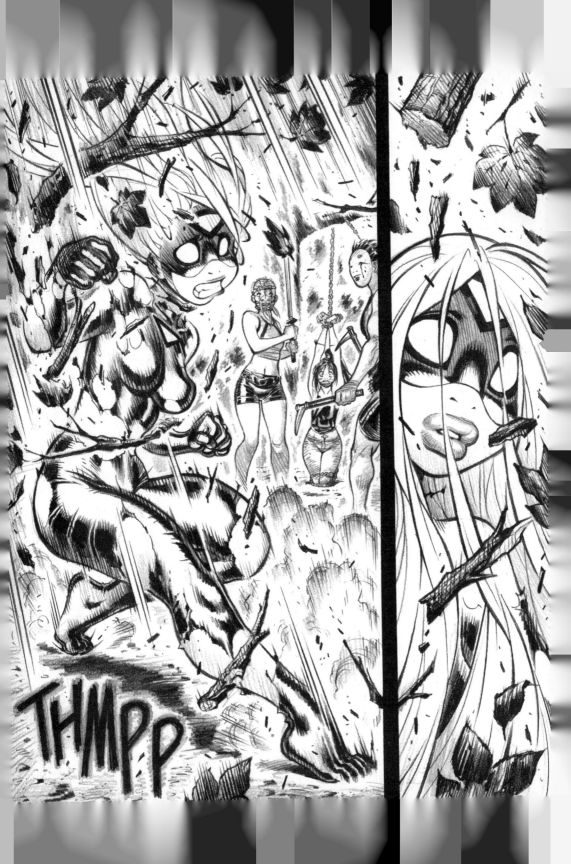

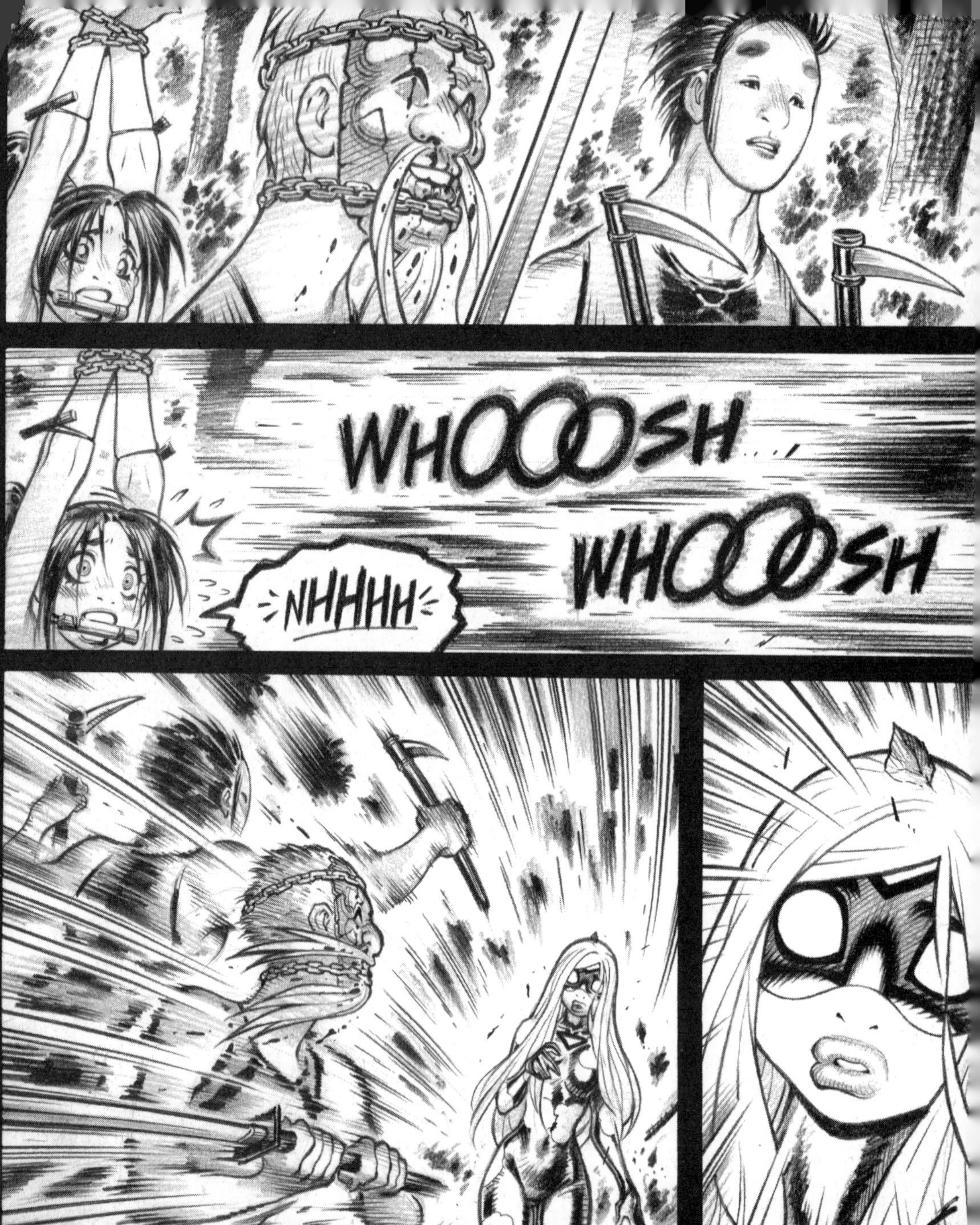
WHOOOOSH...
WHOOOOSH
NHHHH

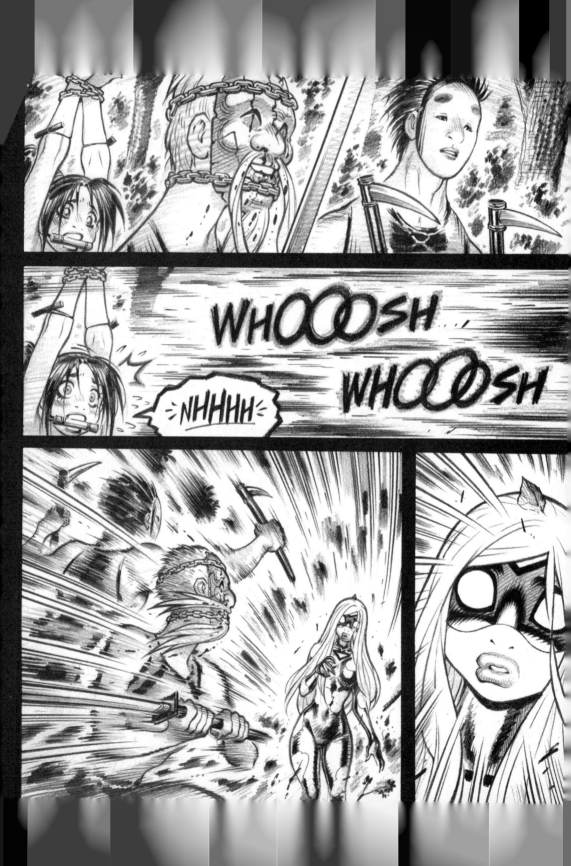

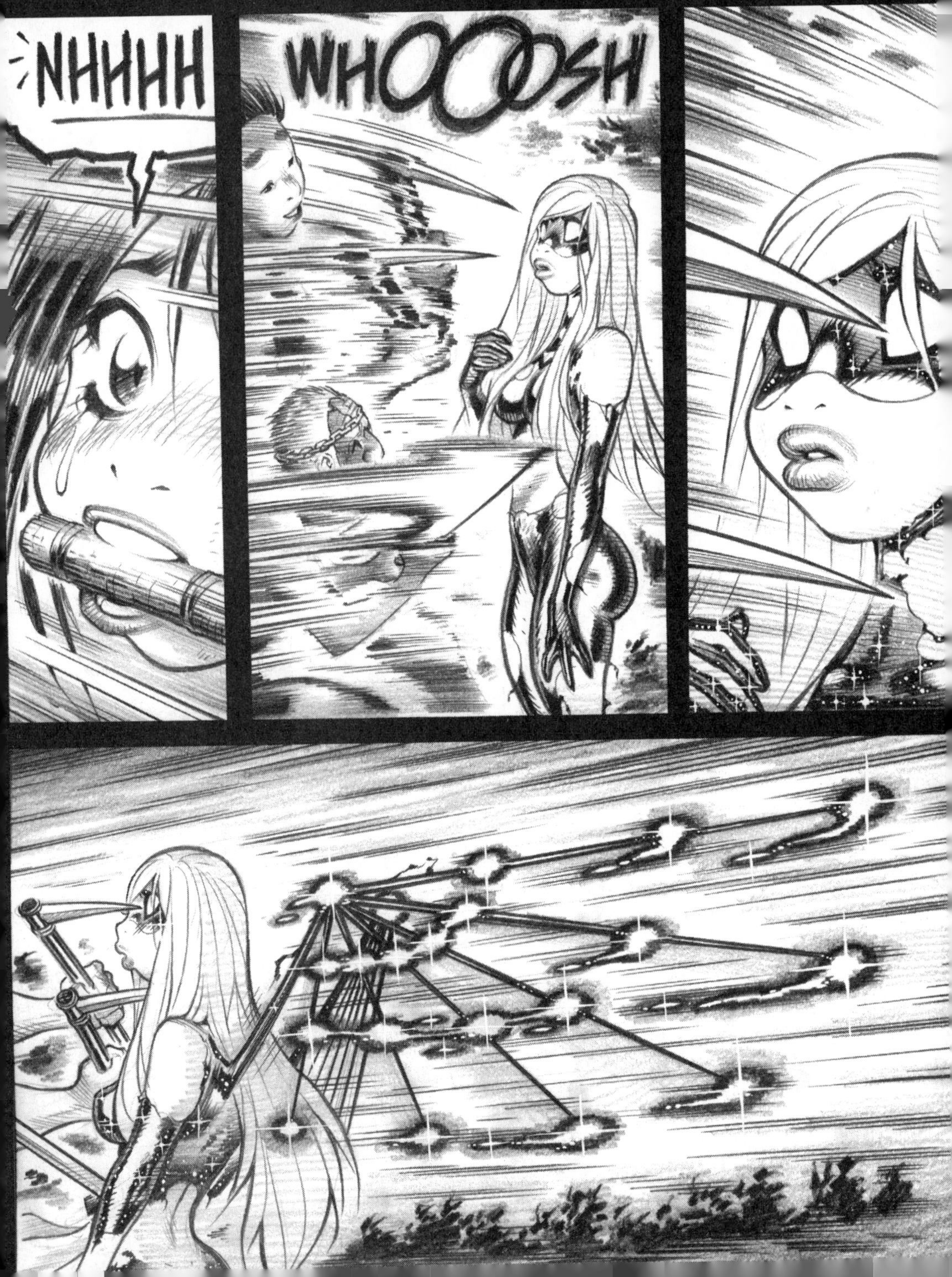
NHHHH
WHOOOSH

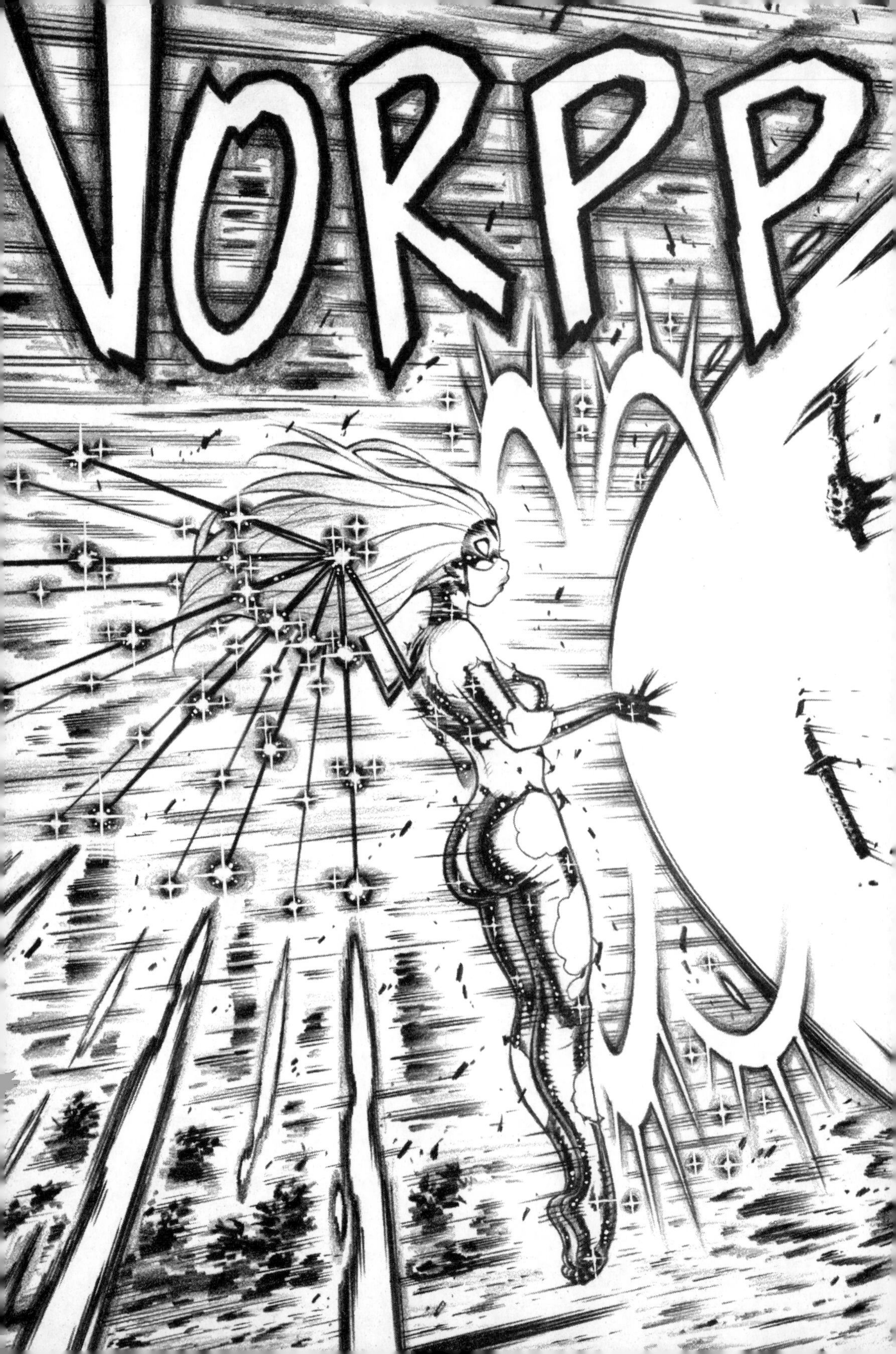
VORPP

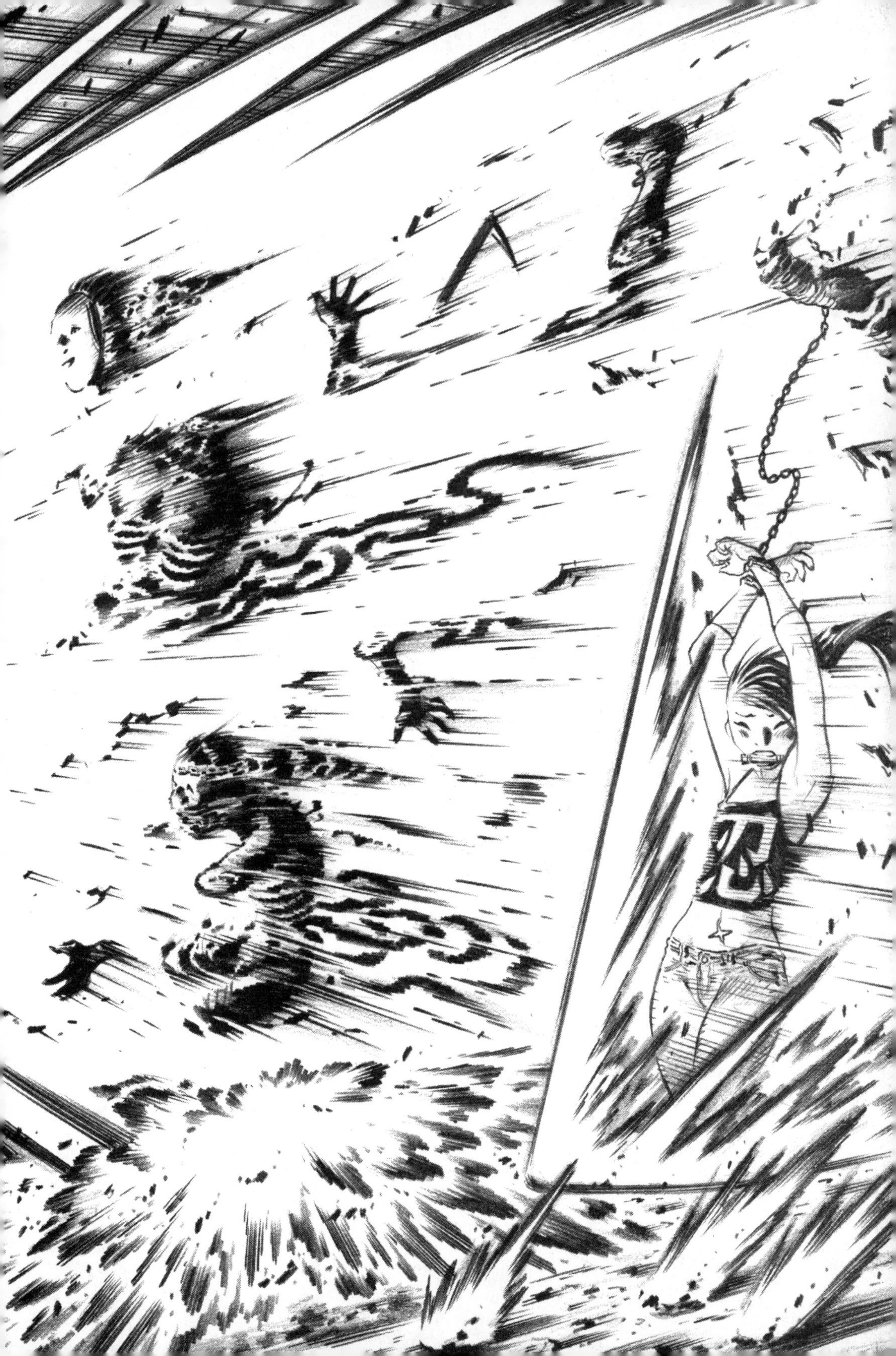

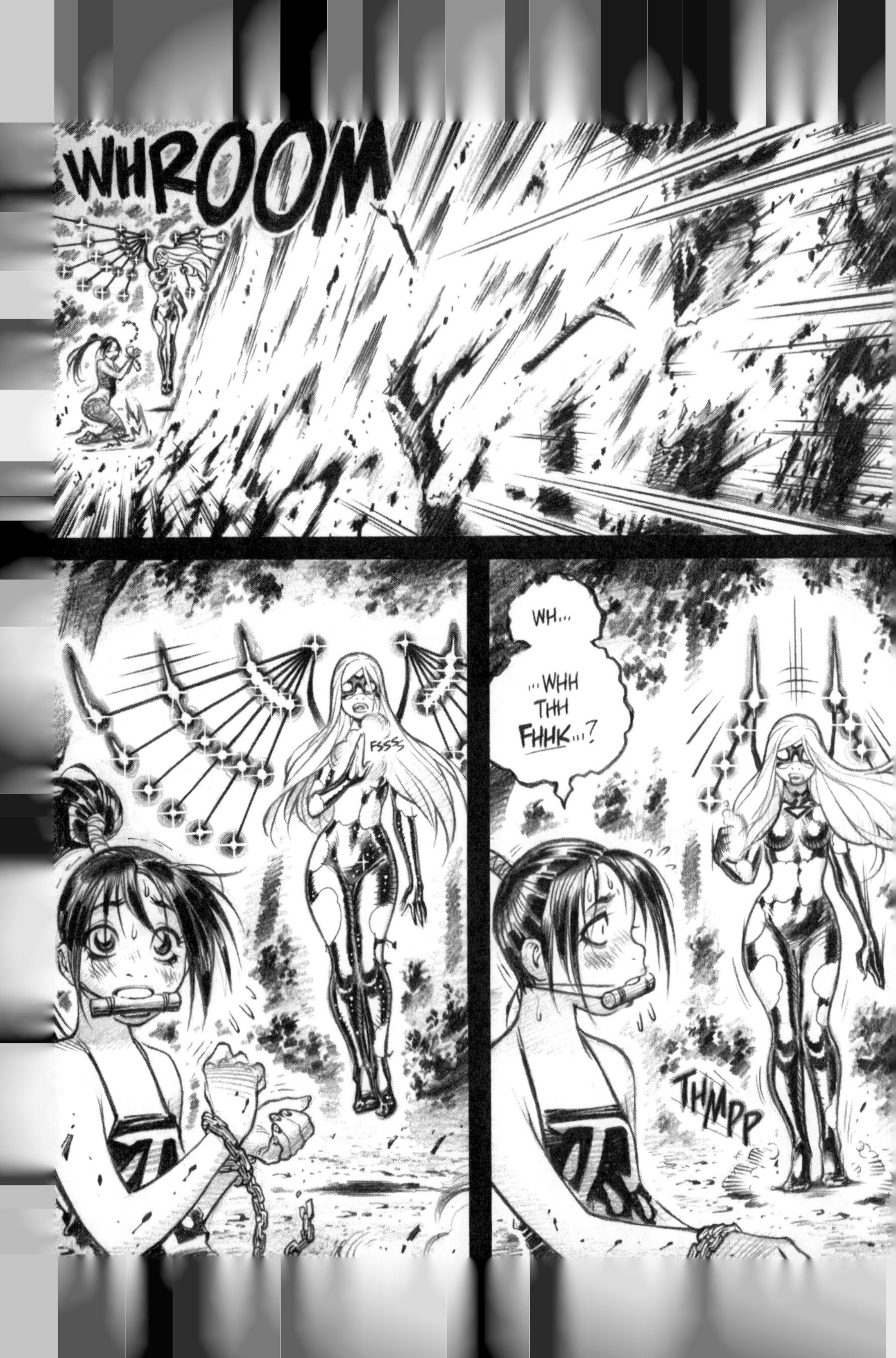
WHROOM
FSSSS
WH...
...WHH THH FHHK...?
THMPP

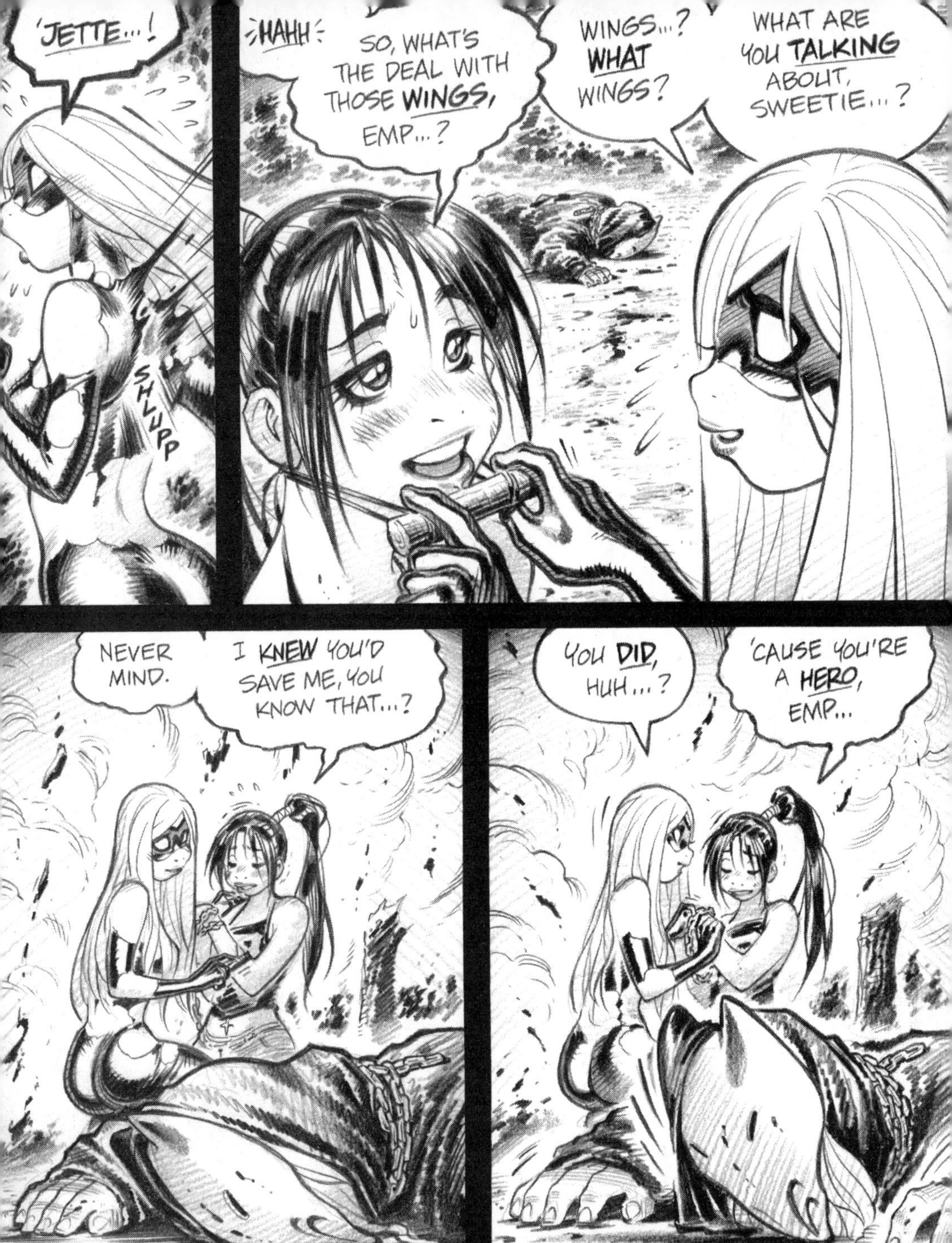
'JETTE...!
SHLUPP
HAHH
SO, WHAT'S THE DEAL WITH THOSE WINGS, EMP...?
WINGS...? WHAT WINGS?
WHAT ARE YOU TALKING ABOUT, SWEETIE...?
NEVER MIND.
I KNEW YOU'D SAVE ME, YOU KNOW THAT...?
YOU DID, HUH...?
'CAUSE YOU'RE A HERO, EMP...

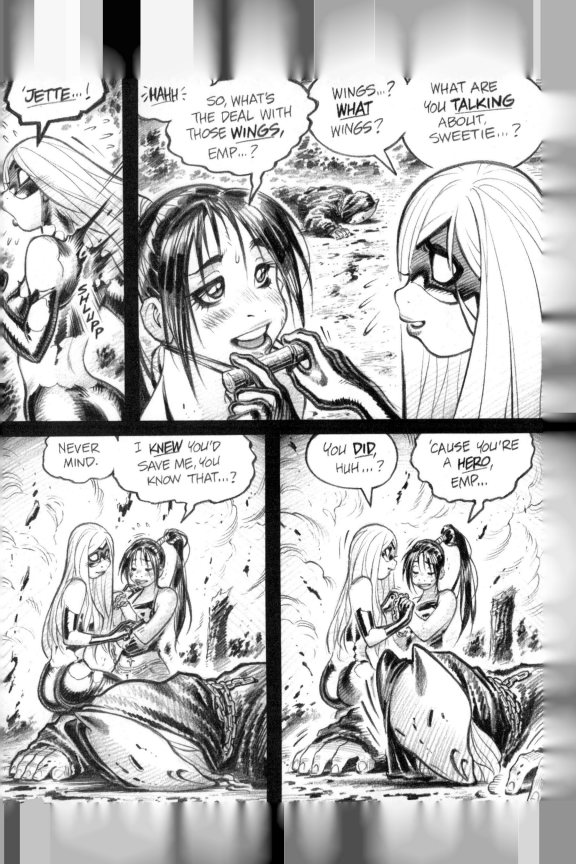

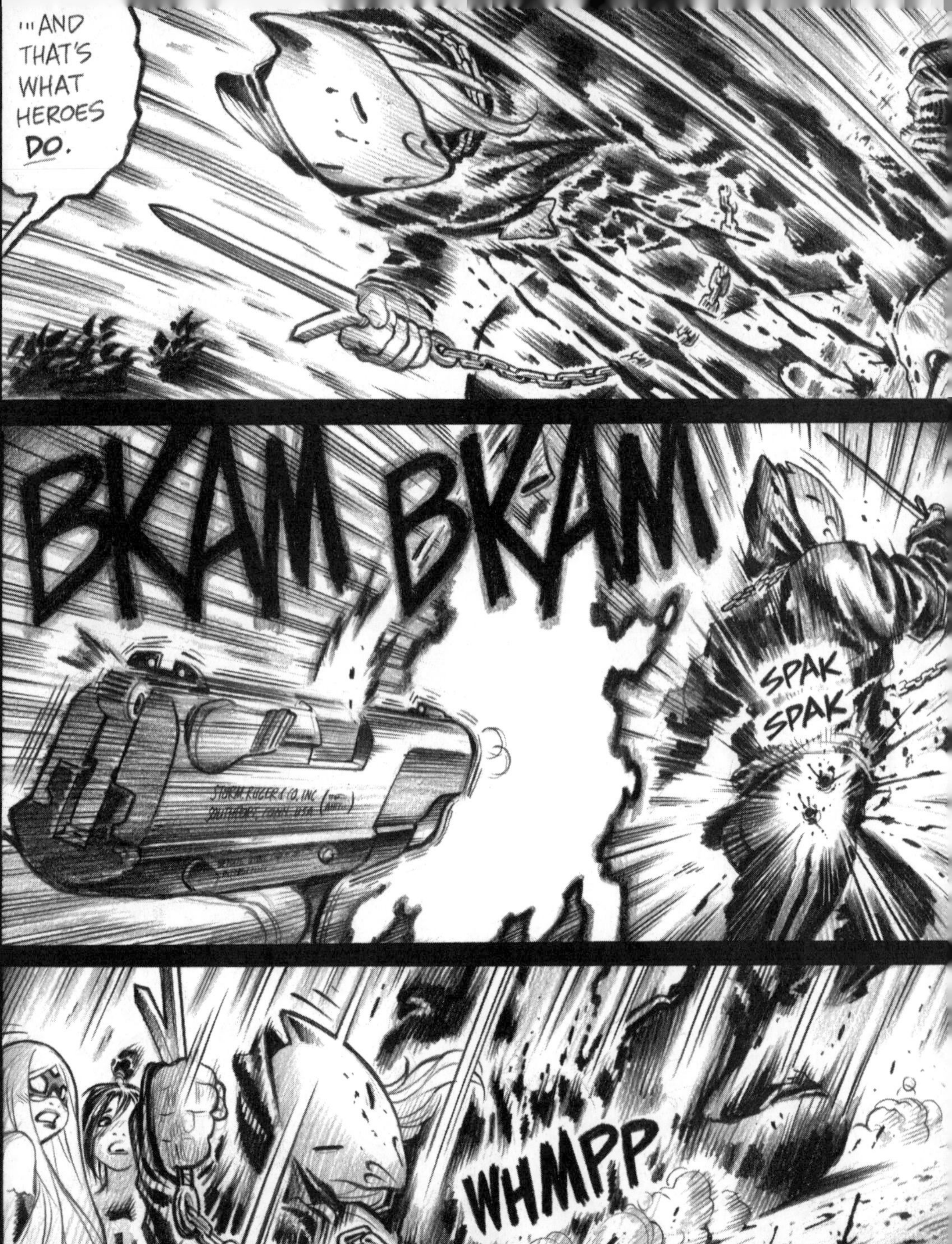
...AND THAT'S WHAT HEROES DO.
BKAM BKAM
SPAK SPAK
WHMPP

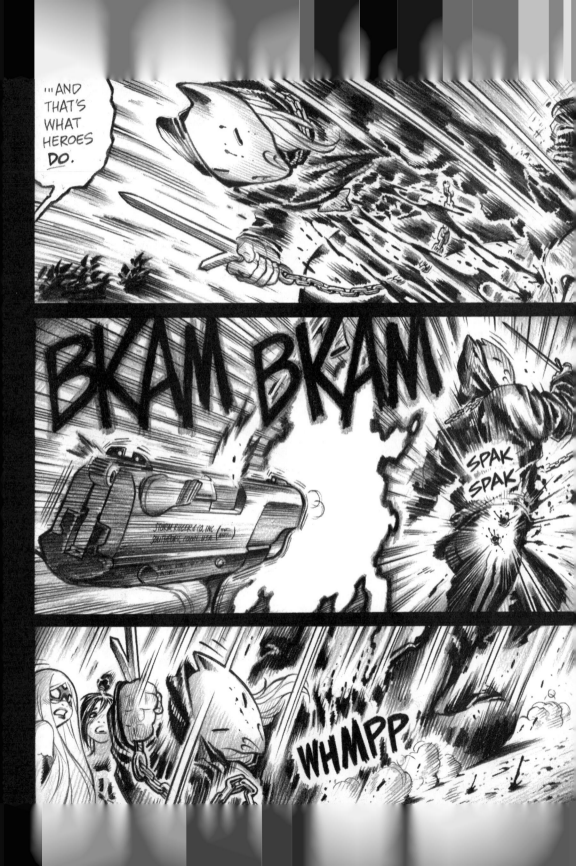

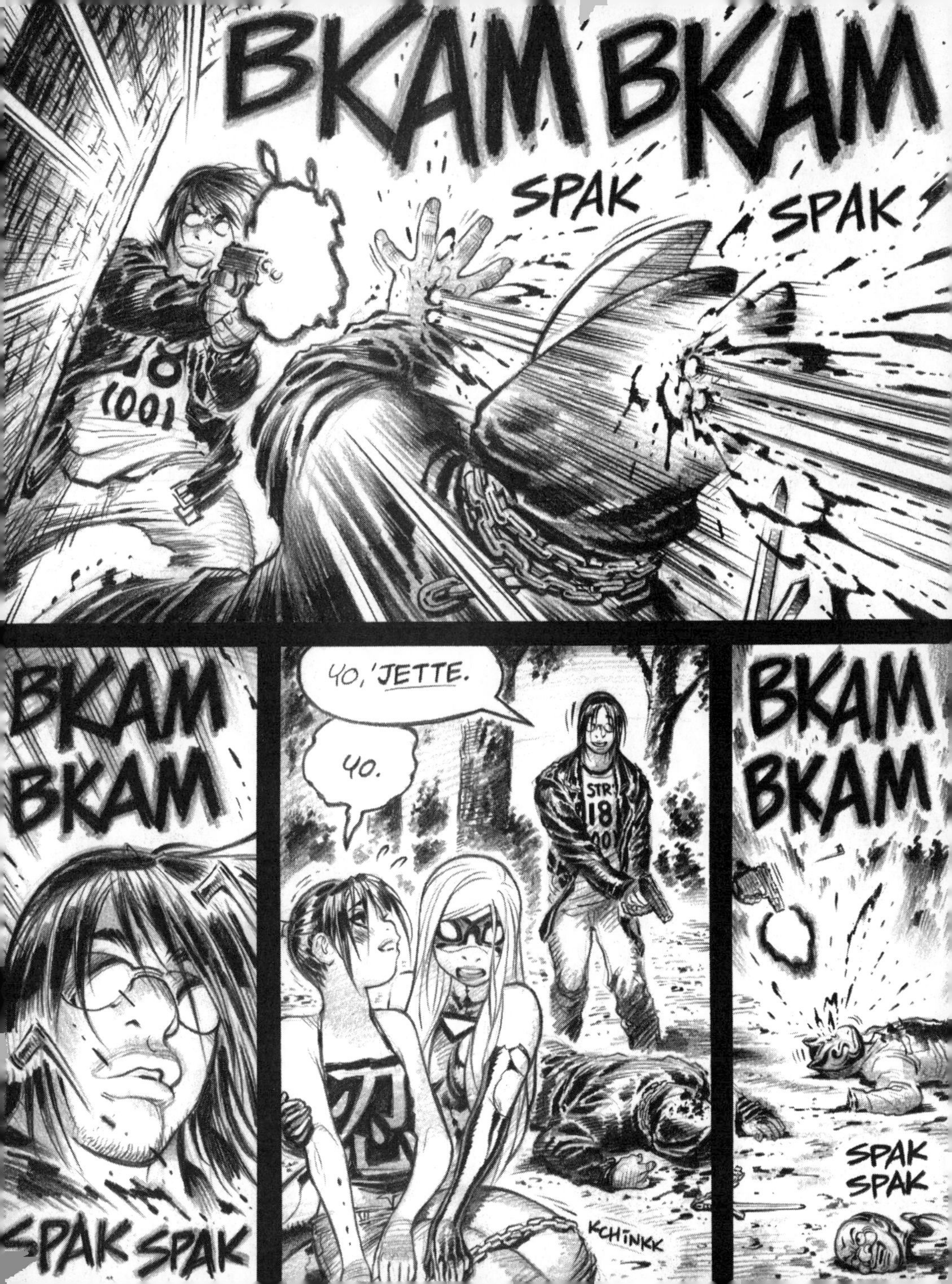
BKAM BKAM
SPAK
SPAK
BKAM
BKAM
SPAK SPAK
YO, 'JETTE.
YO.
KCHINKK
BKAM
BKAM
SPAK
SPAK

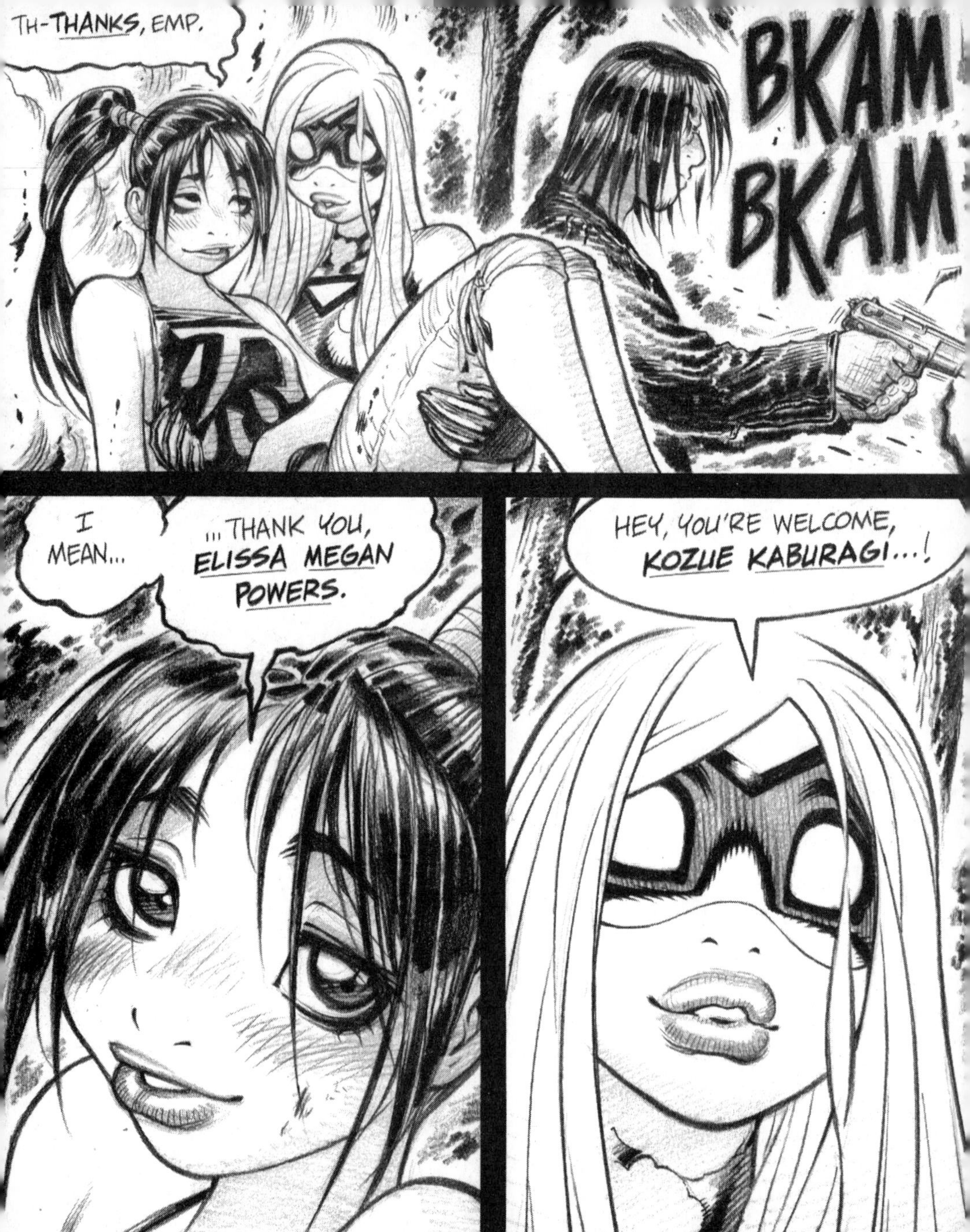
TH-THANKS, EMP.
BKAM BKAM
I MEAN...
...THANK YOU, ELISSA MEGAN POWERS.
HEY, YOU'RE WELCOME, KOZUE KABURAGI...!

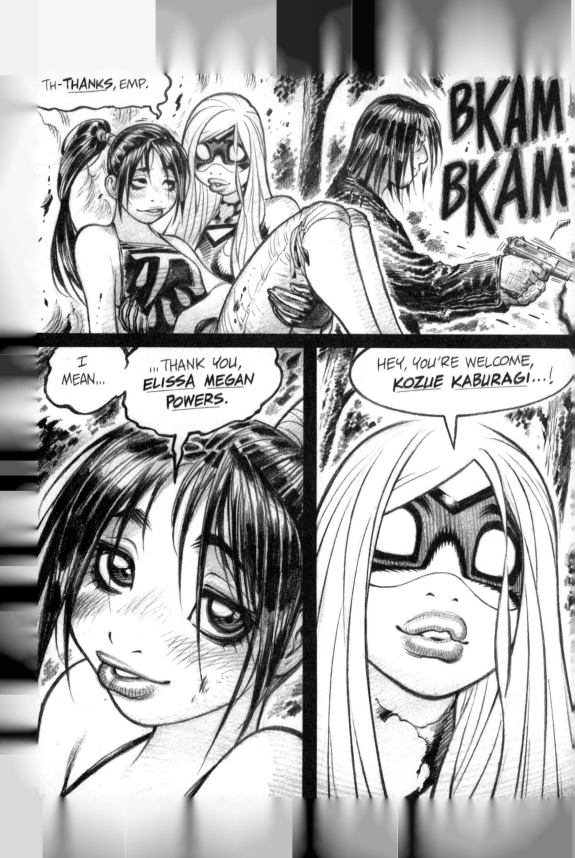

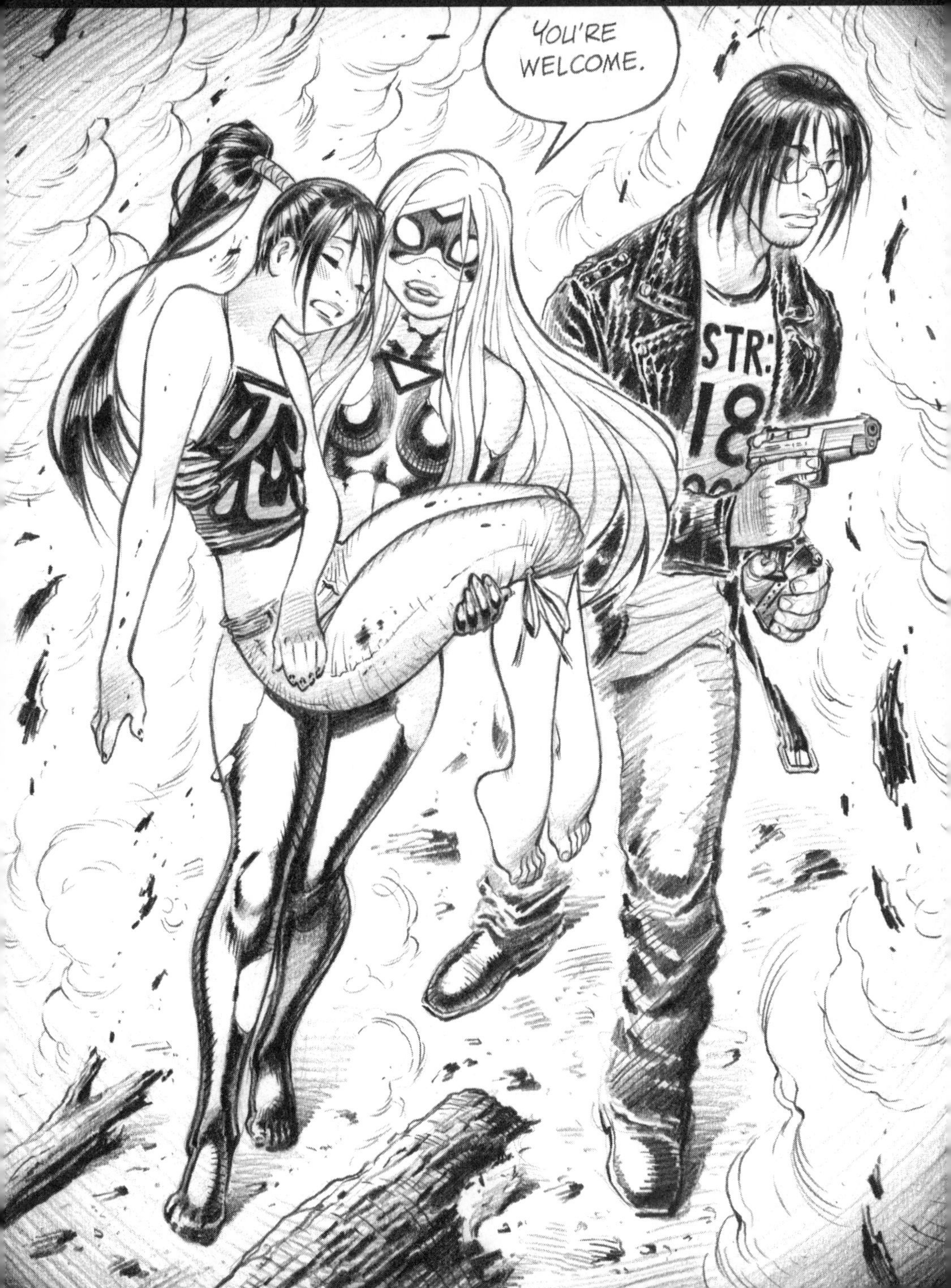
YOU'RE WELCOME.
STR: 18

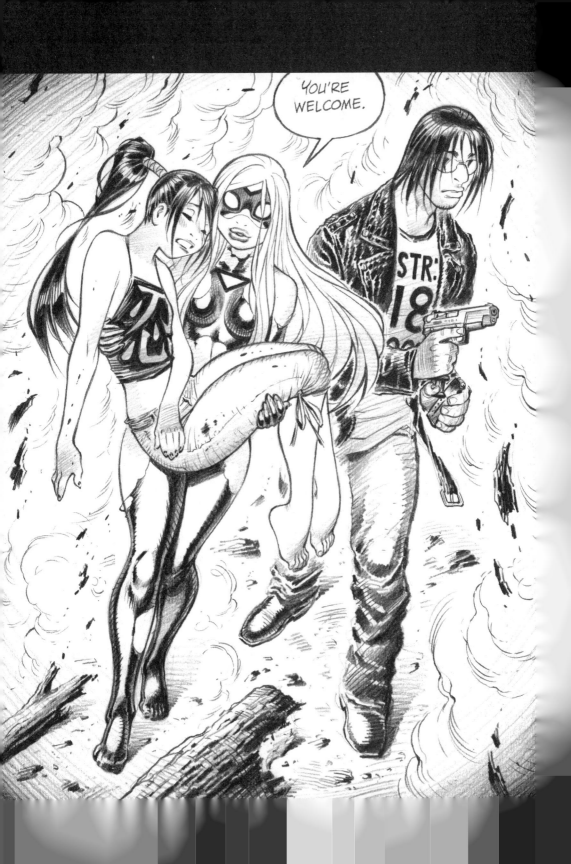

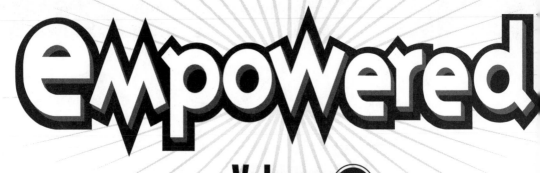

empowered

Volume 3

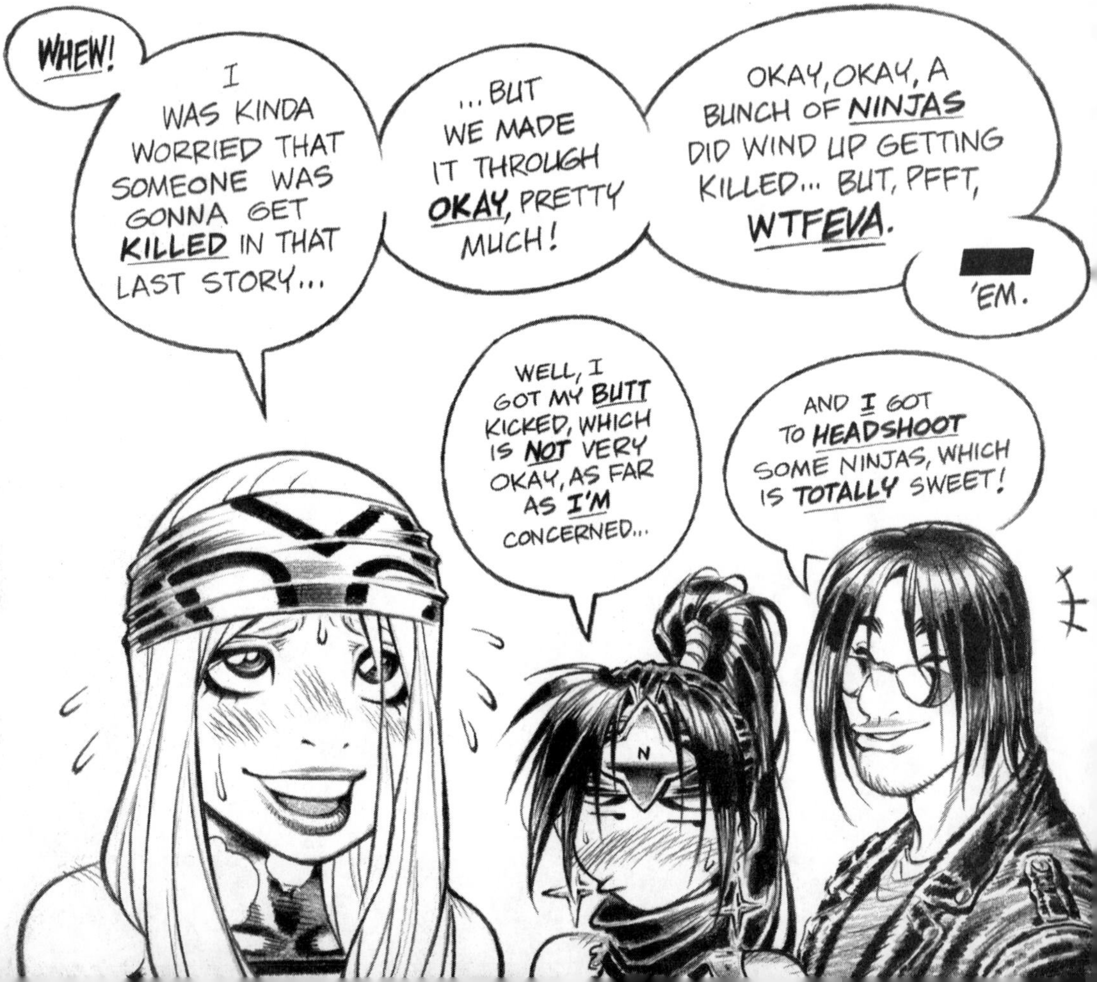
WHEW!
I WAS KINDA WORRIED THAT SOMEONE WAS GONNA GET KILLED IN THAT LAST STORY...
...BUT WE MADE IT THROUGH OKAY, PRETTY MUCH!
OKAY, OKAY, A BUNCH OF NINJAS DID WIND UP GETTING KILLED... BUT, PFFT, WTFEVA.
[redacted] 'EM.
WELL, I GOT MY BUTT KICKED, WHICH IS NOT VERY OKAY, AS FAR AS I'M CONCERNED...
AND I GOT TO HEADSHOOT SOME NINJAS, WHICH IS TOTALLY SWEET!

The End.

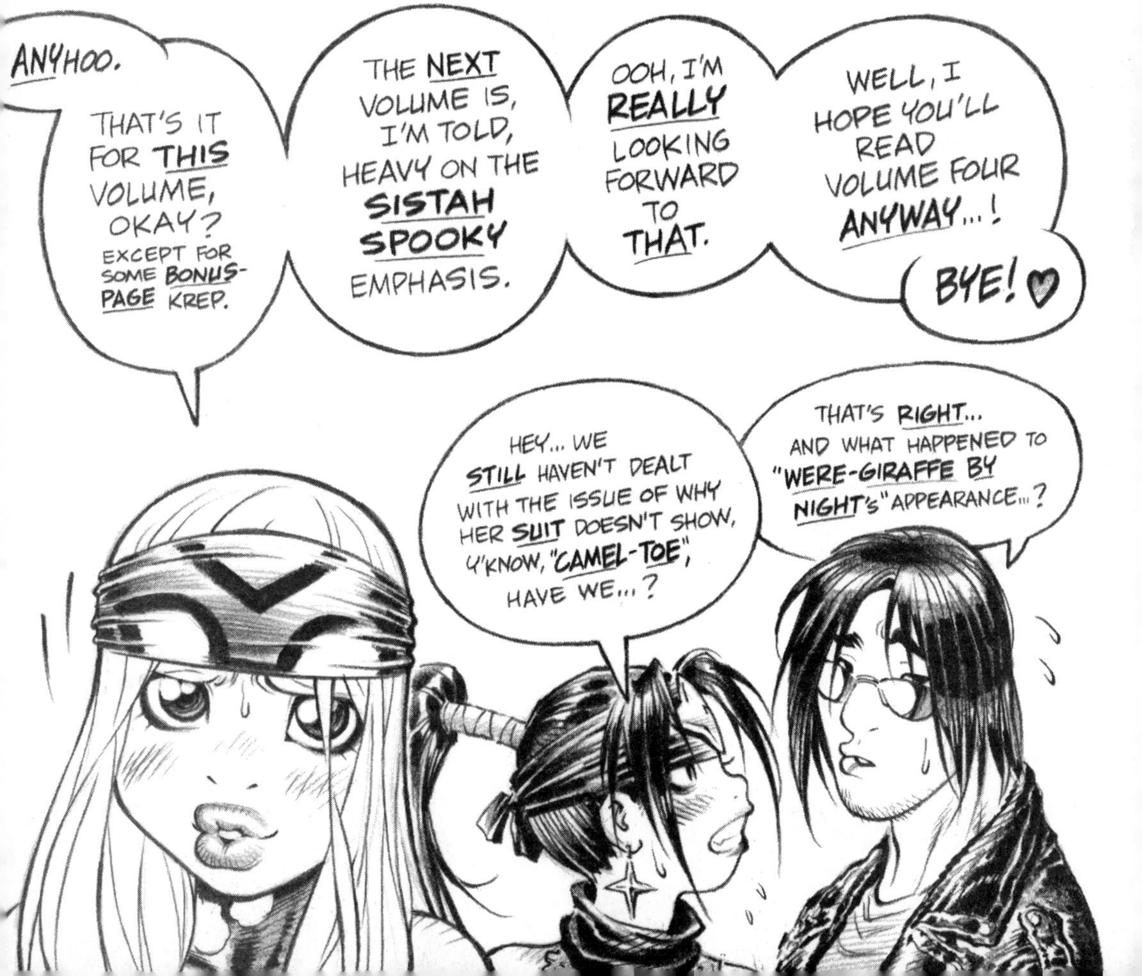
ANYHOO.
THAT'S IT FOR THIS VOLUME, OKAY? EXCEPT FOR SOME BONUS-PAGE KREP.
THE NEXT VOLUME IS, I'M TOLD, HEAVY ON THE SISTAH SPOOKY EMPHASIS.
OOH, I'M REALLY LOOKING FORWARD TO THAT.
WELL, I HOPE YOU'LL READ VOLUME FOUR ANYWAY...!
BYE! ♥
HEY... WE STILL HAVEN'T DEALT WITH THE ISSUE OF WHY HER SUIT DOESN'T SHOW, Y'KNOW, "CAMEL-TOE", HAVE WE...?
THAT'S RIGHT... AND WHAT HAPPENED TO "WERE-GIRAFFE BY NIGHT's" APPEARANCE...?

EMPOWERED EXTRAS

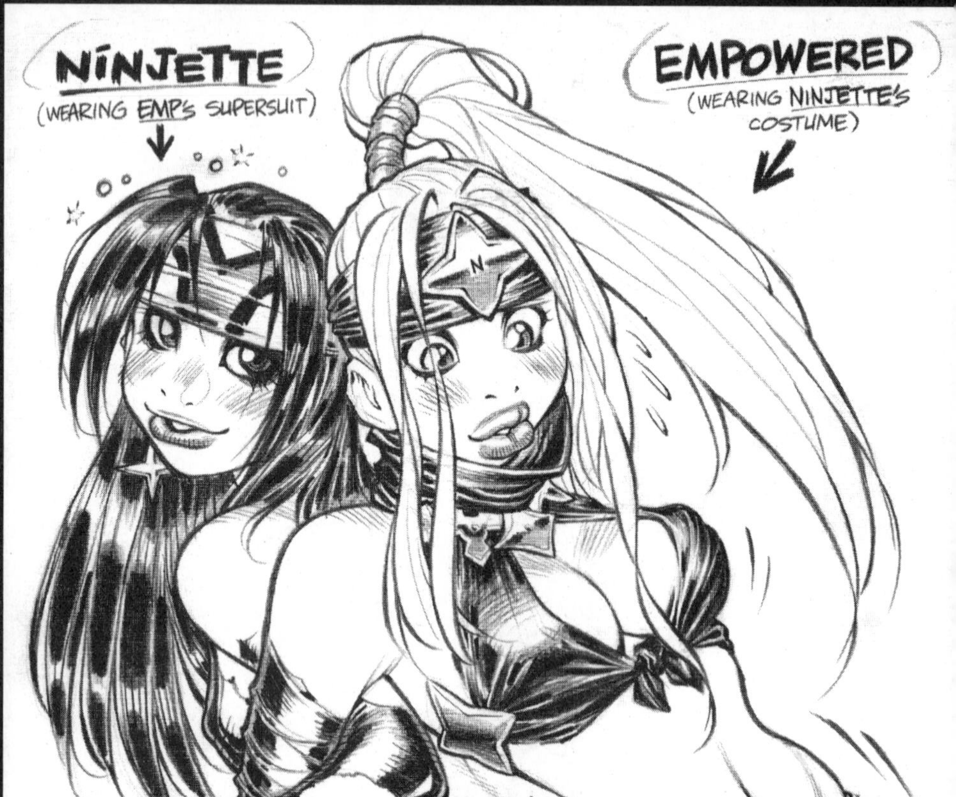
NINJETTE
(WEARING EMP'S SUPERSUIT)
EMPOWERED
(WEARING NINJETTE'S COSTUME)
WARREN 2K7

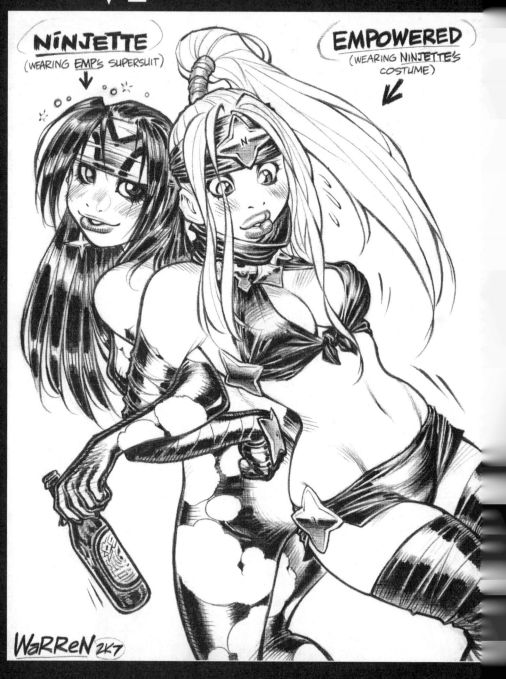

Here's a sketch I did as a prize for an art contest, featuring Emp and Ninjette "cross-dressing" (well, sorta in each other's costumes for some reason . . . (The actual reason being, I thought it would look cute.)

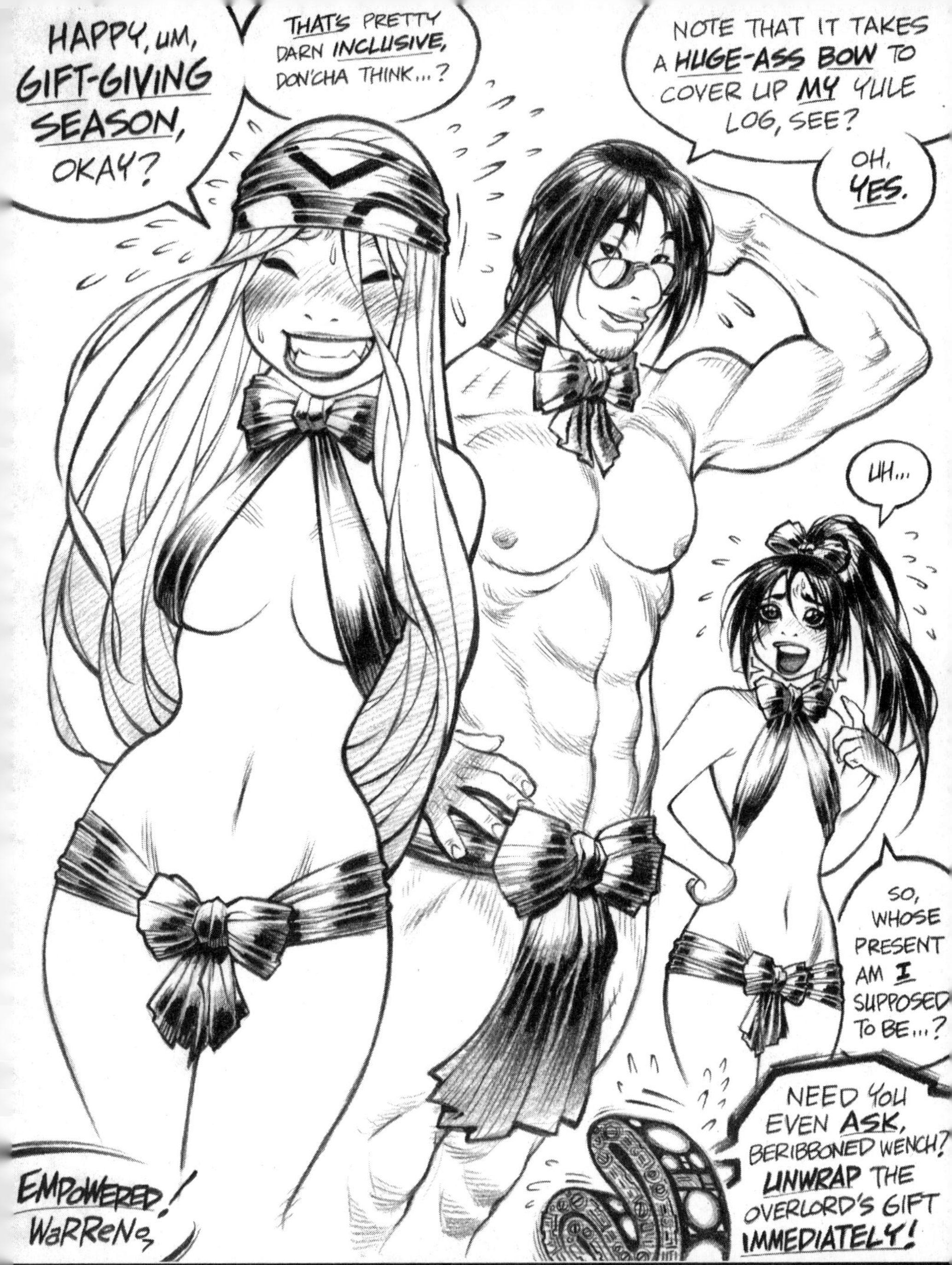
HAPPY, UM, GIFT-GIVING SEASON, OKAY?
THAT'S PRETTY DARN INCLUSIVE, DON'CHA THINK...?
NOTE THAT IT TAKES A HUGE-ASS BOW TO COVER UP MY YULE LOG, SEE?
OH, YES.
UH...
SO, WHOSE PRESENT AM I SUPPOSED TO BE...?
NEED YOU EVEN ASK, BERIBBONED WENCH? UNWRAP THE OVERLORD'S GIFT IMMEDIATELY!
EMPOWERED!
WARREN

Here's my tragically flawed 2007 "Xmas card" piece . . . In the original rough for this page, I drew Emp's head rather too small; as you can see, I overcompensated horrifically on the final version, rendering her well-nigh

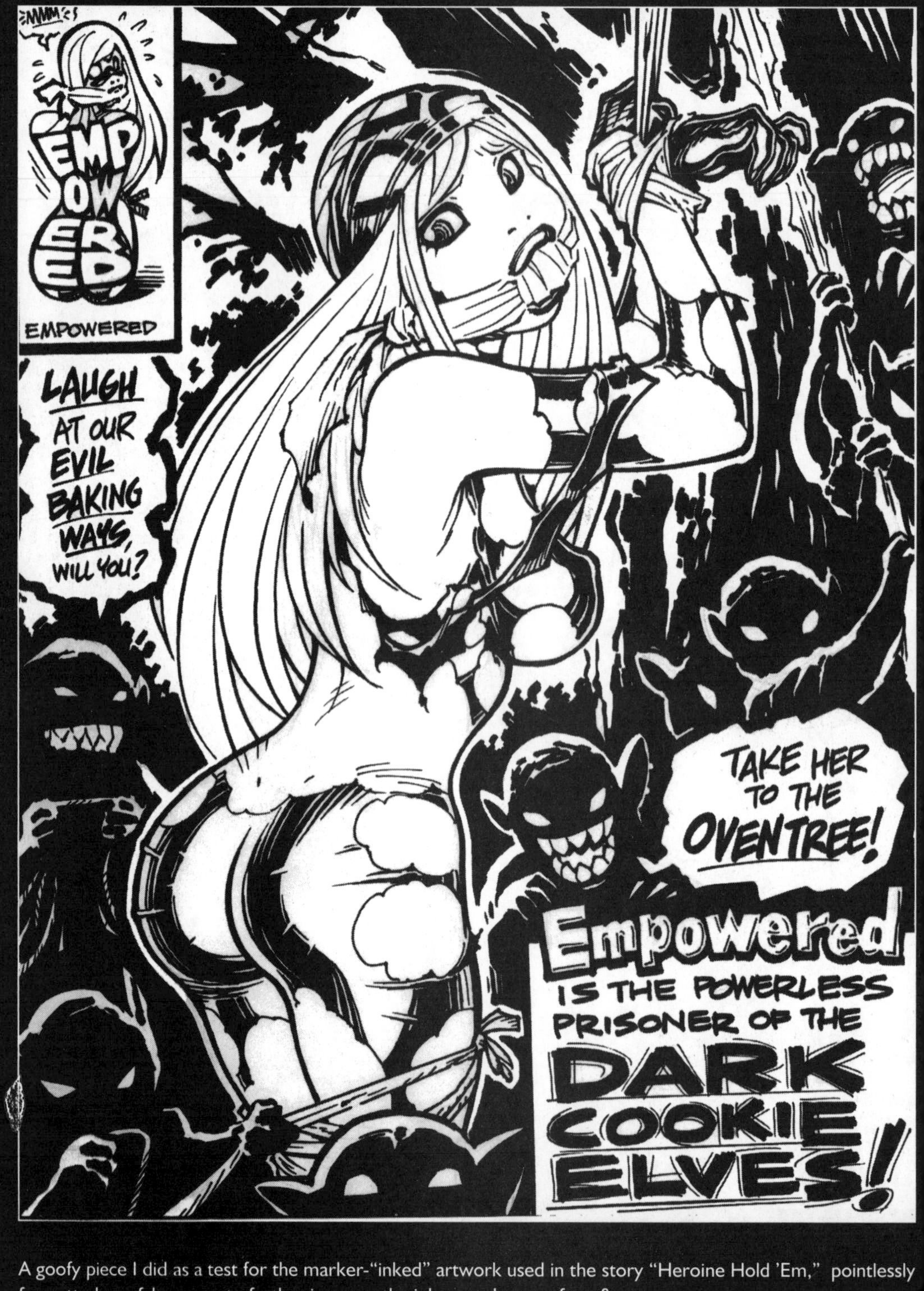

MMM
EMPOWERED
EMPOWERED
LAUGH AT OUR EVIL BAKING WAYS, WILL YOU?
TAKE HER TO THE OVENTREE!
Empowered
IS THE POWERLESS PRISONER OF THE
DARK COOKIE ELVES!

A goofy piece I did as a test for the marker-"inked" artwork used in the story "Heroine Hold 'Em," pointlessly formatted as a fake cover to further increase the inherent degree of goofiness.

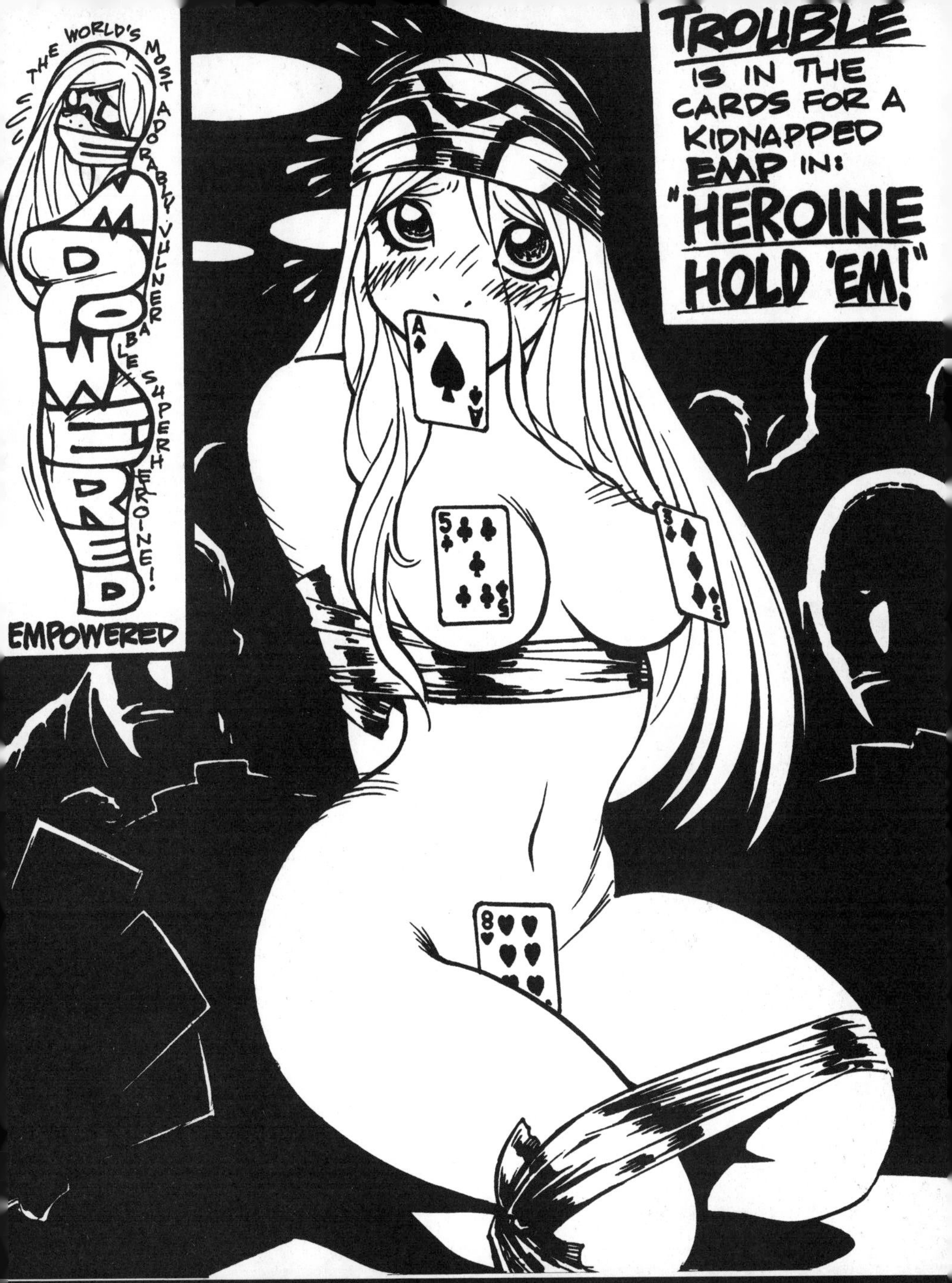
THE WORLD'S MOST ADORABLY VULNERABLE SUPERHEROINE!
POWERED
EMPOWERED
TROUBLE IS IN THE CARDS FOR A KIDNAPPED EMP IN:
"HEROINE HOLD 'EM!"

Speaking of "Heroine Hold 'Em," here's a similarly faux (and very tasteful!) cover illustration I did for that story
I've no explanation for the wacky "Empowered Comics" image in the upper left corner, save perhaps that the

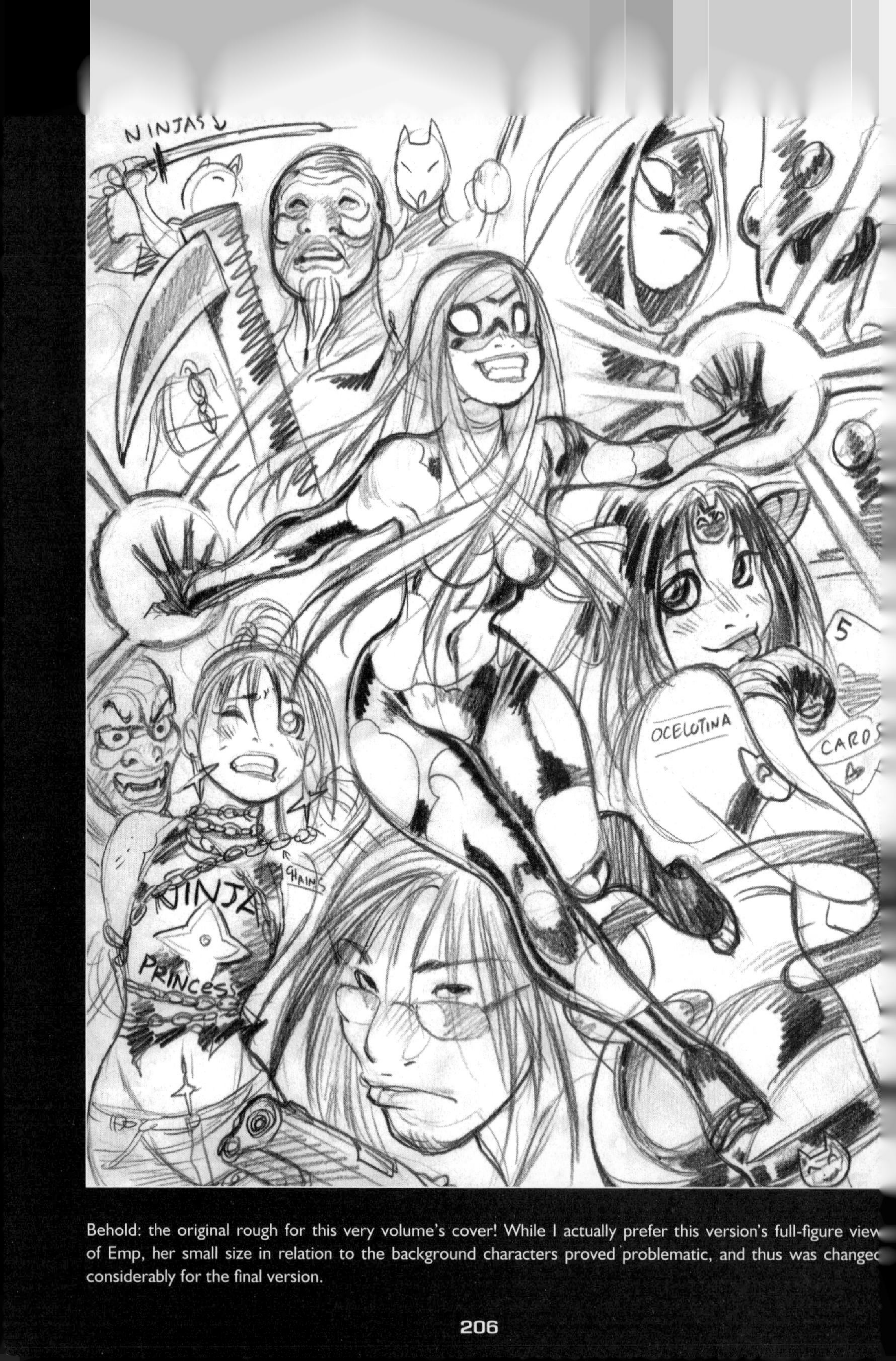
NINJAS
OCELOTINA
CHAINS
NINJA
PRINCESS
5

Behold: the original rough for this very volume's cover! While I actually prefer this version's full-figure view of Emp, her small size in relation to the background characters proved problematic, and thus was changed considerably for the final version.

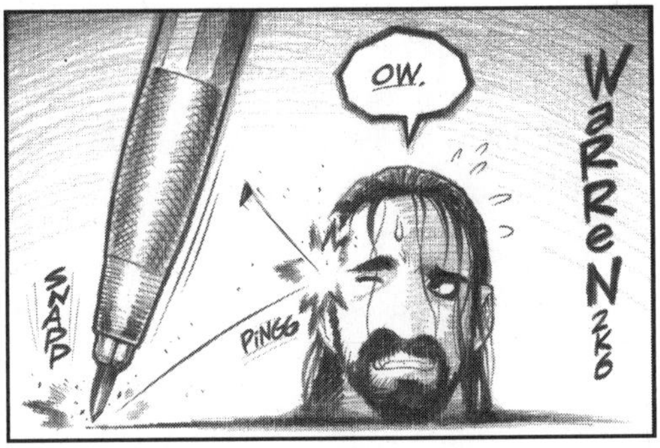
SNAPP
PINGG
OW.
WaRReN 2K6

ADAM WARREN was one of the first writer/artists in the American comics field to integrate the artistic and storytelling techniques of Japanese comics into his work. Yep, he was definitely a manga-influenced pioneer, even going so far as to ride around in a covered wagon and fire his six-shooters in the air while bellowing "Yee-Haw," pioneer-style. Okay, maybe he *didn't* actually go that far.

Off and on since 1988, he's written and drawn an idiosyncratic, English-language comics adaptation of the popular Japanese science-fiction characters known as *The Dirty Pair*, who first appeared in novels by award-winning author Haruka Takachiho and were popularized in a varying series of anime incarnations. The six *Dirty Pair* miniseries Adam worked on were known for their purty, purty artwork, future-shockalicious SF concepts, and obnoxiously satirical sense of humor . . . and should (mostly) be available in trade-paperback collections from Dark Horse (hint, hint).

The rest of Adam's ripped and toned body of comics-related work ranges from forays into the teen-superhero, pop-culture saturation of Wildstorm/DC's *Gen 13*, to a DC prestige-format, far-future iteration of the Teen Titans (*Titans: Scissors, Paper, Stone*), and even a take on old-school anime with a *Bubblegum Crisis* miniseries. More recently, he's created and written the mecha-superteam project *Livewires* for Marvel Comics, along with the miniseries *Iron Man: Hypervelocity*.

Beyond the comics field, he's dabbled in artistic miscellanea such as a dōjinshi "sketchbook" published in Japan and illustrations for magazines such as *Spin, GamePro, Wizard*, and *Stuff*, not to mention several (very) short-lived stabs into the fields of videogames, CD-cover artwork, and TV animation. Currently, he writes and draws a monthly, single-page cartoon feature exploring Playstation-related humor in the back of the videogame magazine *PSM*.

Adam lives a thrillingly reclusive lifestyle somewhere off in the deep woods, where hunting rifles boom, FedEx trucks get stuck in the mud, and grey squirrels the size of Labrador retrievers run up and down the sides of houses all ****ing day long, like the world's loudest and furriest ninja. His hobbies include: pegging himself in the eye with the snapped-off tip from a 3B pencil lead (as seen in the accompanying caricature), dosing up with No-Doz®, dosing down with quality microbrews, reading an average of 4–8 books per week, bailing over to Barnes & Noble to get an average of 4–8 more books per week, working out to *Dance Dance Revolution* for the maximum possible embarrassment value, bitching about the truly critical issues of the day (such as death, taxes, and the New England Patriots' wide-receiver surplus), and damaging what's left of his hearing with an iPod full of songs that are far, far too lame to admit listening to in public. His favorite colors are black and blue, which is almost certainly symbolic of something profoundly negative.

Find out more about Adam and his work
on **DeviantART** and **MySpace**:
http://adamwarren.deviantart.com
http://www.myspace.com/adamwarrencomics

eMPoWered

VOLUME 1
ISBN 978-1-59307-672-6

VOLUME 2
ISBN 978-1-59307-816-4

VOLUME 3
ISBN 978-1-59307-870-6

$14.95 each!

ALSO AVAILABLE FROM ADAM WARREN:

**THE DIRTY PAIR:
SIM HELL 3RD ED. TPB**
ISBN 978-1-56971-742-4
$14.95

**BUBBLEGUM CRISIS:
GRAND MAL TPB**
ISBN 978-1-56971-120-0
$14.95